CHALLENGES FOR LANGUAGE EDUCATION AND POLICY

Valuable for specialists and general readers alike, this extraordinary collection illuminates the personal and social origins and implications of real-life language policies with a level of authority, insight, and specificity not found elsewhere. It connects language policies to the aspirations, benefits, challenges, and tensions experienced by language managers and learners around the world.

Mary McGroarty, Northern Arizona University, USA

Addressing a wide range of issues in applied linguistics, sociolinguistics, and multilingualism, this volume focuses on language users, the "people." Making creative connections between existing scholarship in language policy and contemporary theory and research in other social sciences, authors from around the world offer new critical perspectives for analyzing language phenomena and language theories, suggesting new meeting points among language users and language policymakers, norms, and traditions in diverse cultural, geographical, and historical contexts.

Identifying and expanding on previously neglected aspects of language studies, the book is inspired by the work of Elana Shohamy, whose critical view and innovative work on a broad spectrum of key topics in applied linguistics has influenced many scholars in the field to think "out of the box" and to reconsider some basic commonly held understandings, specifically with regard to the impact of language and languaging on individual language users rather than on the masses.

Bernard Spolsky is Professor Emeritus of English at Bar-Ilan University, Israel.

Ofra Inbar-Lourie is head of the Teachers' Education Unit of Tel Aviv University, School of Education, Israel.

Michal Tannenbaum is Senior Lecturer and head of the Language Education Program at Tel Aviv University, Israel.

CHALLENGES FOR LANGUAGE EDUCATION AND POLICY

Making Space for People

*Edited by Bernard Spolsky,
Ofra Inbar-Lourie, and
Michal Tannenbaum*

NEW YORK AND LONDON

First published 2015
by Routledge
711 Third Avenue, New York, NY 10017

and by Routledge
2 Park Square, Milton Park, Abingdon, Oxon OX14 4RN

Routledge is an imprint of the Taylor & Francis Group, an informa business

© 2015 Taylor & Francis

The right of the editors to be identified as the authors of the editorial
material, and of the authors for their individual chapters, has been
asserted in accordance with sections 77 and 78 of the Copyright,
Designs and Patents Act 1988.

All rights reserved. No part of this book may be reprinted or
reproduced or utilized in any form or by any electronic, mechanical, or
other means, now known or hereafter invented, including photocopying
and recording, or in any information storage or retrieval system, without
permission in writing from the publishers.

Trademark notice: Product or corporate names may be trademarks or
registered trademarks, and are used only for identification and
explanation without intent to infringe.

Library of Congress Cataloging in Publication Data
Challenges for language education and policy: making space for
  people/edited by Bernard Spolsky, Ofra Inbar-Lourie, Michal
  Tannenbaum.
  pages cm
  Includes bibliographical references and index.
  1. English language—Study and teaching—Foreign speakers
  I. Spolsky, Bernard.
  PE1128.C474 2014
  418.0071—dc23
  2014003307

ISBN: 978-0-415-71189-0 (hbk)
ISBN: 978-0-415-71190-6 (pbk)
ISBN: 978-1-315-88428-8 (ebk)

Typeset in Bembo and Stone Sans
by Florence Production Ltd, Stoodleigh, Devon, UK

CONTENTS

Preface: Dear Elana ix
BERNARD SPOLSKY

Introduction: A Portrait of the Researcher in a Never-Ending Journey 1
OFRA INBA-LOURIE AND MICHAL TANNENBAUM

PART 1
Restoring People to Language Assessment 9

1   Language Tests for Residency and Citizenship and the
    Conferring of Individuality 11
    TIM MCNAMARA, KAMRAN KHAN, AND KELLIE FROST

2   Setting Standards for Multilingual Curricula to Teach and
    Test Foreign Languages 23
    BESSIE DENDRINOS AND VOULA GOTSOULIA

3   In the Name of the CEFR: Individuals and Standards 40
    MONICA BARNI

4   Acknowledging the Diversity of the Language Learner
    Population in Australia: Towards Context-Sensitive
    Language Standards 52
    CATHERINE ELDER

vi Contents

5 Students' Voices: The Challenge of Measuring Speaking for
  Academic Contexts 65
  LINDSAY BROOKS AND MERRILL SWAIN

6 Ethical Codes and Responsibility 81
  ALAN DAVIES

PART 2
Focusing on People in Language Policy 93

7 Cultivating an Ecology of Multilingualism in Schools 95
  OFELIA GARCÍA AND KATE MENKEN

8 English in Ethiopia: Making Space for the Individual in
  Language Policy 109
  ELIZABETH LANZA AND HIRUT WOLDEMARIAM

9 Portraits of Language Activists in Indigenous Language
  Revitalization 123
  NANCY H. HORNBERGER

10 Refugees in Canada: On the Loss of Social Capital 135
   THOMAS RICENTO

PART 3
Personalizing the Public Space 149

11 Linguistic Landscapes inside Multilingual Schools 151
   DURK GORTER AND JASONE CENOZ

12 "We Are Not Really a Mixed City"—A De-Jure Bilingual Linguistic
   Landscape: the Case of Jewish-Arab Mixed Cities in Israel 170
   DAFNA YITZHAKI AND THEODORUS DU PLESSIS

13 Hebraization in the Palestinian Language Landscape in Israel 182
   MUHAMMAD AMARA

14 Hebrew in the North American Linguistic Landscape:
   Materializing the Sacred 196
   SHARON AVNI

Contents **vii**

15 *Welcome*: Synthetic Personalization and Commodification of
    Sociability in the Linguistic Landscape of Global Tourism   214
    ADAM JAWORSKI

PART 4
Placing People within Communities and Cultures   **233**

16 A Researcher's Auto-Socioanalysis: Making Space for the Personal   235
    CLAIRE KRAMSCH

17 Understanding the Holocaust: A Personal History, Critical
    Literacy Analysis of a Gestapo File   245
    DAVID I. HANAUER

18 Language Experience Changes Language and Cognitive Ability:
    Implications for Social Policy   259
    ELLEN BIALYSTOK

19 Strategies for the Super-Multilingual in an Increasingly Global
    World   270
    ANDREW D. COHEN

20 Gender, Sexuality, and Multilingualism in the Language Classroom   281
    LYN WRIGHT FOGLE AND KENDALL A. KING

21 Examining Markers of Identity Construction in English Language
    Learning: Some Implications for Palestinian-Israeli and
    Jewish-Israeli Language Learners   294
    JULIA SCHLAM SALMAN, ELITE OLSHTAIN, AND ZVI BEKERMAN

22 Integrational Linguistics and L2 Proficiency   309
    JAMES P. LANTOLF

    About the Contributors   *323*
    Index   *329*

PREFACE

DEAR ELANA

Bernard Spolsky

Societies have formal rites of passage to mark significant dates—the bar mitzvah at 13 years of age for Jewish boys, the Kinaalda at puberty for Navajo girls, the key of the door at 21 in Britain, or the gold watch on retirement in many firms. In the academic world, a traditional way to mark a scholar's voluntary or compulsory retirement (in Israel, university professors like us are still forced to retire in the year that we reach 68) or their attaining some advanced birthday (70 or 80, perhaps) is the publication of a volume of essays written by their former students, colleagues, and friends. Its Germanic origin and continued lack of full integration into English-speaking universities is shown by the name for such a volume: a *Festschrift*. This is not a *Festschrift*, because publishers are wisely quite wary of collections of miscellaneous papers that do not share a theme, but rather a volume of original articles written by your former students, colleagues, and friends to mark the year in which your university's regulations have decided you should move from active to emerita status. As you will quickly learn, this has meant that contributors have not just dug up some unpublished paper to use as a birthday greeting, but rather have used the inspiration they have received from working with you to move in some new direction in their academic development. This provides the theme.

It is this ability to inspire others to meet new challenges that characterizes for all of us our experience with you. You and I first met at a conference in the US where you were introduced to me as one of the brightest new graduates in applied linguistics. I was thrilled to discover shortly afterwards that you had accepted a position at the University of Tel Aviv. Our first joint activity was in cooperation with Andrew Cohen to found an Israeli group of language testers, imitating a similar group that had been formed in Europe.

x Preface

Two decades later, this group still flourishes, meeting annually and encouraging local scholars to develop the field of language testing, a field in which your work has been highly significant. You have developed tests, criticized others, trained students, but most of all you have translated Foucault's distaste for tests (he himself is said to have failed the Bac) into a perceptive and well-organized analysis of the potential danger of large-scale testing and a realization of its destructive role in excluding minorities from academic and economic advancement. What seemed comparatively reasonable when the Chinese Emperor used an elaborate examination system to select a tiny elite of bureaucrats (although its ultimate effect was in producing for Chinese, Korean, and Japanese education a frenzy of examination preparation) proved to be even more harmful when used to control the education of masses of students.

Though you developed high skills in preparing instruments to assess language proficiency, you have remained cautious and cynical about the way test results are used. You appreciate the need for accommodation in the administration of tests—for recognizing that bilinguals and speakers of minority languages are handicapped unless a test is adjusted to meet their requirements. And you understand the role of the individual in a process that bases its interpretation on statistics and group averages. I recall watching you conduct an experimental oral examination with a student; your obvious deep interest in what the student had to say encouraged her to express herself fluently and to concentrate on giving information rather than performing for the examiner. Your senior colleagues appreciate and your juniors learn the double task of language testers: to make sure of the quality of the test, and to share responsibility for its uses. Especially, you have helped us realize the alarming power of tests, for good or evil.

Our next major sphere of collaboration came when we both spent some time at the National Foreign Language Center in Washington, DC, where Richard Lambert was working with colleagues (Richard Brecht and Ronald Walton) and a number of visiting scholars to explore and strengthen the field of language policy, a field we both found to be exciting and important. Our return to Israel coincided fortuitously with the appointment of a new minister of education, one who exceptionally saw the value of language education. With the aid of a grant from the ministry, and working with a number of graduate students, we prepared a survey of language education in the Israeli school system and wrote for the minister a policy statement that he edited and promulgated. Our discussions in the drafting of this policy were long and heated. There were just too many languages to be considered. Hebrew was the hegemonic national language, slowly but surely swamping all the others. Arabic was the language of the largest minority, recognized as an official language for some purposes, used as language of instruction in Israeli Arab schools, but poorly taught in Jewish schools. Everyone wanted English, assuming it to be the source of economic success. "But what about the other languages?" we asked. What should we do about major languages such as French, Russian, Spanish, and German that also were the heritage and sometimes the home languages of large segments of the population? And what about other languages of immigrants, such as Amharic and Tigrinya? What about all the Jewish language varieties that had been developed over 2,000 years in Diaspora and continued to serve as identity languages for many people—Yiddish, Ladino (Judezmo or Haketia), various forms of Judeo-Arabic and Judeo-Aramaic, Juhuri, Jewish Malayalam, to name a few? What about languages of growing economic importance such as Japanese and Chinese? Our final proposal was for teaching the three most important languages (Hebrew, Arabic, and English) and for encouraging the addition of a fourth, whether an immigrant or a heritage or an international language. Here, as in so much of your research and teaching, you constantly asserted the importance of multilingualism, and the need to design policies that support and encourage it.

The policy we drafted was adopted by the minister, but not implemented by the department of education, and has been largely ignored by succeeding ministers. You did not give up, but produced a generation of students and teachers who had learned the central importance of language education; to this, you added influential programs that passed the same knowledge to school inspectors and to school principals. Not restricted to the study or the lecture room, you have continued as an activist for the causes you believe in. Indeed, it is one of the strongest characteristics of your work that it has a firm basis in social and ethical justice.

This was the case in another field in which your initiative has led to considerable activity. In a study that Robert Cooper and I made of language use in the Old City of Jerusalem a number of years ago, we found it interesting to look at the sociolinguistic meaning of public signs. About the same time, two Canadian linguists developed the notion of "linguistic landscape," by which they meant the perception of the relative importance of language choice in public signs. With your skills and enthusiasm in photography, you found this an ideal method to study the relative power of language groups in multilingual societies. A whole new methodology has been developed and enthusiastically adopted by scholars concerned with minority languages throughout the world.

Again, this confirms your commitment to looking behind the public use of language to recognize the way that government, big business, and majority groups exercise power. Whether it is world-dominant English exerting pressure on other languages, or your own native Hebrew developing hegemonic multilingualism that is swallowing up not just its co-official Arabic and the various immigrant and heritage languages with which it chose to compete, including your family's Yiddish, you regularly take the side of the weaker language and minority group.

This has involved, too, your reaction to the interest in language as an individual psychological phenomenon being replaced by the emphasis on its social and communal characteristic. When you came into applied linguistics, the central goal was a psycholinguistic study of the acquisition of individual proficiency; you shared in the revolutionary application of sociolinguistics to the field, the realization that

xii Preface

individual monolingualism was not the focus, but rather the plurilingualism of people living in the multilingual societies.

But you went one step further: as the theme of this volume asserts, and as most of the chapters illustrate, we are now starting to recognize the individual within the community, acknowledging the vital importance of individual differences and making space for the diversity you continually celebrate. The effect of your work has been a personalization of the field; you ask how to go beyond the public performance of the test that depends on group statistics to identify the personal characteristics of those taking the tests. You look behind the dominant language in public signage to ask how policy is expressing the power of the government or of other dominant groups. You are ready at all times to denounce the exertion of power and to call for the equality of weaker individuals and groups.

In the introduction, your former students and colleagues Ofra Inbar-Lourie and Michal Tannenbaum, who were the initiators of this volume celebrating your career to date, will summarize and point out the contribution of each of the chapters. It remains for me to thank them for involving me in the enterprise, to thank the publishers for agreeing to publish the book, and to thank the contributors for the way they have chosen to join in recognition of the significance to applied and educational linguistics of your work. But most of all, to thank you for inspiring us with a creative and ethical approach to our studies, and to look forward to your continued productivity and leadership.

Bernard (Dov)

INTRODUCTION

A PORTRAIT OF THE RESEARCHER IN A NEVER-ENDING JOURNEY

Ofra Inbar-Lourie and Michal Tannenbaum

A meal at Elana Shohamy's is invariably a culinary delight. Delicacies are not prepared ahead and just appear on the table, seemingly without effort. Guests are by then already there, and a lively conversation is ongoing with the hostess actively involved while preparing the food. Dishes are never typically this or that, and do not fit traditional labels. Instead, Elana fearlessly mixes ingredients to create original, surprising, colorful, and tasty dishes that fuel a spirited and challenging exchange. Doing things her own way and "thinking out of the box" is what, in fact, typifies Elana in many other senses, first and foremost, her research, writing, and teaching over the years: it resists boundaries, deconstructs existing definitions, and challenges the conventional with a vision transformed into action.

This book, as the title suggests, is about "people," about language users. It is world-encompassing, heterogeneous, multilingual, and multi-thematic, documenting a range of languages, phenomena, ideologies, and disciplines. It reflects and epitomizes Elana's scholarly endeavors—the world is her kingdom, she is not tied to a particular time or space, her curiosity is endless, her vision far-reaching. She is constantly on the go, journeying to and fro exploring new domains with energy and enthusiasm, noting important controversial local and global issues, reaching out, spreading new ideas about the nature of language and evidence of its use, and leaving her mark wherever she goes.

When deciding on the structure of this book, we first tried to follow what we now realize was a banal course. We divided the chapters according to Elana's areas of research and expertise, gave appropriate titles to the different sections, and strove for internal order. But a review of the chapters revealed that, just as Elana's meals resist conventional categorization, so the themes or ingredients of the various sections rebelled against any imposed order and instead spilled over and flowed into one another. What ensued is an intriguing composition that often

2 Ofra Inbar-Lourie and Michal Tannenbaum

defies the set order, encompassing and reflecting Elana's work in both substance and form.

For Elana, as more than one contributor notes, "language is like life" or often life itself—rich, fluid, dynamic, individualized, unpredictable. This motto underscores her research, her teaching, and her sharp criticism, and diversely emerges as a direct and indirect theme underlying many of the chapters in this book, as illustrated in the decision of some contributors to write on issues related to their personal world and experiences. Some did so explicitly, while others adopted a personal approach toward respondents in their studies, attentive to their predicament, frustrations, and needs.

The fascinating chapter by Claire Kramsch presents her personal life story from a sociolinguistic perspective. Following Bourdieu's reflexive sociology, Kramsch's account fuses the personal and professional paths as reflected in linguistic choices, uses, exposures, and meanings accumulated over the years. Her use of metaphors such as "the ecological landscapes of the heart" conveys the way she addresses both the academic angle of disciplines such as applied linguistics or linguistic landscape, and the emotional realm of the meaning of languages to the individual. This perspective dovetails with Elana's approach to language, where personal experiences and one's life track leave their imprints on language paths.

In the same vein yet in a very different context, David Hanauer presents a personal and chilling family account: he analyzes his grandparents' Gestapo files using critical literacy tools of analysis, in an attempt to grasp the events documented in these files. Here, too, Hanauer shows how life, research, language, tragedy, and meaning are all constantly intertwined, with no need (and perhaps no way) to disentangle these core entities. His analysis presents a seemingly bureaucratic, orderly, and routine documentation of death processes and mechanisms. The racist, mundane discourse in the Gestapo files is the basis for Hanauer's analysis, which explicitly elaborates on how human rights atrocities have a literacy foundation (as well), and postulates that the origins of racism are in language—yet another forceful indication and reminder of how language is an inseparable aspect of both life and death.

If language is life, and life, as we all know, is dynamic, complex, and diverse, then it logically follows that language and language users cannot be placed in and confined to predetermined categories or artificial compartments. Institutions, however, do not do well with fuzziness and fluidity in language use, and need to devise orderly processes or mechanisms to manage and control language use and to channel individuals into neat, uniform boxes. One of the central mechanisms for gaining such control, as Elana has claimed for many years, is the use of tests—in the classroom, in schools, and at national or international levels. Several contributors have focused on testing issues, explicitly and sensitively attending to test takers, criticizing the reality of over-standardization and the artificiality often characterizing language tests.

Monica Barni addresses the misuses of the Common European Framework of Reference (CEFR) framework in the context of plurilingual Europe, where multilingualism is at times seen as a problem rather than as an asset and the language competence of immigrants is ignored. Barni provides examples from the Italian context illustrating how language tests impose monolingual policies, suppressing multilingual diversity by determining and reaffirming language hierarchy. Relying on her analysis, she suggests re-conceptualizing the validity framework of tests used for migrants and re-examining the language knowledge required, hinting at hidden agendas behind language policy.

Similarly, Catherine Elder draws attention to the debilitating impact of judging the language knowledge of individuals according to preset uniform standards that disregard learning cultures and contexts and teachers' professional judgment. In this chapter, Elder illustrates, through the teaching of Chinese in Australia, a more personal approach to descriptors that take into consideration the language acquisition background of the learners and their personal circumstances. The ensuing evaluations are more valid and more democratic and take into consideration the individual learners, as well as their teachers.

Issues of the construct validity of examinations, the match between construct and design, and the possible harms of test results are carefully discussed by Lindsay Brooks and Merril Swain. They compare students' performance in Test of English as a Foreign Language (TOEFL)-like speaking tests with authentic tasks in and outside the classroom as perceived by the test takers, showing the artificiality of the test tasks as opposed to natural authentic interactions. The chapter makes a unique contribution in that it provides room for listening to the students' voices and analyzing the test formats and contents from their own perspective, very much in line with Elana's agenda over the years.

Another study focusing on the potential damaging impact of test results is presented by Tim McNamara, Kamran Khan, and Kellie Frost, who discuss the power of tests to place individuals in social categories. Specifically, they examine the impact of residency and citizenship testing regimes on the identity of individual applicants. Failure in the language test is perceived as a marker of exclusion from the dominant-language society, leading to low self-esteem and lack of confidence regarding language knowledge and skills, with the 'victims' (as Elana might say) accepting the test's decree. As a way of providing some balancing for test coercion, the second part of this chapter applies Bakhtin's notion of authoritative discourse to the complex interaction between the official handbook for the "Life in the UK" test, used to assess assimilation in UK society (i.e. the authoritative discourse), and the individual test taker's "internally persuasive discourse."

Alan Davies raises yet another test-related issue, which has recently been at the center of a broad critical discussion where Elana has played a major role— the responsibility of the language tester. Davies poses the dilemma of just how far this responsibility can go. His analysis focuses on the codes of ethics or guidelines of good practice adopted by three central language testing organizations, noting the issue of collective responsibility among language testers. Davies wonders about the feasibility of taking action against individual testers or organizations that do not abide by the codes, and reaffirms Elana's plea for ethical, democratic test-construction processes. The dilemma regarding the extent to which testers can be held responsible for the unintended consequences of test use, however, remains unresolved.

The avoidance of boxes and categories is also relevant to Elana's strong bent to escape the ivory tower and to her contagious enthusiasm and passion for making a difference in the field. Much of her work has focused on determining policy by actively promoting initiatives that serve the political and social interests of various groups. She translates ideas from one context to another, transforms current models into new, updated, contested ones, and moves from theory to action outside university walls. Her areas of interest and research reflect this, as do her routine teaching practices—often taking students on tours to "see languages" out in the real world—and her contacts with people who can actually make a change in order to discuss new ideas—be they supervisors in the ministry of education, principals whom she regularly teaches, or policymakers.

Indeed, calling for and inspiring leadership has been central to Elana's work throughout the years, encouraging leaders who take risks and advocate a nonconformist stance, as she often does herself. This quality inspired Nancy Hornberger to trace the portraits of brave, committed women leaders who, each in their own context, have attempted to bring about linguistic change against all odds. Each portrait alone and all of them together illustrate the power of individuals in language education and policy, especially in the case of endangered languages where the dominant language is struggling for recognition. They also depict the hidden agendas and the overt and covert mechanisms that propelled them into action, and the significance of bottom-up individual democratic initiatives.

Also explicitly inspired by Elana, though from a somewhat different angle, Ofelia García and Kate Menken present their project of implementing translanguaging policies in multilingual schools. Their initiative targets school principals as leaders in their communities who determine educational language policy. Very much like similar initiatives that Elana has been involved in, García and Menken's aim is to provide the principals with tools needed to determine and implement a school language policy. The aim of the project presented in this book was to instill the concept of multilingualism as a resource, using translanguaging as a means for social justice and for empowering students and teachers.

Another call for action concerning the promotion of multilingual policy appears in the chapter by Bessie Dendrinos and Voula Gotsoulia, who describe an ambitious endeavor to build a data-driven multilingual curriculum linked up with assessment in and across languages in Greece. The data consist of descriptors generated collaboratively with expert teachers, and the detailed plan provides an impressive example of setting and implementing a multilingual educational language policy. The idea of providing an Integrated Foreign Languages Curriculum (IFLC) is essentially similar to the ethos of the proposed language policy document that Spolsky and Shohamy presented to the Israeli ministry of education, which led to the 1996 educational language policy document.

In the last decade, merging two of her passions—languages and photography—Elana has become a world leader in the promotion of the "hot" linguistic landscape scene dealing with the symbolic construction of the public space. Several contributors have written from this perspective, using the LL framework to address such issues as language rights, power relations, and language use in the educational arena.

Jasone Cenoz and Durk Gurter focused their investigation on educational settings, exploring LL in multilingual schools in the Basque Country. Through their quantitative and qualitative analyses, they show how languages are used differently to achieve a range of educational and social aims, including informative functions for students, teachers, and supervisors, serving as teaching aids, and symbolizing other constructs, including identity, culture, group affiliation, and relationships with the "other." By showing how these various functions are mirrored in the linguistic landscape of the schools, their study echoes the significance and advantages embedded in multilingualism as well as the hidden agendas associated with the multilingual aspects of the schools they explored.

A different context that was explored via the LL lens is Hebrew in the North American scene, thoroughly examined by Sharon Avni. Her main point is the decontextualization of language, showing how Hebrew goes beyond the liturgical and canonical textual experiences of religious rituals, as well as beyond its Zionist or Israeli connotations. Avni shows how Hebrew enables a variety of groups and communities to acquire new identifications and values, demonstrating how language crosses over into other categories of social meaning and how it can serve to construct a repertoire of identities, far beyond the usual ones of Jewish, Israeli, Zionist, or religious. Her chapter shows how language is indeed life—dynamic, moving along, and absorbing a range of features and characteristics of other entities it meets on its way.

Adam Jaworski addresses the crossing of borders literally and takes us on a journey outside classrooms, schools, and cities to consider welcoming signs at transitional points, mainly airports, as tools for understanding social phenomena. Analyzing a spectrum of welcoming signs, Jaworski shows that their evident key function is to create a sense of place, a local perspective, as well as a sense of mobility, perhaps from a more global point of view. Inspired by Elana's work, he treats these texts as indicative of the negotiation and contestation of different ideologies, symbolizing issues of ownership and representing different "voices," including gatekeeping and exclusion.

Exploring the linguistic landscape as a vehicle for exposing inequalities, injustice, and discrimination is an area of research that has allowed Elana and other scholars to merge social and political activism with insightful research of various

6 Ofra Inbar-Lourie and Michal Tannenbaum

minority groups (immigrants, working migrants, refugees). One linguistic group that Elana has explored over the years while fighting for their rights is the Arab minority in Israel, and several chapters in the book address issues pertinent to it.

Muhammad Amara suggests new insights on the position of Arabic in Israeli society. Relating to the impact of Jewish and modern Western culture on Palestinian society in Israel, he shows how the linguistic landscape reflects changes in the individual identities of Palestinians in Israel along with the extent and nature of the contact they have with Israeli culture. Amara interprets current features of the LL in various Palestinian areas in Israel as denoting unequal power relations in the "real world," and examines how languages cross borders and penetrate public and private domains, despite conflictual relationships.

Dafna Yitzhaki and Theo du Plessis relate to this group in the context of mixed Jewish and Arab cities in Israel, going on a journey in time and space to explore the notion of successful language planning. Through interviews and discourse analysis, they examine the situation today, 10 years after a benchmark ruling of the Israeli Supreme Court that called for bilingual signage in the public space in mixed cities, revealing serious gaps between declarations and reality. The authors rely on Elana's conceptualization of hidden agendas, which calls for activism to expose these gaps, analyze their sources, and, at times, fight to overcome them.

The third study addressing issues touching on the Arab minority in Israel is by Julia Schlam-Salman, Elite Olshtain, and Zvi Bekerman. Exploring identity construction among Jews and Arabs in a bilingual/binational school, the authors examine perceptions and understandings of Jewish and Palestinian Israeli students concerning power and identity construction vis-à-vis language entities. In harmony with Elana's approach, they too shift from the local to the global, elaborating on the potentially unique roles of English in this social and educational setting, and demonstrating how power relations are reflected in language issues. They show how the students re-appropriated English, "denationalized" or "renationalized" it, and found that this process facilitated their emancipation from locally imposed identity categorizations.

Elizabeth Lanza and Hirut Woldemariam critically present the power of English in a different context. They deal with Ethiopia's intrusive language policy, where English is used as the language of instruction from Grade Five despite the low proficiency of both teachers and students in the language. Issues of language, ideologies, and practices arise as well as hidden social and political agendas when English—the prestigious language, the language of the textbook—drives out the local language. Through this analysis, they point to possible harmful effects of such policy on societal, educational, as well as individual levels.

While acknowledging Elana's rejection of set categories for characterizing language speakers, Kendall King and Lyn Fogle examine a highly conventional categorizing feature—gender. Elana rarely addresses gender issues, as the authors note, perhaps due to her tendency to avoid tags and strict boundaries. In their analysis, however, the authors expand Elana's focus on the experience of the individual language learner and her concern with pedagogical and policy approaches. Analyzing "serendipitous" data excerpts, they explore how gender and sexuality are constructed and construed in different settings of ESL classrooms. By pointing to mechanisms through which the identity of individual learners is enacted in these classrooms, they show how language can privilege or marginalize certain students. They thereby deconstruct existing structures and shed light on political tendencies deeply entrenched everywhere, including in language classrooms.

It is not only language per se that marginalizes individuals, however, but rather the combination of language knowledge and other social and economic forces that act as gatekeepers. This is documented by Tom Ricento in a moving study on refugees in Canada who are struggling to affirm their social and professional capital. The findings demonstrate how, despite their professional qualifications, the local labor market obstructs the validation of their considerable skills. They are denied equal access to employment and social rights in their new country and are left with a sense of powerlessness and despair, with language playing a central role in this state of mind.

While the link between language and cognition has not been one of Elana's main research interests, she has often explicitly referred to its importance. This link is broadly addressed in Ellen Bialystok's chapter. Through a series of studies covering the entire life span, Bialystok shows how bilingualism contributes to cognitive reserve, to executive functions, and to many other cognitive aspects. This area can be viewed as a variation on "language as resource," even though Bialystok does not refer to it explicitly in these terms. This chapter further supports claims about the advantages of bi/multilingualism, a finding fitting Elana's view on this topic, even when approached from various different other angles.

Andrew Cohen, too, addresses the advantages of bilingualism and the centrality of the brain's executive functions. Exploring a unique kind of individual, in terms of language abilities, he analyzes the phenomenon of "super-multilingualism," seeking to understand what is involved in acquiring proficiency in many languages. In tune with Elana's holistic approach to language and her efforts to contextualize the individual, Cohen suggests several internal and external explanatory factors for this phenomenon, as well as actions and programs that can promote its development.

The final chapter, by Jim Lantolf, offers an overview of language, its use, its assessment, and mainly of people within languages. Lantolf elaborates on the view that languages are, in fact, non-entities without their speakers, and that signs do not preexist in some abstract decontextualized space, but constituted in purposeful communicating activity by virtue of their integrational role. This integrational approach is closely related to the view of "language as life": Lantolf focuses on the individual as the central agency for delivering meaning and on effective rather than correct communication. Lantolf also asserts that speakers value the changeable and adaptable features of languages, placing special emphasis on the creativity

8 Ofra Inbar-Lourie and Michal Tannenbaum

involved in listening to and understanding the other, a view that is, in many ways, the very core of this book.

Throughout the years, Elana has offered a critical view on a broad spectrum of key topics in applied linguistics, including language testing, language policy, linguistic landscape, immigrants in schools, language rights, and more, from an interdisciplinary perspective. Her innovative work has inspired many scholars in various areas of applied linguistics to reconsider some commonly held understandings, specifically with regard to the impact of language and languaging on individual language users rather than on the masses, as is strongly evident in this book.

Furthermore, Elana's holistic view of language and the way she merges language, research, and life come forth in the program she has chaired for the last 20 years at Tel Aviv University after taking over from its founder, Elite Olshtain, who is also one of the contributors to this book. The Language Education Program that both of us are part of is unique in that it grapples both with global issues and with specific dilemmas within the multilingual context of Israeli society. The program deals with diversity, immigration, language policies, language testing, curriculum, psychology, linguistics, and other topics against the backdrop of globalization. It also contends with the special historical features and the current linguistic practices of the local Israeli scene, with particular emphasis on the educational system. It brings together educators and scholars from different linguistic backgrounds, all studying together, probing, analyzing, and researching the common and the unique in language education issues from a critical perspective. The ethos of the program—its emphasis on social justice, on language rights, and on multilingualism—is strongly inspired by Elana's endless energies, initiatives, activism, and critical view of current phenomena. She inspires her students, but not less so us, her colleagues and close friends. We see this book as an homage to her work, her vision, and her outstanding contribution to these fields, and as a reflection of her integrative research and vision.

This book does not aim to summarize Elana's work. Perhaps it should be considered an interim summary of the path we have traveled so far, but more so as a hope of many new beginnings. As Constantine Cavafy tells us (translated by D. Mendelsohn):

> *As you set out on the way to Ithaca*
> *Hope that the road is a long one,*
> *Filled with adventures, filled with understanding . . .*

PART 1

Restoring People to Language Assessment

1

LANGUAGE TESTS FOR RESIDENCY AND CITIZENSHIP AND THE CONFERRING OF INDIVIDUALITY

Tim McNamara, Kamran Khan, and Kellie Frost

Introduction

A fundamental aspect of the power of tests (Shohamy, 2001) is their role as gatekeepers to membership of valued social categories. Tests thus have the power to confer on a person a sense of being socially recognizable as acceptable or unacceptable, as belonging or not belonging. Shohamy (2001) was one of the first in our field to draw attention to the famous passage in *Discipline and Punish* (Foucault, 1977) in which Foucault identifies the way in which tests and examination confer individuality:

> The examination as the fixing, at once ritual and "scientific," of individual differences, as the pinning down of each individual in his own particularity . . . clearly indicates the appearance of a new modality of power in which each individual receives as his status his own individuality, and in which he is linked by his status to the features, the measurements, the gaps, the "marks" that characterize him and make him a "case."
>
> (p. 192)

Language requirements in procedures for gaining residency and citizenship, satisfied through passing tests, are examples of the practices identified by Foucault. Such tests, we will argue, are mechanisms of wider ideologies that restrict entrance for migrants and influence particular learner behaviors toward a dominant language (Blackledge, 2009a, 2009b; McNamara & Shohamy, 2008; Shohamy, 2006). McNamara and Roever (2006) describe this interface between ideological mechanism (Shohamy, 2006) and personal experience as "the point of insertion of a policy into individual lives" (p. 192).

12 Tim McNamara et al.

In this chapter, we report case studies of the experience of individuals as they engage with the discourses enacted through such tests. We begin by discussing the relationship of language and social practices in requirements for residency and citizenship, and then consider two contexts: three individuals describing the impact of repeated sitting of language tests to gain permanent residency in Australia, and the experience of a single individual negotiating the language requirements involved in becoming a citizen in the UK.

Language, Residency, and Citizenship

Knowledge of the national language is increasingly becoming a criterion in the determination of rights to immigration and citizenship, evidenced by the growing number of countries adopting formal language testing regimes (Extra, Spotti, & Van Avermaet, 2009). Language testing for immigration and citizenship purposes reflects the "common sense" notion, central to contemporary political and media discourses across Europe and other Western nations, including Australia, that knowledge of the national or official language on the part of migrants is a prerequisite for their successful "integration." It is widely argued that language-testing practices thereby normalize linguistic and cultural homogeneity and reinforce discourses that situate minority languages and multilingual practices as threats to social cohesion and security (Blackledge, 2006, 2009b; Horner, 2009; Shohamy, 2009; Stevenson & Schanze, 2009; Van Avermaet, 2009). For example, Blackledge (2006, 2009b) highlights the ways in which British political discourses imply that "language," or more precisely, a lack of knowledge of English, is the primary factor driving unemployment, crime, and social unrest among particular migrant groups, despite the fact that the groups targeted are typically second- or third-generation "migrants" who are bilingual speakers of the national language. Such discourses, he argues, are often used to justify the use of language tests as a means of promoting "social cohesion," masking the presence of other, state-entrenched obstacles to social participation. Similarly, Shohamy (2001, 2006, 2009) has repeatedly pointed out that tests are used for purposes far broader than simply measuring knowledge, and that the widespread acceptance of the legitimacy of tests means that the often discriminatory and illiberal policy agendas they serve remain hidden.

Language Tests, Immigration, and Residency in Australia

Before being eligible to apply for Australian citizenship, migrants must first be granted permanent residency (PR). PR rights are accessible via a range of migration pathways: economic (or skilled), family, and refugee and humanitarian streams. Currently, only the economic migration pathway involves a language test requirement, although this may soon change (Morrison, 2013).

The language test requirement for PR in Australia forms part of an overall points system in which a minimum of 60 points across a variety of categories, including age, educational qualifications, employment experience, and English language ability, is needed. As of July 2011, the minimum required score was increased from 5 to 6 on the International English Language Testing System (IELTS). No points are attributed to the minimum IELTS score of 6, but extra points are awarded for scores of 7 and 8 on IELTS, 10 and 20 points, respectively, and these extra points are needed in most cases to fulfill the overall requirement. While this has remained a relatively uncontroversial policy—the notion that migrants need to be competent users of English in order to be able to gain skilled employment is, for the most part, uncontested—the reality is that over half those applying for permanent residency via the economic stream are already living in Australia[1]—working in a skilled profession and having completed their higher education in Australia—and yet are unable to readily achieve the points they need for language. What do these migrants make of the experience of being subjected to this testing regime?

Language Tests and the Individual's Experience of the Path to Residency

In the following section, interviews with three migrants attempting to meet language requirements as part of their application for PR in Australia are reported. They were accessed through professional contacts and test preparation courses, and all volunteered to share their experiences. All have lived in Australia for at least three years, have completed tertiary qualifications in Australia, and are in full-time employment. They have each so far satisfied all of the criteria for permanent residency apart from the language test score requirement. The interviews reveal that the test experiences of these individuals affect their perceptions of self and belonging in conflicting ways.

"S" from Sri Lanka has lived in Australia for five years. She completed tertiary education in Australia and has been working full-time in her field for over a year. "S" has spoken English since birth and identifies herself as bilingual (English-Sinhala). She has so far attempted IELTS four times and achieved 8 overall on the third and fourth attempts, but no higher than 7.5 for writing; she requires 8 in all four skills in order to gain the points she requires for permanent residency. Although she believes that language tests are an appropriate means of ensuring migrants are able to communicate with the local population, she identifies language as a marker of identity in conflicting ways. First, her English knowledge positions her as belonging in the dominant community in relation to her Asian friends:

> *I've got a few friends, they're from Asian countries, they've been studying here, I mean, they've finished their degrees but unless you know them very well, it's very*

14 Tim McNamara et al.

difficult to converse with them simply because their English is not too good at all. So, it's a good way of gauging somebody's ability to communicate, but what I think is you shouldn't have a very high score, because after all, um, English is not the mother tongue of most of us, so it's not fair to think us of being of very, very good high standard as maybe a native speaker would.

Although she identifies herself as an English-Sinhala bilingual speaker, in relation to the test she identifies herself as an outsider (non-native speaker) due to her inability to achieve the score she requires on the writing component of the test. This positioning seems consistent with dominant ideologies. She does not challenge the notion that a "native" standard exists, nor that it is superior to other forms of language, but she contests the imposition of such a standard as a benchmark for communicative ability:

It's pretty frustrating when I mean, yeah I can sort of communicate the whole point is to be able to communicate in English properly and I don't have a communication problem as such.

"E" is from Iran and he has lived in Australia for over three years. He completed his Master degree in Australia and has been working in his field for a year. As with "S" above, he does not challenge the government's right to test language, but he sees the score level demanded as perpetuating a circle of exclusion. He reports difficulty making friends, due in part to a lack of confidence communicating in English. This reinforces the exclusion he feels due to the test score requirement, which he perceives as unattainable unless he is first able to access the community of native speakers:

I couldn't find friends here, I was mostly alone and I am alone right now after being, living here for 3½ years. It's a long time for being alone but I, I don't know is it good thing or bad thing but I got used to it eventually . . . other part was obviously the language barrier.

To get [IELTS] 8 the things that makes an 8 is not achieved during the class. You have to, you have to, you have to be here or have a great connection with the people here, the native people.

"M" from Colombia has lived in Australia for four years. She completed her Master degree in Australia, and has been working for two years in an administrative position. She started learning English when she arrived and requires a score of 7 on IELTS for permanent residency. She has made two unsuccessful attempts so far.

It is interesting to compare the way she perceived herself before her second attempt at the test and her reports immediately afterwards. Before the test, she asserted her ability to communicate effectively in English and her successful integration into the Australian community. She rejected the need to justify the legitimacy of her sense of belonging that she feels the test requirement implies:

> *I am functional. I work in an Australian company. And if you ask them, I think, they have no problems with me and my communication . . . I haven't heard any complaint about me from my customers, because I'm in contact with them every day. I pay taxes, like you. I haven't committed any crime here. I consider myself a decent person and my husband is very decent. We were trying just, we are trying just to build a better future.*
>
> *I speak a lot with Neil and Bridget, they are my neighbors. Ah, my neighbors are so lovely. My neighbor is Neil, he's very Aussie. And Bridget is super Aussie. And Rachie, from work, she's super super Aussie, and Michael as well, the way they, the way they speak to me, their slang. This is a different thing than the listening IELTS test. Even if they use slang with me, I can understand everything . . . we couldn't feel the difference between, you know . . .*

Speaking to her after her lack of success on the test for a second time, she was hesitating and self-correcting her grammar and pronunciation. Her response to the question "Do you feel less confident than you did before?" reveals that her test experiences had undermined her sense of confidence and led to her perceiving herself as a learner, or imperfect speaker:

> *Yes, and I have started feeling silly most of the time. Especially with my speaking. Every time I have to think twice . . .*

Her comments in relation to the test scores also suggest her feelings of belonging in the wider community have been undermined by her test experiences. She sees herself positioned as "non-white" and as a non-native speaker of English, and she embraces her "otherness" by mocking what she perceives to be the dominant ideology underlying the test requirements:

> *They just "we're going to make it harder for them, 7, 8, because they are not white people, because they are not as good as Australians and English and Americans are and Irish and they want to steal this country and they want to steal jobs from Australians . . ."*

A number of themes emerge from these cases. First, the value of English is recognized in terms of social inclusion and access to opportunities in Australia. Despite objections to score requirements, all three seemed to accept the necessity of a language test in the immigration process. As described by Shohamy (2001), language tests are socially recognized and legitimized gatekeeping mechanisms that have the power to influence an individual's sense of belonging or not belonging in the community. The migrants viewed their inability to achieve the

16 Tim McNamara et al.

required test score as a marker of their "outsider" status, even when their non-test experiences evidenced quite the contrary—successful integration into the community—as in the cases of "S" and "M" particularly. "E"'s comments further suggest that the success on the test represented successful assimilation with native speakers. Ironically, from his perspective, such success could only be achieved through full inclusion in the native speaker community, which he felt excluded from due, in part, to the perception that his English language skills lacked legitimacy. Even when the test score requirements were deemed unfair by migrants, because they were inconsistent with the language demands faced in their social and working lives, they all seemed to accept the legitimacy of the test as a measure of their English ability. Their failure to achieve the score needed was seen to reflect their status as learners, rather than fully competent speakers of English, even when they did not experience communication difficulties in their daily lives.

Dealing with the Language Demands of the Citizenship Requirements in the UK

In this section, the convergence of policy and the personal in the construction of the subjectivity of "UK citizen" is viewed through the experience of "W," a migrant from Yemen, in his negotiation of the Life in the UK test. "W" was selected for this study as he was in the last phase of the citizenship process and had been attending local ESOL (English for Speakers of Other Languages) classes, where he met the researcher, "K." "W"'s experience will be considered from a Bakhtinian perspective.

In 2005, the Life in the UK (LUK) test was introduced as a language and civic knowledge requirement for migrants wishing to become British citizens. The introduction of the test was a response to social disturbances during the summer of 2001 involving British-Asian youths, white far-right extremists, and the police. In the aftermath of the riots, three reports referred to levels of English language proficiency among Asian migrant communities as a root cause for racial segregation (Cantle Commission, 2002; Denham, 2002; Ritchie, 2001). The policy "panacea" for the perceived breakdown lay in the promotion of English as a common language and British national citizenship to fuse together a supposedly fragmented set of communities (Greenwood & Robins, 2002; Sasse, 2005). Consequently, in 2002, the language requirement for British citizenship was introduced as part of the Nationality, Immigration and Asylum Act. The LUK test became a way of satisfying this requirement.

The LUK test contains 24 multiple-choice questions. A score of 18 out of 24 is required to pass, and the test can be taken as many times as necessary. The test questions target knowledge of life in the UK (TSO, 2007) and are written to a B1 CEFR (Common European Framework of Reference) level of English, to

Language Tests, Citizenship, Individuality **17**

satisfy the "sufficient knowledge of a language for the purpose of an application for naturalisation" requirement (Home Office, 2002).

The content of the test is derived from a handbook named *Life in the United Kingdom: A journey to citizenship* (TSO, 2007). In 2013, the book was renamed *Life in the UK: A guide for new residents* (TSO, 2013), reflecting the extension of the testing regime and language requirement to those seeking permanent residence through indefinite leave to remain (Blackledge, 2009a).

Citizenship testing requires a demonstration that particular values and words have been internalized by the test taker (Löwenheim & Gazit, 2009). Hence, test preparation requires the negotiation of specific discourses. "Ideological becoming" may aptly define this preparation process, which Bakhtin (1981) describes as "the process of selectively assimilating the words of others" (p. 341). A test becomes a "zone of contact" (Bakhtin, 1981), in which the individual may struggle with discourses promoted through the test ("authoritative discourses"). The individual may assimilate these discourses in their own way so that they become "internally persuasive discourse."

Authoritative discourse "demands that we acknowledge it, that we make it our own" and is encountered "with its authority already fused" (Bakhtin, 1981, p. 342). These discourses are endowed with a preexistent power. Thus, the authoritative word is "located in a distanced zone, organically connected with a past that is felt to be hierarchically higher" (Bakhtin, 1981, p. 342). In the case of the British citizenship test, the LUK official handbook is the authoritative discourse to such an extent that it is endorsed as "the ONLY official handbook" (TSO, 2007, front cover, original emphasis). Although unofficial study guides are widely available, the 2007 LUK book distinguishes its place in the hierarchy of competing discourses (Yurchak, 2006) by affirming that "None of these is officially approved" (TSO, 2007, p. 4). The most recent handbook asserts "Everything that you will need to know to pass the Life in the UK test is included in this handbook" (TSO, 2013, p. 10).

The extent to which new discourses are assimilated is what Bakhtin (1981) refers to as "internally persuasive discourse." This discourse "is affirmed through assimilation, tightly woven with 'one's own words.' In the rounds of everyday consciousness, the internally persuasive word is half-ours and half-someone else's" (p. 346). Whereas authoritative discourse is rigid and impermeable to change, internally persuasive discourse is open to "creativity and productiveness" and "does not remain in an isolated, static condition" (p. 345). The following section will examine how "W" used the LUK handbook and made it internally persuasive.

"W" was the first person in his immediate community to take the test, meaning he had to be self-reliant to be successful. In negotiating the LUK handbook, "W" was faced with a problem, which he describes below:

> "W": *I tell you how I start . . . I sit at home and I read the book from the beginning, from the-*

> "K":   What like a story?
> "W":   Yeah, I don't know about around 90 percent of the word I don't know.

"W"'s problem is that he was faced with an authoritative discourse at a level of English beyond his grasp. Such struggle is an essential part of ideological becoming. According to Bakhtin (1981), "the importance of struggling with another's discourse, its influences on an individual's coming to ideological consciousness, is enormous" (p. 348). Various discourses compete in the consciousness of the individual, and for "W," grappling with how to deal with the LUK handbook would contribute directly in assimilating these new words. To resolve this struggle, "W" would have to be creative in making the discourse "half-his." He states his solution in the following exchange:

> "W":   I left and I finished the book . . . everything I write . . . any new word . . . even two . . . I don't know maybe I need
> "K":   You never know
> "W":   I don't know, I don't get . . . I never . . . I had an Arabic dictionary and I started . . . I start in my language. Yeah
> "K":   Do you, do you find it easy to remember the words?
> "W":   Yeah. Of course (OK) when I start . . . memorizing and I think have a good memory to memorize things.
> "K":   Yeah, I think so as well
> "W":   Yeah, and straightaway each word I know then I go back to the Life in the UK and back in Arabic and I have a background about the grammar and how the time, the rules . . . the time . . . the past, the future and the present. Then I read it as Arabic. And in Arabic, I don't care about it, when I go home . . . guess any question.

"W" had been proactive and creative in finding a solution for the initial difficulties in dealing with the LUK handbook. Rather than trying harder in English, "W" used the linguistic resources he had available in Arabic and tackled the problem in a bilingual way. He translated the LUK book into Arabic and read it this way. The test was in English, so "W" worked between his Arabic and English books. This is not to be viewed as a deviant practice, but recognition that despite the ideology of imposing a dominant language, the LUK test aided "W"'s bilingual development. García (2009) states: "These practices are in no way deficient, they simply reflect greater choices" (p. 46). Such bilingual practices serve to undermine the ideological basis of such tests by enabling test takers to utilize their multilingual repertoire rather than privileging the dominant language promoted by the test.

"W" was interviewed numerous times over seven months. On two separate occasions, which were three months apart, he referred to knowledge attributable to the LUK test that remained within his "everyday rounds of consciousness" (Bakhtin, 1981, p. 346). The first is below:

Language Tests, Citizenship, Individuality **19**

> "W": A background. Every day . . . I learn many things new about life in the UK and as well, when I learn—when I learn, when I did the . . . Life in the UK exam, the book guide me to many things like where to go
>
> "K": Yeah, yeah
>
> "W": The role of the UK, the traditional, their habit
>
> "K": Was that many things you didn't know before?
>
> "W": Yes . . . many things I didn't know, but now if you ask me about UK . . . I can guide you to their . . . traditional, their life, their festival (sure) their . . . many things, I know . . . their source of benefit

The latent knowledge from the test remained in the following section. The context is that "W" is wondering how to make sure he can both fulfill his working hours in a factory and study at a local college. This problem is practical one. "K" was a former ESOL (English for Speakers of Other Languages) teacher and "W" asks "K" whether there is financial support from the job center for working part-time hours and attending classes:

> "K": I-I'm not sure . . . because actually sometimes when I was with my students I used to teach . . . some of them used to tell me "I have to go to the job center" . . . but they still came to class
>
> "W": But . . . they give to them only 16 hour . . . maximum
>
> "K": Could be . . . I think so
>
> "W": It should be more than 16 hour . . . they will not allow . . . help you for funding
>
> "K": If you do more than 16?
>
> "W": Yeah
>
> "K": I think that's right yeah
>
> "W": But as I know from the Life in the UK test . . . you know there is for education

Three years after the test has taken place, "W" is able to readily draw upon knowledge from the test material. According to what he has learned, there may be funds available for people in education. This evidences how the discourses from the test were assimilated in resolving an everyday problem for "W."

In terms of subjectivity, this has other implications. Tests can define and recognize subject positions (McNamara & Roever, 2006). Citizenship tests may well be considered unjust, but migrants such as "W" may create conditions that redress the balance of justice through their test preparation and linguistic resources. Thus, the test is negotiated, in some ways, on their own terms. This allows greater latitude in subject positions. Rather than coercion toward a particular set of subject positions, making discourses internally persuasive can also offer alternative subject positions to those provided by authoritative discourses.

Discussion

The picture that emerges from the case studies reported in this chapter is the complexity of effects on self-perception triggered by encounters with language testing regimes in the context of residency and citizenship, and the resources that are developed as a response. The studies in the two settings reported in this chapter differ somewhat in their findings and their emphasis.

In the Australian case, the individuals are confronted with an irrational policy. The underlying driving force of the policy is the fierce political debate that erupted in 2010 about the desirable size of the population, given the strains on infrastructure brought about by increases in population in some of the major cities, with both main political parties agreeing to reduce the overall immigrant intake—and language testing regimes being a suitable mechanism for doing so. The required English levels were raised in 2011 as a result. While the overt justification for the policy is that individuals chosen should have the necessary language skills to pursue their chosen profession, the reality is that individuals who have completed higher degrees in English in Australia, and have successfully managed their professional roles in the Australian environment for some time, are deemed to be inadequately proficient on the basis of their test performance. One response to this would be to confront the irrationality of the policy, but it is precisely due to the disempowering nature of tests that the individual instead loses confidence in his or her own abilities.

For example, "M" from Colombia, in Australia for four years, and working successfully in an administrative position following completion of her master's degree, prior to taking the test required for her to be granted permanent residency, rejected the necessity for the test on the grounds that she was perfectly adequately communicatively competent. Following her failure to get the required IELTS 7, she reports that her confidence has been undermined. Similarly, the bilingual Sinhala-English native speaker from Sri Lanka, who has been in Australia for five years, completing a degree, and now working professionally for a year, sees the requirement for her to get IELTS 8 as not justified by the reality of her communicative behavior in the real world of work and social interaction in Australia. Nevertheless, the impact of the testing regime is to lead her to being positioned as unlike other Australian native speakers of English, a position that she accepts.

The UK case reported here has a rather different emphasis. It shows how the very act of being "called into being" by ideology (Althusser, 2001) triggers the creation of a subjectivity that paradoxically does not conform perfectly to the terms of the ideology. This understanding is central to the work of poststructuralist thinkers such as Jacques Derrida (1998) and Judith Butler (1997), who, while accepting the reality of the potentially determinist role of discourse in the construction of subjectivity, and not resorting too easily to notions of agency independent of discourse, explore the destabilization of the subjectivity so constructed. Butler (1997), for example, writes:

As a form of power, subjection is paradoxical. To be dominated by a power external to oneself is a familiar and agonizing form that power takes. To find, however, that what "one" is, one's very formation as a subject, is in some sense dependent on that power, is quite another . . . Subjection consists precisely in this fundamental dependency on a discourse we never chose but that, paradoxically, initiates and sustains our agency.

(pp. 1–2)

The Bakhtinian notion of "internally persuasive discourse" and its relation to "authoritative discourse" is used to discuss this phenomenon in this chapter; we see the way in which "W" conforms, but not exactly, to what is expected, by and in the very process of responding to the imperatives of discourse. Similar themes are canvassed within work in poststructuralism (McNamara, 2012). For thinkers such as Butler, it is in the individual experience of subjects that the role of discourse in the creation of subjectivity, and paradoxically, too, its limits, are best explored.

Note

1. For the period July–December 2011, out of a total of 87,259 permanent additions, 58,392 came via the economic migration stream. 29,560 of the 58,392 were already temporary residents in Australia (www.immi.gov.au/media/publications/statistics/immigration-update/update-july-dec11.pdf).

References

Althusser, L. (2001). *Lenin and philosophy and other essays*. (B. Brewster, Trans.). New York: Monthly Review Press (original work published 1968).

Bakhtin, M. (1981). *The dialogic imagination: Four essays*. Austin, TX/London: University of Texas Press.

Blackledge, A. (2006). The racialization of language in British political discourse. *Critical Discourse Studies*, *3*(1), 61–79.

Blackledge, A. (2009a). "As a country we do expect": The further extension of testing regimes in the United Kingdom. *Language Assessment Quarterly*, *6*(1), 6–16.

Blackledge, A. (2009b). Inventing English as "convenient" fiction: Language testing regimes in the United Kingdom. In G. Extra, M. Spotti, & P. van Avermaet (Eds.), *Language testing, migration & citizenship* (pp. 66–86). London: Continuum.

Butler, J. (1997). *The psychic life of power: Theories in subjection*. Palo Alto, CA: Stanford University Press.

Cantle Commission (2002). *Challenging local communities to change Oldham*. Coventry: The Institute of Community Cohesion.

Denham, J. (2002). *Building cohesive communities: A report of the ministerial group on public order and community cohesion*. London: Home Office.

Derrida, J. (1998). *Monolingualism of the other; or, the prosthesis of origin*. (P. Mensah, Trans.). Palo Alto, CA: Stanford University Press (original work published 1996).

Extra, G., Spotti, M., & Van Avermaet, P. (Eds.) (2009). *Language testing, migration and citizenship*. London and New York: Continuum.

Foucault, M. (1977). *Discipline and punish: The birth of the prison*. (A. Sheridan, Trans.). London: Allen Lane (original work published 1975).

García, O. (2009). *Bilingual education in the 21st century*. Chichester: Wiley-Blackwell.

Greenwood, J., & Robins, L. (2002). Citizenship tests and education: Embedding a concept. *Parliamentary Affairs*, *55*(3), 505–522.

Home Office (2002). *Nationality, Immigration and Asylum Act*. London: HMSO.

Horner, K. (2009). Regimenting language, mobility and citizenship in Luxembourg. In G. Extra, M. Spotti, & P. Van Avermaet (Eds.), *Language testing, migration and citizenship* (pp. 148–166). London/New York: Continuum.

Löwenheim, O., & Gazit, O. (2009). Power and examination: A critique of citizenship tests. *Security Dialogue*, *40*(2), 145–167.

McNamara, T. (2012). Poststructuralism and its challenges for applied linguistics. *Applied Linguistics*, *33*(5), 473–482.

McNamara, T., & Roever, C. (2006). *Language testing: The social dimension*. Oxford: Blackwell.

McNamara, T., & Shohamy, E. (2008). Language tests and human rights. *International Journal of Applied Linguistics*, *18*(1), 89–95.

Morrison, S. (2013). *Address to the Affinity Intercultural Foundation, Sydney, July*. Retrieved from www.affinity.org.au/wp-content/uploads/2013/07/Morrison-Doing-far-more-to-build-our-nation-170713.pdf (accessed March 1, 2014).

Ritchie, D. (2001). *Oldham independent review. One Oldham—one future*. Manchester: Government for the North West.

Sasse, G. (2005). Securitization or securing rights? Exploring the conceptual foundations of policies towards minorities and migrants in Europe. *Journal of Common Market Studies*, *43*(4), 673–693.

Shohamy, E. (2001). *The power of tests: A critical perspective on the uses of language tests*. London: Pearson.

Shohamy, E. (2006). *Language policy*. Abingdon, UK: Routledge.

Shohamy, E. (2009). Language tests for immigrants: Why language? Why tests? Why citizenship? In G. Hogan-Brun, C. Mar-Molinero, & P. Stevenson (Eds.), *Discourses on language and integration* (pp. 45–60). Amsterdam/Philadelphia, PA: John Benjamins.

Stevenson, P., & Schanze, L. (2009). Language, migration and citizenship in Germany: Discourses on integration and belonging. In G. Extra, M. Spotti, & P. van Avermaet (Eds.), *Language testing, migration and citizenship* (pp. 87–106). London/New York: Continuum.

The Stationery Office (TSO) (2007). *Life in the United Kingdom: A journey to citizenship* (2nd ed.). Richmond: TSO.

The Stationery Office (TSO) (2013). *Life in the United Kingdom: A guide for new residents* (3rd ed.). Richmond: TSO.

Van Avermaet, P. (2009). Fortress Europe? Language policy regimes for immigration and citizenship. In G. Hogan-Brun, C. Mar-Molinero, & P. Stevenson (Eds.), *Discourses on language and integration* (pp. 15–44). Amsterdam/Philadelphia, PA: John Benjamins.

Yurchak, A. (2006). *Everything was forever, until it was no more*. Princeton, NJ/Oxford: Princeton University Press.

2

SETTING STANDARDS FOR MULTILINGUAL CURRICULA TO TEACH AND TEST FOREIGN LANGUAGES

Bessie Dendrinos and Voula Gotsoulia

Social and Educational Context

As a response to the surge for multilingual citizenry in modern societies, particularly in Europe where the promotion of multilingualism has been proclaimed as a key objective by the European Commission, Greece has been trying to honor the 2002 two-plus-one European Council decision and provide opportunities to students to learn two languages in addition to their mother tongue during their compulsory schooling years. English is the first foreign language offered in the early years of primary school. French and German are offered, as options, as of the last two years of primary school. Students may continue with their second language choice in secondary school, where, before the Greek economic crisis, Italian and Spanish were also offered as electives for foreign language study.

Which foreign languages to include or exclude from the school curriculum has rarely been the result of sociolinguistically informed thinking. It depends on the ad hoc decisions of politicians in the Ministry of Education—replaced as soon as the government changes (every four years, at best). That is, even though questions about language inclusion and exclusion are deeply political and may have economic consequences, the issue is not viewed as a component of coherent language education planning by authorized bodies of experts. Sadly, this phenomenon is not unique to Greece, where, for the first time ever, in 2010 a language education planning project was commissioned to the University of Athens,[1] which is executing a number of other projects also, all aiming at institutionalizing multilingual concerns in language teaching, testing, and assessment. One of these projects is concerned with the development of the multilingual curriculum presented in this chapter. The second one is concerned with a multilingual examination suite, leading to the state certificate for language proficiency known with its Greek acronym KPG (Dendrinos, 2013).[2] Both of these have employed the six-level language proficiency scale of the Council of Europe, as it appears in the Common European Framework of Reference for Languages (henceforth, CEFR, Council of Europe, 2001), and have aligned their descriptors to those of the CEFR, recognizing its value as the only document that provides "objective criteria for describing language proficiency . . . [so as to] facilitate the mutual recognition of qualifications gained in different learning contexts, and accordingly . . . aid European mobility" (CEFR, p. 1). In describing, for the first time ever, leveled language knowledge and communication skills, the CEFR—despite its weaknesses, which have to do with its descriptors of language proficiency being too vague and general—initiated the process of standards setting for language teaching, learning, and assessment.

CEFR also made a valuable contribution by distinguishing between the concept of multilingualism and that of plurilingualism. The latter, as understood and defined by the CEFR, shifts attention away from the twentieth-century influential construct of the ideal native speaker and focuses on the language user who has a repertoire of languages or language varieties, and communicative competences of different types and levels. A language user's repertoire is viewed as dynamic, in the sense that it develops and changes throughout one's life. The CEFR's notion of plurilingual education is also useful because it is viewed as a means to developing the learner's "ability to perceive and mediate the relationships which exist among languages and cultures" (Council of Europe, 2014).[3]

The term "plurilingualism" has not been endorsed either by multilingualism studies or by the European Commission. And, although we value the ideas that this term signifies, in this chapter we choose to use the all-inclusive term "multilingualism," as do many academic texts and policy documents, hoping that the different social meanings that this single term conceals will surface. Some of the meanings wrapped up in the term "multilingualism" are as antithetical as the two that are considered at the end of this chapter: polyglots versus speakers with a multilingual ethos of communication; multilingual versus monolingual approaches for teaching and testing foreign languages. Distinctions such as these are crucial for anyone concerned with the study and/or the social practice of multilingualism, just as it is essential to understand that underneath each antithetical notion of multilingualism are two different views of language: the first is a structuralist view of language as "a closed and finite system that does not enable other languages to 'smuggle in'" (Shohamy, 2011, p. 418), which is forever turning the spotlight on the formal properties of language. The second is a semiotic view of language as a system of meaning making through language in use. In the latter view of language, social agents use all the resources available to them, be they different modes of communication, languages, language varieties, and different media, to design meanings (cf. Kress, 2009).

It is in this context that the use of multilingual frameworks and curricula, such as the Integrated Foreign Languages Curriculum (henceforth, IFLC), developed in Greece is presented and discussed here.

The significance of the IFLC is that it serves as a framework of objective criteria for all the foreign language courses being offered in school (cf. Spolsky, 1995) and that it offers comparable descriptions of communicative and linguistic performance in different languages, across distinct levels of language proficiency.

In the sections that follow, the methodology and the tools employed for the development of the IFLC are presented and future actions are discussed. As a conclusion, we briefly discuss how a multilingual curriculum such as this may service multilingual approaches to language teaching, testing, and assessment.

The IFLC

The IFLC was developed as a component of the new National School Curriculum by a team of experts commissioned by the Greek Ministry of Education in 2010–2011.[4] The curriculum document defines the language performance goals, to be achieved at key learning stages, equivalent to the CEFR proficiency levels, in school. Guidelines on to how to deal with the subject matter in the classroom (i.e. which approaches to language teaching, testing, and assessment to use) are provided in a supplementary publication (the "Teacher's Guide").[5]

The IFLC, presently being experimentally implemented in 160 schools throughout the country, is a unified, integrated curriculum for both primary and secondary education (Karavas, 2012). It is the first time that foreign languages are treated as a single discipline in school, with a coherent structure and common aims, essentially decoupled from the organization of the rest of the school curriculum in cycles or grades linked to school years. For the implementation of the new curriculum, schools have been encouraged to group students taking one of the languages offered according to their attested proficiency in the language in question. For instance, fifth grade students diagnosed to be at A2 level of proficiency in English may be grouped together with sixth grade students at the same proficiency level. The critical assumption underlying such practice is directly related to the literacies that language learners have developed, irrespective of classroom teaching, and the experience they have had through or with the target language in informal language learning situations, outside formal school courses, in private language centers, during after-school hours, or in their after-school activities (using Internet, watching television programs, etc.). Greek school students' foreign language proficiency—especially in the most popular foreign languages— differs significantly depending on the language input they have from outside school contexts. Hence, the language proficiency levels are used to explicitly model and systematize language learning, departing from the somewhat vague distinction of language classes conforming to school grades.

The pilot version of the IFLC has entailed systematic efforts by the curriculum developers to specify leveled descriptors of language use in different situational contexts, and more fine-grained linguistic descriptors. The starting point was the KPG examination suite specifications, and the leveled descriptors therein,

26 Bessie Dendrinos and Voula Gotsoulia

organized in terms of communicative language activities (reading and listening comprehension, written and oral production and interaction, written and oral mediation). These descriptors have been empirically trialled for several years through the leveled tasks in test papers, while through a 'Task Analysis project', which attempted to model language use in communicative contexts (cf. Kondyli & Lykou, 2009), the KPG descriptors have been directly linked to test tasks. In order to include the KPG descriptors in the IFLC, these had to be revised as learning objectives, using insights from additional resources such as: (1) previous curricula and syllabi for foreign languages; (2) foreign language coursebooks used in Greek state schools; and (3) learner data drawn from the KPG examinations.

With an underlying view of language as a semiotic system that constitutes an endless resource of meaning making, the IFLC has moved beyond an understanding of the linguistic system as a set of rules determining the well-formedness of sentences. Its can-do statements are formulated in functional terms materially configured in different text types or "genres." The notion of genre (i.e. text as a component of discourse, with generic features) is central in the view of language on which the IFLC rests. Texts are linked to context: the purpose for which each has been produced, the time and space constraints of the social situation to which each pertains, the knowledge, attitudes, and intentions of the participants in a given instance of communication.

Documenting Language Proficiency Descriptors across Languages

The CEFR leveled descriptors attempt to illustrate language use in terms of the user's control of the properties of language, with statements about the range of vocabulary and the grammatical competences the learner is expected to have at each proficiency level. These statements are intuitive rather than data-driven, and therefore subject to interpretations by teachers and testers. This is, in fact, one of the reasons that the CEFR has been strongly criticized (cf. Carlsen, 2010).

Our own concern, while developing the IFLC, has been to provide criterial features characterizing the communicative performance associated with each proficiency level, so as to facilitate syllabus, materials, and test design. We have responded to this goal by adding grammatical, lexical, textual, and other details to the functional descriptors.

In supplementing the functional descriptors with language details, we have avoided descriptions of language features shaped by a structural view of language, linked with a "separatist," monolingual ideology[6]—a view that underlies most of the data-driven "language profiles" compiled before and since the publication of the CEFR, in various European languages (cf. the English T-series, Van Ek & Trim, 1991a, 1991b, 2001; the English Profile Programme, Hawkins

& Filipović, 2012, though the latter includes data from learners of English with various L1s). The supplementation has admittedly been a complex endeavor. Using inverse methodological strategies from those underlying the development of generic functional characterizations of language proficiency (such as those provided by the CEFR), the documentation of the IFLC has involved going back to language data from different languages (hence its originality), formulating precise descriptions of distinct competences in each language, aligning them to validate the initial, cross-language, leveled descriptors, and, subsequently, linking them in a system of comparable linguistic features that can form standards for relating teaching, testing, and assessment in more than one foreign language, and can be explicitly and unambiguously incorporated into educational practice.

The section that follows describes the development of a database to address this task, containing detailed descriptions of elements of communicative performance across levels of language proficiency and across languages offered in Greek state schools.

A Multilingual Database with Descriptions of Elements of Communicative Performance

The IFLC presents language content based on data retrieved from various existent sources, not on intuition. To handle the amount of information available, we developed a database containing detailed descriptions of elements approximating the linguistic and communicative competences across foreign languages included in the Greek school curriculum (i.e. English, French, German, Italian, and Spanish).

The IFLC database is organized in terms of the six-level scale of language proficiency and currently includes the following language components:

1. the IFLC reference level descriptors (can-do statements);
2. the language functions that the learner is expected to perform, at different proficiency levels;
3. the grammar (grammatical patterns) that the learner is expected to use (produce) and comprehend at different levels;
4. the lexis (lexical units) that the learner is expected to use (produce) and comprehend at different levels; and
5. the text types that the learner is expected to produce and comprehend when communicating with a language, at different proficiency levels.

Each of the above components, except for the first, corresponds to one type of language competence, i.e. the functional, grammatical, lexical, and discourse competence. The latter is associated with a range of text types, identified in terms of the sociocultural contexts to which they pertain, determining their linguistic properties. This is essentially in accordance with the priority acknowledged by the theory of language underlying the IFLC to the notion of text as material configuration of discourse. Note that the discourse competence also involves the representation of more fine-grained linguistic elements, such as the thematic organization of discourse (given versus new information), coherence and cohesion in texts, textual characteristics related to style and register, etc. At the moment, this sort of information is not systematically represented in the database entries.

Linguistic information was selected from a variety of relevant resources to inform our database. Specifically, we used: (1) descriptions of competences for each language from "profile books";[7] (2) descriptions of language elements, extracted from foreign language coursebooks currently in use in Greek state (primary and secondary) schools; and (3) descriptions from the KPG specifications.

Elements in each of the database components are described in terms of a common set of metadata: (1) the language with which they are associated, with the exception of the level descriptors common to all languages; (2) the language proficiency level to which they pertain; (3) the communicative activity with which they are associated (comprehension, production, interaction, or mediation); (4) the channel of communication (written or spoken) to which they refer; (5) the source from which they are acquired (profile book, foreign language coursebook, KPG specifications); and (6) the school grade to which they pertain, applicable only to elements drawn from coursebooks. A schematic representation of the structure of the database is shown in Table 2.5 in the Appendix (though for reasons of readability, not all metadata describing the database entries are presented in this table).

In the next subsection, details regarding the representation of competences documenting the language proficiency descriptors of the IFLC are provided.

The Representation of Language Competences

Given the range of different sources and languages from which our data were acquired, a complication that had to be tackled, before the database was populated, is related to the description of language competences. Different sources of data usually describe similar or fairly similar things in somewhat or very different terms, depending on the approach to language they adopt or the organization of linguistic knowledge they implement. A significant part of this project involved the representation of linguistic knowledge for each language, separately, and the alignment (i.e. mapping) of data emerging from different sources and paradigms, so that the linguistic knowledge associated with each proficiency level is eventually represented in a unified manner, across all languages. A common representation model for each database component has emerged from these mappings.

Language competences are generally represented in terms of linguistic *types* (i.e. descriptions that abstract over instances of language use). The database types are organized hierarchically, with more specific inheriting from abstract ones. The concept of inheritance corresponds to a basic *is-a* ontological relation (i.e. if a category y inherits from a category x, it is designated to have equally or more specific characteristics than category x). Language functions are uniformly (i.e. for all languages) described in terms of a small set of broadly specified communication acts and several more-fine-grained macro-functions and micro-functions inheriting from the former. In the current version of the ontology, macro-functions are optionally associated with micro-functions. We acknowledge that this is not the final version of the ontology, as more data will be added in the database, acquired from additional resources. Yet, the ontology of language functions is designed to be fairly simple, incorporating three levels of specificity, as exemplified by the database entries shown in Table 2.1.

The representation of linguistic data in terms of typed descriptions and ontological relations thereof is suitable for modeling the gradual development of linguistic knowledge in learning contexts. Each linguistic type is associated with a certain level, language, communicative activity, and channel of communication. More fine-grained types are generally associated with lower proficiency levels than abstract ones. For instance, the linguistic instantiations of the micro-function "expressing a wish for luck" are expected to be fully developed at a learning stage preceding the development of instantiations of the macro-function "expressing a wish." Cases where an abstract type is developed before a more specific one are cross-checked across languages and have been identified either as inconsistencies emerging from the different sources of information or as special cases that are justified and have been accommodated in the organization of linguistic knowledge across languages. This kind of ontological organization enables the essential consistency checks that will ensure the reliability of the data stored in the database and its metadata, which will eventually be used to feed back the development of prescriptive guidelines for the teacher (and the learner) and the development of syllabi and teaching materials. Additionally, ontologies of linguistic types are intended to support the formulation of generalizations over associations of individual language descriptions (i.e. database entries). Lexical and grammatical elements, for instance, can be linked with specific types of language functions (macro-functions, micro-functions); communication acts, as shown in Table 2.1, will readily abstract over such associations. This kind of abstraction will facilitate the development of learning sequences for a certain language or for more than one language. Learning sequences are envisaged to systematically build on the learner's knowledge and competences, which are gradually acquired in the foreign language(s).

The grammatical knowledge at distinct levels of language proficiency is also represented in terms of ontological structures, including super-types and several subtypes, common for all languages. Contrary to language functions, which essentially encode pragmatic aspects of linguistic communication and are language-independent, grammatical patterns are language-specific (i.e. each sub-type is associated with the description of a grammatical pattern pertaining to one of the

30 Bessie Dendrinos and Voula Gotsoulia

TABLE 2.1 Extract from the ontology of language functions

Communication act	Macro-function	Micro-function
Information exchange	Answering a question	Giving information about the place of an event or action
		Giving information about the time of an event or action
		Giving information about the degree related to an event or action
		Giving information about the manner related to an event or action
		Confirming
		Refuting
		Giving a positive answer
		Giving a negative answer
		Stating ignorance
	Doubting	Doubting a negative assurance
		Doubting a positive assurance
	Reassuring	
	Claiming	Presenting an event or action as possible
		Presenting an event or action as certain
Use of conventions	Answering the phone	Introducing oneself
		Asking who is on the other end of the line
		Asking for someone to hold on
	Expressing a wish	Expressing farewell wishes
		Expressing a wish for luck
		Expressing a wish for success
		Expressing a wish for getting well
	Giving one's regards	
	Apologizing	Expressing formal apology
		Expressing informal apology
Discourse organization	Introducing a subject	
	Discussing a subject	Enumerating
		Narrating
		Describing
		Categorizing
		Comparing
	Changing the subject	
	Participating actively in discussion as listener	Calling for attention
		Requesting a change of subject
		Summarizing a point to check if he or she has understood
		Correcting
	Going back to a topic previously discussed	

five languages currently included in the database). The description of grammatical types is based on part-of-speech labels and patterns of use. We have opted to keep the representation simple and theory-independent, so that it can straightforwardly map onto descriptions incorporating different kinds of theoretical assumptions (e.g. adopted by specific coursebooks or other learning materials). Descriptions of grammatical patterns are allowed to inherit from more than one super-type or sub-type, conforming to a *multiple inheritance* ontological schema. For example, the pattern instantiated by the English phrase "It has been noted that . . ." inherits from the types "verb-tense-the use of present perfect" and "verb-voice-passive voice" for English, depicted in Table 2.2. More abstract, inclusive types are expected to be fully developed at higher proficiency levels than types associated with patterns combining them.

Similarly, the lexical knowledge is uniformly organized in taxonomies that are based on general thematic domains and more fine-grained subdomains, as exemplified in Table 2.3. Language-specific lexical types include words of different parts of speech, evoking a coherent meaning and appearing in related linguistic contexts.

Finally, the text types with which the language learner is expected to communicate are summarized in ontologies such as the one shown in Table 2.4. The parameters of the communicative context in which a text is assumed to function are included in fine-grained descriptions (subtypes) inheriting from general text types (super-types). Note that text types (and language functions) may be associated with particular language activities (comprehension, production, interaction, mediation) and channels of communication (written, oral), whereas grammatical and lexical types are most often underspecified as regards the values of this metadata.

TABLE 2.2 Extract from the ontology of grammatical types

Super-type	Sub-type	Sub-type	Language-specific pattern
Noun	Common noun	Inflectional feature: number	Common noun appearing only in plural: trousers, scissors, tights, people (English)
Noun	Common noun	Inflectional feature: case	Akkusativ (German)
Noun	Common noun	Derivational feature: suffix	Derivation of common noun from adjective: suffix ité (French)
Noun	Proper noun	Inflectional feature: number	Family name: los + surname (Spanish)
Verb		Inflectional feature: tense	The use of present perfect (English)
Verb		Inflectional feature: voice	The use of passive voice (English)

32 Bessie Dendrinos and Voula Gotsoulia

TABLE 2.3 Extract from the ontology of thematically organized lexical types

Super-type	Sub-type	Language-specific lexical type
Economy and industry	Agriculture	sembrar, cosechar, cultivo, explotación, producción, recolección, fruto (Spanish)
Personal relationships	Social life	friend, partner, colleague, guest, to know, to visit, party, present (English)
Geography and environment	Environment	ambiente, deserto, difendere, ghiacciaio, inquinamento, naturale/artificiale, proteggere, salvare (Italian)
Geography and environment	Human environment	casa, centro, chiesa, città, fabbrica, industria, parco, piazza, strada, via (Italian)
Education	Examinations and certificates	Prüfung, Klassenarbeit, Schularbeit (German)

TABLE 2.4 Extract from the ontology of text types

Super-type	Sub-type
E-mail	E-mail for personal communication
	Professional e-mail
	Job request e-mail
Poster	Poster for public show
	Poster for concert
Form	Airplane landing form
	Hotel check-in form

The alignment of linguistic types collected from different sources of data, for different languages, in order to come up with the common representational framework discussed above was not a trivial task. It was treated as a modular task (i.e. common ontologies have initially emerged from mappings of the data from the Profiles for French, German, Spanish, Italian, and English).[8] These ontologies have been employed for description of the contents of foreign language coursebooks. They have been slightly modified and, in some cases, enriched to accommodate such a heterogeneous body of language data retrieved from a variety of coursebooks, written by different authors, espousing disparate language learning and teaching approaches. Finally, the revised ontologies have been mapped onto the descriptions acquired from the KPG specifications, referring to the language functions, grammatical and lexical patterns, and types of texts assessed at each proficiency level in the KPG exams.

Setting Standards for Multilingual Curricula and Multilingual Practices

The database described in the previous section has been designed as the essential methodological apparatus for organizing comparable descriptions of language competences, across foreign languages and across the six-level scale of language proficiency adopted by the IFLC. The description of language components in terms of a common set of metadata and aligned ontologies enables the documentation of the leveled descriptors of the IFLC and can support comparisons and links between the teaching and assessment specifications for different languages. For instance, the set of language functions documenting a certain level for English can be juxtaposed with the set of functions at the same level for another language. Such comparisons are essential for revealing the commonalities and/or differences in teaching and learning languages, and are also crucial for evaluating and refining the IFLC descriptors, so that they determine language proficiency in a precise, unified manner for all languages.[9] In this sense, our work is of particular relevance for the CEFR as well. To our knowledge, it is the first time that an attempt is made to produce explicit, detailed descriptions of a comprehensive set of linguistic data linked with language proficiency levels, in more than one foreign language. These data, associated with the metadata for their organization and filtering, may lend support to slight or more extensive modifications of the CEFR, cross-language descriptors.

In a related vein, comparisons and links between data collected from various, complementary sources comprise an essential step toward setting clear and validated benchmarks for the knowledge pertaining to the distinct levels of language proficiency, for each language, separately.[10] For each language in the database, comprehensive sets of descriptions of linguistic elements, across levels, are derived from the profiles, the coursebooks, and the KPG specifications, and they are mapped onto the reference level descriptors. This process is aimed at producing calibrated language-specific specifications and revealing possible inconsistencies between the originally formulated IFLC descriptors and the actual data.

Ultimately, the documented level descriptors can straightforwardly be transferred and incorporated into educational practice, forming the basis for the development of syllabi and materials, the contents of which will not be based on intuition—thus prone to arbitrary changes and reformulations. Elements from each of the specified language components, sharing common metadata values (level, language, communicative activity, etc.), can be associated with one another and with corresponding level descriptors. Individual can-do statements or sets of can-do statements can be linked with particular language functions, grammatical and lexical elements and types of texts by which they can be reified in certain language or languages, at certain proficiency levels and communicative context. Such associations can form the basis for the development of language teaching—learning units, addressing objectively specified learning outcomes in a single or, more interestingly, in more than one foreign language.

Implications of a Multilingual Curriculum on Foreign Language Teaching and Learning

Multilingual competence is conceptualized presently not as parallel monolingualisms, but as interlingualism and translanguaging, requiring intercultural competence, defined by Byram (2003) as the ability to critically reflect on one's cultural identity and values, and to use his or her awareness of the complex relationships between language, society, and cultural meanings. As such, it is most likely to find a fertile ground for its development in standards-based multilingual curricula—curricula whose descriptors of communicative and linguistic performance are documented in different languages and serve as a basis for multilingual pedagogical approaches and classroom practices. The discussion of such pedagogy, which is still in the making, and its implications for testing are not within the scope of this chapter. Suffice it to say presently that it entails a new paradigm of foreign language education to replace the tradition established by foreign language teaching and learning didactics: a language education project that might adopt a multi-literacies perspective (cf. Kalantzis & Cope, 2012) to motivate learners to perform communicative tasks using all the resources available to them (different languages, language varieties, discourses, registers, genres, and semiotic modes). Ultimately, the goal is the meaning-making process when in intercession with others whose social and cultural experiences may be similar or different.

The new paradigm of foreign language education, based on multilingual curricula, may bear some resemblance to bi/multilingual and bi/multicultural education programs, but it is clearly distinct. While the latter often involve the home/community languages of students for whom the program is designed, the former generally involves only languages that are foreign to all students. In this case, the target language is the object of knowledge, whereas in bi/multilingual programs, the target language(s) are a means through which knowledge is accessed. The latter actually constitute projects that aspire to produce bilinguals or polyglots (e.g. dual language or two-way language immersion, first-language-first, or the multilingual program of the European School), and they are implemented in schools populated with students of different ethnic, cultural, and linguistic backgrounds, deliberately mixed together for as many school subjects and activities as possible, offered in different languages.

It is the former type of programs with which we are concerned in our work: foreign language programs for students developing school literacy in the official language, and also learning two languages in addition to their mother tongue (which may be the same or different than the official language). In these programs, the aim should be to help students learn to do different things in different languages—not necessarily equally well in all languages—and to develop a multilingual ethos of communication (Dendrinos, 2001). This seems to necessitate the explicit aim of interlingual communication (i.e. communication involving the interplay of languages), defined by Dendrinos (2012) as "performance which entails the use of different semiotic resources from more than one language, more than one code and/or semiotic mode when this is required for successful communication" (p. 49).

So long as language (education) policy remains monoglossic (cf. Shohamy, 2006), and language curricula remain monolingual, we cannot easily replace foreign language teaching programs by multi-literacy education. Pedagogic practices will remain as they have been in programs where the teaching and learning of languages is a project of developing parallel monolingualisms.

Conclusion

The aim of this chapter has been to describe an ongoing project developing a multilingual curriculum, which we believe lends itself to a significant shift from monolingual to multilingual foreign language education. As the project continues, the IFLC database will be informed by additional, empirical data, extracted from the KPG corpus, which contains graded scripts produced by candidates participating in the national foreign language examinations. This is another research project being carried out at the Research Centre for Language Teaching, Testing and Assessment (RCeL) of the University of Athens, addressing the linguistic profile of the Greek learner of foreign languages and intending to furnish detailed descriptions of how a specific group of learners (i.e. learners whose common language is Greek) perform in the three European languages documented (cf. Gotsoulia, 2012; Gotsoulia & Dendrinos, 2011). These descriptions, which draw upon actual language data produced by candidates in the KPG exams, will substantially complement the descriptions from the aforementioned sources of data. They will add the insight of what the learner actually does with language, in practice, emphasizing the characteristics of language use, including erroneous usages of linguistic elements. The multilingual database documenting the curriculum level descriptors ideally will serve as a tool for syllabus design, and development of novel teaching/learning material.

Notes

1. The project is being carried out by a team of expert linguists and language educators working at the Research Centre for Language Teaching, Testing and Assessment (RCeL) of the University of Athens (www.rcel.enl.uoa.gr/).
2. For information in English about the KPG exams, visit http://rcel.enl.uoa.gr/kpg.
3. Council of Europe (Language Policy Unit): www.coe.int/t/dg4/linguistic/Division_en.asp.
4. It was developed by a team of 25 language specialists, applied linguists, researchers, and language teachers, directed by Bessie Dendrinos, who gave birth to the idea that a multilingual curriculum replace the curricula used up to the present—a different one for each of the languages offered in state schools.
5. The curriculum document appears only in Greek at http://rcel.enl.uoa.gr/xenesglosses. At the same site, one may also find the Teacher's Guide, which also appears in Greek only.

		Language Component																				IFLC Level Descriptors
		Language Functions					Grammar					Lexis					Text Types					
	Lang Source	EN	FR	GE	IT	SP	EN	FR	GE	IT	SP	EN	FR	GE	IT	SP	EN	FR	GE	IT	SP	
A1	Profile	F-EN-A1-Prof	F-FR-A1-Prof	F-GE-A1-Prof	F-IT-A1-Prof	F-SP-A1-Prof	G-EN-A1-Prof	G-FR-A1-Prof	G-GE-A1-Prof	G-IT-A1-Prof	G-SP-A1-Prof	L-EN-A1-Prof	L-FR-A1-Prof	L-GE-A1-Prof	L-IT-A1-Prof	L-SP-A1-Prof	TT-EN-A1-Prof	TT-FR-A1-Prof	TT-GE-A1-Prof	TT-IT-A1-Prof	TT-SP-A1-Prof	Common for all languages per level
A2		F-EN-A2-Prof	F-FR-A2-Prof	F-GE-A2-Prof	F-IT-A2-Prof	F-SP-A2-Prof	G-EN-A2-Prof	G-FR-A2-Prof	G-GE-A2-Prof	G-IT-A2-Prof	G-SP-A2-Prof	L-EN-A2-Prof	L-FR-A2-Prof	L-GE-A2-Prof	L-IT-A2-Prof	L-SP-A2-Prof	TT-EN-A2-Prof	TT-FR-A2-Prof	TT-GE-A2-Prof	TT-IT-A2-Prof	TT-SP-A2-Prof	
B1		F-EN-B1-Prof	F-FR-B1-Prof	F-GE-B1-Prof	F-IT-B1-Prof	F-SP-B1-Prof	G-EN-B1-Prof	G-FR-B1-Prof	G-GE-B1-Prof	G-IT-B1-Prof	G-SP-B1-Prof	L-EN-B1-Prof	L-FR-B1-Prof	L-GE-B1-Prof	L-IT-B1-Prof	L-SP-B1-Prof	TT-EN-B1-Prof	TT-FR-B1-Prof	TT-GE-B1-Prof	TT-IT-B1-Prof	TT-SP-B1-Prof	
B2		F-EN-B2-Prof	F-FR-B2-Prof	F-GE-B2-Prof	F-IT-B2-Prof	F-SP-B2-Prof	G-EN-B2-Prof	G-FR-B2-Prof	G-GE-B2-Prof	G-IT-B2-Prof	G-SP-B2-Prof	L-EN-B2-Prof	L-FR-B2-Prof	L-GE-B2-Prof	L-IT-B2-Prof	L-SP-B2-Prof	TT-EN-B2-Prof	TT-FR-B2-Prof	TT-GE-B2-Prof	TT-IT-B2-Prof	TT-SP-B2-Prof	
C1		F-EN-C1-Prof	F-FR-C1-Prof	F-GE-C1-Prof	F-IT-C1-Prof	F-SP-C1-Prof	G-EN-C1-Prof	G-FR-C1-Prof	G-GE-C1-Prof	G-IT-C1-Prof	G-SP-C1-Prof	L-EN-C1-Prof	L-FR-C1-Prof	L-GE-C1-Prof	L-IT-C1-Prof	L-SP-C1-Prof	TT-EN-C1-Prof	TT-FR-C1-Prof	TT-GE-C1-Prof	TT-IT-C1-Prof	TT-SP-C1-Prof	
C2		F-EN-C2-Prof	F-FR-C2-Prof	F-GE-C2-Prof	F-IT-C2-Prof	F-SP-C2-Prof	G-EN-C2-Prof	G-FR-C2-Prof	G-GE-C2-Prof	G-IT-C2-Prof	G-SP-C2-Prof	L-EN-C2-Prof	L-FR-C2-Prof	L-GE-C2-Prof	L-IT-C2-Prof	L-SP-C2-Prof	TT-EN-C2-Prof	TT-FR-C2-Prof	TT-GE-C2-Prof	TT-IT-C2-Prof	TT-SP-C2-Prof	
A1	Course Book	F-EN-A1-CB	F-FR-A1-CB	F-GE-A1-CB	F-IT-A1-CB	F-SP-A1-CB	G-EN-A1-CB	G-FR-A1-CB	G-GE-A1-CB	G-IT-A1-CB	G-SP-A1-CB	L-EN-A1-CB	L-FR-A1-CB	L-GE-A1-CB	L-IT-A1-CB	L-SP-A1-CB	TT-EN-A1-CB	TT-FR-A1-CB	TT-GE-A1-CB	TT-IT-A1-CB	TT-SP-A1-CB	
A2		F-EN-A2-CB	F-FR-A2-CB	F-GE-A2-CB	F-IT-A2-CB	F-SP-A2-CB	G-EN-A2-CB	G-FR-A2-CB	G-GE-A2-CB	G-IT-A2-CB	G-SP-A2-CB	L-EN-A2-CB	L-FR-A2-CB	L-GE-A2-CB	L-IT-A2-CB	L-SP-A2-CB	TT-EN-A2-CB	TT-FR-A2-CB	TT-GE-A2-CB	TT-IT-A2-CB	TT-SP-A2-CB	
B1		F-EN-B1-CB	F-FR-B1-CB	F-GE-B1-CB	F-IT-B1-CB	F-SP-B1-CB	G-EN-B1-CB	G-FR-B1-CB	G-GE-B1-CB	G-IT-B1-CB	G-SP-B1-CB	L-EN-B1-CB	L-FR-B1-CB	L-GE-B1-CB	L-IT-B1-CB	L-SP-B1-CB	TT-EN-B1-CB	TT-FR-B1-CB	TT-GE-B1-CB	TT-IT-B1-CB	TT-SP-B1-CB	
B2		F-EN-B2-CB	F-FR-B2-CB	F-GE-B2-CB	F-IT-B2-CB	F-SP-B2-CB	G-EN-B2-CB	G-FR-B2-CB	G-GE-B2-CB	G-IT-B2-CB	G-SP-B2-CB	L-EN-B2-CB	L-FR-B2-CB	L-GE-B2-CB	L-IT-B2-CB	L-SP-B2-CB	TT-EN-B2-CB	TT-FR-B2-CB	TT-GE-B2-CB	TT-IT-B2-CB	TT-SP-B2-CB	

TABLE 2.5 Appendix: The structure and data of the IFLC database

Level		Prof (F-EN)	F-FR	F-GE	F-IT	F-SP	G-EN	G-FR	G-GE	G-IT	G-SP	L-EN	L-FR	L-GE	L-IT	L-SP	TT-EN	TT-FR	TT-GE	TT-IT	TT-SP
C1		F-EN-C1-CB	F-FR-C1-CB	F-GE-C1-CB	F-IT-C1-CB	F-SP-C1-CB	G-EN-C1-CB	G-FR-C1-CB	G-GE-C1-CB	G-IT-C1-CB	G-SP-C1-CB	L-EN-C1-CB	L-FR-C1-CB	L-GE-C1-CB	L-IT-C1-CB	L-SP-C1-CB	TT-EN-C1-CB	TT-FR-C1-CB	TT-GE-C1-CB	TT-IT-C1-CB	TT-SP-C1-CB
C2		F-EN-C2-CB	F-FR-C2-CB	F-GE-C2-CB	F-IT-C2-CB	F-SP-C2-CB	G-EN-C2-CB	G-FR-C2-CB	G-GE-C2-CB	G-IT-C2-CB	G-SP-C2-CB	L-EN-C2-CB	L-FR-C2-CB	L-GE-C2-CB	L-IT-C2-CB	L-SP-C2-CB	TT-EN-C2-CB	TT-FR-C2-CB	TT-GE-C2-CB	TT-IT-C2-CB	TT-SP-C2-CB
A1	KPG	F-EN-A1-KPG	F-FR-A1-KPG	F-GE-A1-KPG	F-IT-A1-KPG	F-SP-A1-KPG	G-EN-A1-KPG	G-FR-A1-KPG	G-GE-A1-KPG	G-IT-A1-KPG	G-SP-A1-KPG	L-EN-A1-KPG	L-FR-A1-KPG	L-GE-A1-KPG	L-IT-A1-KPG	L-SP-A1-KPG	TT-EN-A1-KPG	TT-FR-A1-KPG	TT-GE-A1-KPG	TT-IT-A1-KPG	TT-SP-A1-KPG
A2		F-EN-A2-KPG	F-FR-A2-KPG	F-GE-A2-KPG	F-IT-A2-KPG	F-SP-A2-KPG	G-EN-A2-KPG	G-FR-A2-KPG	G-GE-A2-KPG	G-IT-A2-KPG	G-SP-A2-KPG	L-EN-A2-KPG	L-FR-A2-KPG	L-GE-A2-KPG	L-IT-A2-KPG	L-SP-A2-KPG	TT-EN-A2-KPG	TT-FR-A2-KPG	TT-GE-A2-KPG	TT-IT-A2-KPG	TT-SP-A2-KPG
B1		F-EN-B1-KPG	F-FR-B1-KPG	F-GE-B1-KPG	F-IT-B1-KPG	F-SP-B1-KPG	G-EN-B1-KPG	G-FR-B1-KPG	G-GE-B1-KPG	G-IT-B1-KPG	G-SP-B1-KPG	L-EN-B1-KPG	L-FR-B1-KPG	L-GE-B1-KPG	L-IT-B1-KPG	L-SP-B1-KPG	TT-EN-B1-KPG	TT-FR-B1-KPG	TT-GE-B1-KPG	TT-IT-B1-KPG	TT-SP-B1-KPG
B2		F-EN-B2-KPG	F-FR-B2-KPG	F-GE-B2-KPG	F-IT-B2-KPG	F-SP-B2-KPG	G-EN-B2-KPG	G-FR-B2-KPG	G-GE-B2-KPG	G-IT-B2-KPG	G-SP-B2-KPG	L-EN-B2-KPG	L-FR-B2-KPG	L-GE-B2-KPG	L-IT-B2-KPG	L-SP-B2-KPG	TT-EN-B2-KPG	TT-FR-B2-KPG	TT-GE-B2-KPG	TT-IT-B2-KPG	TT-SP-B2-KPG
C1		F-EN-C1-KPG	F-FR-C1-KPG	F-GE-C1-KPG	F-IT-C1-KPG	F-SP-C1-KPG	G-EN-C1-KPG	G-FR-C1-KPG	G-GE-C1-KPG	G-IT-C1-KPG	G-SP-C1-KPG	L-EN-C1-KPG	L-FR-C1-KPG	L-GE-C1-KPG	L-IT-C1-KPG	L-SP-C1-KPG	TT-EN-C1-KPG	TT-FR-C1-KPG	TT-GE-C1-KPG	TT-IT-C1-KPG	TT-SP-C1-KPG
C2		F-EN-C2-KPG	F-FR-C2-KPG	F-GE-C2-KPG	F-IT-C2-KPG	F-SP-C2-KPG	G-EN-C2-KPG	G-FR-C2-KPG	G-GE-C2-KPG	G-IT-C2-KPG	G-SP-C2-KPG	L-EN-C2-KPG	L-FR-C2-KPG	L-GE-C2-KPG	L-IT-C2-KPG	L-SP-C2-KPG	TT-EN-C2-KPG	TT-FR-C2-KPG	TT-GE-C2-KPG	TT-IT-C2-KPG	TT-SP-C2-KPG

EN = English F = set of Language Functions Prof = Profile
FR = French G = set of Grammatical Structures CB = Course Book
GE = German L = set of Lexical Units KPG = KPG Exam Specs
IT = Italian TT = set of Text Types
SP = Spanish

38 Bessie Dendrinos and Voula Gotsoulia

6. The reason we understand a structural view as "separatist" and a manifestation of monolingual ideology is because it focuses on the formal properties of language—unique to each language—rather than on contextualized language use and the meaning-making process (involving interrelated languages, semiotic systems, genres, and registers). The latter is a view of language that is more consistent with the multilingual ideology that the IFLC is based on, documenting its leveled descriptors with linguistic features not from a single language but from various languages, aided by corpus data informing the documentation process.
7. The following profile books have been used: Van Ek and Trim (1991a, 1991b, 2001) (for English), Instituto Cervantes (2006) (for Spanish), Spinelli and Francesca (2010) (for Italian), Beacco, Bouquet, and Porquier (2004), Beacco and Porquier (2007, 2008), Beacco et al. (2011) (for French), and Glaboniat, Müller, Rusch, Schmitz, and Wertenschlag (2005) (for German).
8. The English T-series has served as the basis for the compilation of the profiles for the rest of the languages considered. Each of the latter implements more or less significant modifications or improvements to the level descriptions developed by Jan Van Ek and John Trim (first published in 1991).
9. This kind of cross-language comparison is depicted in Table 2.5 with shaded cells, across the columns corresponding to the different languages, for language functions drawn from Profile books, at A1 level. Similar relationships between languages can be studied for each language component and each source of data, separately, at each level of proficiency.
10. In Table 2.5 this kind of comparison is exemplified with shaded cells, across the different sources of data, for language functions at A1 level, in English.

References

Beacco, J., Porquier, R. (2007). *A1 Level for French/A Reference Book and CD Audio*. Paris: Les éditions Didier (in French).

Beacco, J., Porquier, R. (2008). *A2 Level for French/A Reference*. Paris: Les éditions Didier (in French).

Beacco, J., Bouquet, S., Porquier, R. (2004). *B2 Level for French/A Reference Book and CD Audio*. Paris: Les éditions Didier (in French).

Beacco, J., Blin, B., Houles, E., Lepage, S., Riba, P. (2011). *B1 Level for French/A Reference Book and CD Audio*. Paris: Les éditions Didier (in French).

Byram, M. (2003). *Intercultural competence*. Strasbourg: Council of Europe Publishing.

Carlsen, C. (2010). CEFR and contrastive rhetoric—what's the link? In J. Mader & Z. Urkun (Eds.), *Putting the CEFR to good use*. Selected articles by the presenters of the IATEFL Testing, Evaluation and Assessment Special Interest Group (TEA SIG) & EALTA Conference in Barcelona, Spain. Retrieved from: www.elc-consult.com/media/ba5b075266ab4423ffff81d6ffffff2.pdf (accessed March 1, 2014).

Council of Europe (2001). *Common European Framework of Reference for Languages: Teaching, learning and assessment*. Cambridge: Council of Europe/Cambridge University Press.

Council of Europe (2014). *Council of Europe Language Education Policy*. Retrieved from: www.coe.int/t/dg4/linguistic/Division_en.asp (accessed March 1, 2014).

Dendrinos, B. (2001). Linguoracism in European foreign language education discourse. In M. Riesigl & R. Wodak (Eds.), *The semiotics of racism: Approaches in critical discourse analysis* (pp. 177–198). Vienna: Passagen Verlag.

Dendrinos, B. (2012). Multi- and monolingualism in foreign language education in Europe. In G. Stickel & M. Carrier (Eds.), *Language education in creating a multilingual*

Europe (pp. 47–60). Duisburg Papers on Research in Language and Culture, Vol. 94. Frankfurt/New York/Oxford/Brussels: Peter Lang.

Dendrinos, B. (2013). Social meanings in global-glocal language proficiency exams. In C. Tsagari, S. Papadima-Sophocleous, & S. Ioannou-Georgiou (Eds.), *Language testing and assessment around the globe: Achievements and experiences* (pp. 47–67). Language Testing and Evaluation series. Frankfurt/New York/Oxford/Brussels: Peter Lang.

Glaboniat, M., Müller, M., Rusch, P., Schmitz, H., & Wertenschlag, L. (2005). *German profile. Common European Framework of Reference for Languages. Description of learning objectives, can-do statements, communicative resources: Levels A1–A2, B1–B2, C1–C2.* Berlin/München/Wien/Zürich/New York: Langenscheidt (in German).

Gotsoulia, V. (2012). Documenting the "linguistic profile" of the Greek foreign language user. *RCeL e-periodical*. Retrieved from: http://rcel.enl.uoa.gr/periodical/research1_en. htm (February article) (accessed March 1, 2014).

Gotsoulia, V., & Dendrinos, B. (2011). Towards a corpus-based approach to modeling language production of foreign language learners in communicative contexts. *Proceedings of the 8th International Conference on Recent Advances in Natural Language Processing.* Retrieved from: http://aclweb.org/anthology-new/R/R11/ (accessed March 1, 2014).

Hawkins, J. A., & Filipović, L. (2012). *Critical Features in L2 English: Specifying the Reference Levels of the Common European Framework. English Profile Studies 1.* Cambridge: Cambridge University Press.

Instituto Cervantes (2006). *Curricular Plan of Cervantes Institute: Levels of reference for Spanish.* Madrid: Instituto Cervantes-Bibliotecanueva (in Spanish).

Kalantzis, M., & Cope, B. (2012). *New learning: Elements of a science education* (2nd ed.). Cambridge: Cambridge University Press.

Karavas, E. (2012). Introducing innovations in periods of financial crisis: Obstacles in the implementation of the new integrated foreign languages curriculum in Greece. *Proceedings of the 5th International Conference of Education, Research and Innovation (iCERI),* Madrid (pp. 5534–5542).

Kondyli, M., & Lykou, C. (2009). Linguistic description of the KPG test tasks: A genre perspective. *RCeL e-periodical* (January Article). Retrieved from: http://rcel.enl.woa.gr/ periodical/research1_en.htm (in Greek) (accessed March 1, 2014).

Kress, G. (2009). *Multimodality: A social semiotic approach to contemporary communication.* London: Routledge.

Shohamy, E. (2006). *Language policy: Hidden agendas and new approaches.* London/New York: Routledge.

Shohamy, E. (2011). Assessing multilingual competencies: Adopting construct valid assessment policies. *Modern Language Journal, 95*(3), 418–429.

Spinelli, B., & Francesca, P. (2010). *Profile of the Italian language: CEFR levels A1, A2, B1, B2.* Milano: La nuova Italia (in Italian).

Spolsky, B. (1995). *Measured words: The development of objective language teaching.* Oxford: Oxford University Press.

Van Ek, J. A., & Trim, J. L. M. (1991a). *Threshold 1990.* Cambridge: Council of Europe/ Cambridge University Press.

Van Ek, J. A., & Trim, J. L. M. (1991b). *Waystage 1990.* Cambridge: Council of Europe/ Cambridge University Press.

Van Ek, J. A., & Trim, J. L. M. (2001). *Vantage.* Cambridge: Council of Europe/Cambridge University Press.

3

IN THE NAME OF THE CEFR

INDIVIDUALS AND STANDARDS

Monica Barni

Diversity, Standards, and Tests: Links and Paradoxes

In the past decade, we have witnessed three major developments that have produced consequences upon language uses and policies in Europe and that, in our opinion, are strictly linked to one other. The first is a social phenomenon: mobility and migration are easier and increasing, and there is also a greater ease in international and intra-national communication. Increased and easier mobility and communication have direct implications on language use and on language policy: linguistic and cultural diversity are key features of the EU, of its member states, and of its institutions. They characterize the daily interactions of its citizens. Diversity—or, as it has been recently defined, "super-diversity" (Vertovec, 2006, 2007) or "hyper-diversity" (Baynham & Moyer, 2012; Kelly, 2008)—and the management thereof present a challenge for Europe and for all its citizens, generating widespread concern about social cohesion and integration. The EU institutions' concern regarding the construction of social cohesion also encompasses the dimension of the management of linguistic diversity. For migrants, in most cases, the official language of the host country is an L2, while one, two, or more language(s) and also mixtures of languages are used in their daily linguistic exchanges. The approach adopted by the EU aims to develop opportunities that see multilingualism as a resource that, if harnessed, will allow for the active inclusion of all citizens (see, among others, Council of the European Union 2002; European Commission, 2008). Yet despite the fact that in most of the EU documents and recommendations (Council of the European Union, 2002) multilingualism is addressed as an asset, most often it is dealt with as a problem (see Blommaert, Leppänen, & Spotti, 2012), in particular in the case of migrants. Not all kinds of multilingualism are considered as having the same value: evidence of this is the fact that the Eurocentric policy gives little consideration to immigrant languages. As Extra and Yagmur (2012) highlight, at nation state level, "immigrant languages are the least recognised, protected and/or promoted, in spite of all the affirmative action at the European level" (p. 12). This is evident in national language policy in education, but also at the social level. There, an attempt is made to resolve questions of linguistic diversity, social integration, and social cohesion through imposing upon immigrants the obligation to learn the national language(s) of the country where they have decided to live and work. Pupils' and citizens' own failure to use the national language(s), the right language(s), the most appropriate language variety(ies), and/or the best suited genre during a given communicative encounter are seen as proof that they lack the necessary instruments for achieving a communicative goal. This is often perceived as a lack of willingness to integrate into the country.

The second fact we have witnessed in Europe is the publication in 2001 of the CEFR, drawn up under the auspices of a prestigious European-level organization such as the Council of Europe and adopted by the European Commission itself in its language policies (e.g. Committee of Ministers, 2008; EC Action Plan, 2004–2006). Since that date, the CEFR—and mostly its descriptors of communicative language competence—has become the most important reference document in the fields of language learning, teaching, and assessment, both in Europe and beyond. It has become an operational tool used to justify choices in language policies, both at the educational and, more in general, the social level. As Byram and Parmenter (2012) note:

> the CEFR is clearly a policy document bearing values and intentions. Yet, like any texts, the intentions of its authors may not be read by its users and not be taken in entirety but used in part for the purposes of the users.
>
> (p. 4)

To this consideration, we should add the fact that the part of the document that has been read and used the most and that has had the strongest impact on education and society at large is the one containing the scales of proficiency. Consequently, the CEFR is mainly seen only in terms of levels of proficiency in a language. As we will show below, this aspect paradoxically presents a gap with the theoretical approach as defined in the first chapters of the document. The descriptors are based on a monolingual approach to language competence that ignores the plurilingual approach sketched in the first part of the document.

The third fact is the "shift in the understanding of the functions, status and roles of language tests. From tools used to measure language knowledge, they are viewed today more and more as instruments connected to and embedded in political, social and educational contexts" (Shohamy, 2007, p. 117). Starting with Shohamy's book in 2001, the power of tests has been revealed, as has their application as instruments of policy, especially in reference to migrants. Language

42 Monica Barni

tests are increasingly being used as policy instruments for declared and undeclared policies (Shohamy, 2006): "establishing entrance criteria that include a test of another language, a new de facto policy is created, the implication of which is that the 'tested' language becomes the most important language to acquire and master" (Shohamy, 2007, p. 120). Furthermore, the tests, in their criteria and constructs, embody and support the most appropriate language variety that should be used by people, and in this sense, language tests impose monolingual policies and consequently suppress multilingual diversity.

In the next paragraphs, we will try to explore more deeply the just sketched interrelations among these three facts and reflect on how individual characteristics and language choices impact standards and tests in complex societies.

Language Use and Norms

Diversity (or super-diversity, as Vertovec (2006, 2007) highlights) is the norm today, as is linguistic diversity. A cluster of varied ways of using language is formed whenever people communicate (see also, among others, Jørgensen, 2008, 2010; Jørgensen, Karrebæk, Madsen, & Møller, 2011). Many of the texts so produced bear "the traces of worldwide migration flows and their specific demographic, social and cultural dynamics. Migration makes communicative resources like language varieties and scripts globally mobile" (Blommaert & Rampton, 2011, p. 2). As De Mauro (2006) highlighted, we now are facing a crisis of the monolithic consideration of language uses, language ideology, and language policy that requires a paradigm shift in the study of language in society, in which "rather than working with homogeneity, stability and boundness as the starting assumptions, mobility, mixing, political dynamics and historical embedding" should now be "central concerns in the study of languages, language groups and communication" (Blommaert & Rampton, 2011, p. 3).

But, as the same authors state (Blommaert & Rampton, 2011), languages continue to be considered as bounded systems linked with bounded communities, such as "proper" language is bounded, pure, and composed of structured sounds, grammar, and vocabulary designed to refer to things (Gal & Irvine, 1995; Joseph & Taylor, 1990). Despite this increasing call for a deeper theoretical framework on language (see, among many others, De Mauro, 2006; Meeuwis & Blommaert, 1998), this model continues to play a hegemonic force in public discourse, in bureaucratic and educational policy and practice, and in commonly held beliefs. As a consequence, linguistic competence is still mainly described from a monolingual perspective. A plurilingual repertoire is just considered as the sum of different monolingualisms (language 1 plus language 2 . . . plus language N); people are still considered plurilingual when they are able to speak different languages and, in interactions, are able to switch from one language to another. This monolingual perspective guided the construction of the descriptors of competence in the CEFR, in striking contrast with what was declared in its theoretical approach.

The Paradox in CEFR: The Pluri/Multilingual Approach and the Operational Standards

As we have noted (Barni & Machetti, 2005), in the first chapters of the CEFR, where its theoretical foundations are illustrated, a dynamic view of the presence and use of languages is presented, with its basis in the metaphor of a continuum of competence (L1/L2, native/non-native) as a shared space. The experiences of language of a learner/user integrate with each other: the competence of natives and learners cannot be compared to finite sets and closed clusters of structures and vocabulary. As an open set, the continuum should rather act as an area of penetration, overlap, and comparison, characterized by a strong dialectic contact. In the words of the CEFR:

> the plurilingual approach emphasises the fact that as an individual person's experience of language in its cultural contexts expands, from the language of the home to that of society at large and then to the languages of other peoples (whether learnt at school or college, or by direct experience), he or she does not keep these languages and cultures in strictly separated mental compartments, but rather builds up a communicative competence to which all knowledge and experience of language contributes and in which languages interrelate and interact.
>
> (Council of Europe, 2001, p. 4)

In Chapter 8 of the document, devoted to the illustration of its operational applications, the concept of plurilingual and pluricultural competence as a continuum is reaffirmed. In fact, it tends to:

- move away from the supposed balanced dichotomy established by the customary L1/L2 pairing by stressing plurilingualism where bilingualism is just one particular case;
- consider that a given individual does not have a collection of distinct and separate competences to communicate depending on the languages he/she knows, but rather a plurilingual and pluricultural competence encompassing the full range of the languages available to him/her.

(Council of Europe, 2001, p. 168)

The model of a continuum of linguistic and communicative competence, viewed as an opportunity to manage communicative acts using the different linguistic codes at one's disposal, seems to answer the request for the paradigm shift in the study of language in society.

In actual fact, however, it does not even produce effects at the operational level of the document. Byram and Parmenter (2012) ascribe this to the fact that "like any text, the intentions of its authors may not be taken in entirety but only

44 Monica Barni

used in part for the purposes of the users" (p. 4). In the CEFR, this is the case not only because of the difficulties arising from reading it (Komorowska, 2004; Martyniuk & Noijons, 2007), but for the vagueness of the document itself and the inconsistencies it presents. In fact, although plurilingualism continues to be addressed as a value, a resource to be exploited, the information provided to take advantage of this resource (Council of Europe, 2001, p. 170 ff.) is vague and sometimes contradictory. The impression one gets from reading these pages is that the idea of a plurilingual approach remains an empty concept, a mere flag to wave. The operational implications arising from the issues of languages in contact are never clearly spelled out.

This impression becomes stronger when we come to the descriptors and scales of proficiency in (a) language. We should not overlook the fact that this is the most attractive and used part of the document:

> when people referred to "the CEFR" they were often thinking only of the scales of proficiency, and this was not helped by academic debate about the validity and reliability of the scales, which turned attention from the rest of the CEFR.
>
> (Byram & Parmenter, 2012, p. 5; see also Fulcher, 2008)

As the same authors highlight (Byram & Parmenter, 2012, p. 114), the main "entry" to the CEFR by its users is via the levels and the scales and in connection with assessment, and some aspects of the document, and in particular, the notion of plurilingualism and its value for curriculum design have been neglected and are not influential or accepted. Another notion linked to plurilingualism that is included in the CEFR, but underdeveloped, is that of competence in mediation (Dendrinos, 2006), which, on the contrary, should be a necessary and permanent condition in any semiotic activity for the negotiation of meaning when different codes co-occur and are co-used, as it is outlined in the theoretical approach.

The attractiveness and strength of the levels and the emphasis on assessment practices, connected with renewed ideologies of nationalism and language, call for the integration of immigrants, and provoked an increase in the use of language tests based on the CEFR descriptors across the whole of Europe (Extra, Spotti, & Van Avermaet, 2010; Mar-Molinero & Stevenson, 2006; Van Avermaet, 2010). These tests are shielded by policies based on the ideological premise that success in language tests not only shows a clear willingness to integrate on the part of the person taking the test, but also provides the key to success in the workplace and in society as a whole. The language descriptors of the CEFR are used as benchmarks in migrant competence, even though they were not designed for them (McNamara, 2011) and are mainly based on a monolingual and objectified view of the language one is supposed to use, being the "standard" language. As a consequence of this, those who undergo the language testing regime for integration are to be measured against a standard departing from a static mono-normative and artefactualized concept of language, in which their individual characteristics and their plurilingual repertoires are not taken into consideration.

As a result, people with very rich linguistic repertoires and with a learning background far from formal education are either denied access to a country altogether or cannot obtain a residence permit because they lack sufficient competence in "the" language of "the" country. Therefore, the "tested language" becomes the most important language to acquire and master.

As Shohamy (2004) affirms, the consequences of the political use of language tests include determining prestige, a hierarchy of languages and suppressing diversity, standardizing, homogenizing languages, and perpetuating criteria of correctness. Shohamy (2007) observes that:

> One of the most salient uses of tests affecting language policies is in perpetuating language homogeneity, a construct which is detached from the reality of what languages are and how they are being used, especially in multilingual societies. Most tests impose homogeneous criteria of correctness and thus deliver a message that languages are uniform, standard and follow the same written norms.
>
> (p. 124)

The power of tests becomes ever stronger when test criteria such as rating scales affect language policy, and the definitions of "what it means to know a language" adhere to generic descriptions, detached from any context and from the contextualized nature of language and language performance in multilingual environments. As Leung and Lewkowicz (2012) suggest, the models of language underpinning construct validity in many established assessment frameworks appear to have remained static. This implies a potential misrecognition or under-recognition of "competence" in actual communication in a rapidly changing communication and language landscape, and a consequent call for a new validity framework in language tests.

But, in spite of this call, tests based on a monolingual framework such as the CEFR continue to be used to make decisions about people's lives. As evidence of such a use, we will briefly describe the language testing regime for immigrants in Italy.

Linguistic Issues of Foreign Immigration into Italy

The consequences of the implicational link between the CEFR and its standards and tests become more evident and problematic when tests are used as a gatekeeper against immigrants. This is very much the case in a particular context such as that of Italy, where: (1) a coherent and structured policy regarding language(s) both in the educational domain and in society at large is lacking (Barni, 2012; Vedovelli, 2010); (2) even sporadic decisions about language(s) at a political level

46 Monica Barni

are taken without the involvement of experts and there is no awareness of their impact and consequences; and (3) there is a tremendous lack of competence in, and awareness of, language testing and assessment and of its consequences, as has been highlighted in some surveys (Barni & Machetti, 2006).

Nevertheless, in Italy, as almost everywhere in Europe, CEFR levels are now enshrined in laws and in policies incorporating the use of language tests in granting immigrants rights of entry, residency, and, ultimately, citizenship (Van Avermaet, 2010). The Italian situation can thus be considered emblematic of the lack of reflection on the CEFR, its use and misuse, and of the fact that too often it is just used to foster, justify, and support decisions. Any sort of decision is permitted "in the name of the CEFR." This use implies that reference to the CEFR and its levels is often merely used as a label without any further meaning, with no consideration of the impact and consequences of such a use.

To understand the inconsistency of the choices made, we will briefly describe the context of the migratory phenomenon in Italy, both on a social level and with reference to education.

The presence of immigrants in Italy began to make itself known in the mid-1970s (Ferrarotti, 1979), but starting in the early years of the 1990s, the numerical size of the phenomenon increased exponentially. This was and is partly thanks to the unique geographical position of the Italian peninsula, which functions as a bridge to Europe. Today, around 5 million foreigners live in Italy (8 percent of the Italian population; Caritas, 2012), and around 800,000 foreign students are present in the educational system (8.4 percent of the entire number of enrolled students; MIUR/ISMU, 2013). Schools in which no foreign students attend do not exist. These most recent statistics demonstrate the tendency of immigrants to settle permanently in Italy. They also bring to light the fact that, by now, the phenomenon of immigration has become a structural element of the social makeup of Italy. The interventions made in response to this structural element as far as a linguistic plan is concerned have been of an emergency nature (Barni, 2012). There is no structured plan in public education for Italian language learning on the part of foreign adults, except for the lifelong learning centers called Permanent Territorial Centers, which, even from a solely numerical point of view (there are only 560 of them in all of Italy), are inadequate to meet the language formation needs of the immigrant population. The same lack of a structured plan for language learning characterizes the public school system. Decisions about extra support for the national language for newcomers are left to the schools, and sometimes even to the individual teachers, often unprepared to be language teachers (Barni, 2012).

Notwithstanding this, the lack of Italian language competence on the part of foreign pupils is always pointed to as the cause of their failure to succeed academically. With regard to adults, it is interpreted as a sign of their unwillingness to integrate into society. More and more, emphasis on the necessity of learning the Italian language goes hand in hand with references to the CEFR and its levels of competence, and with their improper use for political aims.

The Language Testing Regime for Immigrants in Italy

The paradigmatic example of the problems and the misuses of the CEFR is the introduction of language tests for long residence permits in Italy. Using the CEFR as a standard for assessing people's competence means using it for a policy-related goal: in effect, its introduction in Italy has been used politically to push for monolingualism, faulting immigrants' use of the language(s) of origin at home, and enhancing their need to learn the language of their host country. In schools, it is used to emphasize the role of the proficiency in Italian among pupils from families with foreign origins. The absence of this proficiency is blamed for these pupils' lack of academic success at school. This use of the CEFR is in line with a context of growing public anxiety about security and cultural diversity and a movement toward hiding other people's languages in schools and in society (Barni, 2012).

An example of the political use of the CEFR and its levels is the Ministerial Decree of June 4, 2010, which mandates the introduction of a test in Italian for those requesting a long-term residence permit. In the preamble to the decree, the CEFR itself is listed among the reasons behind the introduction of the test, as a document that is believed to give the mandate for such tests. The CEFR level chosen for immigrants is A2.

A subsequent agreement, signed in November 2011 between the Italian Ministry for the Internal Affairs and the Ministry for Education, establishes the articulation of the test in three sections: listening comprehension, reading comprehension, and written production. The choice of these abilities clearly shows that no reflection has been made on the nature of language proficiency useful to this kind of language user in order to inform the test's construct, and that the social actions that the test should eventually support are not articulated in the test design. The test construct and design are policy-based, and practical financial considerations are given priority over social significance, as the administration and assessment of written tests are much less demanding than oral and open ones.

Furthermore, the same agreement states that the tests are to be implemented, administered, and assessed by teachers in each of the adult education centers in Italy. So now dozens of different tests and dozens of different markers are used, and everything is justified by the CEFR and by European language policies. It seems a typical hypocrisy: Italy has to have a test because other countries have one; the test is imposed and justified through reference to the CEFR and European language policies, but all of the decisions are left to individual teachers. As such, the state leaves the decisions to them and washes its hands of everything à la Pontius Pilate.

48 Monica Barni

If we look at the test results, we see that the consequences of this policy, and the use of the CEFR as its mandate, are very problematic. Analyzing the results made available only by newspapers (*Il Sole 24 Ore*, May 16, 2011)—as of now, no central monitoring of choices made and procedures adopted in each exam center is called for—we discover that between December 2010 and May 2011 (the most recent available data), the average rate of failure on the test nationally was 13.6 percent. The city of Turin showed the highest number of candidates passing, with a 96.5 percent pass rate, and similar figures were seen in Rome (96 percent) and Naples (95 percent). Much lower percentages were seen in Milan (86 percent), Venice (70 percent), Vicenza (72 percent), and Verona, where only 65 percent passed the test.

Do these results reflect immigrants' proficiency in Italian, or are they influenced by the characteristics of the person conducting the assessment? Such characteristics include not only theoretical knowledge and technical skill about language testing and assessment, but also the attitude towards the persons being assessed. In other words, is it possible that political factors related to the context where the exam center is located played a role in the assessment of immigrants' proficiency in Italian? Why are the highest failure rates in cities of Northeast Italy, where political discourse revolves around law and order, and where ethnic, linguistic, and cultural diversity are considered law-and-order risks and assimilation is preached to immigrants? To investigate the situation more thoroughly, we are currently carrying out a survey in the various centers where the tests are produced and administered.

Through the answers to a questionnaire sent to teachers directly involved in the testing and assessment procedures in more than 50 CTPs selected throughout Italy, covering large and small urban centers in the North, Centre, and South (Barni, 2012), we have discovered that all of them indicated the CEFR as the instrument guiding and justifying their choices. We asked teachers to give their opinions on the introduction of tests of proficiency in Italian for immigrants and whether proficiency in the language of the country is a necessary prerequisite for living and working there. According to 87 percent of teachers, proficiency in Italian is fundamental for immigrants in Italy and a necessary prerequisite for a long-term resident permit. The majority of teachers (63 percent) said that they are in favor of the introduction of the test, also because the tests promote Italian language learning.

We are still analyzing the tests produced in the various centers, but from an early analysis it emerges that the majority of tests follow exactly the instructions given by the ministry, and that they therefore focus entirely on listening and reading comprehension, and written production. Furthermore, in some cases, tests of grammar are added and correctness in Italian is the primary parameter that informs their assessment. Plurilingual uses are penalized as not pertaining to "the" Italian language. What emerges is the fact that standards set by policy form the basis for the test, without any critical discussion by teachers.

Conclusions

Some years ago, Shohamy (2007) claimed that:

> Language tests should mediate ideologies and practices in more open, democratic and negotiable ways, and prevent the use of tests as powerful mechanisms capable of imposing draconic policies that have no empirical base. This happens especially when language tests violate diversity, when a false view of language development is being dictated through tests, when language is viewed in isolated ways detached from actual use of multilingual codes in communities, or when there are empirical data about the advantage of different accommodations that is being denied.
>
> (p. 128)

Our investigation in Italy has revealed that open, democratic, and negotiable ways of viewing competence in language are still far from being achieved. Once competence standards have been fixed, they constitute an instrument of power that can easily be incorporated into laws. This has happened with the CEFR and its descriptors of competence, which have become the standard for assessing the proficiency of people for whom they were never intended, with test construct and design not reflecting the needs of those taking the tests, but instead bowing slavishly to practical requirements regarding how tests are to be administered and assessed. Furthermore, the plurilingual competences of immigrants and their actual uses in communication are ignored.

The evolution of notions of language proficiency is not reflected in current test designs, and it will take a long time to change this. An accountable framework such as the CEFR, with its proficiency descriptors, is now embedded in policy processes, and it is only through policy processes that it can be challenged or updated. It is also deeply embedded in existing administrative procedures, and there will be a natural reluctance to change them because of all the administrative—and even legislative—work that this would entail (McNamara, 2011).

We believe, on the contrary, that a deeper reflection on the concept of plurilingual competence and on individual patterns of language acquisition and learning is now needed, and the approach that is only sketched out in the CEFR itself should be a starting point for further development.

References

Barni, B., & Machetti, S. (2005). *The (lack of) professionalism in language assessment in Italy.* Poster presented at the 2nd EALTA Conference, Voss, Norway, June 2–5, 2005.

Barni, M. (2012). Italy. In G. Extra & K. Yagmur (Eds.), *Language rich Europe. Trends in policies and practices for multilingualism in Europe* (pp. 146–153). Cambridge: Cambridge University Press.

50 Monica Barni

Barni, M., & Machetti, S. (2006). Language policy and languages in contact: Theoretical and operational problems. In E. Banfi, L. Gavioli, C. Guardiano, & M. Vedovelli (Eds.), *Atti del V Congresso AItLA*, Bari, 17–18 February 2005 (pp. 89–111). Perugia: Guerra Edizioni (in Italian).

Baynham, M., & Moyer, M. (2012). *Language and hyperdiversity in the global city: Re-thinking urban contexts*. Thematic Session at SS19, Berlin, 24–26 August 2012.

Blommaert, J., & Rampton, B. (2011). Language and superdiversity. *Diversities*, *13*(2), 1–21.

Blommaert, J., Leppänen, S., & Spotti, M. (2012). Endangering multilingualism. In J. Blommaert, S. Leppänen, P. Pahta, & T. Raisanen (Eds.), *Dangerous multilingualism* (pp. 1–21). London: Palgrave.

Byram, M., & Parmenter, L. (2012). *The Common European Framework of Reference: The globalization of language education policy*. Bristol, UK/Buffalo, NY/Toronto: Multilingual Matters.

Caritas (2012). *Immigration: Statistical survey. 2012*. Rome: Idos (in Italian).

Committee of Ministers (2008). *Recommendations to member states on the use of the Council of Europe's Common European Framework of Reference for languages (CEFR) and the promotion of plurilingualism*. Strasbourg: Council of Europe.

Council of Europe (2001). *Common European Framework of Reference for Languages: Learning, teaching, assessment*. Cambridge: Cambridge University Press.

Council of the European Union (2002). *Resolution on linguistic diversity and language learning*. Brussels: European Commission.

De Mauro, T. (2006). Crisis of language monolithism and less spoken languages. *LIDI. Lingue e idiomi d'Italia*, *1*(1), 11–37 (in Italian).

Dendrinos, B. (2006). Mediation in communication, language teaching and testing. *Journal of Applied Linguistics*, *22*, 9–35.

EC Action Plan (2004–2006). *Promoting language learning and linguistic diversity*. Brussels: European Communities.

European Commission (2008). *Communication from the Commission to the European Parliament, the Council, the European Economic and Social Committee, and the Committee of the Regions. Multilingualism: An asset for Europe and a shared commitment*. Brussels: European Communities.

Extra, G., & Yagmur, K. (Eds.) (2012). *Language rich Europe: Trends in policies and practices for multilingualism in Europe*. Cambridge: Cambridge University Press.

Extra, G., Spotti, M., & Van Avermaet, P. (Eds.) (2010). *Language testing, migration and citizenship: Cross-national perspectives*. London/New York: Continuum Press.

Ferrarotti, F. (1979). Basic statements for a survey on foreign workers in Italy. *Esperienze e proposte*, *38* (in Italian).

Fondazione ISMU e MIUR (2013). Students with non Italian citizenship. National Report 2011–2012. *Quaderni ISMU*, *1* (in Italian).

Fulcher, G. (2008). Testing times ahead? *Liaison Magazine*, *1*. Southampton: Subject Centre for Languages, Linguistics and Area Studies.

Gal, S., & Irvine, J. (1995). The boundaries of languages and disciplines: How ideologies construct difference. *Social Research*, *62*(4), 967–1001.

Jørgensen, J. N. (2008). Polylingual languaging around and among children and adolescents. *International Journal of Multilingualism*, *5*(3), 161–176.

Jørgensen, J. N. (2010). Languaging: Nine years of poly-lingual development of young Turkish-Danish grade school students. *Copenhagen Studies in Bilingualism*. Køge Series. Vols. K15–K16. Copenhagen: University of Copenhagen.

Jørgensen, J. N., Karrebæk, M. S., Madsen, L. M., & Møller, J. S. (2011). Polylanguaging in superdiversity. *Diversities*, *13*(2), 23–37.

Joseph, J., & Taylor, T. (1990). *Ideologies of language*. London: Longman.

Kelly, M. (2008). *Hyperdiversity: The challenge of linguistic globalisation*. Paper presented at Languages of the Wider World: Valuing Diversity, SOAS, University of London.

Komorowska, H. (2004). CEF in pre- and in-service teacher education. In K. Morrow (Ed.), *Insights into the Common European Framework* (pp. 55–64). Oxford: Oxford University Press.

Leung, C., & Lewkowicz, J. (2012). *The validity of assessing speaking*. Paper presented at the Ninth Annual Conference of EALTA, Innsbruck, Austria.

McNamara, T. (2011). Managing learning: Authority and language assessment. *Language Teaching*, *44*(4), 500–515.

Mar-Molinero, C., & Stevenson, P. (Eds.) (2006). *Language ideologies, policies and practices: The future of language in Europe*. Basingstoke: Palgrave Macmillan.

Martyniuk, W., & Noijons, J. (2007). *The use of the CEFR at national level in the Council of Europe Member States*. Retrieved from: www.coe.int/t/dg4/linguistic/Forum07_webdocs_EN.asp#TopOfPage (accessed March 1, 2014).

Meeuwis, M., & Blommaert, J. (1998). A monolectal view of code-switching: Layered code-switching among Zairians in Belgium. In P. Auer (Ed.), *Code-switching in conversation. Language, interaction and identity* (pp. 76–98). London/New York: Routledge.

Shohamy, E. (2001). *The power of tests: A critical perspective on the uses of language tests*. London: Longman.

Shohamy, E. (2004). Assessment in multicultural societies: Applying democratic principles and practices to language testing. In B. Norton & K. Toohey (Eds.), *Critical pedagogies and language learning* (pp. 72–93). New York/London: Cambridge University Press.

Shohamy, E. (2006). *Language policy: Hidden agendas and new approaches*. New York: Routledge.

Shohamy, E. (2007). Language tests as language policy tools. *Assessment in Education*, *14*(1), 117–130.

Van Avermaet, P. (2010). *Language requirements for adult migrants: Results of a survey – observations and challenges*. Strasbourg: Council of Europe.

Vedovelli, M. (2010). *Future indicative first person plural: We will be. Linguistic destiny of Italy from Babelic noncomprehension to Pentecostal plurality*. Rome: EdUP (in Italian).

Vertovec, S. (2006). The emergence of super-diversity in Britain. *Centre for Migration, Policy and Society, Working Paper, 25*. Oxford: University of Oxford.

Vertovec, S. (2007). Superdiversity and its implications. *Ethnic and Racial Studies*, *30*(6), 1024–1054.

4

ACKNOWLEDGING THE DIVERSITY OF THE LANGUAGE LEARNER POPULATION IN AUSTRALIA

TOWARDS CONTEXT-SENSITIVE LANGUAGE STANDARDS

Catherine Elder

Introduction

The language standards or outcomes-based frameworks that have dominated language education since the 1980s are by their nature normative. They consist of hierarchically arranged behavioral descriptions of proficiency or achievement that serve as benchmarks for gauging learning and teaching outcomes or readiness to meet the language demands of particular academic or workplace contexts. Aligning learners to these norm-referenced frameworks is the basis for high-stakes decisions at both the individual and institutional level. The Common European Framework of Reference (CEFR), now used extensively both within and beyond Europe, is a prime example. Evidence relating to the various CEFR scale levels (B1, B2, C1, C2, etc.) is increasingly required by administrators for recognition and portability of qualifications from diverse educational systems within and beyond Europe, for establishing entry to or exit for entry to particular courses or professions, and even in determining eligibility for immigration or citizenship (McNamara, 2011). Language standards, such as those associated with the *No Child Left Behind* policy in the US (Deville & Chalhoub Deville, 2011), may also be adopted for accountability purposes, often in association with language tests, to guide decisions about allocation of funding and to determine whether public investment in language learning is conforming to expectations. Language standards are also used by educators for curriculum planning and professional development purposes, to assist teachers in goal setting, diagnosing needs, and reporting achievement of individual learners or groups (Llosa, 2011). In all cases, the reference point for making judgments is the typical behavior of the norming group as codified in the wording of the scale descriptors or standards.

Critiques of Generic Standards

Precisely because they are normative and oriented to typical rather than individual behaviors, outcomes-based frameworks have been criticized for being overly generic. Indeed, as Hudson (2012) points out, "one of the most problematic facets of language ability standards is the lack of precision in linking relatively abstract definitions to test scores" (p. 479). Fulcher (2004) goes further in pointing to the "validity chaos" that occurs when pegging preexisting tests designed for specific purposes to a scale (the CEFR) that is entirely decontextualized. Teachers' difficulties in linking learners' achievements to centralized standards have been less well documented, but an example from the Australian context, in which the current chapter is located, illustrates the point. Scarino (2000) cites a teacher of French grappling with the imprecise wording of the Curriculum Profile for Australian schools, a national scale designed to map school progress in language learning on a single line of development from beginners to advanced:

> "Writes texts drawing on an expanding repertoire of language"
> *What do you mean? An expanded vocabulary?*
> ". . . to meet the demands of a small range of communicative purposes."
> *They're too vague. They're too vague! What do you mean by a small range of communicative purposes? What in God's name do you mean? Talking? Writing? Writing to who? Talking to who? Do you want to a two year old? Or do you want to a university professor?*
>
> (p. 18)

And if this vagueness is a problem for the reporting of language learning in general, it is all the more true for individual languages, the learning of which may be differentially challenging or engaging for learners depending on a variety of factors, including the linguistic distance of the target from their mother tongue, the nature and extent of their investment in learning, and, not least, the social context in which the language is taught, including the teaching approach and values attached to the target language in that context (Stroud & Heugh, 2011). McNamara (2011) emphasizes this point in relation to English learning and the CEFR, stating that "The imposition of a single set of cultural meanings and social values for language education for each setting in which the CEFR is adopted eviscerates the traditions of language teaching which are incompatible with the CEFR . . ." (p. 7).

It can thus be argued that the unifying or universalizing tendency that makes language standards attractive for educational systems is also their Achilles heel. They are abstractions, generalizing across learners and learning cultures in a way that limits both their validity for particular contexts and their utility for users (Scarino, 2012). Even in societies where diversity is valued rhetorically, as Shohamy (2001) notes, "there is rarely recognition of the specific and unique

54 Catherine Elder

knowledge of the different groups in schools as educational leaders often continue to strive for homogenous knowledge for all" (p. 384).

Language Standards in the Australian Context

In the Australian educational arena, serious attempts have been made to resist this tendency toward homogenization, with a strong argument made for ESL-specific standards as means of describing the developmental stages of second language learners, rather than measuring them against English literacy standards formulated for majority learners. The ESL Bandscales developed in the early 1990s (McKay, Hudson, & Sapuppo, 1994) attempted to imbue its descriptors with contextual detail reflecting stages of second language development, with information on the conditions of learning and with reminders of the bilingual and bicultural origins of ESL learners as manifest in the continued use of the home language with their peers (McKay, 2000). These standards are still widely used and have been subject to further refinements including a substantially modified set of scales for indigenous speakers of non-standard varieties of English and English-lexified creoles (Education Queensland, 1999/2002).

Educators in languages other than English have not been so well served. The National Curriculum Profile (Curriculum Corporation of Australia, 1994) mentioned above (along with the subsequent state-based standards derived from it) treats all additional languages taught at school as foreign, on the mistaken assumption that English, the official language of Australian schooling, is the common point of departure for all. Some background information on the learning of languages other than English in Australia is in order to explain why such overgeneralization is particularly problematic.

Learning Languages Other than English in Australian Schools

Australia has been regarded as pioneering in its inclusion of an unusually broad range of languages within the mainstream education system, including those spoken by indigenous learners and by recent and long-term immigrants. The quality of learning in these programs may affect individual life chances, as the credits obtained for language study at the upper levels of schooling can count significantly toward the overall entrance ranking for university selection. Of the 350 languages (including 50 indigenous languages) offered in some kind of formal education program in Australia (Lo Bianco & Slaughter, 2009), many are studied both by those with a home background and/or cultural affiliation with the target language (TL) or a variety of it, and those who have traditionally been termed foreign language learners, with no prior TL exposure outside the classroom. Chinese, currently one of the eight most heavily subscribed languages in Australian schools, is a case in point, and will be used for illustrative purposes hereafter.

Until the late 1980s, Modern Standard Chinese was studied largely as a foreign language by relatively small numbers of students from English-speaking backgrounds. This situation changed in the 1990s in response to a dramatic rise in the rate of Chinese immigration to Australia, such that the majority of students now studying Chinese in Australian schools are either international students on temporary study visas or the children of immigrants born and raised either in "greater China" (i.e. mainland China, Taiwan, and Hong Kong) or in other Chinese communities in Southeast Asia (Scrimgeour, 2012). Such students cannot, however, all be assumed to have age-appropriate literacy in Modern Standard Chinese, the language taught in Australian schools, given the variations in their age at immigration (sometimes after a very short period of schooling) and the different varieties (Cantonese, Hakka, etc.) used in the home community or country. Although the written code is essentially the same for all Chinese varieties, the spoken varieties may be mutually unintelligible in some cases. Furthermore, frequent contact with English, which, for most, becomes the dominant language, may mean that the home or "heritage" language either attrites or is never fully acquired (Polinsky, 2008). Also contributing to variation in language proficiency is the fact that some learners with a home background or prior schooling in Chinese may maintain or continue to develop their language skills outside mainstream classrooms through regular attendance at after-hours community language programs, although the nature and quality of instruction in such programs varies widely (Liddicoat et al., 2007).

The implications of this complex "langscape" (Angelo, 2006) for achievement in school Chinese learning have been considered in studies conducted in the Australian state of Victoria by Clyne, Fernandez, Chen, and Summo O'Connell (1997) and by Elder (1996, 1997, 2000), respectively. Clyne et al. (1997) examined the performance of a small sample of "background speaker learners" enrolled in secondary school Mandarin programs in Victoria, identifying instances of syntactic transference from both English and non-standard dialects as one of a number of areas where targeted pedagogical intervention was required. Elder (1996, 2000) conducted a large-scale comparison of the performance of different categories of Chinese learners on secondary school "foreign" language examinations. She found large score differences between different categories of learners, as well as evidence of test bias with disturbing implications for the decisions made on the basis of test scores (Elder, 1997, 2000). Research from the US on heritage language learning has offered similar evidence of diversity, although the findings here relate largely to university settings. Wu (2008), for example, explores the diverse prior experiences and current needs of Chinese heritage learners at college level in relation to "Chinese true beginner learners," showing that a number of grammatical forms easily mastered by the former are particularly challenging for second language learners due to their distinctiveness from related grammar rules in English. She also discusses the different distribution of languages skills among heritage language learners (who typically have stronger oral than print literacy skills), their greater comfort with language unknowns, their different approaches to learning grammar, and heightened cultural awareness compared to second language learners. On the other hand, according to Xiao (2010), when heritage learners are compared to native speakers of Mandarin there is evidence of reduced fluency when dealing with more abstract concepts and using formal genres seldom encountered in everyday language use domains. Efforts to theorize the process of heritage language learning in ways that differentiate it from second and first language learning (e.g. O'Grady, Kwak, Lee, & Lee, 2011) point to the importance of appropriately tailored teaching and assessment approaches for heritage language learners. Such recognition has, however, been slow to take hold in the Australian educational context.

Some acknowledgement of the diverse and changing profile of students learning Chinese in Australia is now reflected in differentiated courses and assessment with specific "eligibility criteria" for different groups of learners at the upper levels of schooling. However, this differentiation is not based on a clear articulation of the variable learning needs of the different groups. More importantly, the differentiation is not made at all levels of the education system or recognized in current standards-based frameworks used to guide the construction of curriculum and the conduct of assessment in language classrooms (Scarino, 2012). This means that teachers have no agreed mechanism for setting appropriate curricular goals or reporting on the diverse levels of achievement of their learners. Indeed, the different needs and abilities of these learners may be virtually invisible. This can have negative consequences. On the one hand, both recent immigrants who have been partially schooled in Chinese in their home countries and the background or heritage learners of Chinese parentage who use one or other variety of Chinese at home may gain little in proficiency from attending language programs built around syllabi and textbooks designed for the assumed second language beginner learner (Scrimgeour, 2012, p. 313). On the other hand, at the higher levels of schooling, there is a disturbingly high attrition rate among second or foreign language learners whose learning needs may not be met and who may perceive the competition from their Chinese-speaking counterparts to be unduly daunting (Orton, 2008).

For this language, then, and also for others taught within the Australian school system, there is a clear need for context-sensitive standards that acknowledge the diverse nature and range of achievements to be expected in school language programs and go beyond the current generalized outcome statements currently in operation.

The SAALE Study

How to derive such standards in the face of scant research on how learning proceeds in such situations? The Student Achievement in Asian Languages

(SAALE) project (Scarino et al. 2011), which will be briefly described in the following pages, offers a partial solution, aiming to draw out some of the complexities associated with the complex local ecologies of four Asian languages (Chinese, Indonesian, Japanese, and Korean) currently offered within the Australian school system, using evidence gathered from the learners themselves. As advocated by Shohamy (2001) in her proposal for democratic assessment, it draws on evidence from diverse groups within the learner population and develops descriptions of their achievement in collaboration with expert teachers well placed to understand these learners' special needs.

Methodology

The project brief required us to develop and administer tests to the learners at three year levels (end of primary school [Year 6/7], mid-secondary school [Year 10], and end of secondary school [Year 12]), to identify salient differences in performance among subgroups within the sample and use evidence from their performance to develop profiles of achievement. The particular challenge for the study was to devise a common measure of reading, writing, and oral interaction for each year level for each of the four languages that would also allow comparison of the achievements of learners from different language backgrounds and with different amounts of instructional exposure. Each measure therefore needed to span a broad range of abilities to encompass the kind of diversity described in relation to Chinese learners above. The tests, which were communicative in orientation, in keeping with the current culture of teaching in schools, were developed to the same broad specifications in consultation with panels of expert teachers of the respective languages to ensure that their content was aligned with what was likely to have been taught and learned in the particular language.[1] They were administered to school-age learners across four states of Australia and then marked by panels of expert teachers against an agreed set of criteria that were the same across languages and year levels (i.e. *content, vocabulary, forms/structures; fluency, intelligibility, comprehension* for the oral test; and *content, vocabulary, forms/structures, discourse,* and *script/characters* [depending on the language] for writing). Scores derived from this process were then cross-referenced to background information elicited from learners and participating schools about "time-on-task" variables (frequency, duration, and intensity of language instruction both in Australia and elsewhere), as well as about aspects of their language background (e.g. parents' first language, country of birth, years of instruction, age at immigration), which our reading of relevant research literature suggested might have a bearing on their language learning outcomes. This assisted us in creating sub-groupings based on empirical evidence of differences in learner performance.

58 Catherine Elder

Project Outcomes

Learner Subgroups

It should be noted that language background proved to be a much more powerful and consistent predictor of achievement in all languages than time-on-task, so learner subgroups were based on language background differences rather than on differences in the duration and intensity of instruction.[2] For Chinese, which again will be used for illustrative purposes, we identified three broad language background groupings using the following working definitions of first, background, and second language learner, respectively:

First language learner. Born in a country where target language (or a variety of it) is the official medium *AND* arrived in Australia at age 8 or more *AND* the target language was the first language used before starting school *AND/OR* uses the target language at home.

Background language learner. Born in Australia but with one or more parents born in a country where target language is official medium *AND* target language was first language used before starting school *AND/OR* uses the target language at home *OR* born in a country where target language (or a variety of it) is official medium *BUT* arrived in Australia before age 8 (and therefore has limited experience of target language medium instruction).

Second language learner. Born in a country where the target language (or a variety of it) is *NOT* the official medium *AND* no more than one parent is born in the country where the target language is official medium *AND* first language before school *AND/OR* language used at home is *NOT* the target language or a variety of it.

Grouping learners in this way yielded results (mean scores) that were statistically different from one another overall, although not for all skill areas or for all assessment criteria (for further details, see Scarino et al., 2011). The trend at all year levels was for the "first language learners" as defined above to outperform all other learners, as might be expected given their substantial experience of mother tongue schooling in the home country, and for the "background language learners," with home exposure to the target language or a variety of it but little or no prior experience of mother tongue schooling, to outperform the "second language learners," whose opportunities for target language input and instruction were confined mainly to the Australian school classroom. Separate descriptions of achievement were therefore devised for each of these groups.

Descriptions of Achievement

Descriptions were developed at a three-day intensive workshop involving the same panel of expert teachers that had already provided feedback at the test development stage. Before the workshop, writing papers and recorded speech

Context-Sensitive Language Standards **59**

samples were ordered by overall test score. The panels, working collectively, selected 8–12 samples of performance at average and high score levels for each group. Comments on the selected samples were pooled to produce two sets of descriptions within each language background subgroup, one representing the norm (middle score range) and the other representing what had been achieved by the higher performers (top score range). By way of example, an extract from the Year 10 (mid-secondary level) writing descriptions for average level background language learners is provided below. The extract relates to the assessment rubric Characters:[3]

> *Characters are generally accurate and legible. Characters are occasionally incomplete or incorrect, with similar (or homophonic) characters employed mainly because of difficulties mapping oral language information onto appropriate print forms, for example,* 看 (春) 天, 下 (夏) 天, 开时 (始). *Pinyin is occasionally used to replace low-frequency or complex characters, though pinyin spelling is often incorrect and influenced by oral dialect sounds, for example, rung* (让)人开心; *yinwai* (因为). *Pinyin or English is sometimes used for place names (e.g. Opera House). Use of squared paper for character writing is effective in both indenting paragraphs and allocating spaces to punctuation.*

The "background language learners" described here have some facility with spoken Chinese, most likely acquired in the home and/or community domain, but having had limited experience with mother tongue schooling, they sometimes struggle to render these oral forms in writing due to their restricted repertoire of characters. They therefore resort to Hanyu Pinyin Romanization, and the influence of their home variety is visible in their spelling. The corresponding descriptions for the other two learner groups are not displayed here due to space constraints, but these show abilities that are quite different in nature. The "first language learners" have a much larger repertoire of characters and show greater ease with character formation, and indeed a personal handwriting style developed during several years of mother tongue education in the home country. The "second language learners," understandably, rely in their writing on a far more restricted repertoire of taught language. The challenges they experience in writing are primarily of a mechanical nature relating to the formation of characters (stroke number and arrangement) and to unfamiliarity with Chinese writing conventions.

As can be seen from the extract provided, examples of common errors are included in the descriptions so that teachers can easily relate to the described features. In addition, there are individual exemplars of both written and spoken production. The commentary attached to each exemplar details some of the salient features of achievement (which can be linked to the general descriptions)[4] along with information about the learner's language background and prior Chinese learning experience, for example:

60 Catherine Elder

> *The student was born in Australia of Chinese-born parents and speaks Cantonese at home. The student has studied Chinese since Year 1 (six years) and has also attended community school for five years. The Chinese program has two 60-minute lessons per week (approximately 80 hours per year).*

This biographical information and the associated commentary on their writing draw attention to the variability within each learner subgroup and to the importance of taking individual histories into account when planning teaching and monitoring learning.

Discussion

The descriptions developed for the SAALE project attempt to overcome some of the limitations of generic standards frameworks by drawing on evidence of actual achievement in specific languages with particular linguistic features (not only Chinese, as illustrated here, but also Indonesian, Japanese, and Korean) and in a learning context where the population of learners is highly heterogeneous, as described for Chinese above. The descriptions have been generated collaboratively with expert teachers with a view to rendering them meaningful for use in diagnosing needs, planning instruction, recognizing achievements, and reporting on learner progress. It is intended that these empirically derived descriptions will overcome the masking effect of generic frameworks and encourage noticing of important differences between learners that might otherwise be overlooked. Such descriptions can also serve to alert policymakers to the need for appropriate policies, goals, and expectations for the learning of Chinese (and the other Asian languages for which these data-driven descriptions have been produced). They acknowledge and legitimize the presence of first language learners and background/heritage language learners, as well as foreign or second language learners in mainstream classrooms, and offer evidence of the variation in both the nature and level of achievement for each group, thereby serving as a baseline or reference point for future planning.

There are, nevertheless, limitations attached to this attempt to counter some of the problems with overly generic frameworks. First of all, there is a paradox inherent in the design of a project that attempts to document the diversity of learner achievements but does this via common measures (see further discussion of this methodology in Elder, Kim, & Knoch, 2012). While a comparative design was needed to demonstrate the gaps in ability between different groups of learners, clearly much will have been lost by the fact of having all learners perform the same tasks. First language learners with high levels of mother-tongue literacy can certainly use language for a range of purposes other than those reflected in the tests developed for this project, and the lower level second language learners may have been better able to display their emergent abilities on less formal classroom tasks, with scaffolding from the teacher or other learners as required.

Additional evidence from classroom observation, as well as from performance on a broader range of tasks, will be needed in subsequent iterations of the project in order to extend the generalizability of these descriptions.

Second, the descriptions lack a longitudinal dimension, providing only cross-sectional snapshots of average and high level achievement for each language background grouping at the different year levels rather than documenting the specific markers of language development on a continuum over time. Tracking studies of different cohorts of learners could potentially offer more fine-grained evidence of progression in language learning for different learner groups.

In addition, it should be acknowledged that the current descriptions reflect achievement within a limited sample of volunteering schools and the collective insights of a single group of expert teachers. The nature of the sample, comprising a disproportionate number of strong and stable language programs, may have skewed the test results. The judgments of each expert panel may likewise reflect a view of language learning that is not universally shared among language teachers. Additional trialing and feedback from a broader sample of schools and potential users will be necessary before any descriptions could be considered sufficiently representative to claim legitimacy as common standards.

Also relevant to the question of usability is the fact that, as both Breen et al. (1997) and McKay (2000) have noted in relation to standards for ESL students, teachers respond best to frameworks that are accompanied by suggestions on appropriate teaching and assessment strategies. Such advice is particularly urgent for the background or heritage language learners, who constitute a largely untapped resource of community bilingualism and who, as noted by Kim (2012), may struggle to maintain and develop their mother tongue even after years of language study, due to lack of professional awareness of and attention to their specific learning needs.

Conclusion

The chapter has described a recent attempt to solve the widely documented problem with generic standards in the form of empirically driven descriptions of achievement tailor-made for use in a particular context—that of the teaching and assessment of Asian languages in Australian schools. While the language-specific descriptions yielded for this project should be seen as very tentative and require further refinement in light of additional evidence from broader classroom observation and research, they are an important first step in the process of balancing the institutional need for accountability in planning and monitoring language teaching and learning with due respect for local conditions and for the needs of particular learners.

It could, of course, be argued, given concerns about the homogenizing effect of frameworks articulated at the outset of this chapter, that the problem of overgeneralization persists, in the sense that the original norming group has

62 Catherine Elder

simply been replaced by three rather crudely differentiated subgroups (i.e. first, background, and second language learners), each of which functions as a new normative reference point for what is likely to be highly variable individual learner behavior. The descriptions for first and heritage language learners, for example, while acknowledging that the learner's L1 may be different from spoken *Puthuonga*/Mandarin, do not describe the features of specific varieties that may aid or impede acquisition of the taught standard. Thus, although every effort has been made in this project to come up with subcategories that are both recognizable and statistically distinguishable from one another, language teachers will inevitably experience some difficulties in matching the profiles of individual learners to the general descriptions.

This problem is surely inescapable and inherent in all standards. Some degree of generalization and categorization is necessary in all educational enterprises and even the most individualized interventions must always be made with reference to some idealized construct of what progress entails for a typical group of learners. The value of standards is that they make the construct explicit and available for interrogation. But the risk of any centralized system of standards, when used for accountability purposes, is that the construct becomes reified, inducing perfunctory compliance rather than promoting critical engagement—a situation that, it is hoped, will be avoided with these particular language descriptions via an ongoing program of professional development and research.

Notes

1. At Year 12, rather than developing custom-built tests, we relied on existing end-of-school examination data, administered by the relevant state assessment authority and made available to us for the project. To collect oral data at Year 6, we relied on a classroom observation protocol rather than a formal test. Further details are provided in the project report (Scarino et al., 2011).
2. Only at Year 6, where there are relatively small numbers of learners from Chinese speaking backgrounds, were the descriptions for first and background language learners combined.
3. Additional descriptions were also drawn up for each of the remaining assessment criteria (i.e. *forms and structures, discourse, vocabulary and content*) but are not provided here due to space considerations.
4. Both descriptions and exemplars produced for the project can be found at www.saale.unisa.edu.au.

References

Angelo, D. (2006). *Shifting langscape of northern Queensland*. Paper presented at the Workshop on Australian Aboriginal Languages, University of Sydney.

Breen, M. P., Barratt-Pugh, C., Derewianka, B., House, H., Hudson, C., Lumley, T., & Rohl, M. (1997). *Profiling ESL children. How teachers interpret and use national and state assessment frameworks (Vol. 1)*. Canberra, Australia: Department of Employment Education, Training and Youth Affairs.

Clyne, M., Fernandez, S., Chen, I., & Summo O'Connell, R. (1997). *Background speakers: Diversity and its management in LOTE programs.* Canberra, Australia: National Languages and Literacy Institute of Australia.

Curriculum Corporation of Australia (1994). *Languages other than English: A curriculum profile for Australian schools.* Melbourne: Curriculum Corporation.

Deville, C., & Chalhoub Deville, M. (2011). Accountability-assessment under No Child Left Behind: Agenda, practice, and future. *Language Testing, 28*(3), 307–321.

Education Queensland (1999/2002). *Bandscales for Aboriginal and Torres Strait Islander learners.* Retrieved from: http://education.qld.gov.au/students/evaluation/monitoring/bandscales (accessed March 1, 2014).

Elder, C. (1996). The effect of language background on "foreign" language test performance: The case of Chinese, Italian and Modern Greek. *Language Learning, 46*(2), 233–282.

Elder, C. (1997). What does test bias have to do with fairness? *Language Testing, 14*(3), 261–277.

Elder, C. (2000). Outing the "native speaker": The problem of diverse learner backgrounds in "foreign language" classrooms. *Language Curriculum and Culture, 13*(1), 86–108.

Elder, C. Kim, H., & Knoch, U. (2012). Documenting the diversity of learner achievements using common measures. *Australian Review of Applied Linguistics, 35*(3), 251–270.

Fulcher, G. (2004). Deluded by artifices: The Common European Framework and harmonization. *Language Assessment Quarterly, 1*(4), 253–266.

Hudson, T. (2012). Standards-based testing. In G. Fulcher & F. Davidson (Eds.), *The Routledge handbook of language testing* (pp. 479–494). London/New York: Routledge.

Kim, S. H. O. (2012). Learner background and the acquisition of discourse features of Korean in the Australian secondary school context. *Australian Review of Applied Linguistics, 35*(3), 339–358.

Liddicoat, A. J., Scarino, A., Curnow, T. J., Kohler, M. Scrimgeour, A., & Morgan, A. M. (2007). *An investigation of the state and nature of languages in Australian schools. Report to the Department of Education.* Canberra, Australia: Department of Education, Employment and Workplace Relations.

Llosa, L. (2011). Standards-based classroom assessment of English proficiency: A review of issues, current developments and future directions for research. *Language Testing, 38*(3), 367–382.

Lo Bianco, J., & Slaughter, Y. (2009). Second languages and Australian schooling. *Australian Education Review, 54*, 1–84. Victoria, Australia: Australian Council for Educational Research.

McKay, P. (2000). On ESL standards for school-age learners. *Language Testing, 17*(2), 185–214.

McKay, P., Hudson, C., & Sapuppo, M. (1994). ESL Bandscales. In P. McKay (Coordinator), *NLLIA ESL development: Language and literacy in schools project (Vol. 1)* (pp. B1–D52). Canberra: National Languages and Literacy Institute of Australia.

McNamara, T. (2011). Managing learning: Authority and language assessment. *Language Teaching, 44*(4), 500–515.

O'Grady, W., Kwak, H.-Y., Lee, O.-S., & Lee, M. (2011). An emergentist perspective on heritage language acquisition. *Studies in Second Language Acquisition, 33*, 223–245.

Orton, J. (2008). *Chinese language education in Australian schools.* Melbourne: The University of Melbourne.

Polinsky, M. (2008). Heritage language narratives. In D. Brinton, O. Kagan, & S. Bauckus (Eds.), *Heritage language education: A new field emerging* (pp. 149–164). New York: Routledge.

Scarino, A. (2000). Complexities in describing and using standards in languages education in the school setting: Whose conceptions and values are at work? *Australian Review of Applied Linguistics, 23*(2), 7–20.

Scarino, A. (2012). A rationale for acknowledging the diversity of achievement in particular languages in school education in Australia. *Australian Review of Applied Linguistics, 35*(3), 231–250.

Scarino, A., Elder, C., Iwashita, N., Kim, S. H. O., Kohler, M., & Scrimgeour, A. (2011). *Student achievement in Asian languages education. Full report.* Canberra, Australia: Department of Education, Employment and Workplace Relations.

Scrimgeour, A. (2012). Understanding the nature of performance: The influence of learner background on school-age learner achievement in Chinese. *Australian Review of Applied Linguistics, 35*(3), 312–338.

Shohamy, E. (2001). Democratic assessment as an alternative. *Language Testing, 18*(4), 373–391.

Stroud, C., & Heugh, K. (2011). Languages in education. In R. Mesthrie (Ed.), *Cambridge handbook of sociolinguistics* (pp. 413–429). Cambridge: Cambridge University Press.

Wu, S.-M. (2008). Robust language learning for Chinese Heritage learners: Technology, motivation and linguistics. In K. Kondo-Brown & J. D. Brown (Eds.), *Teaching Chinese, Japanese and Korean heritage language students* (pp. 271–279). New York: Lawrence Erlbaum.

Xiao, Y. (2010). Discourse features and development in Chinese L2 writing. In M. Everson & H. H. Shen (Eds.), *Research among learners of Chinese as a foreign language. Chinese Language Teachers' Association monograph series (Vol. 4)* (pp. 133–151). Honolulu, HI: National Language Resource Centre.

5

STUDENTS' VOICES

THE CHALLENGE OF MEASURING SPEAKING FOR ACADEMIC CONTEXTS

Lindsay Brooks and Merrill Swain

Elana Shohamy has been a colleague and friend for as long as either of us can remember. She has been a powerful force in both those roles. The danger, of course, is that at some point, her critical insight might be used to analyze us, but to date, she has applied her critiques to other domains. For example, her book *The Power of Tests* (2001) opened up the possibility of critical discussion about the uses of language tests. In that book, she wrote, "It is through the voices of test takers who report on the testing experiences and their consequences that the features of the use of tests can be identified" (p. 7). We would add that it is through the voices of test takers that we are also given insights into the similarities and differences between experiencing tests and the real-life contexts the tests are attempting to reflect. In this chapter, we will discuss test takers' perceptions of a specific high-stakes speaking test (speaking section of the Test of English as a Foreign Language internet-Based Test (TOEFL iBT) and compare their views of speaking during the test as compared to speaking in real-life academic contexts.

Test Takers' Perceptions of and Reactions to Speaking Tests

Many studies have recognized the importance and value of listening to test taker feedback (Alderson, 1988; Brooks, 1999; Brown, 1993; Cheng, 2005; Cheng & DeLuca, 2011; Elder, Iwashita, & McNamara, 2002; Hill, 1997; Nevo, 1985; O'Loughlin, 2001; Yu, 2007; Zeidner, 1990; Zeidner & Bensoussan, 1988). Test takers are important stakeholders in testing (Davies & Elder, 2005) and can provide significant insights into tests (Shohamy, 2001). In turn, these insights can inform and improve the test-taking experience (Fulcher, 2003; Jennings, Fox, Graves, & Shohamy, 1999). Feedback from test takers can be used to identify aspects of a test situation that may be problematic, and this information can subsequently

66 Lindsay Brooks and Merrill Swain

be used in the test development cycle to refine tests and tasks. Eliciting test takers' perceptions of a test is also important as a check on its authenticity, or whether the tasks correspond to target use (Bachman & Palmer, 2010).

Inseparable from test taker perceptions is their affective response to, and during, a testing context. Whether students like a topic, interlocutor, or test format can potentially positively or negatively influence their performance (Bachman & Palmer, 2010). Although he did not examine effects on performance, Qian (2009) investigated test takers' reactions to direct (face-to-face) testing, and semi-direct (person-to-machine) testing. He found that 33 percent favored face-to-face testing, while only approximately 10 percent preferred semi-direct testing. The lack of interaction in the semi-direct test was cited as the main reason for the test takers' preference for direct testing. However, almost 41 percent had no preference, responding positively to both test formats. The remaining 16 percent either responded negatively to both test formats (10 percent) or held no opinion on either format (6 percent). In another study comparing test taker perceptions of direct and semi-direct tests, Kiddle and Kormos (2011) found that test takers' ratings of all features of direct and semi-direct test formats were generally positive. However, the students rated the direct format more highly in terms of fairness, and the authors suggested that this might be because the test takers did not regard the two test formats as equivalent. Stricker and Attali (2010) surveyed test takers on their attitudes to the TOEFL iBT and found that the speaking section was rated the least favorably of all four skill areas. They stated that it remains to be answered whether "these attitudes are common to all speaking tests or are triggered by unusual features of the TOEFL section, such as the absence of interaction" (p. 14).

What appears to be absent from the literature are test takers' perceptions of high-stakes tests such as the TOEFL iBT and the comparability of the speaking as measured in the test to the types of speaking in the contexts the test was designed to reflect. In this chapter, we provide a space for students' voices by addressing the research question as to whether the students feel there are differences in their speaking activities and their own performances in the contexts of the TOEFL iBT and in their real-life academic studies, both in class and out of class.

Gathering the Voices

The students whose views are represented in this chapter were international graduate students enrolled in a Canadian university. The students volunteered to participate in the study after being informed of our research through their departments and through a newsletter for international students. Fifteen students were from science disciplines (engineering, dentistry, biochemistry, and physics) and 15 students were from social science disciplines (education and psychology). These students came from 11 different language backgrounds: Mandarin, Farsi, Arabic, German, Hindi, Italian, Kurdish, Nepalese, Portuguese, Russian,

Measuring Speaking for Academic Contexts **67**

and Spanish. Each participant was given a pseudonym appropriate to his or her first language background. Table 5.1 provides an overview of additional information about the participants. The TOEFL iBT scores in Table 5.1 are those that the participants obtained in the research version of the speaking section that was part of our data collection procedures.

We asked the students to record themselves during class time doing an activity reflective of the activities they normally engaged in during class time (21 recorded presentations, nine recorded paired or small group discussions). We also asked the students to record themselves during an out-of-class activity that was related to their academic studies (two recorded presentations, 28 recorded paired or small group discussions). The students were also recorded while doing a research version of the speaking section of the TOEFL iBT provided to us by ETS. The research version of the TOEFL iBT consisted of two independent (Tasks 1 and 2) and four integrated (Tasks 3–6) speaking tasks. Table 5.2 provides an overview of the six tasks.

As soon as possible after each recording was made (immediately after the test; within about 24 hours after the in-class and out-of-class activities), we conducted a stimulated recall session with 14 of the participants. In the stimulated recalls, the students reflected on their speaking in the three contexts. The strategies they

TABLE 5.1 Participants' backgrounds

		Sciences (N = 15)	Social sciences (N = 15)
Gender	F	4	12
	M	11	3
Age in years	Median	23	25
	Range	22–30	22–43
Time in Canada	Median	2.5	6
(months)	Range	2–17	1–19
TOEFL iBT speaking score	Median	24	23
(maximum score of 30)	Range	19–30	17–29

TABLE 5.2 Overview of the six tasks in the TOEFL iBT

Task	Language skills required	Topic	Preparation time (in sec.)	Response time (in sec.)
1	Speaking	Familiar topic	15	45
2	Speaking	Familiar topic	15	45
3	Reading, listening, speaking	Campus life situations	20	60
4	Reading, listening, speaking	Academics course content	30	60
5	Listening, speaking	Campus life situations	30	60
6	Listening, speaking	Academic course content	20	60

68 Lindsay Brooks and Merrill Swain

used are reported in Brooks and Swain (2013a). Additionally, each participant responded to a semi-structured interview (see Appendix) lasting, on average, 35 minutes. We asked students to reflect on their perceptions of the speaking version of the TOEFL iBT and their real-life academic speaking, their reactions to the test tasks, their speaking in their academic studies, and to make any other additional comments they wished. The data we report on in the remainder of this chapter come from the interviews.

For the analysis of student perceptions, we first transcribed the participants' interviews. Using the interview questions as a guide to identifying themes in the transcripts, we developed a preliminary coding scheme. For questions that elicited a direct answer, this just involved identifying the participants' responses to those questions. Therefore, the results for those questions have an N of 30. For questions that were open-ended, such as those in which participants reflected on the similarities and differences between the TOEFL iBT and their real-life academic speaking, we developed a list of themes that emerged from the participants' responses. Because not every participant mentioned each theme, those results have an N of less than 30. Using an iterative process, we then further refined the coding scheme so that the codes reflected whether the participants held positive, negative, or mixed views. We also identified whether each comment was about the speaking section of the TOEFL iBT or a real-life academic speaking context. Our coding captures the percentage of participants who commented on a particular theme in a given context. Therefore, multiple mentions of a theme were only counted once. However, we coded all instances so that we could check, for example, if a participant expressing a positive view on a theme in a particular context later in the interview expressed a negative view about that theme and context. In such cases, the coding decisions were collapsed and coded as a "mixed view" for that theme and context.

To establish inter-coder reliability, two research assistants (RAs) met, and after independently coding one participant's interview, compared their coding decisions and discussed any discrepancies. Then, they independently coded an additional five transcripts. The inter-coder reliability based on coding these six transcripts (20 percent of the interviews) was calculated using the Spearman-Brown prophesy formula and was .98, with an inter-coder agreement of 90 percent. One of the RAs then independently coded the remaining 24 transcripts using NVivo 9.

Students' Perceptions

Our research question addressed the differences in the students' perceptions of their speaking activities and their own speaking performances across contexts. In the following two sections, we present: (1) the perceptions of the students with respect to the speaking section of the TOEFL iBT; and (2) their perceptions of the comparability of their speaking in the TOEFL iBT and their in-class and out-of-class contexts.

Measuring Speaking for Academic Contexts **69**

Perceptions of the Speaking Section of the TOEFL iBT

As an overview of the participants' impressions of the speaking section of the TOEFL iBT, we asked students whether the test: (1) reflected the academic English required for studies at university; (2) was effective in assessing their English language proficiency; and (3) provided sufficient evidence about their speaking proficiency (see questions 2 a, b, and c in the Appendix). Because the questions tended to elicit yes/no answers (or, in some cases, a combination of both), the results we report have an N of 30 (100 percent of the participants).

The results presented in Table 5.3 show that 43 percent of the participants commented positively that, in general, the tasks and the types of speaking were representative of what they were required to do in their academic studies. A slightly higher percentage of students (47 percent) expressed mixed views, as illustrated by Sofia's comments in Excerpt 1.

Excerpt 1

> *I think not very well for graduate studies. Maybe for undergraduate I would find it more suitable because I remember doing those tasks when I was in my undergraduate. Like that's the kind of tasks that I think you do. But graduate, it's different because it's kind of more creative. Things have to come up from your own rather than showing that you understood what other people say . . . For example, I felt that I was using more memory stuff, like how much I could remember about the lecture and then kind of reproduce it or rephrase it but not arguing about it.*

> (Sofia, interview)

When asked whether any of the task types were more reflective of what they did in their studies, 21 of the 23 students who expressed a view reported that the integrated tasks were more reflective and authentic, while only two students felt that the independent tasks were more reflective because they were not tied to any particular discipline. A representative sample of the students' differing perceptions of the integrated and independent tasks is shown in Faraz's comments in Excerpt 2.

TABLE 5.3 Perceptions of the speaking section of the TOEFL iBT ($N = 30$)

	Positive		*Mixed views*		*Negative*	
	N	*%*	*N*	*%*	*N*	*%*
Reflective of academic English at university	13	43	14	47	3	10
Effective in assessing proficiency	11	37	12	40	7	23
Sufficient evidence of proficiency	7	23	9	30	14	47

Excerpt 2

> *I guess two first parts, I mean those general topics were kind of ridiculous section because I mean sometimes you don't have any idea about this stuff. You cannot do it. But other four parts are really good. I guess they kind of reflect academic environment because you're going to read something and listen to something and you have to talk about that with your supervisor. Or you're in the class, you have to listen to professor and then ask and discuss so those parts are good in general.*

> (Faraz, interview)

In answering whether they thought the speaking section of the TOEFL iBT was effective in assessing their English language proficiency, 37 percent of the students responded positively and 23 percent felt that it was not effective. Huan was among the 40 percent who had mixed views (see Excerpt 3). Although she felt the test was mostly effective, it was not entirely effective because it only assessed her language in that "particular setting."

Excerpt 3

> *I want to say, 60 percent, maybe because I don't know, I feel like when I was in the test, and the pace is usually quite different from what I am in the daily setting, maybe because it just assess particular setting I was taking the test.*

> (Huan, interview)

Only 23 percent of the students felt that the speaking section of the TOEFL iBT provided sufficient evidence of their language proficiency, while 30 percent held mixed views and 47 percent felt that the tasks did not allow performances indicative of their oral proficiency in academic English. Students cited the lack of interaction, including not being able to ask questions or interrupt ($N = 11$), the lack of opportunity to show humor, creativity, and personality ($N = 6$), and the inability to demonstrate their "everyday" speaking ($N = 5$) as the top reasons why they felt the test underrepresented their speaking proficiency. Mina, one of the participants, summed up the perceptions of those holding negative or mixed views in her comment that the TOEFL iBT "is not complete."

Perceptions of the Comparability of the Speaking Section of the TOEFL iBT and Real-Life Academic Contexts

In this next section, we summarize the participants' perceptions of the *similarities* between their speaking during the TOEFL iBT and during their real-life academic studies. This is followed by a section on the *differences* the participants perceived between their speaking in the TOEFL iBT and real-life academic contexts. Two of the themes (confidence and performance) are directly from the questions we

Measuring Speaking for Academic Contexts **71**

asked them (see Appendix), so all 30 participants commented on those. The remaining themes that we report on emerged from the students' responses to the questions about the similarities and differences. Because of this, the total number of participants commenting on each theme varies.

Similarities. For similarities, only two themes emerged from the participants' responses: content and task type. Forty percent of the students mentioned that the content was similar to their real-life academic contexts. As for task type, 57 percent of the participants mentioned that the task types were similar. Excerpt 4 contains a representative sample of the types of comments students made with respect to similarities between the speaking section of the TOEFL iBT and real-life contexts.

Excerpt 4

> *They cover lectures for example . . . simulating recorded classes, they also cover some uh daily life of students for example, in the library or uh in dormitory or talking with friends about the courses or other things so mainly they cover these two. If the aim is to see how a student can perform well in an academic life I think it's somehow good.*

(Sami, interview)

Differences. For differences, many more themes emerged from the participants' reflections. Our participants perceived that their speaking in the TOEFL iBT and in their real-life academic studies differed in terms of the confidence they felt, the degree of interaction, the time, the level of nervousness, the attention to language (versus content), and, ultimately, in their performances. When reflecting on their confidence, the participants distinguished between the TOEFL iBT, in-class, and out-of-class contexts. That is why we report on this difference separately in Table 5.4. For the other differences, the students often made no distinction between in-class and out-of-class contexts and instead compared the TOEFL iBT to real-life academic contexts in general.

As shown in Table 5.4, the highest percentage of students (73 percent) reported feeling the most confident in the out-of-class context. As Luli stated in her interview, "Out-of-class I still can speak very fluently, more casually, lots of words come to my mind . . . I feel really comfortable."

A relatively high percentage of participants expressed mixed views about their confidence in the in-class context (67 percent). Their comments reflected their consideration of the type of in-class speaking involved (level of formality), and their level of comfort with the course content and classmates and/or professors. For example, 63 percent reported confidence in speaking to their professors either in class or out of class, 33 percent had mixed feelings, and 3 percent (one participant) reported not feeling confident interacting with professors.

72 Lindsay Brooks and Merrill Swain

TABLE 5.4 Students' reported confidence in the three contexts ($N = 30$)

	Confident		Mixed views		Not confident	
	N	%	N	%	N	%
TOEFL iBT	11	37	4	13	15	50
In-class	9	30	20	67	1	3
Out-of-class	22	73	8	27	–	–

The other differences that emerged from our participants' responses are listed in Table 5.5. Only the five most common themes appear in the table; six or fewer participants mentioned the remaining themes, so we have not included those themes in our results.

Of the 27 participants who mentioned interaction as a difference between the TOEFL iBT and real-life contexts, 25 of them expressed a negative reaction to the lack of interaction in the speaking section of the TOEFL iBT. For two participants, however, the lack of interaction was a positive feature of the TOEFL iBT. Students overwhelmingly felt that a lack of interaction was the main difference between the test and their real-life academic speaking. When asked about differences, Wenyan commented on the lack of interaction in the TOEFL iBT and the resultant effect on his confidence (Excerpt 5).

Excerpt 5

> *The computer won't respond to you. Sometime people will say "Yeah right" and that's just a word, but it helps you to build confidence.*
>
> (Wenyan, interview)

TABLE 5.5 Students' perceptions of the differences between the TOEFL iBT and real-life contexts

Difference	TOEFL iBT		Real life		Both/same	
	N^a	$\%^b$	N	%	N	%
Lack of interaction	27	90	–	–	–	–
Short time	24	80	1	3	–	–
Increased nervousness	17	57	4	13	6	20
More attention to language	13	43	2	7	–	–
Better performance	2	7	21	70	7	23

[a] Number of participants commenting on difference

[b] Percentage of total participants ($N = 30$) expressing difference

Similarly, Tao commented (see Excerpt 6) that the lack of interaction in the TOEFL iBT was different from the interaction and co-construction that is a part of real-life contexts. He felt that the stress and the lack of feedback in the TOEFL iBT context negatively impacted his performance.

Excerpt 6

> *Yeah, but uh, another uh big difference is I'm talking to a machine instead of a real person . . . that's a lot different . . . You know when you talk to people you see their face and their uh expression . . . And, accordingly . . . either go further into this topic or switch to another topic . . . or, you know there are more interactions. Talking with a machine and also under certain formality limit and it's different [laughs]. I think I can speak better than I'm reflected in the scores of my oral test . . . due to the pressure.*

(Tao, interview)

The second most frequently mentioned difference involved time, both in terms of the limited total length of speaking time in the TOEFL iBT and the time limitation of having to respond within 45 or 60 seconds (see Excerpt 7). One student commented that she felt pressured for time in her in-class presentation. Similar to Excerpts 5 and 6, in which more than one theme emerged from the students' reflections, Excerpt 7 demonstrates the time limitation theme, but also shows the cascade of themes in that the time limitation caused Faraz to feel stressed, which, in turn, affected his performance.

Excerpt 7

> *So, I guess time limitation in TOEFL exam makes you nervous and stressful, so sometimes you cannot speak in a way that you are actual . . . I just want to repeat uh one more time that please remove the time limit . . . because it's not natural. In real life, you're not limited to speak in 45 seconds, anywhere.*

(Faraz, interview)

As shown in the previous excerpts in this section and in Table 5.5, the theme of nervousness figured prominently in the students' comments as the third most frequently mentioned difference between the TOEFL iBT and real-life speaking contexts. A majority of students (57 percent) felt more nervous in the TOEFL iBT than in their real-life academic speaking, 13 percent said that they were more nervous in their in-class presentations, and 20 percent said that they felt nervous in both the test and in-class contexts. No students mentioned feeling nervous out of class.

In Excerpt 8, Sara's comments reveal the two themes of affect and attention to language, another thread where we see the inseparability of affect and cognition (Swain, 2013).

74 Lindsay Brooks and Merrill Swain

Excerpt 8

Because my circle of people . . . even I interact with them like in English, most of them are not Anglophone English speakers so the anxiety level of producing correct English as far as you can is very low. In the test though, the anxiety level is higher . . . You are asked to produce one, two, three, four, five and you're like aware of it. So you prepare for the test and then during the test, did I produce that kind of sentence? Did I use the passive? Did I use like because you know you're supposed to use more than two, three tenses because you're being scored on that.

(Sara, interview)

Another one of our participants, Tala, commented on her attention to using more formal language in the TOEFL iBT and in her in-class presentation than in her out-of-class discussion (see Excerpt 9).

Excerpt 9

But in a group it was different because we could just use informal language. But of course in TOEFL when you have a test, you use more formal language. And, yes, in presentation again you are trying to use more formal language. It's in more complete sentences, but in a group discussion, you may not complete your sentences and you don't worry about that.

(Tala, interview)

As shown in Table 5.5, students felt their performance differed in the contexts: 70 percent felt their speaking was better in real-life contexts than in the TOEFL iBT, whereas 23 percent felt that their performances were the same, and 7 percent felt that their performance was better in responding to the TOEFL iBT speaking tasks. Of the 21 students (70 percent) who said that their speaking was better in real life, eight reported that it was better out of class than in class, while three reported that it was better in class than out of class; 10 reported no distinction between their in-class and out-of-class performances.

Just as nervousness was a common theme in the students' comments on the differences between the TOEFL iBT and real-life contexts, comments about performance and affect came together, in tandem. A total of 23 students mentioned affect and its influence on their performance. That is, inseparable from their comments on performance was some mention of affect. In Excerpt 10, in response to a question about her in-class speaking, Sofia responded that her performance in class was better than in the TOEFL iBT. What this excerpt reveals is that her goals in speaking differed in the two contexts and rather than focusing on what she was saying in the test, her focus was on how she was saying it and the "worry" that doing so caused.

Measuring Speaking for Academic Contexts **75**

Excerpt 10

> *[Spontaneous in-class speaking] Oh! I think I do better in that than the TOEFL [laughs]. I don't know, maybe because . . . I'm concerned about what I'm saying so, because it's interesting and we're doing it for the sake of the discussion. But in the TOEFL I'm so worried about the form and the grammar and the stuff.*
>
> (Sofia, interview)

In Excerpt 11, Bo also commented on the connection between performance and affect, saying that because he was under no time pressure, his accuracy was better in real-life contexts as he had time to find the word that he wanted or, if he could not, in real life, somebody would be there to interact with him and co-construct his message.

Excerpt 11

> *I think [my accuracy in real life is] a little bit better because I'm totally free from the stress of the timing so I can chose freely and actually when not, when I am not that nervous, not anxious, I can find the word that I want. Maybe it takes a while, one more second but I can always found the word. And if I could not found the word . . . somebody will give me the word, that's what I'll say and I'll continue.*
>
> (Bo, interview)

Discussion

As we mentioned earlier, to our knowledge, there have been no studies in which students have been asked for their perceptions of their speaking in a test performance and their speaking in real-life academic contexts. In this chapter, we have provided a space for the voices of our participants as they compared their speaking in the TOEFL iBT and in their real-life academic studies. The highest percentage of our participants expressed mixed views with respect to whether the TOEFL iBT was reflective of the academic English required in a university setting. Several of the participants said that studying for the test before arriving in Canada allowed them a glimpse into the academic culture they would be facing. As one of our participants, Lian, stated, "it opened the door" for her introduction to North American university life. Overall, they felt that the tasks (the integrated tasks rather than the independent tasks) called upon some of the same skills they were required to use at the university. However, one of our participants, Sofia, mentioned (see Excerpt 1) that the tasks may have been more appropriate for undergraduate students. Since all of our participants were graduate students, it is not clear whether undergraduate students would have voiced similar views.

76 Lindsay Brooks and Merrill Swain

In response to whether the TOEFL iBT effectively measured their oral proficiency, 40 percent of the students had mixed views, while 37 percent responded positively. Some of the participants with mixed views felt the test was mostly effective but was limited (see Excerpt 3). As Sami, one of our participants, acknowledged, because of "the limitations in the kind of technology, for example it's done with a computer; it's not the real life, it's the simulation of the real life" (see also Excerpt 4). In his comment, Sami highlights one of the inherent challenges of measuring speaking, particularly semi-direct measures, in that the technology allows for simulation but not replication of real life.

As to whether the speaking section of the TOEFL iBT provided sufficient evidence of their speaking skills, our participants also commented on some of the limitations, with the highest percentage of the students (47 percent) saying that the test did not provide a complete picture of their speaking. What students felt was missing was interaction and the chance to demonstrate aspects of their personality, including humor and creativity. As one of the students, Shan, commented, "the TOEFL tasks cannot assess students' ability to give response or instant feedback, so it might be limited in this kind of way," and, as Wenyan said, "I don't think they allow me to make jokes."

When we asked students about the similarities between their speaking in the test and their speaking in real-life academic contexts, the similarities they mentioned, content and tasks, mirrored the comments they made in response to their perceptions of whether the TOEFL iBT reflected the type of speaking they did in their studies. In their comments, 57 percent of the students felt the tasks, especially the integrated tasks, were similar to those they typically did in their academic studies. As Suyin commented, "when we read articles and then discuss with our peers and classmates, so that's the similarity and for the fifth and sixth parts, yeah, it happens when we are finishing lectures, we'll have some discussions."

In comparison to the comments on the similarities, the students had a lot more to say about differences. Although we have presented the differences separately, we have shown that the perceptions are often interrelated and what brings them together is affect (Swain, 2013). Half of the students commented that they did not feel confident about their speaking in the TOEFL iBT, in part due to having to speak to a computer. The students held overwhelmingly negative views on this lack of interaction in the TOEFL iBT, commenting that it made them nervous, impacting their performances for the worse. Other studies have found that students also responded negatively to semi-direct computer-mediated testing (e.g. Qian, 2009). Stricker and Attali (2010) questioned whether the test takers in their study rated the speaking section of the TOEFL iBT unfavorably because of the "absence of interaction" (p. 14), and our study suggests that this may partially account for their finding, but perhaps other features of the test may have played a role too. According to our participants, the timed nature of the TOEFL iBT

Measuring Speaking for Academic Contexts **77**

was anxiety-provoking, and this, coupled with no interaction, was profoundly different from the speaking they did in their academic studies.[1] Despite the fact that the TOEFL iBT was not high-stakes for our participants, most reported that they felt more nervous doing the test than they did in their real-life speaking at the university. Perhaps most importantly, the students' perceptions of the differences when responding to the TOEFL iBT in contrast to speaking in real-life academic contexts wove together a complex synthesis of affect and cognition. Reasons were rarely given without being accompanied by a comment about feelings such as confidence and nervousness. Many of the students reported that in responding to the speaking section of the TOEFL iBT, they paid more attention to their language use, but because of the stress in that context, their performances suffered (Brooks & Swain, 2013b).

Although our study is limited to the voices of a small number of students, our participants' comments and insights have highlighted some of the challenges of measuring speaking in academic contexts and thus provided important feedback that can be used by test developers. Among the challenges are the constraints imposed by the test context itself, both in terms of the representation of the speaking construct and the attempt to simulate real-life speaking. Our participants' reflections have made it clear that they perceive not only these limitations in the test, but distinct differences between the testing and real-life academic speaking contexts. One of the main differences was the lack of interaction in the testing context, about which participants were overwhelmingly negative. Our students told us that the lack of interaction in the speaking section of the TOEFL iBT was frustrating and upsetting to them, reinforcing Shohamy (in Lazaraton, 2010), who stated, "when it comes to language I could not accept that any construct that does not involve interacting with actual 'real life' language with actual people could provide [meaningful measurement]" (p. 261).[2] We would argue that the absence of interaction poses a serious challenge to the meaningfulness of extrapolating from test performance to real-life performance in that interaction is such an important part of real-life speaking. Additionally, the other differences suggest that students are engaging in entirely different activities as they move from high-stakes testing contexts to real-life academic ones (see also Brooks & Swain, 2013b). We leave the last word to Mei, another participant in our study:

> *Sometimes [in real life] there will be situation that I was interrupted and then I need to start the topic and continue my discussion so I feel, yeah, maybe that's the part missing from the test, but it's so hard to uh simulate [laughs] the same situation in a test. It's still a test.*

Appendix

Student Interview Questions

1. **Background questions/information**
2. **Questions related to TOEFL iBT Speaking tasks** (adapted from Cumming, Grant, Mulcahy-Ernt, & Powers, 2005)
   a) Overall, how well do you think the tasks reflect the academic English required for studies at university? Why? Which tasks do this best? What do you think is missing?
   b) How effective do you think the tasks are in assessing your English language proficiency in academic settings? Why/why not?
   c) Do you think the task(s) (individually and together) provide sufficient evidence about your speaking proficiency?
3. **Questions related to real–life speaking**
   a) What are the similarities between TOEFL iBT speaking tasks and real-life academic speaking?
   b) What are the differences between TOEFL iBT speaking tasks and real-life academic speaking?
   c) Overall, how would you compare your performance on the TOEFL iBT speaking tasks with your performance in your real-life academic studies?
   d) How confident do you feel about your speaking on the TOEFL iBT speaking tasks?
   e) How confident do you feel about your speaking in your academic studies? With peers? With professors?
4. **Other comments**
   Do you have any other comments you'd like to make about the TOEFL iBT speaking tasks, your real-life academic speaking, or is there anything else you'd like to say?

Acknowledgments

We would like to express our gratitude to the TOEFL program at ETS for their financial support of this study. However, the opinions or interpretations are ours and do not necessarily reflect those of the TOEFL program. Additionally, we wish to thank the following people who contributed to this project: Mohammed Al-Alawi, Seung Won Jun, Ali Malcolm, Paul Quinn, and Choongil Yoon for their help in transcribing and coding the data; Yongfang Jia for her help with transcribing; and a special thank you to Khaled Barkaoui for his advice throughout the project. We also extend our thanks to Robert Kohls, Sharon Lapkin, and Maryam Wagner, and the reviewers at ETS, who all provided us with helpful feedback. We also acknowledge with thanks our participants for their time and insights.

Notes

1. Simulating real life may be elusive because even when students are engaged in authentic assessment activities, the fact that they are being assessed "fundamentally changes the nature of a task, and thus compromises authenticity" (Spence-Brown, 2001, p. 463). Several of our participants commented that although they considered interacting with an interlocutor as they did in other tests of oral proficiency more realistic and authentic, it was still anxiety-provoking due to: (1) the reactions of the interlocutor; and (2) the fact that they were engaged in a test situation.

2. In the original construct framework of the speaking section of what was to become the TOEFL iBT, speaking was conceptualized "as the use of oral language to interact directly and immediately with others" (Butler, Eignor, Jones, McNamara, & Suomi, 2000, p. 2). However, due to practical constraints, the decision was made to make the test semi-direct. The final speaking framework included this limitation, and therefore the expected performance in both the independent and integrated speaking tasks is to "produce monologic discourse" (Jamieson, Eignor, Grabe, & Kunnan, 2008, p. 75).

References

Alderson, J. C. (1988). New procedures for validating proficiency tests of ESP? Theory and practice. *Language Testing, 5,* 220–232.

Bachman, L. F., & Palmer, A. S. (2010). *Language assessment in practice.* Oxford: Oxford University Press.

Brooks, L. (1999). *Adult ESL student attitudes towards performance-based assessment.* Unpublished MA dissertation. University of Toronto, Canada.

Brooks, L., & Swain, M. (2013a). *Strategic speaking clusters in testing and real-life contexts.* Paper presented at the AAAL Conference, Dallas, Texas, March.

Brooks, L., & Swain, M. (2013b). *Contextualizing performances: Comparing performances during TOEFL iBT and real-life academic speaking activities.* Manuscript submitted for publication.

Brown, A. (1993). The role of test-taker feedback in the test development process: Test-takers' reactions to a tape-mediated test of proficiency in spoken Japanese. *Language Testing, 10,* 277–303.

Butler, F. A., Eignor, D., Jones, S., McNamara, T., & Suomi, B. K. (2000). *TOEFL 2000 speaking framework: A working paper (TOEFL Monograph No. 20).* Princeton, NJ: Educational Testing Service.

Cheng, L. (2005). *Changing language teaching through language testing.* Cambridge: Cambridge University Press.

Cheng, L., & DeLuca, C. (2011). Voices from test-takers: Further evidence for language assessment validation and use. *Educational Assessment, 16,* 104–122.

Cumming, A., Grant, L., Mulcahy-Ernt, P., & Powers, D. E. (2005). *A teacher-verification study of speaking and writing prototype tasks for a new TOEFL (TOEFL Monograph No. 26).* Princeton, NJ: Educational Testing Service.

Davies, A., & Elder, C. (2005). Validity and validation in language testing. In E. Hinkel (Ed.), *Handbook of research in second language teaching and learning* (pp. 795–813). Mahwah, NJ: Lawrence Erlbaum.

Elder, C., Iwashita, N., & McNamara, T. (2002). Estimating the difficulty of oral proficiency tasks: What does the test-taker have to offer? *Language Testing, 19,* 347–368.

Fulcher, G. (2003). *Testing second language speaking.* London: Pearson.

Hill, K. (1997). The role of questionnaire feedback in the validation of the oral interaction module. In G. Brindley & G. Wigglesworth (Eds.), *Access: Issues in language test design and delivery* (pp. 147–174). Sydney: National Centre for English Language Teaching and Research, Macquarie University.

Jamieson, J. M., Eignor, D., Grabe, W., & Kunnan, A. J. (2008). Frameworks for a new TOEFL. In C. A. Chapelle, M. K. Enright, & J. M. Jamieson (Eds.), *Building a validity argument for the Test of English as a Foreign Language™* (pp. 55–95). New York: Routledge.

Jennings, M., Fox, J., Graves, B., & Shohamy, E. (1999). The test-takers' choice: An investigation of the effect of topic on language-test performance. *Language Testing, 16*, 426–456.

Kiddle, T., & Kormos, J. (2011). The effect of mode of response on a semidirect test of oral proficiency. *Language Assessment Quarterly, 8*, 342–360.

Lazaraton, A. (2010). From cloze to consequences and beyond: An interview with Elana Shohamy. *Language Assessment Quarterly, 7*, 255–279.

Nevo, B. (1985). Face validity revisited. *Journal of Educational Measurement, 22*, 287–293.

O'Loughlin, K. (2001). *The equivalence of direct and semi-direct speaking tests.* Cambridge: Cambridge University Press.

Qian, D. D. (2009). Comparing direct and semi-direct modes for speaking assessment: Affective effects on test takers. *Language Assessment Quarterly, 6*, 113–125.

Shohamy, E. (2001). *The power of tests.* Harlow, England: Longman.

Spence-Brown, R. (2001). The eye of the beholder: Authenticity in an embedded assessment task. *Language Testing, 18*, 463–481.

Stricker, L. J., & Attali, Y. (2010). *Test takers' attitudes about the TOEFL iBT™ (TOEFL iBT™ Research No. iBT-13).* Princeton, NJ: Educational Testing Service.

Swain, M. (2013). The inseparability of cognition and emotion in second language learning. *Language Teaching, 46*, 195–207.

Yu, G. (2007). Students' voices in the evaluation of their written summaries: Empowerment and democracy for test takers? *Language Testing, 24*, 539–572.

Zeidner, M. (1990). College students' reactions towards key facets of classroom testing. *Assessment and Evaluation in Higher Education, 15*, 151–169.

Zeidner, M., & Bensoussan, M. (1988). College students' attitudes towards written versus oral tests of English as a Foreign Language. *Language Testing, 5*, 100–114.

6

ETHICAL CODES AND RESPONSIBILITY

Alan Davies

Elana Shohamy's admirable 2001 book about the power of tests carefully avoids the trap that critical language testing (CLT) advocates all too easily fall into, the trap of rejection. What Shohamy does is to go beyond the default critical language testing position, which reveals the extent to which CLT uncovers existing structures of power and then stops short, implying that language testing must be abandoned. Shohamy accepts the critical testing critique and has, indeed, been at its cutting edge. But she goes further, taking seriously the need for language testers to be responsible professionals:

> The message conveyed in this book should not be interpreted in anarchistic terms. *It is not a call for the abolition of tests altogether;* rather, it is a call for the practice of quality tests which . . . imply also the practice of democratic testing. Such testing requires shared authority, collaboration, involvement of different stakeholders—test takers included—as well as meeting the various criteria of validity. Following such procedures will lead to responsible testing. In simple terms, this means: *Do it, but do it with care.*
> (Shohamy, 2001, p. 161, added emphasis)

The Power of Tests is, above all, a demand for responsibility in language testing. Such a demand can be met by observing the procedures described in the book by Shohamy. Responsibility has always been the goal of (language) testing, but as a set of somewhat discrete components (reliability, validity, practicality . . .). What Shohamy does is to consider responsibility as a unified and achievable whole, and for that she deserves our gratitude.

In this chapter, I continue the discussion of responsible language testing, and ask how far the responsibility of the language tester goes—are there any limits

82 Alan Davies

to it? A good place to start will be the Codes of Ethics and of Practice, which have proliferated in recent years among the various language testing associations, eager to professionalize themselves.

ALTE (the Association of Language Testers in Europe)

ALTE distinguishes between the responsibilities of ALTE members and the responsibilities of examination users. What ALTE members are enjoined to do is to follow orthodox language testing principles and procedures in the design of their tests, to publish those principles and procedures for test users, to interpret examination results for the benefit of test users and test takers, to take the necessary measures to ensure fairness, and, where necessary, make appropriate accommodations on behalf of handicapped candidates and to provide candidates with full disclosure on the level and content of the examination and on the rights of candidates. The Code also sets out the responsibilities of examination users. This concerns the appropriate use of the information provided for the test users by the examination developers. It is hard to see how the ALTE organization can exercise control over test users—it is not clear how this could be implemented.

In recent years, ALTE have revised their Code of Practice as detailed questionnaires in the form of checklists. These self-assessment checklists are set out in the areas of test design and construction, administration, processing (marking, grading of results), and analysis and review. The questioning method is somewhat similar to the method employed in the European Association for Language Testing and Assessment (EALTA) Code, to which I come shortly. But it needs to be emphasized first that the rationale of the ALTE Code is quite different from that of the International Language Testing Association (ILTA) Code, and indeed from the EALTA Code in that it presents ethics as a matter of professional test development, with particular reference—as is to be expected with a membership of test providers—to responsible and accountable test construction, delivery, and analysis. It does, as noted earlier, embrace examination users (and of that, more later). What is omitted from the ALTE Code is the individual language tester and the ethical questions he or she may ask. The ILTA and the EALTA Codes concern individual behaviors by members of their organizations; the basic question they pose to a member is: What is expected of me as a professional member of ILTA or EALTA? While the basic ALTE question is: What are the technical requirements of a responsible testing/examination organization?

EALTA (the European Association for Language Testing and Assessment)

EALTA's mission statement is as follows: "The purpose of EALTA is to promote the understanding of theoretical principles of language testing and assessment, and the improvement and sharing of testing and assessment practices throughout Europe."

Ethical Codes and Responsibility **83**

EALTA's guidelines for good practice are introduced thus:

> Reflecting its policy of inclusiveness, EALTA wishes to serve the needs of a very broad membership. EALTA's guidelines for good practice in testing and assessment are accordingly addressed primarily to three different audiences: those involved in (a) the training of teachers in testing and assessment, (b) classroom testing and assessment, and (c) the development of tests in national and institutional testing units or centres . . . For all these groups, a number of general principles apply: respect for the students/ examinees, responsibility, fairness, reliability, validity and collaboration among the parties involved.

EALTA's own guidelines to good practice in language testing and assessment contain 71 questions addressed to EALTA members. They cluster under three main headings relevant to the three audiences set out in the rationale quoted above:

1. considerations for teacher pre-service and in-service training in testing and assessment;
2. considerations for classroom testing and assessment; and
3. considerations for test development in national or institutional testing units or centres.

These EALTA guidelines cover some of the ground in the ILTA guidelines for practice and some in the ALTE Code. They are less concerned than the ILTA Code with ethical principles, but they give wide coverage to ethical practices, although they do not consider the conflict of interest that language testers can find themselves in. They cover much of the same ground—albeit in terms of individual language testers—as the ALTE Code. The most striking difference of the EALTA Code is that it is wholly presented in question format. Does that mean that there is no EALTA view of appropriate conduct and behavior of its members? The answer is probably no, since, in many cases, the expected response to a question in the guidelines is fairly obvious, for example: C 3/2: "Are the tests piloted?" It would be a brave (misguided?) language tester who would answer "no" to that question and not know it was the wrong answer.

The EALTA questions, just as the ALTE checklists, contain the issues that language testers need to think about and, where appropriate, act on. What they do not do, except insofar as the expected response is obvious and self-evident, is provide an account, a narrative to EALTA members—of what is normally expected, what type of ethical behavior is expected EALTA behavior. There are two responses to this: the first is that by not providing a set of EALTA norms, there is allowance for a variety of legitimate replies that empower individual members. The second response is that this question format assumes that EALTA takes its professional responsibility seriously through its workshops, conferences

84 Alan Davies

and other meetings, and its publications, thereby making clear to the members what the issues are and what responses could be expected from a serious member of the association. From that point of view, the 71 questions are indeed an aide-memoire, a checklist to make sure that all relevant matters have been taken care of.

ILTA (the International Language Testing Association)

When ILTA was established in the early 1990s, one of the early projects was to develop a Code of Standards (also known as a Code of Practice). A draft Code was produced in 1997, but the project was not taken further, largely, it seems, because it appeared too difficult to agree on a single ILTA Code. ILTA may have been a small organization, but it had a global membership, and therefore wished to reach agreement on a single—global—Code. Somewhat later, the project was restarted. It was decided that in the first instance, a Code of Ethics (CoE) should be developed and not a Code of Practice (CoP), on the grounds that it would be more abstract and therefore more likely to gain universal acceptance. The CoE was developed and accepted by ILTA as its CoE in 2000.

Several years later, ILTA decided that a CoP was also necessary. A new committee was established in 2003 to develop a Code of Practice for ILTA. The Japanese Association (JLTA) agreed to develop its own Code and to share its thinking with ILTA. It would then be possible for ILTA either to develop the JLTA Code of Practice in full or amended form, or to consider an alternative if the JLTA Code was thought too local. Such an alternative might be to encourage local associations and groups to develop their own CoP in conformity to the ILTA CoP, on the understanding that such local CoPs would be submitted for approval by ILTA. In the event, the CoP committee agreed to recommend to the ILTA AGM in Ottawa in 2005 that an amended version of the JLTA Code should be accepted. The draft was finally adopted as the ILTA CoP in 2007.

As a global body, ILTA had a more difficult task in reaching this agreement than did EALTA or ALTE. It is true that both are Europe-wide bodies, but the intercultural links are probably less difficult to make than the global ones of ILTA. The Codes of ALTE and EALTA are, in any case, quite different. ALTE, unlike both ILTA and EALTA, is an association of test/examination organizations and providers, while ILTA and EALTA are both associations of individual language testers.

The ILTA Code of Ethics justifies itself thus:

> [it] . . . is a set of principles which draws upon moral philosophy and serves to guide good moral conduct. It is neither a statute nor a regulation, and it does not provide guidelines for practice, but it is intended to offer a benchmark of satisfactory ethical behaviours by all language testers.

It mentions sanctions but it makes clear that good professional behavior is dependent on judgment; there are no formal rules and what the Code of Ethics relies on, in the absence of sanctions, is the willingness of ILTA members to act responsibly in accordance with the Code of Ethics (CoE) because they are professionals. In other words, professional training and experience equip you to behave responsibly. Those who fall short may be stripped of their ILTA membership. That mirrors the procedure in, for example, law and medicine, but in those professions the sanctions are very much more effective. Without membership of the relevant legal or medical professional bodies, it is not possible to practice as a lawyer or a doctor. That is just not the case in language testing, where the sanctions are weak and not supported by the law. Thus, there is nothing to prevent an ex-member of ILTA from continuing to practice as a language tester. While the law and medicine are strong professions, language testing is a weak profession, where the burden of being professional is more an individual than a collective responsibility.

While the CoE stays aloof at the abstract level, the ILTA Code of Practice (CoP) attempts to fill in the detail. Thus, Principle 8 of the CoE states: "language testers shall share the responsibility of upholding the integrity of the language testing profession," which is followed by Part B of the CoP: "Responsibilities of test designers and test writers," followed by such detailed instructions as: "Test materials should be kept in a safe place, and handled in such a way that no test taker is allowed to gain an unfair advantage over other test takers."

AERA (the American Educational Research Association)

By way of comparison, I turn to the American Educational Research Association (AERA), which is a much larger body than the three language testing organizations discussed so far. It is much broader in scope, although it does include testing and assessment within its brief. It is an important organization, and its Ethical Standards are influential.

The Standards (also referred to as the Code) contain six sections:

1. responsibilities to the field;
2. research populations, educational institutions and the public;
3. intellectual ownership;
4. editing, reviewing and appraising research;
5. sponsors, policymakers and other uses of research; and
6. students and student researchers.

Two examples of these Standards are:

2 B.8: Researchers should carefully consider and minimize the use of research techniques that might have negative consequences, for example,

86 Alan Davies

experimental interventions that might deprive students of important parts of the standard curriculum.

5 B.9: Educational researchers should disclose to appropriate parties all cases where they could stand to benefit financially from their research or cases where their affiliations might tend to bias their interpretation of their research or their professional judgments.

The Standards are intended "to stimulate collegial debate and to evoke voluntary compliance by moral persuasion . . . it is not the intention of the Association to monitor adherence to the Standards or to investigate allegations of violation of the Code." Voluntary compliance by moral persuasion could be read as the slogan/motto of all weak professions. The closest any of the organizations discussed here comes to asserting its strengths as a responsible and authorized professional body is the ILTA annotation to Principle 6: "Failure to uphold this Code of Ethics will be regarded with the utmost seriousness and could lead to severe penalties, including withdrawal of ILTA membership."

These are fine and necessary words, but it would be difficult to take action against an individual for not upholding the CoE—difficult to demonstrate and difficult to prove. And would the individual care, given that ILTA is a tiny and not hugely influential organization? AERA is influential, but takes what is surely the more mature position by calling on "voluntary compliance by moral persuasion." In other words, putting the responsibility on professionals to act as professionals. No doubt, it would be desirable for ILTA and the other language testing associations to be stronger and to be in a position to impose sanctions on those members who fail to uphold their CoE. But for that to happen, it is first necessary for the external stakeholders to recognize their need for a trusted and authoritative and accountable organization. Such development comes in two ways: first, from within, by pursuing the principles and procedures of good practice in development, delivery, analysis, and interacting with tests and clients (all included in the ALTE Code); and second, from without, through public awareness of their need for the services they can trust, and where they can obtain those services, which is the case for doctors and lawyers.

Clearly, tests are used for political purposes and language tests perhaps more than other tests, as they perform a social function. Those who use tests are being political: Who makes the political decisions about the use of language tests, and to what extent are test developers responsible, ethically if not legally, for that use (Shohamy, 2001)? Fulcher and Davidson (2007) agree with Messick (1989) that decisions about test use need to be considered in terms of their consequences, very much a teleological approach: "The intention of a decision should be to maximize the good for the democratic society in which we live, and all the individuals within it . . . we may define any test as its consequences" (Fulcher & Davidson, 2007, pp. 142–143).

Ethical Codes and Responsibility **87**

Tests have both intended and unintended consequences, but a test must be judged only by its intended consequences. That, after all, is the nature of validity. Tests are developed for a particular purpose, for a particular audience. But what about unintended consequences? Are language testers, ethically (if not legally) responsible for the unintended consequences of the tests they develop? What does taking responsibility for one's actions mean? If I write a book, how far does my responsibility for its use go? If the book is a ghost story, can I be responsible if a reader has nightmares after reading my book? If the book is a biography of a famous religious leader, am I responsible for the actions of devotees who burn my book and attack my family?

In the case of the infamous Dictation Test (Davies, 2004; McNamara, 2006), employed in Australia in the first half of the twentieth century for the purpose of excluding unwanted immigrants, those who developed the test, just as those who used it, were clearly responsible, ethically responsible, because its explicit use as a test was intended. Bachman and Palmer (2010) balance the demands on the test developer and the test user and make no mention of unintended test use. This is only to be expected, given the comments by Fulcher and Davidson (2007):

> an unintended use may take one of two forms: (1) an unintended use that the test developers do not know about or do not approve of, or (2) an unintended use that the test developers know about and approve of . . . Both are equally invalid unless a new argument is constructed for the new testing purpose and evidence collected to show that the retrofitting is valid, so that the same test may be shown to be useful in a new decision-making context . . . retrofitting test purpose without the construction and investigation of a new validity and utilization argument constitutes an implicit claim that any test can be used for any purpose, which is to introduce validity chaos.
>
> (p. 175)

McNamara and Roever (2006) consider a range of language tests used for establishing social identity, ranging from the celebrated biblical story of the shibboleth (Lado, 1949; McNamara, 2005; Spolsky, 1995) to present-day language tests used to determine the claims of asylum seekers. They write:

> The politics and ethics of the use of these tests are complex . . . The procedures involved are widely used in Europe, Australia and elsewhere in the pioneering of claims of undocumented asylum seekers . . . the lack of validity considerations in their implementation leads to serious injustice, a situation that would be remedied in large part by attention to the quality of the testing procedure.
>
> (McNamara & Roever, 2006, p. 165)

88 Alan Davies

The objection, then, that McNamara and Roever (2006) have to these procedures, which involve assessing whether the claimant really does come from the country that he or she claims to come from by matching his or her accent/dialect to that country or region, is in terms of their validity. They criticize the sociolinguistic construct that all too commonly assumes a homogeneity of accent/dialect where none exists and they criticize the methods used in the assessment. In other words, they have no objection to the testing of asylum seekers to determine their honesty. This is what they write:

> Although some applied linguists and language testers have objected to the use of such procedures altogether, it is reasonable to think that the evidence that they provide, when that evidence is properly obtained and interpretable, might be as useful in supporting a valid claim to asylum as in denying an invalid one.
>
> (p. 172)

McNamara and Roever are not among the objectors to language tests for establishing social identity. They refer to the guidelines for the proper use of language analysis in relations to questions of national origin in refugee status (Language and National Origin Group, 2004). Where does this leave their assertion, already quoted, that "the politics and ethics of these tests are complex" (McNamara & Roever, 2006, p. 165)?

The politics of their argument is straightforward: it concerns the national decision to offer asylum only to those who are genuine refugees and to exclude those who are not. The implementation of that intention in the procedures they discuss is a matter of validity and, as they show, they fail that test. Where, then, are the ethical concerns? Presumably, they have to do with the use of such procedures and are a judgment on the exclusion measures. As McNamara and Roever have shown, there is no agreement on this in the language testing profession—and it may be (as the ILTA Code of Ethics makes clear) that while the profession accepts the need for such testing, which is, after all, quite legal, there will be acceptance of those individuals in the profession who choose not to participate on grounds of conscience. So, are these tests ethical? It would seem that, according to McNamara and Roever, they are potentially externally valid but they lack internal ethicality, hence they should be judged not to be valid.

Can a language test be fair, and is fairness an ethical consideration? McNamara and Roever (2006) discuss fairness in the context of the ETS Fairness Review Guidelines (ETS, 2003) and of the various Codes of Ethics and Practice discussed earlier in this chapter. They recognize the difficulty of setting a global norm for fairness (McNamara & Roever, 2006, p. 137). Fairness, they propose, is a professional obligation. If fairness is an ethical component, they are right. But what exactly is fairness? Examining Rawls (2001) on fairness and justice, Davies

(2010) argues that in language testing, it is validity rather than fairness that must be the criterion:

> A test that is valid for group A (say adults) cannot be valid for group B (say children) because they belong to different populations. It is not whether such a test is fair or unfair for group B: the test is just invalid for group B. The search for test fairness is chimerical.
>
> (p. 175)

This leads back to the earlier discussion on language testing for asylum seekers and raises the issue of language tests for citizenship. The proposed legislation for pre-entry language tests was debated in the UK House of Lords on October 25, 2010. Briefing points were quoted from Blackledge of the University of Birmingham, who argued that such tests were not valid for purpose. Charles Alderson was also mentioned in the debate. Alderson commented that "the UK Border Agency's August 2010 list of approved providers of the English test has been developed by unknown agencies with absolutely no evidence of their validity, reliability etc." (Hansard 25 Oct 2010, 1102; ILPA, 2010).

These two critics approach the issue from the two different ethical positions discussed earlier, one from the point of view of ethics for use (no test for this purpose could be valid) and the other from the point of view of the internal validity of the test (this test lacks the necessary requirements of a language test). What Alderson appears to be claiming here—unlike Blackledge, but like McNamara on the testing of asylum seekers—is that such a test could be ethical if it were a satisfactory test.

The moral philosopher Peter Singer (2002) contends:

> what is it to make moral judgments or to argue about an ethical issue or to live according to ethical standards? Why do we regard a woman's decision to have an abortion as raising an ethical issue but not her decision to change her job?
>
> (p. 13)

Singer's answer is the golden rule: an ethical belief or action or decision is one that is based on a belief that it is right to do what is being done. Ethics, Singer argues, is a set of social practices that has a purpose, namely the promotion of the common welfare. "Moral reasoning, therefore, is simply a matter of trying to find out what is best for everyone, achieving the good of everyone alike— the golden mean" (Davies, 2004, p. 98).

Professional ethics is about the ethics of the profession, unlike morality, which is a matter for the individual. In becoming a member of a profession, the new entrant agrees to uphold the ethics of the group—with which his or her own conscience may not always agree. The various Codes (of Ethics, of Practice, of

90 Alan Davies

Standards . . .) make public what it is members are prepared to agree to, what it is they "swear" by, and they reach this agreement through compromise. They accept responsibility for the development of the language tests they work on and for the intended consequences of those tests. But they do not accept responsibility for any unintended consequences. Nor should they.

Conclusions and Future Directions

So, what are the Codes for, what is their value, what their role? What they do is limited. They are not a set of rules, not a legal document. What they are is a promise, an oath, to which members bind themselves, a way of asserting and claiming fraternity and sorority, not in secret, but in public. The onus is on individual members to demonstrate their professionalism, their status as professionals by adherence to their Code. Paradoxically, while the ethics is group-related, the upholding is a matter for individual morality.

As for responsibility for test use, this must be limited, as Fulcher and Davidson (2007) point out, to the purpose for which the designer has validated the test. Where does this leave tests for asylum and citizenship, and the use by government agencies of invalid tests (ILPA, 2010)? In the case of the first (asylum and citizenship), what is ethical in language testing—what the Codes require—is that the tests should be properly designed, valid for their purpose. Or, in Shohamy's (2001) formulation: "Following such procedures will lead to responsible testing" (p. 161). The profession does not oppose such tests. However, as ILTA CoE Principle 9 quoted above makes clear, while not opposing such tests, the profession does not require members to take part in their construction if they have a conscientious objection against them. The imposition of such tests is a political matter, and the Codes have nothing to say about politics. What is ethical for the profession is not necessarily moral for every individual member. In the case of the second (government use of invalid tests), the Codes again insist that it is professionally irresponsible to use invalid tests. However, correct though that argument is, it can succeed only if government and other agencies are willing to heed professional advice. Otherwise, just as the Australian government's attitude to the Dictation Test shows, what decides is politics, and not ethics.

The responsibility of language testers is not, I have argued, unlimited: it encompasses the intended consequences of a test, but not the unintended consequences. Here, it seems, Shohamy and I may not be in accord. Or perhaps it is more appropriate to recognize that Shohamy is more catholic in her view of responsibility. It is not that she is prepared to accept responsibility for all possible consequences (intended as well as unintended), but rather that she wants to make sure that language testers are fully prepared for all possible consequences:

> The responsibility of testers, then, is to admit the limitations of their profession, and construct knowledge in a responsible way, by working

together with a number of groups of users who accumulate evidences of the knowledge that is being assessed.

(p. 148)

Such a responsibility requirement is demanding. How far it is realistic remains unclear.

References

AERA (American Educational Research Association) (1992). *Ethical standards.* Retrieved from: www.aera.net (accessed October 30, 2010).

ALTE (Association of Language Testers in Europe) (2001). *Principles of good practice for ALTE examinations.* Retrieved from: www.alte.org (accessed October 30, 2010).

Bachman, L. F., & Palmer, A. (2010). *Language assessment in practice.* Oxford: Oxford University Press.

Davies, A. (2004). Introduction: Language testing and the golden rule. *Language Assessment Quarterly, 1*(2/3), 97–107.

Davies, A. (2010). Test fairness: A response. *Language Testing, 27*(2), 171–176.

EALTA (European Association for Language Testing and Assessment) (2006). *EALTA Guidelines for good practice in language testing and assessment.* Retrieved from www.ealta.eu. org (accessed October 30, 2010).

ETS (Educational Testing Service) (2003). *Fairness review guidelines.* Princeton, NJ: ETS.

Fulcher, G., & Davidson, F. (2007). *Language testing and assessment: An advanced resource book.* London: Routledge.

Hansard (2010). 25 October, vol. 721, cols 1101, 1102.

ILPA (Immigration Law Practitioners' Association) (2010). *House of Lords motion re: Statement of changes in immigration rules* (Cm 7944) October 25, 2010. Retrieved from: www.ilpa.org.uk (accessed October 30, 2010).

ILTA CoE (International Language Testing Association Code of Ethics) (2000). *Code of ethics for ILTA.* Retrieved from: www.iltaonline.com (accessed October 30, 2010).

ILTA CoP (International Language Testing Association Code of Practice) (2000). *ILTA Guidelines for practice.* Retrieved from: www.iltaonline.com (accessed October 30, 2010).

Lado, R. (1949). *Measurement in English as a foreign language.* Unpublished doctoral dissertation, University of Michigan, Ann Arbor.

Language and National Origin Group (2004). Guidelines for the use of language analysis in relation to questions of national origin in refugee cases. *The International Journal of Speech, Language and the Law, 11*(2), 261–266.

McNamara, T. (2005). 21st century shibboleth: Language tests, identity and intergroup conflict. *Language Policy, 4*(4), 1–20.

McNamara, T. (2006). Validity in language testing: the challenge of Sam Messick's legacy. *Language Assessment Quarterly, 3*(1), 31–51.

McNamara, T., & Roever, C. (2006). *Language testing: The social dimension.* Oxford: Blackwell.

Messick, S. (1989). Validity. In R. L. Linn (Ed.), *Educational measurement* (3rd ed.) (pp. 13–103). Washington, DC: The American Council on Education and the National Council on Measurement in Education.

Rawls, J. (2001). *Justice as fairness: A restatement.* Cambridge MA: Harvard University Press.

Shohamy, E. (2001). *The power of tests.* Harlow: Pearson Education.

Singer, P. (2002). *Writings on an ethical life.* New York: HarperCollins.

Spolsky, B. (1995). *Measured words.* Oxford: Oxford University Press.

PART 2

Focusing on People in Language Policy

7

CULTIVATING AN ECOLOGY OF MULTILINGUALISM IN SCHOOLS

Ofelia García and Kate Menken

Introduction

Schools as institutions are shaped by educational policies from the top, but also by the ideologies and enactments of individual educators (Menken & García, 2010). Most important among all individuals who exert authority in schools are the principals, leading a school's educational efforts and managing its organization.

This chapter focuses on schools serving emergent bilinguals; in the US, where our work takes place, such students are typically designated "English language learners" by the school districts in which they are enrolled. As Shohamy (2001, 2006) has noted, school principals wield enormous power in shaping language policies enacted within schools. For example, in New York City—the site for the project described in this chapter—school principals are called upon to determine if their school will provide bilingual education or monolingual English education, which greatly impacts the students' educational experiences, opportunities, and language practices both within school and throughout their lives. In spite of the importance of such a decision, it is one that most principals are ill-prepared to make (Menken & Solorza, 2014). And yet the role of school leaders as language policymakers has been overlooked both in research and in educational practices. Hornberger (2010) thus makes a plea for "sociolinguistically informed educators . . . [who can] open up ideological and implementational space for multilingualism and social justice, from the bottom-up" (pp. 562–563).

The present chapter describes a project, in which García and Menken are involved as co-principal investigators, that develops the knowledge base of school principals, as well as other school staff, in order to transform the linguistic practices in schools enrolling large numbers of emergent bilingual students. The initiative, known as the City University of New York—New York State Initiative on the Education of Emergent Bilinguals (CUNY-NYSIEB), focuses on transforming ideologies about bilingualism held by individuals—specifically principals and other school leaders, teachers, parents, and students—while creating an ecological community of practice in which bilingualism is used as a resource and multilingualism is valued in schools. A large team of scholars makes up the leadership component of the CUNY-NYSIEB initiative.[1]

This project has been deeply informed by both the work and scholarship of Elana Shohamy. With her contagious enthusiasm, Shohamy has described to us the course on bilingualism that she has offered for school principals in Israel in recent years, and her firm belief that such courses engender a powerful impact within schools. We start by briefly describing the situated context for the project in New York City, and then detail our shared work with individual school principals and staff. The purpose of this chapter is to share the work we have done, which is so closely aligned to Shohamy's own beliefs and work, so that further efforts with school leaders can extend into contexts beyond the US and Israel.

The Context

The first cohort of schools selected to participate in our project were overwhelmingly located in New York City; thus, in this chapter, we limit our discussion to the 23 city schools (out of a total of 27 schools statewide) with which we worked during the first 1.5 years of the project (January 2012–June 2013).[2] New York City is one of the most multilingual cities in the world (García & Fishman, 2002). Despite the linguistic richness of New York City, languages other than English (LOTEs) are hardly ever recognized as resources[3] in schools. Rather, they are typically only considered—and problematized—when students are institutionally classified as "English language learners."

Whereas linguistic diversity is the citywide norm, only a small proportion of emergent bilinguals benefit from the provision of bilingual education; thus, the vast majority of these students in New York City receive instruction in English as a second language (ESL) programs, where instruction is typically solely in English (New York City Department of Education, 2013). The number of bilingual education programs has dramatically decreased in city schools in recent years; whereas emergent bilinguals were equally divided between bilingual education and ESL programs in 2000, 76 percent are currently enrolled in ESL programs, with just 22 percent in bilingual education programs (Menken, 2013a; New York City Department of Education, 2013).

Project Participants

Schools selected for participation in the CUNY-NYSIEB project were all listed as failing schools due to the underperformance of their students designated as

"English language learners" on state exams. The schools also served an above average number of these students. All 23 NYC schools that applied for the CUNY-NYSIEB project were selected for participation at the project's inception in January 2012. Thus, participation in the project was voluntary for the principals who applied on behalf of their schools.

The participating schools reflected the diversity of New York City, and were as follows: seven elementary schools (Kindergarten–5th grade), two elementary/middle schools (Kindergarten–8th grade), 10 middle schools (6th–8th grade), and four high schools (9th–12th grade). In terms of location throughout the city, six of the schools were in Manhattan, nine were in the Bronx, seven in Queens, and one in Brooklyn. In some of the schools, the overwhelming majority of emergent bilinguals were Spanish-speaking, but there were also schools that were highly linguistically heterogeneous. At the start of the project, the majority of participating schools offered either ESL or transitional bilingual education programs in which the children were transferred to monolingual English-only programs once they had received a passing score on the English proficiency test given by New York State.

We wanted to ensure that every school transformed their practices surrounding the education of bilingual students according to their resources, the needs of their student population, and their school community. At the same time, we wanted to communicate a coherent shared vision of dynamic bilingualism as a resource, something that all schools, regardless of program type or school population, would be able to follow.

CUNY-NYSIEB Vision and Non-Negotiable Principles

The CUNY-NYSIEB team is comprised of faculty members and doctoral students who, from the start of our work together, were knowledgeable about bilingualism and the education of emergent bilinguals, including the range of school programmatic structures and pedagogies, but who approached the work from differing angles. School principals were well informed about the many regulations that have been put in place by New York State in order to shape the teaching and learning of these students, but few had received any preparation to work with this population of students. What was therefore needed was a way to build a dialogue across our individual differences and experiences as scholars, researchers, and educational practitioners. To build this dialogue, we relied on time together in a series of institute sessions, meetings, and on-site supports that enabled all of us to better understand each other's positionalities and to construct a program of individual action that met the needs of the students and teachers within each school (described below). To guide our efforts to come together, we developed a coherent vision that moves beyond some of the common assumptions about bilingualism.

Vision

Bilingualism in U.S. schools is often seen as a problem, and English-only programs have grown, especially in the last decade as bilingual programs have come under attack (García, 2009a; García & Kleifgen, 2010; Menken, 2008, 2013a). Instructional programs therefore typically encourage subtractive bilingualism, as exemplified in the reality that the vast majority of emergent bilinguals in U.S. schools are enrolled in English as a second language, with instruction and materials typically only provided in English. The small proportion of emergent bilinguals who receive bilingual education usually do so through transitional bilingual education, in which a student's home language is to be used for a short period of time that decreases as the student learns English. When bilingualism in U.S. schools is encouraged and developed, it has most often been through what are called dual language bilingual programs. Some of these programs are two-way bilingual programs, initially bringing together equal numbers of students who are developing English with those who are developing the language other than English. Other dual language programs are one-way and can be better described as developmental bilingual education programs. Regardless of the student composition, these dual language bilingual programs in the U.S. separate languages strictly and adhere to a philosophy of additive bilingualism, in which one language is separately added to a "first" language (for a critical perspective, see García, 2014).

Our philosophy of bilingualism, however, differs from the subtractive or additive approaches of these program structures (García, 2009a), in an effort to break away from their rigidity and carve out spaces within schools to build on the complex and fluid ways that emergent bilinguals actually use language. As we describe below, our vision for CUNY-NYSIEB adheres to the following three tenets:

1. the creative emergence of individual language practices;
2. the dynamics of bilingualism; and
3. the dynamic processes of teaching and learning of emergent bilinguals (for a complete statement of our vision, visit www.cuny-nysieb.org).

The naming of the CUNY-NYSIEB initiative in referring to students as "emergent bilinguals" instead of "English language learners" expresses our view that bilingualism is the desired norm for all American students, and that rather than a "problem," it is an asset that all students in New York State should possess to meet the demands of the twenty-first century (see García, 2009b; García & Kleifgen, 2010). What is more, the use of students' home languages in school is essential for their academic success in all of the areas that currently "count" in the current high-stakes testing environment defining U.S. schooling today, especially their development of English literacy (for instance, see August & Shanahan, 2006; Goldenberg, 2008; Hornberger & Link, 2012). In focusing on the emergence of the students' bilingualism, we hold that bilingual development

Multilingualism in Schools **99**

is not linear, static, or able to reach an ultimate endpoint of completion; rather, it is always emergent, continuous, never-ending, and shaped by relationships with people, texts, and situations.

Bilingualism is dynamic, and not simply additive (García, 2009a). Contesting traditional views of bilinguals normed on the language practices of monolinguals and misperceived as possessing a rigid separation between their languages, and like Shohamy (2006), among others (see, for instance, Cenoz & Gorter, 2011; García, 2009a, 2014; Makoni & Pennycook, 2007), our work is grounded in the view that bilinguals language fluidly, using language differently from monolinguals. Thus, educators need to continuously provide affordances for the actual language practices of emergent bilinguals and for new understandings to emerge. Bilingual students, we argue, need to language bilingually, or translanguage, using their entire linguistic repertoire to make meaning and to meet their communicative and academic needs.

Translanguaging as the discursive norm of all bilinguals, as well as a pedagogical scaffolding for emergent bilinguals, is the centerpiece of our vision (García, 2009a). The term translanguaging was coined in Welsh (Trawsieithu) by Cen Williams (1994). In its original use, it referred to a pedagogical practice where students are asked to alternate languages for the purposes of reading and writing, or for receptive or productive use; for example, students might be asked to read in English and write in Welsh, and vice-versa, and it is that meaning that still is prevalent in the Welsh bilingual education literature (for a review, see Lewis, Jones, & Baker, 2012a, 2012b). García (2009a) has extended the term to refer to the flexible use of linguistic resources by bilinguals in order to make sense of their worlds, and has applied it mostly to classrooms because of its potential in liberating the voices of language-minoritized students. Translanguaging is related to other fluid languaging practices that scholars have called by different terms, such as polylingualism (Jørgensen, 2008), transidiomatic practices (Jacquemet, 2005), metrolingualism (Otsuji & Pennycook, 2010), and codemeshing (Canagarajah, 2011).

Aligned to others promoting translanguaging pedagogies (e.g. Blackledge & Creese, 2010; Canagarajah, 2011; Creese & Blackledge, 2010), we assert that emergent bilinguals need to be encouraged to perform fluid and dynamic language practices that go beyond separate conceptualizations of "first" and "second" languages. Instead of focusing on the addition of English as a second language, educators must engage bilingual students' entire range of language practices, including features and practices associated with languages other than English, as well as those associated with English, as their very own.

Non-Negotiable Principles for Principals (and All School Staff)

To carry out these principles of *emergence*, *dynamic bilingualism*, and *dynamic bilingual teaching and learning*, we established two non-negotiable principles for all CUNY-NYSIEB schools:

1. Bilingualism as a Resource in Education

Regardless of program structure (i.e. whether the program is called ESL or bilingual), the home language practices of emergent bilingual students are not only recognized, but also leveraged as a crucial instructional tool and, to the greatest extent possible, nurtured and developed. The entire linguistic repertoire of bilingual children is used flexibly and strategically in instruction.

2. Support of a Multilingual Ecology for the Whole School

The entire range of language practices of *all* children and families are evident in the school's textual landscape (e.g. in signs throughout the school, in texts in the library and classrooms), as well as in the interactions of all members of the school community.

Many professional development programs may hold a similar vision about bilingualism and using bilingualism in education, but it has been our collaborative structure, with its many contact hours, that has enabled this coherent vision to shape the ideologies and practices of the participants in the project. Before we identify some of the changes that have taken place in participating schools to date, we describe the collaborative structures that we put into place.

CUNY-NYSIEB Structures

To implement our project, CUNY-NYSIEB involved the following structures over 1.5 years, from January 2012 to June 2013: teamwork (CUNY-NYSIEB Teams and School Emergent Bilingual Leadership Teams), seminars, and on-site support. All three structures aim to foster individual voices, through shared collaboration over an extended period of time in different formats. Our work with schools took place over two phases: a foundational stage from January to June 2012, and an implementational stage from July 2012 to June 2013. Schools were required to develop a school improvement plan during the foundational stage, focused on the education of emergent bilinguals and aligned to our non-negotiable principles, which was then implemented with CUNY-NYSIEB support during the implementational stage, over the course of the 2012–2013 school year.

CUNY-NYSIEB Team

The CUNY-NYSIEB team was comprised of six faculty members from various City University of New York (CUNY) campuses who specialize in different aspects of the education of emergent bilinguals, and six doctoral students specializing in Language and Education in the Urban Education program at the Graduate Center of CUNY (see note 1 for identification of persons in the teams). One faculty member was paired with a doctoral student and assigned to four schools for on-site visits. Each pair provided support to their schools through monthly site visits, and was in regular contact throughout the project period. The team also met with the Co-Principal Investigators of the project and the Project Director every two weeks to share experiences, review protocols and processes, and generate ideas and resources.

Seminars and Collaborative Descriptive Inquiry

The principals were required to participate in five monthly all-day seminars during the foundational stage that were held from January through June 2012, and two half-day seminars during the implementational stage from September through December 2012. During the foundational stage, the morning session consisted of a formal lecture on topics relevant to our vision, including dynamic bilingualism and translanguaging, programmatic structures, and pedagogical practices.

For the afternoon, the schools were divided by level (e.g. elementary, middle, and high schools) and were engaged in a process that we call collaborative descriptive inquiry (CDI). Collaborative descriptive inquiry is a disciplined, democratic process for collective teaching and learning, derived from the work of Patricia Carini in the 1970s and continued to this day by many educators (see, for example, García & Traugh, 2002; García & Velasco, 2011; Himley & Carini, 2000). The development of an individual voice and trust in the group contributed to our increased understandings.

During the implementational stage, seminars mainly involved CDI, with brief lectures at the start of the day. The CUNY-NYSIEB *Guide for Professional Development* details and expands the curriculum used for the seminar meetings during the foundational stage, January–June 2012 (Witt & Mehr, 2012).

Emergent Bilingual Leadership Teams in Schools

After the second seminar during the foundational stage, principals were asked to form *Emergent Bilingual Leadership Teams*, a group within their school made up of school leaders and teachers who would collectively focus on improving the education of the emergent bilinguals in the building. The principals and two or more members of the school's Emergent Bilingual Leadership Teams attended remaining seminars and developed their school improvement plans with support from CUNY-NYSIEB. This group was responsible for the school-wide implementation of the improvement plans during the 2012–2013 school year.

On-Site Support

Each CUNY-NYSIEB team made monthly visits to the schools during the foundational stage, first obtaining information about the school by interviewing school leaders and educators and by observing classes. The CUNY-NYSIEB teams also worked with the Emergent Bilingual Leadership Teams on developing their school improvement plans, focusing on goals for implementation in the following academic year.

The CUNY-NYSIEB teams made monthly or bimonthly school visits during the implementational stage. In addition, they provided teachers with professional development in translanguaging strategies and offered support specific to each school's efforts to improve the education of emergent bilinguals.

Changing Ideologies and Enactments

To engender changes within participating schools, where many administrators and teachers possessed limited knowledge about emergent bilinguals and saw these students solely through a deficit lens at the start of our work together, we used a quote from Martin Luther King that we found in one of the schools: "You don't have to see the whole staircase, just take the first step." The bulk of the changes thus far have taken place, step by step, in the following three areas: (1) school ecology and community/family engagement; (2) programmatic structures; and (3) translanguaging pedagogical practices.

School Ecology and Community/Family Engagement

One of the first changes that schools enacted involved identifying, acknowledging, and then displaying the multilingual ecology of their school. At the start of the project, we found that many principals and teachers were simply unaware of the languages spoken by their students; now, educators routinely ask children and parents about the languages they speak at home and have learned about the languages. To do so, many use the CUNY-NYSIEB Guide, *The Languages of New York* (Funk, 2012). For example, one principal told us during his initial interview that his students speak "African." Today, this principal can talk with pride about the multilingualism of those very children, marveling over one student's abilities in Pulaar, French, Mandinka, Wolof, and English.

All of the schools in the project now have multilingual welcome signs prominently displaying the languages of all their students. Some schools have labeled key locations in the building with multilingual signage, and/or used the children's languages in morning announcements, poems, and songs for the whole school. One school created a welcome packet in the school's most commonly spoken languages—Spanish, Polish and Chinese—to be given to all newcomers.

Despite the fact that many schools still offer ESL programs, teachers have found ways of identifying, acknowledging, valuing, and incorporating their students' home language practices in instruction, to support their academic skills as well as English literacy ability. For instance, the schools have purchased texts in the children's many languages and, where texts were unavailable, some have involved bilingual parents and community members to make audio recordings of classroom literature in the students' languages for all of the children to enjoy.

Many of the schools have engaged the parents not only in putting on international and multilingual activities, but in teaching their languages, their cultures, their dances, their songs, their ways of making meaning and life.

This deeper understanding of their school's multilingualism is not limited to classrooms in which there are emergent bilinguals; rather, the resources of *all* bilingual children are recognized. Taken together, smaller and larger changes serve to mainstream the multilingual ecology of the schools, turning the schools' multilingualism into a source of pride. These examples of the schools' appropriations of multilingualism are significant, as instead of schools standing as an unwelcoming border where English monolingualism is imposed on multilingual communities and only one part of the children's linguistic and cognitive repertoire is acknowledged, such efforts move schools into borderland spaces that embody the complexity of the communities they serve.

Programmatic Structures

In sharp contrast to the rapid closure of numerous bilingual education programs over the past decade (Menken, 2011, 2013a), our schools are transforming their programmatic structures to support the students' bilingualism. In some of the schools, the ESL programs have been transformed through the use of translanguaging strategies (described below); thus, ESL programs are no longer English only, but are significantly building on the students' home language practices. In other schools, transitional bilingual education programs have become focused on the sustained use of home languages to develop the students' bilingualism. Yet, in others, transitional bilingual education programs are giving way to dual language bilingual education programs, the only possible type of program within New York City that allows for sustaining and developing the bilingualism of children over time. But unlike other dual language bilingual education programs in the city where languages are compartmentalized, within these programs translanguaging is used as a pedagogical tool to make meaning and ensure the students' cognitive engagement and self-regulation of learning.

The following is an example of one team's summary about a middle school they have worked with:

> *The school has embraced the CUNY-NYSIEB principle of using students' bilingualism as a resource and has opened two dual languages classes (Spanish and English) to serve students in the upper grades. The teachers in this new bilingual structure make up the Emergent Bilingual Leadership Team and meet regularly . . . teachers have begun to recognize and value bilingualism and biliteracy as the goal for their emergent bilinguals. They have eagerly embraced translanguaging as a transformative pedagogy.*
>
> (Herrera & Ebe, summary, December 2012)

Translanguaging as a pedagogy is the subject of the next section.

Translanguaging

What makes translanguaging different from these other fluid languaging practices is that it is *transformative*, attempting to wipe out the hierarchy of languaging practices that deem some more valuable than others. Thus, translanguaging is a mechanism for social justice, especially when incorporated in teaching language minoritized students (García, forthcoming).

Because little has been written about translanguaging as pedagogy in the past (García & Li Wei, 2014, forthcoming; Menken, 2013b), the CUNY-NYSIEB project has issued a *Translanguaging Guide* (Celic & Seltzer, 2012) in an effort to support educators and educational leaders in their efforts to negotiate and extend translanguaging practices in the classroom. With a theoretical introduction by García, the guide helps teachers construct translanguaging classrooms, as well as use translanguaging strategies for content, language, and literacy development. Because CUNY-NYSIEB work is deeply rooted in the individual school's ecology, the guide also describes the process of collaborative descriptive inquiry (García & Ascenzi-Moreno, 2012). That is, the use of the guide, like translanguaging and dynamic bilingualism, is not meant to be linear, but to respond to the desires, aspirations, wishes, and needs of individual educators in a particular space as they work with unique emergent bilinguals. As this chapter goes to press, the project is in the implementation phase; as such, schools are currently at differing stages in their uses of translanguaging strategies in the classroom.

One CUNY-NYSIEB team noted the following examples of further translanguaging strategies they observed at a high school serving Spanish-speaking emergent bilinguals:

> *In a beginner ESL class the teacher—who speaks five languages—used his knowledge of Spanish to highlight cognates and similarities in structures. A bilingual computer teacher preparing students for A+ certification maneuvered between English test questions and discussion about the concepts in Spanish. A monolingual English-speaking science teacher asked students to identify Spanish cognates and then attempted to build a sentence summarizing a concept in Spanish (which was met by applause by the students). Therefore, translanguaging is a pedagogical approach used by all teachers across the school as a means to support content learning, side-by-side language comparison and as a way to become bilingual.*
>
> (Guzmán Valerio & Kleyn, CUNY-NYSIEB summary,
> December 2012)

While still in the early phases, these examples show teachers are now offering their emergent bilingual students space to use their linguistic resources more flexibly than ever before in participating schools, and how the students' home language practices are being leveraged strategically in the students' development of content and language for academic purposes.

Conclusion

This chapter focuses on how we have applied what we learned from Shohamy to our work with schools that have large numbers of emergent bilinguals. The going back and forth between the individual voices of principals and a shared collective vision of emergence of language practices, dynamic bilingualism, and dynamic development of teaching and learning have enabled us to build a generous collaborative space where, over time, schools and the lives of emergent bilingual children have been transformed. This is the story of the structures we have put into place and the people we have called upon in order to accomplish this.

Our story is not of total success. After a year and a half, some of the schools are still failing, according to children's scores on standardized tests, and others are struggling in more qualitative ways to overcome the challenges they face in their efforts to implement the changes they had planned. But overall we have found that the ethos of the schools has been transformed to one of potential—potential to succeed, to learn from the community and the children, to view bilingualism as a resource. These schools have become, in other words, not just places that teach disadvantaged children, but sites to learn about the advantages of being multilingual. The enthusiasm for multilingualism is contagious, and teachers are constructing teaching and learning from the individuality of the children, as well as a shared vision of the strength of having a multilingual school ecology.

Our story is also of the efforts it takes to work collaboratively to act on a coherent vision across our differences and individualities—individualities as scholars, teachers, and students. The road taken is not always one of certainty. Our scholarship and theoretical frameworks have often come up against everyday practices in schools. For us, as scholars, this work has taken us to a different place—one of questioning "expert" knowledge and of the humbling realization that we are all learners when it comes to the enterprise of schooling emergent bilinguals. This work has put us in the position of learners, as we—academics and school personnel—collectively learn from each other the complexities of language education policies and the languaging practices of emergent bilingual students. To improve the education of emergent bilinguals, we must work collaboratively as learners and listen to individual voices, as we nourish a vision of pride and hope in a bilingual future for all American children.

Acknowledgments

We thank the New York State Education Department for funding the CUNY-NYSIEB project, and our amazing team members (noted below). We also thank Kate Seltzer and Tatyana Kleyn, as well as other members of our team, for their valuable feedback on an earlier draft of this chapter.

Notes

1. CUNY-NYSIEB is funded by New York State. The Principal Investigator is Prof. Ricardo Otheguy. At its inception, Nelson Flores served as Acting Project Coordinator, a position now held by Dr. María Teresa Sánchez. The team of the Leadership component is composed of the following CUNY faculty: Professors Laura Ascenzi-Moreno, Brian Collins, Ann Ebe, Tatyana Kleyn, and Vanessa Pérez; a Field Supervisor, Christina Celic; and Research Assistants: Kathryn Carpenter, Luis Guzmán, Luz Herrera, Sarah Hesson, Liza Pappas, and Heather Woodley. There are two other components of the project that are not examined in this chapter; more can be learned about the entire project at www.cuny-nysieb.org.
2. It is worth noting that the CUNY-NYSIEB project is ongoing, and has recently received funding to continue.
3. For our use of the term resource in this chapter, we credit Ruiz (1984) for long ago offering the field differing orientations to language that drive policy and programming decisions. Two of these orientations are, in our view, opposing: a language-as-problem orientation, in which linguistic diversity is regarded as a problem that must be resolved through imposed monolingualism, versus language-as-resource, in which each language is seen as a rich resource that should be developed and conserved. It is this latter perspective that we promote in schools.

References

August, D., & Shanahan, T. (Eds.) (2006). *Developing literacy in second-language learners: Report of the National Literacy Panel on Language-Minority Children and Youth.* Mahwah, NJ: Lawrence Erlbaum Associates.

Blackledge, A., & Creese, A. (2010). *Multilingualism: A critical perspective.* London: Continuum.

Canagarajah, S. (2011). Translanguaging in the classroom: Emerging issues for research and pedagogy. *Applied Linguistics Review, 2,* 1–28.

Celic, C., & Seltzer, K. (2012). *Translanguaging: A CUNY-NYSIEB guide for educators.* New York: CUNY-NYSIEB. Retrieved from: www.nysieb.ws.gc.cuny.edu/files/2012/06/FINAL-Translanguaging-Guide-With-Cover-1.pdf (accessed May 4, 2014).

Cenoz, J., & Gorter, D. (2011). A holistic approach to multilingual education: Introduction. *The Modern Language Journal, 95*(3), 339–343.

Creese, A., & Blackledge, A. (2010). Translanguaging in the bilingual classroom: A pedagogy for learning and teaching? *The Modern Language Journal, 94*(1), 103–115.

Funk, A. (2012). *The languages of New York State: A CUNY-NYSIEB guide for educators.* New York: CUNY-NYSIEB. Retrieved from: www.nysieb.ws.gc.cuny.edu/files/2012/07/NYSLanguageProfiles.pdf (accessed May 4, 2014).

García, O. (2009a). *Bilingual education in the 21st century: A global perspective.* Malden, MA: Wiley-Blackwell.

García, O. (2009b). Emergent bilinguals and TESOL. What's in a Name? *TESOL Quarterly, 43*(2), 322–326.

García, O. (2014). Countering the dual: Transglossia, dynamic bilingualism and translanguaging in education. In R. Rubdy & L. Alsagoff (Eds.), *The global-local interface, language choice and hybridity* (pp. 100–118). Bristol, UK: Multilingual Matters.

García, O. (forthcoming). Theorizing and enacting translanguaging for social justice. In A. Creese & A. Blackledge (Eds.), *Heteroglossia as practice and pedagogy.* London: Springer.

García, O., & Ascenzi-Moreno, L. (2012). How to use this guide: Collaborative descriptive inquiry. In *Translanguaging: A CUNY-NYSIEB guide for educators*. New York: CUNY-NYSIEB. Retrieved from: www.nysieb.ws.gc.cuny.edu/files/2012/06/FINAL-Trans languaging-Guide-With-Cover-1.pdf (accessed May 4, 2014).

García, O., & Fishman, J. (Eds.) (2002). *The multilingual apple: Languages in New York City* (2nd ed.). Berlin: Mouton de Gruyter.

García, O., & Kleifgen, J. (2010). *Educating emergent bilinguals: Policies, programs and practices for English Language Learners*. New York: Teachers College Press.

García, O., & Li Wei (2014). *Translanguaging: Language, bilingualism and education*. London: Palgrave Macmillan.

García, O., & Li Wei (forthcoming). Translanguaging, bilingualism and bilingual education. In W. Wright, B. Sovicheth, & O. García (Eds.), *Handbook of bilingual education*. Malden, MA: Wiley-Blackwell.

García, O., & Traugh, C. (2002). Using descriptive inquiry to transform the education of linguistically diverse U.S. teachers and students. In Li Wei, J. M. Dewaele, & A. Housen (Eds.), *Opportunities and challenges of (societal) bilingualism* (pp. 311–328). Berlin/New York: Walter de Gruyter.

García, O., & Velasco, P. (2011). Observing, collaborating and describing: Giving back power to the teachers. In A. M. de Mejía & C. Hélot (Eds.), *Empowering teachers across cultures* (pp. 1–16). Bern: Peter Lang (in Spanish).

Goldenberg, C. (2008). Teaching English language learners: What the research does—and does not—say. *American Educator*, Summer 2008, 8–44. Retrieved from: www.aft.org/pubs-reports/american_educator/issues/summer08/goldenberg.pdf (accessed March 1, 2014).

Himley, M., & Carini, P. (Eds.) (2000). *From another angle: Children's strengths and school standards. The Prospect Center's descriptive review of the child*. New York: Teachers College Press.

Hornberger, N. (2010). Language and education: A Limpopo lens. In N. Hornberger & S. McKay (Eds.), *Sociolinguistics and language education* (pp. 549–563). Bristol, UK: Multilingual Matters.

Hornberger, N., & Link, H. (2012). Translanguaging and transnational literacies in multilingual classrooms: A biliteracy lens. *International Journal of Bilingual Education and Bilingualism*, *15*(3), 261–278.

Jacquemet, M. (2005). Transidiomatic practices: Language and power in the age of globalization. *Language and Communication*, *25*, 257–277.

Jørgensen, J. N. (2008). Polylingual languaging around and among children and adolescents. *International Journal of Multilingualism*, *5*(3), 161–176.

Lewis, G., Jones, B., & Baker, C. (2012a). Translanguaging: Developing its conceptualisation and contextualisation. *Educational Research and Evaluation*, *18*(7), 655–670.

Lewis, G., Jones, B., & Baker, C. (2012b). Translanguaging: Origins and development from school to street and beyond. *Educational Research and Evaluation*, *18*(7), 641–654.

Makoni, S., & Pennycook, A. (2007). *Disinventing and reconstituting languages*. Bristol, UK: Multilingual Matters.

Menken, K. (2008). *English learners left behind: Standardized testing as language policy*. Bristol, UK: Multilingual Matters.

Menken, K. (2011). From policy to practice in the multilingual apple: Bilingual education in New York City. Editorial Introduction. *International Journal of Bilingual Education and Bilingualism*, *14*(2), 123–133.

Menken, K. (2013a). Restrictive language education policies and emergent bilingual youth: A perfect storm with imperfect outcomes. *Theory into Practice*, *52*(3), 160–168.

Menken, K. (2013b). Emergent bilingual students in secondary school: Along the academic language and literacy continuum. *Language Teaching*, *46*(4), 438–476.

Menken, K., & García, O. (Eds.) (2010). *Negotiating language policies in schools: Educators as policymakers*. New York: Routledge.

Menken, K., & Solorza, C. (2014). No child left bilingual: Accountability and the elimination of bilingual education programs in New York City Schools. *Educational Policy*, *28*(1), 96–125.

New York City Department of Education, Office of English Language Learners (2013). *2013 demographic report*. New York: New York City Department of Education.

Otsuji, E., & Pennycook, A. (2010). Metrolingualism: Fixity, fluidity and language in flux. *International Journal of Multilingualism*, *7*(3), 240–254.

Ruiz, R. (1984). Orientations in language planning. *NABE Journal*, *8*(2), 15–34.

Shohamy, E. (2001). *The power of tests: A critical perspective on the uses of language tests*. London: Longman/Pearson.

Shohamy, E. (2006). *Language policy: Hidden agendas and new approaches*. London: Routledge.

Williams, C. (1994). *Evaluation of methods of learning and teaching in the context of bilingual secondary education*. Unpublished PhD dissertation, University of Wales, Bangor (in Welsh).

Witt, D., & Mehr, M. (2012). *School leaders and bilingualism: A CUNY-NYSIEB guide for professional development*. New York: CUNY-NYSIEB. Retrieved from: www.nysieb.ws. gc.cuny.edu/files/2012/03/leadershipcurriculum_final.pdf (accessed March 1, 2014).

8

ENGLISH IN ETHIOPIA

MAKING SPACE FOR THE INDIVIDUAL IN LANGUAGE POLICY

Elizabeth Lanza and Hirut Woldemariam

This study examined the incongruous situation associated with English in Ethiopia. On the one hand, discourses of globalization contribute to the widespread recognition of its importance for the country, and Ethiopia's current language policy accords it a prominent place in education. On the other hand, there is a recognized general low degree of proficiency in the language among its users to such an extent that these users are, in many cases, unable to fulfill the anticipated needs for the use of English as decreed by the national language policy. The educational language policy mandates English to be used as a medium of instruction (hereafter, MOI) after primary education. Nonetheless, due to the generally low degree of proficiency of English, students and teachers alike actually use Amharic and other local languages for the purpose of classroom interaction in order to bridge the skill gap and focus on content instruction, a practice not in line with the country's educational language policy. Hence, English remains a commonly used language of textbooks while the actual MOI appears to be determined by the linguistic background of teachers and students. This study addresses the role of English in Ethiopia, highlighting the prestige accorded to the language in Ethiopian society at large, and the attitudes of teachers and students toward English and proficiency in the language. We point to individually based approaches, or linguistic practices, taken to surmount the challenges associated with the low degree of proficiency in English. Hence, in this chapter, we focus on the need to make space for the individual in language policy.

Our study is based on a range of data collected through semi-structured interviews, focus group discussions, and classroom observations from different regions, as well as data on the linguistic landscape, the use of signs in the public sphere (Landry & Bourhis, 1997; Shohamy, Ben-Rafael, & Barni, 2010; Shohamy & Gorter, 2008). In the following, we first present an overview of the languages,

110 Elizabeth Lanza and Hirut Woldemariam

language policy, and language ideology in Ethiopia, and highlight potential "hidden agendas" (cf. Shohamy, 2006), in order to embed the discussion of the role of English in Ethiopia. Subsequently, we address the perceived problem of low proficiency in English among Ethiopians, particularly teachers and students, in the country's various regions. In conclusion, we discuss the conflicting language ideologies and practices regarding English in light of a theoretical approach to language in late modernity.

Language Policy and Language Ideology in Ethiopia

Language policy and language ideology go hand in hand. Language ideologies, a set of beliefs about language, serve to rationalize existing social structures and dominant linguistic practices, particularly through their institutionalization in official language policy (Lanza & Woldemariam, 2008). Language ideologies are grounded in history and can be overt through policy decisions, but they can also be covert with various mechanisms leading to "de facto language policy" (Shohamy, 2006).

Located in the Horn of Africa, Ethiopia is a multilingual, multiethnic, and culturally pluralistic country with a population of about 80 million. According to *Ethnologue* (Lewis, Simons, & Fennig, 2013), there are 87 living languages spoken, stemming from four different language families (see Crass & Meyer, 2008). The most dominant Ethiopian language in the country is Amharic, a Semitic language. Although the Amhara are a minority in the country, from an historical perspective they have dominated the country politically and linguistically. According to Mazrui (2004), sub-Saharan Africans are rarely "strong linguistic nationalists (such as in Asia, the Middle East and Europe, for example) [who] tend to resist any massive dependence on languages other than their own" (p. 6). However, noting exceptions to this trend, he highlights the Amhara, along with the Somali and the Afrikaners.

Amharic is currently used as a lingua franca by all peoples of various ethnic backgrounds, a practice that is encouraged by a range of opportunities and circumstances, and Amharic continues to spread, both as a first language and as a second language (Cohen, 2006). This dominance of Amharic, however, has been challenged through language policy initiatives that evolved during the 1990s.

Language policy in Ethiopia has undergone significant milestones, which have coincided with important historical upheavals in the country. Until 1991, Amharic was used as the MOI and literacy in primary education, having taken on the role as the language of education during the rule of Emperor Haile Selassie (1955–1974). Haile Selassie's regime was overthrown by a Soviet-supported communist junta (the *Dergue*) in 1974, yet the use of Amharic also prevailed during the *Dergue*. After its overthrow in 1991, revolutionaries led by the Tigrayans from the north became responsible for important changes in the country, particularly a new constitution advocating a policy of "ethnic federalism." As Cooper (1989) clearly demonstrates, language planning is always enacted for the attainment of non-linguistic ends, and is related to other aspects of social planning and change. The political nature of Ethiopia's language policy is evident, "when minority ethnic groups see their political rights best preserved through their membership in ethnic groups, most commonly understood in linguistic terms" (Smith, 2008, p. 235). Ethiopia's Federal Constitution guarantees that persons belonging to various ethnic and linguistic minorities shall not be denied the right to enjoy their own culture and to use their own language. Regional administrations have been assigned to take on formal and practical responsibilities for running their own affairs, including language development and education. Each region typically has a dominant ethnic group, and hence an official regional language.

The newly formed government in the 1990s introduced a national educational policy based on the use of "mother tongues" as the MOI. The stated purpose of the policy was to foster national unity, identity, and development while respecting cultural diversity. Today, regional and local languages are widely used in the educational, administrative, and judiciary systems, as well as in the media. Also, in the regional cities, local languages have become visible in the public sphere— a situation that is relatively new in the Ethiopian context (Lanza & Woldemariam, 2008). Ethiopia's language policy of ethnic federalism, as applied to education, has its critics, who argue that education in the regional languages will inhibit social and national mobility (Vaughan, 2007). Shohamy (2006) illustrates clearly how various mechanisms are at play in the link between ideology and practice, and this includes language education. Nonetheless, despite the poverty of the country, the educational policy espousing mother tongue instruction in the various regions has achieved some admirable results. The achievement scores of those students who received the highest number of years of mother tongue instruction were the highest scores across the curriculum for Grade 8 in a study undertaken in 2004 (Heugh, Benson, Bogale, & Yohannes, 2007).

The new educational language policy in the country is actually trilingual involving Amharic, regional languages, and English. English takes over as a MOI from Grades 5, 7, or 9, depending upon the region. Although the continent of Africa has been marked by an epoch of colonialism, Ethiopia takes special pride in having remained free (cf. Lanza & Woldemariam, 2011). Nonetheless, English is used as an MOI, as a language of business advertisement, media, and for many other purposes. Indeed, English is not perceived as a hegemonic colonial language in Ethiopia, despite its wide influence in this era of globalization.

On the other hand, Amharic has been perceived by non-Amharas to have played a hegemonic role in relation to other indigenous languages, similar to "colonial languages." With the current political system dominated by non-Amhara leaders, however, Amharic has lost its prominent role in education throughout the country. The language is in fact perceived by many Amharic speakers as an "endangered" language, not only due to the rising importance of regional languages, but also to the prominence given to English.

The Role of English in Ethiopia: A Second Language or a Foreign Language?

The role and status of English in Ethiopia is quite complex and, in a way, unique compared to the situation in other African countries where postcolonial varieties have evolved. Prior to Amharic's dominant role in education before the current language policy, English had played a role in education between 1941 and the late 1950s. English plays a dominant role in language policy in a globalized educational context (see Gardner, 2012; Walter & Benson, 2012) and in Ethiopia. English is, as noted, used as an MOI, as a language of the media, and as a language of business, and in writing laws. Nevertheless, unlike the situation with countries using English as a second language, English in Ethiopia is not used as a lingua franca, nor as a language of wider local communication. However, among the small group of elite, code-switching from Amharic or other languages to English can be observed (cf. Reda, 2013).

Constitutionally, there is in fact no mention of the status of English in either the federal or the regional constitutions of Ethiopia. Nevertheless, its role in the educational context is pointed out in the Educational and Training Policy (Ministry of Education, 1994). The current policies of language use (English, Amharic, and local languages) vary across the diverse regions. English is taught as a subject from Grade 1 in all regions, without exception, and textbooks are written in English. From Grade 9 onwards, English is to be the exclusive MOI common to all the regions.

In the education sector, English has thus been accorded a higher position than Amharic, which, contrary to English, is introduced only at Grade 3 in most regions in the country. In the Oromo region (see Figure 8.2), home to the largest ethnic group in Ethiopia, Amharic is introduced at Grade 5. Interestingly, in the earlier policy, the reverse was true in that Amharic was introduced from Grade 1, while English was introduced from Grade 3, thus indicating the reversal of roles and status. The introduction of English as a subject before Amharic, and its use as MOI as of Grade 5, bears witness to the prestige attributed to the language.

In general, one may say that English is foreign to most Ethiopians, and that it is only used for communication by a small minority of the educated elite. The designation of English as a "second official language" in Ethiopia thus is not appropriate as it is not a local medium of communication. Its role resembles more that of a foreign language. The use of English in Ethiopia is limited to fewer arenas than is the case in many other African countries in which the language enjoys high status, aspiration value, and use (Bogale, 2009).

While English has taken on the role of a "global" language, we may nonetheless ask how a global language becomes part of local repertoires. In other words, there is a need to examine both the global and the local levels at which language, or rather linguistic repertoires, operate (cf. Lanza & Woldemariam, 2013). While we may evaluate the role of English in language policy in general, we need to

English in Ethiopia   113

address the role of the individual in language policy, by actually examining linguistic practices. Spolsky (2004) points out that "the real language policy of a community is more likely to be found in its practices than in management" (p. 222). He identifies three inherent components in his framework for language policy: beliefs (ideology), practice, and management. A closer look at beliefs or ideologies provides us a better overview of the role of English in Ethiopia.

Language ideology regarding English is evident in the linguistic landscape (hereafter, LL) of the country. Lanza and Woldemariam (2008) illustrated the use of English in a peripheral region of Ethiopia in which the informational content was limited, yet the indexical nature of its use was quite clear for locals—as an indicator of prestige. Consistently, the shop owners proclaimed that by using English, they were being "modern"; hence, their use of the language indexed their aspirations toward an identity associated with prestige and modernity, similar to the situation in Addis Ababa (Lanza & Woldemariam, 2013).

Shohamy (2006, 2012) notes that the public space can be an arena for ideological battles, thus arguing for the relevance of examining the LL of an area for assessing the hierarchies of languages. In Figure 8.1, a picture taken in Addis Ababa, the language school advertisement reflects the prevalent ideology among Ethiopians, despite the fact that the sign is a private artifact. The importance of English is emphasized through the large lettering at the top of the sign. At the language school, instruction in other languages is also offered, as illustrated at the

FIGURE 8.1 A private language school advertisement in Addis Ababa

bottom of the upper part of the sign. Interestingly, four other languages are listed before Amharic, the federal working language. The sign appears to be aimed primarily at Ethiopians, given the prevalent use of Amharic in addition to English.

The LL in various cities of Ethiopia reveals that English is the most favored language in Ethiopia (see also Bekele, 2012; Raga, 2012; Woldemariam & Lanza, in press).

Perceived Low Proficiency in English

English is accorded high prestige in Ethiopia and is used by many in its written form, as evidenced in the LL. Blommaert (2003) points out that "the English acquired by urban Africans may offer them considerable prestige and access to middle-class identities in African towns. It may be an 'expensive' resource to them" (p. 616). Yet, outside the local African context, such a resource conforming to peripheral norms (Blommaert, 2010) may not have the same indexical value (i.e. may not point toward the same social value). However, even within the local African context, in this case, Ethiopia, local norms for the use of English are not looked upon favorably by policymakers.

Many Ethiopian scholars are in agreement that the level of English language proficiency among teachers and students in Ethiopia is very low and that the situation affects the teaching and learning process through the medium of English. In fact, it has been claimed that the lack of proficiency in English among Ethiopian teachers has been the main reason for the decline of the quality of education, coupled with the limited capacity of students to follow their lessons in English (Negash, 2006). This concern is also being addressed in current teacher training (cf. Institute of International Education, 2012).

The official language policy of ethnic federalism aims to provide quality education through the use of local languages as MOI, at least in the early levels of education. However, the government's goal of internationalization appears to supersede the goal of quality education through its insistence on English as MOI. As Heugh et al. (2007) point out:

> the teaching of English in the first cycle of primary is seriously under-resourced. The teaching of English as a subject and its use as a medium of instruction during the second cycle of primary, is also seriously under-resourced. In both instances, teacher under-preparedness is a major challenge.
>
> (p. 55)

Teachers are confronted with a challenging situation. The question is how both teachers and students accommodate to this situation.

The Subversive Use of Amharic and Other Vernaculars Instead of English

Given the general scenario portrayed above, we may elaborate on specific examples. Figure 8.2 is a map of Ethiopia indicating the various federal regions and the capital Addis Ababa. Recall that each federal region has a regional language policy promoting the dominant regional language and some local languages, as well as English. Furthermore, when to introduce Amharic is also decided at the regional level. Language ideology and linguistic practices are, at times, at odds with one another.

In the Southern Nations, Nationalities and Peoples (SNNP) region, the most multilingual region of them all, local languages are used as MOI in their respective localities from Grades 1–4, while English is used as MOI from Grade 5 onwards. The use of English as MOI at Grade 5 provides students with only four years of English study as a subject, which is unlikely to prepare students for academic use. In general, parents show a very positive attitude toward the English medium policy. According to a study in the Gamo-Gofa zone of the SNNP region, parents prefer English and Amharic over the mother tongue as the MOI because they perceive the economic and social advantage of these languages, particularly English (Woldemariam, 2007). However, according to interviews with Gamo teachers,

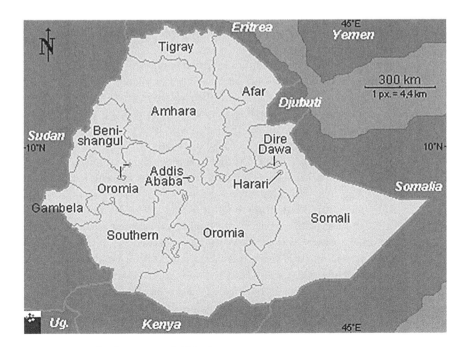

FIGURE 8.2 Federal regions of Ethiopia

both teachers and students have serious problem using English as MOI, and turning to a local language cannot always serve the classroom situation, as the linguistic/dialectal background of teachers and students may vary. According to the teachers in Gamo schools, neither the teacher nor the students have the necessary proficiency in English, and practically all of the classes are conducted rather in Amharic, a common language. Encountering local linguistic variation, teachers prefer to switch to Amharic than the local language.

Similarly, in Sidama of the SNNP region, parents were pleased that their children were receiving instruction in their mother tongue, yet they were also pleased that the MOI for the second cycle had become English only (Bogale, 2009), a finding also reflected in Lanza and Woldemariam (2009). According to Bogale (2009), "parents believe learning in the mother tongue is economically disadvantageous to their children, and see Amharic—and better yet English—as languages that are good for future employment" (p. 1097) (see also Heugh, 2009). Meanwhile, the same teachers admitted that using English as MOI created problems for comprehension in the classroom, and they often felt compelled to interpret the content of their instruction into the mother tongue of the student.

The case in other regions also shows the turn to Amharic. In Gambella, one issue affecting mother tongue instruction at the lower primary level is a shortage of teachers who are native speakers of Nuer and Anguak (Bogale, 2009). Teachers who do not know the language of instruction very well reportedly use Amharic. Hence, Amharic is brought in also at lower levels before the introduction of English in situations in which the teacher does not have the local language of instruction in his or her own linguistic repertoire.

Lanza and Woldemariam (2009) investigated language use and language attitudes in Tigray, based on an oral interview questionnaire administered to Grade 5 school children, their parents, and their teachers in 2005. English also then enjoyed status in the educational setting. Currently, it is still introduced as a subject from Grade 1, while Amharic is introduced later at Grade 3. Tigrinya is used as MOI from Grade 1 to Grade 6, while English is used as MOI from Grade 7. The use of Tigrinya as MOI is highly appreciated by teachers. Almost all (97 percent) of the teacher respondents believed that it was useful for children to be taught in Tigrinya. Attitudes toward the use of English were, in general, positive, with many parents desiring English as the MOI for their children. However, as in the rest of the country, the English proficiency of the students, teachers, and other speakers was perceived to be very low.

In the Oromia region, Afan Oromo is used as MOI from Grade 1 to Grade 8, and from Grade 9 onwards, English takes over. However, based on information from teachers from the region, in most cases, classroom interactions take place practically all of the time in Afan Oromo, while English mainly remains the language of textbooks. In fact, it is clearly stated in the Teacher's Guide that language switching to the mother tongue can be allowed whenever necessary to facilitate communication in the classroom interaction.

Even at the university level, as pointed out by many instructors, most students have a serious problem understanding lectures given exclusively in English, and instructors' providing interpretations in Amharic and holding discussions in Amharic are frequently used strategies employed to facilitate classroom interactions. According to an interview with an instructor from Jima University, one of the public universities in Ethiopia, the instructor said he had encountered graduate students called in to undertake a recruitment interview for a graduate assistant position at the university who asked if they could take the interview in Afan Oromo or Amharic rather than in English.

The proficiency in English among university graduate students has also been noted to be below expected standards. As part of its reform process, Addis Ababa University, the oldest and largest university in Ethiopia, has started offering a new training program in Academic English for graduate students. Since the academic year 2008–2009, incoming graduate students take the training for five weeks in an intensive manner with the aim of enhancing their academic English and general proficiency in the language so as to enable them to follow graduate programs better.

There are no studies showing the level of proficiency of English among secondary school students; however, a sample survey that the second author undertook strongly indicates that the proficiency level is low. Interviews were conducted among sample instructors from Addis Ababa University, high school teachers from schools in Nazreth (Oromia), Gamo (SNNP), and the Addis Ababa area. Although English is officially the MOI, and textbooks are prepared in English, in practice, in many parts of the country, subjects are taught in the vernacular. According to the interviews with teachers at different class levels, and even those at the university level, in practice, class discussions are undertaken in Amharic and/or local languages depending on the region. Observation also confirms that even English as a subject is taught in Amharic or another vernacular language. In most cases, code-switching between English and Amharic or another local language is done in order to assist the students in grasping the subject matter, a practice that, in principle, runs contrary to the expectations of the language policy. Interestingly, more recent international studies in bilingual education actually highlight the potentials of such "translanguaging" (García & Li Wei, 2013):

> an approach to the use of language, bilingualism and the education of bilinguals that considers the language practices of bilinguals not as two autonomous language systems as has been traditionally the case, but as one linguistic repertoire with features that have been societally constructed as belonging to two separate languages.
>
> (p. 1)

All the teachers and university instructors interviewed agreed that most students would fail to understand a lesson if it were only presented in English, so that providing an interpretation in a local language is expected. Drawing on the total linguistic repertoires of both the teacher and the students in instruction is not part and parcel of the educational language policy in Ethiopia; however, it is a solution to a practical problem that inevitably facilitates learning. Such a pragmatic solution is a viable one until a fundamental solution to the challenge can be addressed.

The difficulty with the use of English in education was actually noted even prior to the new language policy in education. In a British Council report, Stoddart (1986) pointed out all the difficulty with implementing English in the classroom, concluding: "In such a situation it is no longer appropriate to call English a medium of instruction; rather it has become a medium of obstruction" (pp. 6–7).

Despite several efforts that have been made to address the challenges of English proficiency in Ethiopia, including setting up English Language Improvement Centers in many teacher training colleges and universities, a significant gap remains (see also Institute of International Education, 2012). Using English as MOI has not guaranteed an improved proficiency in that language, and recommendations for language policy and planning in Ethiopia have been made (Heugh, 2011), yet remain to be implemented.

Considering the problem with the English proficiency of students, during the previous regime, the Ministry of Education in 1980 had entertained the idea of replacing English with Amharic. Different panels were organized by the then Ethiopian National Language Academy working on coining scientific and technical terminologies to develop Amharic to fulfill the same role as English. However, that direction has been changed in the current Language and Training Policy. In fact, the use of regional languages and English as MOI in cases in which Amharic was previously used significantly reduces the dominance of Amharic, which enjoyed its exclusive role in the educational and public arena until the new Constitution. The idea of developing Amharic to be used as MOI in place of English was not acceptable for the new government in the 1990s, as it also had other agendas with its proposed policy. Ironically, however, in practical cases, Amharic, as well as other local languages, is being employed in an informal way to bridge the gap between the students' proficiency in English and their mastery of subject matter. We thus witness how individuals, notably teachers, are creating new de facto language policy through their linguistic practices.

Conclusion

Shohamy (2006) points out that language education policy "cannot stand alone but is rather connected to political, social and economic dimensions" (p. 77). This is clearly demonstrated in the Ethiopian context. Despite the language policy in place and a language ideology that favors extensive usage of English in education and other public settings, what actually occurs is that due to the low proficiency of the users, in practice, individuals determine language use in settings

English in Ethiopia **119**

formally determined as contexts for English. Hence, English remains in the textbook while actual classroom discussions take place in either Amharic or other vernacular languages, or a combination of both, depending on the circumstances and the region.

With the new political regime and the language and training policy, one could say that the role of English in Ethiopia has increased compared to previous times, whereas the proficiency level is still the same. The current political perspective precludes the exclusive use of Amharic in different domains and different regions, resulting in a tendency to use more English in the domains that hitherto belonged to Amharic with attempts being made to make English a lingua franca. Amharic, however, is already a relatively developed lingua franca that has been used as MOI in primary education, but it cannot be employed officially in this context within the current political framework. Moreover, there are challenges to expanding the use of vernaculars to high school and tertiary levels, considering the scarcity of expertise and resources to develop all of the languages. This situation favors the continued use of English. In fact, the expansion of the English language's role seems to serve as a double-edged sword: as a gateway to an international access and as a means of keeping a distance from Amharic, the language that served as MOI at the elementary school in the previous regime. As the current regime comprises politicians with another ethnic background than Amhara, we may interpret the current regime's education policy as having a "hidden agenda" (Shohamy, 2006).

Based on their study of English in Singapore with a focus on style and identity, Stroud and Wee (2012) propose the notion of "sociolinguistic consumption" as "a way of approaching the question of language in late modernity," situating "language choice as consumption firmly within a framework of social class, access and privilege" (p. 205). In order to understand sociolinguistic consumption, they point out, there is a need to make a distinction between language as "the direct object of consumption" and language that one is socialized into through the consumption of some particular type of activity. In Ethiopia, English is recognized as a valuable asset for social prestige and advancement, and language instruction programs for adults and private English-language schools for children have their place on the market. Hence, English is the direct object of consumption. However, it is also the language that is invoked in particular activities associated with modernity, and, in the Ethiopian context, this involves education that prepares the student for a globalized Ethiopia. As such, the notion of "sociolinguistic consumption" is an apt metaphor for both types of language consumption in the Ethiopian context. The use of English, the selling of English as a commodity through language instruction, and having an education in English all index valuable material assets, as promoted ideologically by language policy in the country. The reality, however, of how successful this consumption is on the linguistic market is at odds with the intention. The observations and reports of how teachers subversively resort to other means for securing learning in the classroom emphasize the role that individuals play in de facto language policy—in this case, linguistic practices as language policy.

Shohamy (2006) notes that "While mechanisms of ideological control exercised through language policy have been examined extensively at a global level, they have been less fully explored at the level of day-to-day interaction" (p. 90). Though, policy wise, English is decreed as the MOI, in the actual implementation, Amharic and other vernaculars serve the purpose behind the closed doors of classrooms. We witness, then, that language education policy "provides an arena for resistance but also an arena for negotiation" (p. 92). There is a need to take a step toward strengthening the quality of teaching English as a subject in Ethiopia in such a way that students' English language proficiency can be improved. Until then, however, the use of bilingual education that officially allows Amharic and other vernaculars along with English should be a viable option to facilitate the teaching–learning process in areas where Amharic is the common language of the students. Whether official policy will eventually follow current linguistic practices remains to be seen.

Acknowledgments

This work was partly supported by the Research Council of Norway through its Centres of Excellence funding scheme, project number 223265.

References

Bekele, S. (2012). *The linguistic landscape in Bole and Merkato*. MA thesis, Addis Ababa University.

Blommaert, J. (2003). Commentary: A sociolinguistics of globalization. *Journal of Sociolinguistics*, 7, 607–623.

Blommaert, J. (2010). *The sociolinguistics of globalization*. Cambridge: Cambridge University Press.

Bogale, B. (2009). Language determination in Ethiopia: What medium of instruction? In S. Ege, H. Aspen, B. Teferra, & S. Bekele (Eds.), *Proceedings of the 16th International Conference of Ethiopian Studies*. (pp. 1089–1101). Trondheim: Department of Social Anthropology, Norwegian University of Science and Technology.

Cohen, G. (2006). The development of regional and local languages in Ethiopia's federal system. In D. Turton (Ed.), *Ethnic federalism: The Ethiopian experience in comparative perspective* (pp. 165–180). Addis Ababa: Addis Ababa University Press.

Cooper, R. (1989). *Language planning and social change*. Cambridge: Cambridge University Press.

Crass, J., & Meyer, R. (2008). Ethiopia. In B. Heine & D. Nurse (Eds.), *A linguistic geography of Africa* (pp. 228–250). Cambridge: Cambridge University Press.

García, O., & Li Wei (2013). *Translanguaging: Language, bilingualism and education*. Basingstoke: Palgrave.

Gardner, S. (2012). Global English and bilingual education. In M. Martin-Jones, A. Blackledge, & A. Creese (Eds.), *The Routledge handbook of multilingualism* (pp. 247–264). Oxford: Routledge.

Heugh, K. (2009). Into the cauldron: An interplay of indigenous and globalized knowledge with strong and weak notions of literacy and language education in Ethiopia and South Africa. *Language Matters: Studies in the Languages of Africa, 40*(2), 166–189.

Heugh, K. (2011). Productive engagement with linguistic diversity in tension with globalized discourses in Ethiopia. *Current Issues in Language Planning, 11*(4), 378–396.

Heugh, K., Benson, C., Bogale, B., & Yohannes, M. (2007). *Final report study on medium of instruction in primary schools in Ethiopia.* Commissioned by the Ministry of Education, September–December 2006.

Institute of International Education (2012). *Enhancing the quality of English language education in Ethiopia.* Report on a Future Search Conference sponsored by the Embassy of the USA in collaboration with the Ministry of Education of the Government of the Federal Democratic Republic of Ethiopia, the Institute of International Education, and Ambo University.

Landry, R., & Bourhis, R. (1997). Linguistic landscape and ethnolinguistic vitality: An empirical study. *Journal of Language and Social Psychology, 16*, 23–49.

Lanza, E., & Woldemariam, H. (2008). Language ideology and linguistic landscape: Language policy and globalization in a regional capital of Ethiopia. In E. Shohamy & D. Gorter (Eds.), *Linguistic landscape: Expanding the scenery* (pp. 189–205). New York: Routledge.

Lanza, E., & Woldemariam, H. (2009). *Language ideology and language policy at the crossroads: Globalization and regionalism in Ethiopia.* Paper presented at Language Policy and Language Learning Conference, Limerick, Ireland, June 18–20.

Lanza, E., & Woldemariam, H. (2011). Colonial languages in an African country without a colonial past? In K. V. Lexander, C. Lyche, & A. M. Knutsen (Eds.), *Pluralité des langues, pluralité des cultures: Regards sur l'Afrique et au-delà. Mélanges offerts à Ingse Skattum à l'occasion de son 70ème anniversaire* (pp. 291–301). Oslo: Novus Forlag.

Lanza, E., & Woldemariam, H. (2013). Indexing modernity: English and branding in the linguistic landscape of an African capital. *International Journal of Bilingualism.* OnlineFirst, May 3, 2013. doi:10.1177/1367006913484204.

Lewis, M. P., Simons, G. F., & Fennig, C. D. (Eds.) (2013). *Ethnologue: Languages of the World* (17th ed.). Dallas, TX: SIL International. Retrieved from: www.ethnologue.com (accessed March 1, 2014).

Ministry of Education (1994). *Education and training policy.* Addis Ababa: Ministry of Education.

Mazrui, A. M. (2004). *English in Africa after the Cold War.* Bristol, UK: Multilingual Matters.

Negash, T. (2006). *From crisis to the brink of collapse.* Discussion Paper 33. Nordiska Afrikainstitutet, Uppsala.

Raga, A. (2012). Linguistic landscape and language attitude: A case study on Jimma town's linguistic landscape inscribers' attitude for Afan Oromo. *International Journal of Sociology and Anthropology, 4*(7), 218–225.

Reda, F. G. (2013). *Tigrinya-English/Amharic codeswitching.* Unpublished doctoral dissertation. University of Oslo, Norway.

Shohamy, E. (2006). *Language policy: Hidden agendas and new approaches.* London/New York: Routledge.

Shohamy, E. (2012). Linguistic landscapes and multilingualism. In M. Martin-Jones, A. Blackledge, & A. Creese (Eds.), *The Routledge handbook of multilingualism* (pp. 538–551). Oxford: Routledge.

Shohamy, E., & Gorter, D. (2008). *Linguistic landscape: Expanding the scenery.* Oxford: Routledge.

Shohamy, E., Ben-Rafael, E., & Barni, M. (Eds.) (2010). *Linguistic landscape in the city.* Bristol, UK: Multilingual Matters.

Smith, L. (2008). The politics of contemporary language policy in Ethiopia. *Journal of Developing Societies, 24*(2), 207–243.

Spolsky, B. (2004). *Language policy.* Cambridge: Cambridge University Press.

Stoddart, J. (1986). *The use and study of English in Ethiopian schools.* (Unpublished report). Addis Ababa: The British Council, English Language Services Department.

Stroud, C., & Wee, L. (2012). *Style, identity and literacy: English in Singapore.* Bristol, UK: Multilingual Matters.

Vaughan, S. (2007). Le féderalisme ethnique et la démocratisation depuis 1991 (Ethnic federalism and democratization since 1991). In G. Prunier (Ed.), *L'Ethiopie contemporaine (Contemporary Ethiopia)* (pp. 369–395). Paris: Karthala.

Walter, S., & Benson, C. (2012). Language policy and medium of instruction in formal education. In B. Spolsky (Ed.), *Handbook of language policy* (pp. 278–300). Cambridge: Cambridge University Press.

Woldemariam, H. (2007). The challenges of mother-tongue education in Ethiopia: The case of North Omo area. *Language Matters: Studies in the Languages of Africa, 38*(2), 210–235.

Woldemariam, H., & Lanza, E. (in press). Language contact, agency and power in the linguistic landscape of two regional capitals in Ethiopia. *International Journal of the Sociology of Language.*

9

PORTRAITS OF LANGUAGE ACTIVISTS IN INDIGENOUS LANGUAGE REVITALIZATION

Nancy H. Hornberger

Introduction

As an ethnographer of language education policy and practice in multilingual classrooms, schools, and communities, I pay attention to context, consistent with the precepts of my field. Yet, at the center of those contexts, and of my ethnographic gaze, is the individual actor. Whether writing about pupil participation and teacher techniques as criteria for success in an experimental bilingual education program in Peru; successful contexts for bilingual literacy in two Philadelphia elementary classrooms; ideological paradox and intercultural possibility in Andean bilingual education policy and practice; the continua of biliteracy as ecological framework for understanding multilingual language policies; voice and contentious educational practices in Indigenous language revitalization; or methodological rich points in the ethnography of language policy, I find inspiration and illumination in the actions and philosophies of individual teachers, learners, and language activists I have the privilege to know.

In honor of Elana Shohamy—brilliant scholar, generous colleague, dear friend, I reflect here on how her groundbreaking work in language assessment, language policy, and linguistic landscape similarly uncovers and celebrates individual agency. Commenting first on her academic contributions in these research terrains, I consider three present-day Indigenous language activists whose work plows these same fields and exemplifies the power of individual people in language education and policy.[1]

Elana Shohamy and the Power of Language Tests, Language Policy, and Linguistic Landscape

Elana and I first met at the 1997 American Association for Applied Linguistics conference in Orlando, where we both gave invited plenaries. Elana was at the forefront of the critical language testing movement, bringing attention to ways language tests (and all tests) serve as tools in perpetuating dominant languages and knowledges by failing to recognize minoritized group learners' previous language or content learning (Shohamy, 2001, 2004). Some years later, she and I co-edited a volume on language assessment for the *Encyclopedia of Language and Education* (Shohamy & Hornberger, 2008)—a stunningly comprehensive and authoritative reference compendium, thanks to Elana.

Elana had been meanwhile collaborating with Bernard Spolsky on language policy research in Israel, daring to open up the question of the "other" languages beyond Hebrew (Spolsky & Shohamy, 1999). One of Elana's key contributions to language policy (LP) has been her attention to its hidden agendas (Shohamy, 2006). Building on Schiffman's (1996) distinction between overt and covert LP, Kloss's (1969) and Cooper's (1989) corpus-status-acquisition typology, and Spolsky's (2004) model of language practices, beliefs, and management, Shohamy sees LPs as mechanisms for organizing, managing, and manipulating language use, learning, and forms—including mechanisms such as language tests and language in public space (Shohamy, 2006). Notably, this formulation draws attention to individual actors' roles in LP enactment.

Linguistic landscape "refers to linguistic objects that mark the public space," put in place by public authorities, but also private individuals, associations, or firms, and reflecting symbolic construction of public space influenced by: rational considerations of attractiveness to the public; expressions of identity; and underlying power relations among competing sociopolitical forces (Ben-Rafael, Shohamy, Amara, & Trumper-Hecht, 2006). Here, as in her scholarship on language tests and language policy, Elana's work brings individual actors into focus, as agents shaping and influencing the linguistic landscapes in which they carry out their lives.

Below, I present brief portraits from my research alongside Quechua, South African, and Sámi Indigenous language activists.[2] Inspired by portraiture (Lawrence-Lightfoot & Davis, 1997) and "history in person" (Holland & Lave, 2001), I seek to portray these individual activists' perspectives, experiences, and voices in social and cultural context, as emergent and shaped in part through dialogue with me (Lawrence-Lightfoot & Davis, 1997, p. xv), and to highlight the mutually constitutive nature of language and the enduring struggles of Indigenous peoples that are crucibles for the forging of their identities (Holland & Lave, 2001, p. 109). I have chosen activists who have engaged, in one way or another, with themes of assessment, policy, and landscape, as a way of illuminating terrains Elana has explored and paths these individuals are charting.

Neri Mamani and Linguistic Landscape in Highland Andes

A Quechua language activist whose vision for Quechua language revitalization recurringly calls attention to linguistic signs that mark public space is Neri Mamani—bilingual teacher, teacher educator, researcher, and advocate for Indigenous identity and language revitalization across rural, urban, and peri-urban spaces of the Andes. Mamani grew up in southern highland Peru and, when I met her in 2005, was a bilingual intercultural education (EIB) practitioner enrolled in the PROEIB-Andes master's program for Indigenous educators at San Simón University in Cochabamba, Bolivia. PROEIB-Andes, founded in 1996, serves the Andean region of South America, enrolling Indigenous bilingual intercultural educators whose languages range from Quechua with several varieties and millions of speakers to Amazonian languages with far, far fewer speakers—all of them, nonetheless, persistently marginalized and endangered (Hornberger, 2013; Hornberger & Coronel-Molina, 2004; Hornberger & King, 2001; López, 2006, 2008).[3]

Neri's early pride in her family's Quechua roots coexisted with a rural/urban, Quechua/Spanish, Indigenous/Western dichotomy. Growing up in the town of Sicuani, she maintained contact with the rural community of her birth, Callalli, during school vacations spent with her grandparents there, herding sheep and alpacas. She and her sisters would dress in the colorful hand-embroidered clothing of the region, changing out of it to return to their studies in Sicuani. A sharp distinction between Spanish language, Western dress, and urban space, on one hand, and Quechua language, Indigenous dress, the countryside, and agricultural work, on the other, existed for Neri as a child, but without a conscious sense that this represented "Indigenousness." Through her experiences, mobility, studies, and work as bilingual teacher, teacher educator, and researcher, those distinctions gradually blurred in her practices even as her identity became more consciously Indigenous. Now, she assumes a personal language policy of using Quechua and engaging in traditional Indigenous practices in public, urban, and literate spaces in her daily life in order to break down longstanding language and identity compartmentalizations. Although these linguistic and cultural practices do not perhaps constitute linguistic landscape in its usual sense of visible written signs, they are visible and audible expressions of what Shohamy and colleagues refer to as the symbolic construction of public space—expressions of identity consciously influenced by considerations of public attention, presentation of self, and contestation of underlying power relations.

Mamani argues that Quechua use is a highly visible marker of Indigenous identity and that the strengthening of both depends on daily use of Quechua as a viable language of communication in public spaces:

> *If we don't use our language, talking on the phone, writing on the Internet, riding public transport . . . going to the supermarket . . . who's going to do it?*

126 Nancy H. Hornberger

She acknowledges schooling as a transformative site for shifting the language's indexical value away from exclusive association with rural life and agricultural labor. As a student in a prestigious master's program that includes an Indigenous language requirement as criterion for admittance and in which she and her peers deploy a complex, fluid set of linguistic resources in their academic work, Neri is keenly aware of the benefits of multilingual repertoire. Furthermore, she and her peers extend their use of Indigenous languages beyond dichotomized, diglossic, domain-restricted use in education, to visual, aural, digital, expressive, tangible uses in public spaces.

Neri's master's thesis research in what she calls a "peri-urban" Quechua-speaking community at Cusco's periphery reinforced, for her, the close connection between language revitalization and cultural practices. Musing on one elder's narration of wedding practices in an "exquisitely sweet" Quechua, on traditional festivities surrounding the handing on of the mayoral *vara* "baton" in some Cusco communities, or on the *faena* "communal work day" at her own fieldwork site involving all community members in replacing water pipes, she contemplates the continuity and change in language and cultural practice around Indigenous tradition and worries about loss of these practices:

> No one shirks the obligation. I think this is already being lost in the cities. If you don't want to go, you don't. Let's say for the school faena "work day"—I don't go and I just pay the fine. But in the community everyone shows up.

Mamani believes that "devolving and protecting" Indigenous resources (Smith, 1999) includes public cultural practices such as these, as much as language, on the one hand, or natural resources and material artifacts, on the other.

For Neri, interculturality is not some unattainable ideal, but lived practice in public space—cultural dialogue between cultures co-present and interwoven in the same space, coexisting not as separate, pure cultures, but with mutual dialogue and respect. Indigenous families in a peri-urban community observing cultural practices brought with them from their rural home in Cusco's remote provinces are expressions of this interculturality. These include, for example, young girls from Chumbivilcas who gather firewood as they walk with her in the hills, a habit built in to the life of a rural child, but not part of a city child's thinking, or the dexterous horseback riding competitions for which Canas province is famous, now enacted in Cusco. She had not expected to see practices such as these in the city.

On the other hand, she observes the permeation of "Western" ways in Indigenous people's thinking and is concerned that urban Indigenous youth grow up without a conscious sense of their Indigenous roots or identity. She advocates for consciousness-raising efforts to counter that trend:

> There may be many Indigenous people who don't know they are Indigenous . . . in the cities, for example. Migrants come, their children grow up, now they think

> *they are from Cusco . . . They no longer identify with their community, where their parents came from, their grandparents . . . Maybe they were born there, but now, they have nothing to do with their past. I say for people like that there should be some awareness-raising, maybe, of who we are, some recognition . . . do something so that they too realize that yes, they are Indigenous.*

It is not that Neri rejects any and all Western influences. She agrees with Smith's Indigenous project of critically reading Western history, but this does not mean that "everything western since the Conquest is now no good." Rather, she emphasizes notions of dialogue and encounter—fluid movement, mutual respect, and influence among cultures.

Nor is it that Mamani knows definitively what it means to be Indigenous. She reflects that PROEIB students engage in continual and never fully resolved conversations about Indigeneity. Someone points a finger at someone else for being too citified, not "pure" Indigenous. Others identify themselves not as Indigenous, but Amazonian; they start classifying themselves and each other or questioning each other's practices:

> *We are continually questioning ourselves, our acts, our way of saying things, of dressing, of eating, everything. At times, there are colleagues who don't want to eat a little food from the street, let's say . . . They'll say—No, I don't want to go to the market because it stinks there . . . Then, immediately someone comes out and says—what kind of Indigenous person are you? . . . just like that . . . So, the person who hears that also says—oh, you're right. And so, he/she is obliged to reflect and the next minute says—ok, let's go.*

Neri herself is not immune to these questionings and self-questionings; it is in her daily practice and constant self-reflection that she works out what it means, to her, to be an Indigenous person and a Quechua speaker in the private, professional, and public spaces—the linguistic landscape—of Cusco and the Andes.

Nobuhle Hlongwa and Multilingual Language Policy at University of Kwazulu-Natal, South Africa

Professor Nobuhle Ndimande-Hlongwa has been integrally involved in implementing isiZulu as medium of instruction at the University of KwaZulu-Natal in Durban, South Africa, throughout her academic career. As former Head of the School of isiZulu Studies and current Humanities Dean of Teaching and Learning, but also as language teacher, teacher educator, and researcher, Hlongwa has undertaken a range of initiatives to advance isiZulu at UKZN. In addition to her isiZulu teaching and administrative responsibilities, Professor Hlongwa developed a graduate language planning seminar taught through isiZulu medium

128 Nancy H. Hornberger

for which she wrote an introductory textbook in isiZulu, *Ukuhlelwa Kolimi* (Ndimande-Hlongwa, 2009). Hlongwa was a key participant in a three-year interdisciplinary faculty research project funded by the South Africa–Norway Tertiary Education Development Program (SANTED) and directed toward creation of discipline-specific modules in isiZulu, isiZulu terminology development, and translation activities (Engelbrecht, Shangase, Majeke, Mthembu, & Zondi, 2010; Engelbrecht & Wildsmith-Cromarty, 2010; Ndimande-Hlongwa, Balfour, Mkhize, & Engelbrecht, 2010; Ndimande-Hlongwa & Wildsmith-Cromarty, 2010; Wildsmith-Cromarty, 2008).

In keeping with South Africa's multilingual language policy of 1996 and the increasing attention to implementing it in higher education (Van der Walt, 2013; Van der Walt & Brink, 2005), UKZN faculty approved, in 2006, a language policy affirming respect for all of South Africa's official, heritage, and other languages. Elevation of the status and use of isiZulu in higher education is a major aim of the UKZN language policy, in recognition that 80 percent of KwaZulu-Natal's population speaks isiZulu. Embroiled perhaps in what Shohamy might call hidden agendas, the 2006 policy lay dormant until 2010, when UKZN Deputy Vice Chancellor (DVC) for Teaching and Learning Vithal assumed responsibility for pushing ahead to make the university truly multilingual in teaching, learning, and research. As part of that initiative, I spent a few weeks at UKZN that year to facilitate dialogue across the schools and faculties on next steps for policy implementation and, in that context, I met Professor Hlongwa.[4]

I spent a few days with Hlongwa at the School of isiZulu Studies at UKZN's Howard College campus in the Memorial Tower Building, a corridor of layered meanings for me since it adjoins the corridor that housed the (now defunct) Department of Linguistics where I had spent three weeks 15 years earlier when it was the University of Natal—a whole history of post-apartheid institutional transformation lies behind those layers. Nobuhle had recently been promoted from Head of the School of isiZulu Studies to Deputy Dean of Humanities and, in that capacity, we met with her newly appointed Dean and the current Head of isiZulu Studies to get their thoughts and reflections on furthering implementation of isiZulu-medium instruction at UKZN. Among the strategies we discussed at some length that day was the development of an institution-wide isiZulu Terminology Development Platform, an interactive electronic clearinghouse and website for dissemination and feedback across the university and out to the public— a kernel of an idea I later learned had been put into action the following year (R. Dhunpath, personal communication, November 14, 2011).

Nobuhle also invited me—and several faculty colleagues—to a session of her graduate seminar in language planning. We had a lively discussion among about 15–20 faculty and master's students (all school teachers). Issues raised included: the difficulty of categorizing South Africans' language proficiencies as first language (L1) or second language (L2) and the need to deconstruct such designations; rural and urban varieties of isiZulu and codeswitching; school learners writing

Zulu-ized English words rather than pure isiZulu in their isiZulu-medium classes; parents' reactions to new school policies of teaching isiZulu-medium rather than English in primary grades; the stigmatization of doing a master's in isiZulu; and the need for mother-tongue-based multilingual education in schools and at UKZN to counter the hegemony of English—not to replace English with isiZulu, but in an additive model.

These were concerns—mechanisms of language policy, in Shohamy's terms—that emerged over and over again in dialogue with faculty across the university, issues Nobuhle and her colleagues continually grapple with as they seek to shift educational discourses toward welcoming and accommodating instruction through the medium of isiZulu and other African languages in K-12 schools and in higher education. Tensions of particular significance for Nobuhle revolved around the special role of isiZulu and the School of isiZulu Studies in implementing the policy. There were concerns lest isiZulu become the sole, rather than primary, focus—what about other South African languages? What about languages spoken by immigrants or foreign students, such as French, Portuguese, kiSwahili? There were concerns as to the appropriate role for the School of isiZulu Studies in the implementation of isiZulu-medium teaching across the university: isiZulu faculty expertise is clearly central to the undertaking, but they are neither enough in number nor do they necessarily cover all areas of expertise required to meet the need. Nobuhle herself is undeniably stretched to the limit in her multiple roles as teacher, researcher, and dean. A 2011 reorganization creating a School of Arts and, within it, an African Languages Cluster housing both isiZulu and kiSwahili may go some way toward addressing these tensions (N. Hlongwa, personal communication, July 19, 2013).

Nobuhle is the only college professor in her family, encouraged early on by a teacher who went on to pay her registration fee when she enrolled for her bachelor's degree in 1993; and she gratefully acknowledges the strong support of her husband. Conscious that her family is proud of her, she also feels the weight of personal responsibility; she recently bought a house where the orphaned children of a sister who died in 2009 can live with their aunts. Her commitment, then, is not just to her academic field and the promotion of her language, but above all to her family and her people—a heavy burden at times.

As a person of Zulu heritage, fluent isiZulu speaker, experienced teacher of the language as both subject and medium, and accomplished researcher in isiZulu linguistics and language planning, Nobuhle is in great demand and feels the weight of responsibility to keep the language policy moving ahead. With her growing number of publications, Hlongwa's national and international career is taking off—she gave her first international keynote at a 2010 onomastics conference in Norway (her PhD is on onomastics of African languages), and serves as executive member of the newly established International Council on Indigenous Place Names. She is a member of the Ministerial Advisory Panel on the development of African Languages in Higher Education and a recently named Commissioner on South

130 Nancy H. Hornberger

Africa's new Linguistic Human Rights Tribunal. She is, in short, a key figure not only in the implementation of isiZulu at UKZN, but of multilingual language policy in South African higher education more generally, and Indigenous language policy internationally.

Hanna Outakoski and Literacy Assessment in Sápmi, Scandinavia

Hanna Outakoski bears the name of the village in which she was raised in the far north of Finland, deep within the Arctic Circle—a part of the world known to (North) Sámi speakers as Sápmi, stretching across northern Sweden, Norway, Finland, and Russia. This wide expanse of tundra is the centuries-old home to reindeer-herding Sámi people. Hanna's father and grandfather spoke some Sámi with her from early on, but it was when she began to spend extended time beginning age 7 or 9 with her reindeer-herding relatives who spoke only Sámi at home that she became fluent (an opportunity her younger brother did not get, to his regret). Outakoski is today a PhD student and adjunct lecturer in North Sámi language at the University of Umeå in Sweden and a strong advocate for Sámi language and people—a role she is inevitably drawn to, though one not always comfortable for her.[5]

Hanna comes from a long line of teachers—her parents and grandparents were teachers, and indeed her grandfather's grandfather founded the school in Outakoski. At the university, she teaches beginning, intermediate, and advanced North Sámi to new beginners and mother tongue heritage learners, developing and continually updating her own materials; she also designs and teaches courses for distance learning on the Second Life platform. Hanna travels long distances to meet with her students—often taking the train nine hours each way. Though Umeå is in the north of Sweden, most of her students are even further north and widely dispersed, so she locates her courses in different towns each year to reach as many as possible. North Sámi is the largest Sámi group, numbering about 35,000 of approximately 100,000 Sámi. While no accurate count exists of the total number of speakers of Sámi's nine varieties, Hanna estimates that about two-thirds of North Sámi speak the language.

Another consequence of Umeå's relative distance from the heartland of the Sámi-speaking population, and a source of frustration for Hanna, is that the municipality of Umeå provides little offering in Sámi, despite Sweden's 2010 policy on National Minorities and National Minority Languages entailing a legal obligation to protect minorities and promote their languages, including Sámi (Swedish Code of Statutes, 2009, p. 724). Hanna explained to me in August 2012 that Umeå municipality had chosen to interpret "basic knowledge" of Sámi to mean that the learner must already know how to read and write Sámi in order to qualify for mother tongue instruction—an interpretation that is nowhere in the law nor in the European Convention underlying the law, and that has the

Portraits of Language Activists **131**

effect of excluding Sámi children in Umeå who might otherwise get instruction in their mother tongue—including Hanna's own sons, ages 8 and 6, who are too little to have learned to read and write, even though they speak a little and understand almost everything. She and colleagues in the municipality had applied for and been awarded extra funds for Sámi language instruction in 2012, which they then could not spend because "there are not enough Sámi children"; the money would have to be returned to the government, thus also hampering the chances of its being re-awarded in the future. Hanna spoke out on this via the media, as well as in person, with municipal officials, together with other Sámi and representatives for Finnish and Meänkieli, also included in the national minority languages law. Happily, she later reported that:

> we actually got the municipality to change the political decision they had made about mother tongue teaching! It is great news for our kids and a great achievement . . . this time the Sámi fought together with the Finns and we did get our say in the matter.
>
> (personal communication, September 30, 2012)

Similarly, Hanna brought pressure on the municipality to create a children's room for Sámi literature in the municipal library, which now exists and is quite well stocked; frustratingly, it is a rather dark and uninviting space compared to the "other" children's room in the library, which is bright and cheery. Though discouraged by the politics (and hidden agendas and mechanisms of language policy), Outakoski stays in the fray for Sámi's sake.

A fluent speaker of Finnish, Swedish, and English in addition to North Sámi, Hanna and her husband are raising their sons multilingually. Since Umeå has had no Sámi language instruction nor immersion pre-school (a language revitalization strategy difficult or impossible to realize for the widely dispersed Sámi population), Hanna enrolled the boys in an immersion pre-school in Finnish, to access another part of their heritage. At home, Hanna speaks to them in Sámi, their dad speaks to them in Swedish, and they generally reply in Finnish. She worries sometimes that her children need to be closer to other Sámi speakers in order to become fluent speakers. As for so many Indigenous language activists, her roles as teacher, researcher, and advocate are sometimes at odds with those as parent and inter-generational transmitter of her language; just as Nobuhle, Hanna, too, is stretched in her many roles and responsibilities, and at the same time is unquestionably a powerful actor in language education and policy for Indigenous language revitalization.

Outakoski is a key player in the Literacy in Sápmi research project—a three-country study of youth literacy in North Sámi, English, and the national language (Swedish, Norwegian, and Finnish, respectively), by means of a literacy assessment in which youth write texts in each of their three languages, one descriptive and one argumentative, for a total of six texts per youth. This comprehensive study

132 Nancy H. Hornberger

also entails interviews, questionnaires, language diaries, and observation, but the core data are the texts written by youth in roughly four age categories—9, 12, 15, and 18 years old, who study, or have studied, North Sámi as a subject in school.[6] Driving hundreds of miles across Sápmi to visit 13 schools or school districts, staying a week at each school (during a four-month data collection period), Hanna brought along a carload of two dozen laptop computers (with a keystroke logging program installed) on which youth wrote their texts in several sessions; there are more than 800 texts composed by 150 youth, in five languages. Though sometimes accompanied by other team members, as the only Sámi speaker on the team and the one with personal contacts in many of the schools they visited, Hanna was crucial to the data collection and is currently coordinating the transcription and translation phase as well.

This is not an assessment study in the usual sense of individual assessment. Given that many of the participants are children of a national minority and Indigenous heritage in a context of contested minority/language politics, there will be no identification of, nor comparisons between, individual writers or schools; comparisons made will be across languages, countries, text types, or anonymized case studies. It is a descriptive, qualitative study, not a standardized, quantitative number-crunching one. Yet, given its purposes of shedding light on the kinds and characteristics of writing Sámi-speaking youth engage in in today's world, the study offers possibilities for assessment of a different kind—a democratic, inclusive assessment in the sense that Shohamy (2004) calls for, carried out in collaboration and cooperation with the youth and their teachers, headmasters, and families; designed to provide space for youth to incorporate their own local knowledge in writing in any or all of their three languages; and protecting and guarding their rights through anonymity. Further, since the study includes attention to the policy, program, and curricular contexts in which Sámi is taught to these youth, there is also opportunity for the researchers to examine assumptions and consequences of these policy mechanisms for Sámi youth's writing, and, as so compellingly articulated in Shohamy's words and in Outakoski's daily practice, to assume responsibility for the mechanisms and their uses.

Final Reflection

Though these brief portraits give only a glimmer of the rich and complex lives, scholarship, and commitment of the people portrayed, they clearly demonstrate the power of individual people in shaping language assessment, policy, and landscape, and the paths and spaces opened up in their doing so (Hornberger, 2005). In drawing these portraits of three young language activists in Indigenous language revitalization, I hope I have done some justice to Elana's clear-sighted vision and insights. Most of all, I hope the portraits convey, in some small way, the depth and inspiration Neri, Nobuhle, and Hanna's lives and words hold for me and for many others.

Notes

1. For Elana and the three Indigenous language activists I portray here, I use first and last name interchangeably, in recognition of both the personal and scholarly dimensions of the portraits.
2. I am grateful to the three activists, whose real names and stories I tell here with their permission and encouragement.
3. My ongoing thanks to Luis Enrique López, founding director of PROEIB-Andes, and to all the faculty, staff, and students there who have so warmly welcomed me over the years, beginning even before the master's program was officially launched and continuing to the present. My very special thanks go to Neri Mamani for our friendship and conversations together. The following paragraphs draw from my interviews with Neri on September 11, 2004, and June 20 and 28, 2005, and from my participant observation with her cohort during 2004–2006.
4. I am grateful to DVC Renuka Vithal and Director Rubby Dhunpath of the University of KwaZulu-Natal Teaching and Learning Office for graciously inviting, organizing, and hosting my visit, and to all the faculty, staff, and students (former and current) who welcomed and met with me during my stay. My particular thanks here to Nobuhle Ndimande-Hlongwa for generously sharing her time and thoughts with me. The following paragraphs draw from my visit in August 2010 and e-mail exchanges since then.
5. I am grateful to Görel Sandstrom, Head of the Department of Language Studies at University of Umeå, for inviting, appointing, and hosting me as Visiting Professor beginning in 2012, and to faculty, staff, and students there for very warm hospitality from the first day. Among the several colleagues who are collaborating with me, my special appreciation goes to Hanna Outakoski for her unfailing warmth, generosity, and tenacious dedication to the development and promotion of Sámi language and Sámi language education. The following paragraphs draw from my visits in August–September 2012 and May–June 2013, and ongoing e-mail exchanges and research collaborations.
6. The project is funded by the Swedish Research Council and undertaken by a four-person research team led by Professor Kirk Sullivan and including faculty members Eva Lindgren and Asbjørg Westum. My thanks to Kirk and Eva for permission to mention the project and for including me in it.

References

Ben-Rafael, E., Shohamy, E., Amara, M., & Trumper-Hecht, N. (2006). Linguistic landscape as symbolic construction of the public space: The case of Israel. *International Journal of Multilingualism, 3*(1), 7–30.

Cooper, R. L. (1989). *Language planning and social change.* Cambridge: Cambridge University Press.

Engelbrecht, C., & Wildsmith-Cromarty, R. (2010). Exploring multilingualism in a problem-based learning setting: Implications for classroom and clinical practice in the nursing discipline. *AlterNation, 17*(1), 108–137.

Engelbrecht, C., Shangase, N., Majeke, S., Mthembu, S., & Zondi, Z. (2010). Zulu terminology development in nursing and midwifery: The subject specialists' perspective. *AlterNation, 17*(1), 249–272.

Holland, D., & Lave, J. (Eds.). (2001). *History in person: Enduring struggles, contentious practice, intimate identities.* Santa Fe, NM: School of American Research Press.

Hornberger, N. H. (2005). Opening and filling up implementational and ideological spaces in heritage language education. *Modern Language Journal, 89*(4), 605–609.

134   Nancy H. Hornberger

Hornberger, N. H. (2013). Negotiating methodological rich points in the ethnography of language policy. *International Journal of the Sociology of Language, 219*, 101–122.

Hornberger, N. H., & King, K. A. (2001). Reversing Quechua language shift in South America. In J. A. Fishman (Ed.), *Can threatened languages be saved? "Reversing Language Shift" Revisited: A 21st century perspective* (pp. 166–194). Bristol, UK: Multilingual Matters.

Hornberger, N. H., & Coronel-Molina, S. M. (2004). Quechua language shift, maintenance and revitalization in the Andes: The case for language planning. *International Journal of the Sociology of Language, 167*, 9–67.

Kloss, H. (1969). *Research possibilities on group bilingualism: A report (Publication No. b-18).* Quebec, Canada: International Center for Research on Bilingualism, Laval University.

Lawrence-Lightfoot, S., & Davis, J. H. (1997). *The art and science of portraiture.* San Francisco, CA: John Wiley & Sons.

López, L. E. (2006). Cultural diversity, multilingualism and indigenous education in Latin America. In T. Skutnabb-Kangas, O. García & M. Torres-Guzmán (Eds.), *Imagining multilingual schools: Languages in education and glocalization* (pp. 238–261). Bristol, UK: Multilingual Matters.

López, L. E. (2008). Top-down and bottom-up: Counterpoised visions of bilingual intercultural education in Latin America. In N. H. Hornberger (Ed.), *Can schools save indigenous languages? Policy and practice on four continents* (pp. 42–65). New York: Palgrave Macmillan.

Ndimande-Hlongwa, N. (2009). *Ukuhlelwa kolimi (Language planning).* Pietermaritzburg: Shuter & Shooter.

Ndimande-Hlongwa, N., & Wildsmith-Cromarty, R. (Eds.) (2010). Multilingualism for access, language development and language intellectualization. *Alternation, 17*(1). Retrieved from: http://alternation.ukzn.ac.za/docs (accessed March 1, 2014).

Ndimande-Hlongwa, N., Balfour, R., Mkhize, N., & Engelbrecht, C. (2010). Progress and challenges for language policy implementation at the University of KwaZulu-Natal. *Language Learning Journal, 38*(3), 347–358.

Schiffman, H. F. (1996). *Linguistic culture and language policy.* New York: Routledge.

Shohamy, E. (2001). *The power of tests: A critical perspective on the uses of language tests.* London: Longman.

Shohamy, E. (2004). Assessment in multicultural societies: Applying democratic principles and practices to language testing. In B. Norton & K. Toohey (Eds.), *Critical pedagogies and language learning* (pp. 72–92). Cambridge: Cambridge University Press.

Shohamy, E. (2006). *Language policy: Hidden agendas and new approaches.* London: Routledge.

Shohamy, E., & Hornberger, N. H. (Eds.) (2008). *Encyclopedia of language and education (2nd Edition), Vol. 7: Language Testing and Assessment.* New York: Springer.

Smith, L. T. (1999). *Decolonizing methodologies: Research and indigenous peoples.* London: Zed.

Spolsky, B. (2004). *Language policy.* Cambridge: Cambridge University Press.

Spolsky, B., & Shohamy, E. (1999). *The languages of Israel: Policy, ideology, and practice.* Bristol, UK: Multilingual Matters.

Swedish Code of Statutes (2009). Act on national minorities and national minority languages, 724 (in Swedish). Retrieved from: www.government.se/content/1/c6/13/67/58/19668cda.pdf (accessed May 4, 2014).

Van der Walt, C. (2013). *Multilingual higher education: Beyond English medium orientations.* Bristol, UK: Multilingual Matters.

Van der Walt, C., & Brink, C. (2005). Multilingual universities: A national and international overview. *South African Journal of Higher Education, 19*(4), 822–851.

Wildsmith-Cromarty, R. (2008). Can academic/scientific discourse really be translated across English and African languages? *Southern African Linguistics and Applied Language Studies, 26*(1), 147–169.

10

REFUGEES IN CANADA

ON THE LOSS OF SOCIAL CAPITAL

Thomas Ricento

Introduction

Social scientists, including applied linguists, have used the construct of "capital" (e.g. human capital, cultural capital, and social capital) to characterize the mechanisms that influence the life chances of individuals and the well-being of communities (Lin, 2000). Research has found that inequality often correlates with unequal access to social goods and services that provide opportunities for socioeconomic upward mobility. Although Marxist class-based analysis tends to emphasize structural class-based causality for such inequalities, neo-capital theories tend to look to the choices and decisions made by individuals, mediated by systemic forms of overt or covert discrimination—such as race or gender discrimination—to account for differential outcomes in life experiences and socioeconomic well-being. Within the neo-capital framework, at least in modern liberal democratic states, government is expected to ensure equality of opportunity for all citizens[1] to gain access to the benefits that a society may provide to facilitate "life, liberty, and the pursuit of happiness." Beyond creating a "level playing field," however, many liberal political theorists argue, government should not be in the business of providing special advantages to some individuals or groups who may have benefitted less—often far less—than other individuals or groups, because that would violate the "rules" of the game by giving an unfair advantage to particular individuals or groups. In cases in which strong historical and empirical evidence of discrimination based on gender, race, or national origin has been documented, for example, governments and their legislative bodies have adopted policies and passed laws outlawing such discrimination.[2] Yet, those policies and laws have frequently been opposed by individuals, political parties, and advocacy organizations who believe that such policies are discriminatory and "illiberal" because they provide an unfair advantage to some "protected groups," but not others. These conflicts occur, in part, because there is no easy or fair way to characterize what constitutes a "level playing field." For example, discrimination in hiring practices can be quite subtle and may reflect unconscious biases toward individuals based on factors such as foreign accent, place of origin, or civil status (e.g. refugee, landed immigrant, permanent resident).

When theorists from sociology discuss or define social capital, they are usually referring to individuals and groups who are legal citizens within sovereign states, with historical roots and some ongoing connection with a geographical space, having established some sense of belonging to a greater collectivity—usually national—and usually measured in multiple generations of residency. However, this framework and the associated socio-demographic labels and categories that are employed in scholarly research that focuses on hierarchies of inequality that correlate with, for example, gender, ethnicity, race, and educational attainment, run into some difficulty when applied to individuals and groups whose social capital may not be fully recognized because of their "foreignness" (i.e. because they are "outsiders" whose credentials and bona fides were obtained, recognized, and rewarded in their home country, but are not recognized or valued in their new country). One of the salient and overt characteristics of "foreignness" is the language spoken by outsiders and especially the degree to which their language differs from the expected, standard norm used by the dominant national group (Blommaert, 2010). However, it is not only perceived deficiencies in language that render foreigners "outsiders" and suspect with regard to their legitimacy as citizens, although that can often be an important factor that perpetuates the outsider status of foreigners. In the case of refugees, the discounting or erasure of earned social capital is often more of a barrier to socioeconomic integration than possible deficiencies in the dominant/official language(s) of their new country.

Researchers have found that refugees face a number of challenges that are specific to their status as persons fleeing war, persecution, various types of physical abuse, and economic privation (Abu-Laban, Derwing, Krahn, Mulder, & Wilkinson, 1999; Martin & Curran, 2007; Pruebber & Tanasescu, 2007; Schellenberg & Maheux, 2007). There are some similarities between the refugee and broader non-refugee immigrant population in Canada. Both categories have a higher unemployment rate than the Canadian-born population. In a 1999 study funded by Citizenship and Immigration Canada (Abu-Laban et al., 1999), based on a sample of 616 refugees, managerial and professional occupations, along with skilled trades, accounted for 37 percent of adult refugee employment, while 32 percent worked in semi-skilled jobs and 31 percent in unskilled jobs. The unemployment rate for the refugee men was 14 percent and 19 percent for women, while 58 percent considered themselves to be underemployed. The unemployment rate was somewhat higher for refugees compared to the rate for the overall immigrant population.

But the picture is more complex in that some immigrant groups tend to do much better in the labor market in Canada than other groups. Several studies have found that non-European immigrants are especially disadvantaged in the Canadian labor market (Bloom, Grenier, & Gunderson, 1995; Hiebert, 1999; Pendakur & Pendakur, 1998). Bauder (2003), based in part on data from interviews with institutional administrators and employers in Greater Vancouver who service or employ immigrants from South Asia, argues rather convincingly that "professional associations and the state actively exclude immigrant labour from the most highly desired occupations in order to reserve these occupations for Canadian-born and Canadian-educated workers" (p. 699). Even though the level of education among immigrants has steadily increased since the 1950s (Akabari, 1999), immigrants have not benefitted from their educational attainments and have lower returns on education than Canadian-born workers (Reitz, 2001a, 2001b).

An earned credential in one of the recognized professions, such as medicine, engineering, or law, obtained in certain countries, does not easily, or often, embody or convey the same social capital when the possessor of such a credential arrives in Canada, or other industrialized high-income countries, as a refugee. This process, known as de-skilling (Bauder, 2003), has led to exclusion of highly trained and experienced individuals from upper labor-market sectors to which Canadian-educated workers have access. A division of labor is enforced based on national origin and place of education (Collins, 1979). Although social capital, especially in liberal democracies such as Canada, is claimed to be something one achieves through education, training, and experience, along with membership and participation in particular networks—professional and personal—that list of achieved attributes is diminished or even erased when individuals cross national borders. For example, the provable fact of having an earned medical degree from a prestigious medical school in Colombia, along with Board Certification in a specialty (e.g. neonatal surgery), with many years of relevant experience and evidence of ongoing professional training and upgrading of skills and knowledge,[3] is insufficient evidence to allow for certification to practice medicine in the province of Alberta, Canada, not just in the short term, but even permanently. As will be described later in this chapter, in the case of "outsiders" who may be fully credentialed and with very high social capital, as measured by all of the normal indices, that social capital can be, and frequently is, negated by gatekeeping agencies that serve the economic interests of "insiders." The mismatch between the achieved status and identities of "foreign" professionals, and the refusal to acknowledge these achievements on the part of credentialing bodies, requires a rethinking of central assumptions about the concept of "social capital," at least when applied to individuals such as refugees.

The Life of Refugees in Calgary

From August 2009 through July 2011, I was the Principal Investigator in a research project conducted in Calgary, Alberta, Canada, titled "Linguistic and cultural barriers to refugees' access to medical and social services." The purpose of the

138 Thomas Ricento

study was to gain a more sophisticated and comprehensive understanding of the sorts of challenges and barriers faced by refugees in their transition to living and working in Calgary, Canada. From an initial intake of 30 families in Phase I of the project, representing 120 people, we chose six focal families for Phase II, which involved monthly visits to their homes, at which time structured and semi-structured interviews were conducted with family members (adults and children over 12 years of age) in one of six languages: Karen, Nepali, Somali, Dari, Spanish, or French. The countries of origin for the interviewees were Myanmar, Bhutan, Somalia, Afghanistan, Colombia, and Congo, respectively. Over the course of nine months, we gained many insights into the obstacles faced by these individuals who had lived in Calgary anywhere from a few months to more than two years. We amassed over 100 hours of interviews with this remarkable group of people and came to learn about their immense courage and ability to persevere in the face of unimaginable horrors and travails, which included the witnessing of the murder and kidnapping of family members, and, in several cases, survival in relocation camps for more than 10 years. All of them expressed gratitude for having escaped the war, political unrest, and lack of human rights that prevailed in their countries and that resulted in often harrowing journeys to staging countries before their arrival in Canada. Yet, the transition for the families into a normal life was, understandably, filled with anxiety, frustrations, and setbacks, despite the availability of support programs and community organizations that do their best to help this vulnerable population succeed.

The impact of border crossings on the lives of individuals, such as refugees, has many dimensions. One of the most significant findings from the Calgary project was the impact of dislocation from their native country on the ability of individuals to gain footing in a labor market that favors persons with Canadian work experience, which correlates with easier access to financial capital (e.g. a credit history, which facilitates borrowing money to start a business), and with appropriate (usually native) English language skills, in the case of Alberta. The label "refugee" itself is often a barrier to employment, and for foreign-born persons who are "visible minorities" (an official term in Canada that generally means "non-white"), the barrier to employment is even higher.

To illustrate how individual refugees have experienced their transition to life in Canada, I provide vignettes of three persons who participated in the study. One (Fernando) is a highly trained professional from Colombia, a physician who is hoping to someday become a pharmacy technician in Canada. The barriers Fernando faced include deficiencies in English, but this was not the only, nor even the most significant, factor in his case. Rather, regulatory institutions in Canada, especially the College of Physicians and Surgeons, Alberta, was unresponsive to his repeated attempts to get information and guidance about how to obtain certification to practice medicine in Canada. This was not the first or only example of the intransigence of the College of Physicians and Surgeons in Alberta when an applicant was from a country other than the US, England, Australia, New

Zealand, or South Africa (countries that have reciprocity agreements with Canada that recognize medical degrees from those countries *prima facie*); another physician from Colombia[4] that I interviewed in 2008 had been ignored by the licensing agency for five years until a physician colleague for whom he had served as a physician's assistant made a telephone call, and within 10 minutes this physician had been cleared for a medical internship, which led, eventually, to full licensure to practice medicine, after taking and passing three written exams and a laborious and protracted oral exam (Dr. X, personal communication, December, 2008).

The other two individuals whose stories will be related are a married couple from the Democratic Republic of the Congo. Robert (all names are pseudonyms), 47 years old, had a good life as a businessman in the informal economy of a poor, African country until the onset of war and threats to his and his wife's security required that they leave the country and come to Canada as government-sponsored refugees. Although Robert had much less formal education than Fernando when he arrived in Montreal, his inability to borrow money from a bank necessary to buy a truck to become an independent businessman resulted in a severe diminution of his ability to use his skills and knowledge to participate in the Canadian economy. His wife, Jacqueline, has not been able to obtain permanent resident status after trying for more than 10 years. The stress of not obtaining permanent resident status, which barred her from many social services and prevented her from getting a job, led to serious mental anguish, resulting in a period of hospitalization. In the Congo, even poor people can enjoy a rich social support network, something that does not exist for Robert or Jacqueline in Calgary.

Fernando

Fernando Diaz is a 51-year-old pediatric surgeon who had been living in Calgary for three years and six months at the time the research project began. He, his wife, and two children fled Colombia to escape guerillas who had kidnapped his brother and demanded monthly extortion payments as a condition to leave his family alone. He was notified on a Friday by the Canadian embassy that he would have to leave Colombia for good the following Tuesday. Fernando had an excellent lifestyle in Colombia. He was a pediatric surgeon who had his own clinic in Colombia and had worked in four other clinics. He had a very high monthly income. His wife was a certified accountant and had her own business, doing assessments for various companies. Once in Calgary, Fernando sent his medical diplomas to Ottawa for an evaluation. He is still waiting for a response. He has also contacted the College of Physicians and Surgeons of Alberta and has received no help from them, other than being told that "we have enough physicians in Alberta," an assertion that is refuted by reliable data. In the meantime, he has been networking and talking to people in the medical field in Calgary to gain information about the licensure process. He was told that it might take him four to five years to get licensure, if he is lucky. He also found out that many immigrant

140 Thomas Ricento

physicians pass all the exams and are still not accepted for internships. There are only six surgeons in Calgary who perform the kind of surgeries that Fernando used to perform in Colombia (on newborn and prematurely born infants), yet the social capital that Fernando possesses is simply not recognized by gatekeepers who have their own agenda and reasons (mostly economic) for restricting access to the practice of medicine in the province (Bauder, 2003).

Fernando applied for various survival jobs, even cleaning jobs, but he could not get any, because he mentioned that he was a surgeon in Colombia. An advisor told him to say that he is only a high school graduate if he wants to get a survival job; otherwise, they will consider him overqualified. When asked by the research project interviewer, "What do you find negative about your life in Canada?" Fernando answered:

> *What I find negative of my life in Canada is the language barrier . . . In order to get recognition of my certificates as a Medical Surgeon, I am asked to fulfill so many difficult requirements. It is easier to win the lotto than to be accepted as a professional in Canada.*
>
> (September 30, 2010)

When he arrived in Canada, both Fernando and his 44-year-old wife had "level zero of English," although Fernando did have some English reading skills in his medical specialization. The classes he took in the LINC (Language Instruction for Newcomers to Canada) program were not appropriate for his needs, and he felt much of it was a waste of time. In various interviews, he provided quite specific comments about the English language instruction that was provided in the local LINC program. For example, he noted that the different needs, ages, and backgrounds of students should be taken into account in the development of courses and curricula: "For example, it is not the same to teach English to my mother, who is a senior of 78 years, than to teach to my children or myself, who have completely different ages, interests and background" (September 30, 2010). The obstacles that Fernando faces appear insurmountable. The likelihood that he will be able to get a license to practice medicine in Canada is extremely low. Physicians with medical degrees and licenses from the United Kingdom, the United States, South Africa, Australia, and New Zealand have far fewer barriers to gain medical licenses than do physicians from any other country, the result of bilateral agreements with medical licensing agencies, and the fact that the degrees were obtained in English-dominant countries. Fernando is frustrated by the lack of opportunities to interact with English-speaking Canadians, by the barriers to getting any type of job, and by the fact that the English classes he can enroll in are inappropriate for his language needs; in addition, he is also effectively blocked from many of the services and benefits that citizens take for granted that might help him improve his financial and social situation. These include the inability to get a credit card, and the inability to get credit from a local bank in order to start a business, since he does not have a job and has no credit history. Another source of frustration and an affront to his dignity is that Fernando's knowledge and experience as a highly trained surgeon is totally disregarded by the medical establishment in Calgary. For example, when his teenage daughter was taken by Fernando to the emergency floor of a local hospital, as a pediatric surgeon, he understood that her symptoms indicated a diagnosis of appendicitis, "and I told the doctor that she was having appendicitis and the doctor did not believe me; we brought her to the hospital at 8:00 a.m. and she was diagnosed and not taken to surgery until 1:00 a.m. the next day" (November 2, 2010). In Colombia:

> *If any of my children got sick, they were seen with priority by my colleagues. Here it is the opposite; my daughter has been sick for two weeks now and the doctor didn't prescribe anything; even though I know what her problem is, I cannot do anything because I cannot get the right drugs for her without a prescription; that makes the situation more difficult.*
>
> (December 9, 2010)

In both of these examples, it was not only a language barrier that frustrated Fernando, but rather the humiliation he experienced by the total erasure of his identity and expertise as a highly trained pediatric surgeon who only wanted to provide important information about his young daughter's medical condition.

With the modest financial support that the federal government provides to Fernando running out, with little prospect for obtaining a license to practice medicine of any type—let alone as a certified neonatal surgeon—with no ability to borrow money to start a small business (he has contemplated opening a restaurant), and with the language barrier still a major factor in all aspects of his daily life, including interactions with his children's teachers, Fernando has seriously considered returning to the dangers of Colombia rather than continuing to live under current conditions: "If I had imagined even 5 percent of this reality, I would rather have taken the risk of being killed over there [Colombia] rather than enduring the situation in which I find myself" (December 9, 2010). He has applied for positions in some hospitals in Panama City, and has even considered the possibility of volunteering for two weeks in Haiti in order to maintain his skills; but without money, he could not afford to go to Haiti. Even though returning to Colombia would involve a high risk of being kidnapped again or killed if he did not meet the ransom demands, Fernando reasoned:

> *Despite all of the dangers that we might face back in Colombia, I think that it is better to take that risk given all of the frustrations we have experienced here. At least we would have the opportunity to have our careers and a decent life in our country . . . The way we are living here we feel as if we have lost our dignity while we have to beg for help in order to survive.*
>
> (December 9, 2010)

142 Thomas Ricento

Despite being close to despair when we spoke with Fernando in December 2010, in our interview with him and his family on January 12, 2011, Fernando was much more upbeat about his prospects. He told us that he had the opportunity to speak with native English speakers and that he had improved his communication skills and had greater confidence:

> *I am not afraid anymore to go to do things by myself, like going to the bank or shopping at the supermarket, making a telephone call to an office or attending an appointment. I do it myself and am able to communicate in English 80 to 90 percent.*
> (January 12, 2011)

He is currently studying to become a pharmacy technician; his children are doing well in school and will likely attend university in Canada and their future prospects are bright. His wife continues to improve her English skills as well. Yet, Fernando's case is not the exception; there are tens of thousands of highly trained, highly educated refugees in Canada, like Fernando and his wife, who have escaped war, persecution, various types of physical abuse, and economic privation, and who have found that there is yet another sort of hidden price to be paid for living in a secure environment in a country in which their lack of appropriate language skills and non-transferable professional credentials severely curtail their ability to enjoy the "full blessings of liberty" that is the unquestioned birthright of citizens in liberal democracies, such as Canada. The term "dis-citizenship" aptly captures the "in between worlds" of refugees such as Fernando who have learned that the price to be paid for freedom and security may be far steeper than they had ever imagined possible.

Robert and Jacqueline

Robert and Jacqueline have lived in Canada for 17 years; prior to moving to Calgary in 2007, they had lived in Montreal, Quebec, for 14 years. Robert and his wife fled the Democratic Republic of the Congo (formerly Zaire) to escape the civil unrest that escalated into a devastating war. While he and his wife are grateful to be in Canada, they have had to endure extensive bureaucratic barriers to gaining permanent residence (for his wife, Jacqueline) and citizenship (for Robert). Lack of proficiency in English has contributed to other barriers in gaining work for both of them; for example, in the case of Robert, his experience as a small businessman in a developing, low-income country (Congo) is simply not recognized or valued in the formal, credentialed, and salaried economy of Canada, whereas Jacqueline cannot work because she lacks appropriate legal status, a situation that has been ongoing for 10 years, with no end in sight.

Before the civil unrest started, Robert was able to enjoy a decent lifestyle in the Congo. He rented a small house downtown and had his own business, selling vegetables and preparing fast food for restaurants (e.g. sandwiches). However, when

Refugees in Canada   **143**

the war started, things changed drastically. He saw people being killed in front of his eyes and dying of starvation. Due to the lack of safety and transportation, people could not even go to the hospital:

> *The great difficulties and challenges back home was war; before war . . . I could survive and there were not lots of difficulties. With small business in the street, like buying vegetables here and sell them there, you can live without any problem.*
>
> (August 30, 2010)

Robert's knowledge of Canada prior to his arrival was limited; yet he believed that as long as he could live in peace in a democratic country, he would be able to fulfill his dreams:

> *When I first heard about Canada I was at school . . . when you are still young, you have some kinds of dreams: I will become a doctor, I will go to this place or other. That is why I decided to travel (i.e. to leave the Congo when he was young, prior to the war there).*
>
> (August 30, 2010)

He came originally to Quebec mainly because, as a Francophone, he believed he and his wife would have more opportunity for education and a bright future. He became a permanent resident in 2001 and applied for citizenship in 2006; however, as he had moved to a new address, he did not get the papers from immigration, and did not learn until 2009 that they had been sent to his old address. He has reapplied and hopes to gain citizenship in the near future.

After he obtained permanent resident status in Quebec, he went to a technical college in Montreal and got a two-year degree in engineering. However, he was not able to get a job even after looking for five years; instead, he did odd jobs, working for various social services agencies that help families to readjust to life in Canada. The fact that he was a fluent Francophone living in the only Canadian province in which French is the *sole* official language did not "level the playing field" for him. As a visible minority, and as an "outsider," fluency in French did not provide any advantage. Eventually, he moved west to Alberta, hoping to find more opportunities to work in the field for which he was trained.

After three years in Calgary, Robert and his wife have been struggling, living on $900 per month[5] for all expenses, well below the official poverty level; they also depend on a local food bank to make ends meet. While Robert and Jacqueline both appreciate the safety and security that living in Calgary affords, and believe in the principle that everyone should be treated equally and fairly, their status as refugees limits their access to the kinds of benefits, services, and job opportunities that citizens, especially native-born Canadians, expect and take for granted. They do not like being dependent on government support and charity

144 Thomas Ricento

in order to survive. Robert has continued to try to find work that will enable him to support himself and his wife:

> *I tried to do my best, like renting a big truck and look for a market in transportation companies, work by myself, but it was very difficult. I contacted DHL, FED EX . . . it was very difficult . . . rent a car for $1,500, gas, insurance. I could not afford all those things . . . Now my future life in Canada, I am still looking for it . . .*
> (October 7, 2010)

The stress of their circumstances contributed to hospitalization for Jacqueline, who had been experiencing psychological problems; as Robert recounted:

> *When she [Jacqueline] arrived here [in Montreal], immigration said that you cannot get papers except your kids and husband that sponsored you, but the sponsorship doesn't count, so she had to wait. It is stressful if you don't have papers. We tried even to get a lawyer who can intervene so that she can at least get a health card, but that doesn't work . . . These [events] caused my wife to be disturbed mentally and she got admitted for mental problems to the hospital due to the stress.*
> (October 7, 2010)

Eventually, thanks to the intervention of the Women's Association in Calgary, Jacqueline was able to get her Alberta healthcare card. However, she has yet to receive her permanent resident card 10 years after applying for it, and she has no idea when she will get it:

> *Sometimes when I make a call [to the immigration authorities] they say that my case is pending, just be patient . . . so I don't know how long it is going to take . . .*
> (August 30, 2010)

> *Without permanent residence, I am nothing, I don't have any rights . . . because I am not in social service, I don't have a right to get a lawyer or a judge . . . I don't have a right to work and I never apply for it.*
> (November 23, 2010)

Another resource that was available in Congo that is not available in Canada is the social network and community support system that enabled Robert and Jacqueline to persevere during difficult times in their lives. As Jacqueline described it:

> *In the country [Congo] even if there is poverty, there is also something better, like living in that society. There, people are not closed in their houses, not like here where you are like isolated and like you are living alone. But there, all people are outside, either you have or don't have food, but you are outside; sometimes*

somebody has a potato in his hand, he can give it to you, and everybody say "hi" and how are you doing, whether you know him or her or you don't, and if you are sick you will say "No, I am not doing well," and that person will inform any person he or she will meet and say "I said hi to someone and he or she said that I am sick"; everyone will come and say "We heard that you are sick," and if you don't have foods, they will bring them. Moreover, if you have kids, you cannot suffer. You can leave the kids to anybody who is available there. We don't have daycare because we can't pay for it.

(August 30, 2010)

Because free ESL classes are available through the LINC program only to immigrants who have permanent resident status, and Jacqueline is ineligible, she cannot study English, nor can she work. As Robert rather succinctly put it: "You are like in an open prison. You see others living, but you are not living. As soon as you are living that situation, it finally makes you sick" (October 7, 2010). Robert also noted that some people who arrive in Canada illegally, circumventing the legal processes, are able to stay in the country, while he and his wife have played by the rules and are still in limbo. When they hired a lawyer, he took their money and went to France. Without financial resources to hire another lawyer, with difficulties in communicating effectively with bureaucrats in Edmonton (location of the provincial capital in Alberta) and Ottawa (the federal capital city) orally or through e-mail, and without social support networks that they had been accustomed to in their home country to provide psychological and social support, the freedom and security of Canada offers little solace. Asked how he hoped his life in Canada would be 10 years from now, Robert replied:

I expect to have peace, I expect to get a job, take care of my kids, open their own accounts. I don't worry because I am still alive . . . If you don't have a job, you don't have peace. I remember when I was in Montreal, my wife got sick and I decided to quit my job, so that I could take care of my kids; with that condition, you don't have peace. All that is caused by immigration . . . that stresses us and is affecting our whole family, it keeps us in poverty . . . you cannot move forward.

(October 7, 2010)

Conclusion

When people move across national borders in search of better economic and social opportunities, often traversing great distances, it is inevitable that they will face many challenges. With regard to matters of language, Blommaert (2010) notes that:

Movement of people across space is . . . never a move across empty spaces. The spaces are always someone's space, and they are filled with norms,

146 Thomas Ricento

> expectations, conceptions of what counts as proper and normal (indexical) language use and what does not count as such.
>
> (p. 6)

Those who move from a place in which their language is dominant to a place in which it is not dominant, or even recognized, will find their identity and status challenged in unexpected ways (Blommaert, 2008). These observations apply in the cases of Fernando, Robert, and Jacqueline whose deficiencies in English have impacted their ability to integrate into mainstream Anglophone Canadian society. However, while language proficiency is an important index of one's social capital in a particular time and place, what counts as proper and normal educational, professional, and experiential capital in those spaces is also dependent on the norms, expectations, and conceptions of the people who already inhabit those places, and especially those people with the authority to adjudicate the value of credentials and the worthiness of life histories that may fall outside the normal patterns and expectations.

Limitations of space prevent me from providing additional details about the lives of Fernando, Robert, and Jacqueline and their encounters with school system bureaucracies, housing, and transportation issues, along with many other challenges, and how their current disempowered status has affected their children's lives. Nonetheless, the details provided convey the essential point of this chapter, which has been to illustrate the ways in which the involuntary diminution of social capital all three have experienced has contributed to a sense of powerlessness in their respective lives, severely limiting possible and realistic paths to a normal life that each had hoped to recapture in moving to Canada. Their resilience in the face of adversity speaks to their strength of character that has enabled them to maintain hope when despair seemed like the only possible option. The governments (federal and provincial) of Canada have provided them with at least some resources and opportunities to improve their situation,[6] but what these refugees require more than government aid is broader societal recognition and validation of their considerable skills, training, and experiences so that they can become fully engaged citizens in Canada, with the same rights and responsibilities as other citizens, which includes equal access to employment and the social goods and services that their earned social capital should entitle them to.

Notes

1. Citizenship is a legal designation as well as a generic term for persons living in a geographical area. However, a person's legal status (e.g. temporary worker, undocumented "alien," permanent resident) may contribute to a person's sense of alienation and of dis-citizenship (Ramanathan, 2012), along with various forms of marginalization and possible disengagement with the host society.
2. For example, in the United States, affirmative action policies have been used to remedy historical patterns of discrimination against persons based on race, gender, or national origin.

3. In fact, these are the credentials held by Fernando Diaz (a pseudonym), a 51-year-old pediatric surgeon, who had been living in Calgary for three years and six months at the time the research project on refugees in Calgary began.
4. I am unable to provide the identity of this person because he requested that I not use his name or affiliation due to fears that his family in Colombia would be at risk.
5. This is the amount provided to them by the federal government.
6. For example, permanent residents in Canada are eligible for 1,200 hours of free ESL instruction for a period of three years.

References

Abu-Laban, B., Derwing, T., Krahn, H., Mulder, M., & Wilkinson, L. (1999). *The settlement experiences of refugees in Alberta*. Prairie Centre of Excellence for Research on Immigration and Integration and Population Research Laboratory. Retrieved from: http://pcerii.metropolis.net/Virtual%20Library/RefugeeStudy/ (accessed March 13, 2009).

Akabari, A. H. (1999). Immigrant "quality" in Canada: More direct evidence of human capital content. *International Migration Review, 33*, 156–175.

Bauder, H. (2003). "Brain abuse," or the devaluation of immigrant labour in Canada. *Antipode, 35*(4), 699–717.

Blommaert, J. (2008). *Grassroots literacy: Writing, identity and voice in Central Africa*. New York: Routledge.

Blommaert, J. (2010). *The sociolinguistics of globalization*. Cambridge: Cambridge University Press.

Bloom, D. E., Grenier, G., & Gunderson, M. (1995). The changing labour market position of Canadian immigrants. *Canadian Journal of Economics, XXVIII*(4b), 987–1001.

Collins, R. (1979). *The credential society: A historical sociology of education and stratification*. New York: Academic Press.

Hiebert, D. (1999). Local geographies of labor market segmentation: Montreal, Toronto, and Vancouver, 199. *Economic Geography, 75*, 339–369.

Lin, N. (2000). Inequality in social capital. *Contemporary Sociology, 29*(6), 785–795.

Martin, F., & Curran, J. (2007). Separated children: A comparison of the treatment of separated child refugees entering Australia and Canada. *International Journal of Refugee Law, 19*(4), 440–470.

Pendakur, K., & Pendakur, R. (1998). The colour of money: Wage differentials across ethnic groups. *Canadian Journal of Economics, 31*, 518–548.

Pruebber, V. J., & Tanasescu, A. (2007). *Housing issues of immigrants and refugees in Canada*. Retrieved from: www.calgary.ca/docgallery/bu/cns/homelessness/housing_issues_immigrants_refugees.pdf (accessed March 14, 2009).

Ramanathan, V. (2012). *Language policy and (dis)citizenship: Rights, access, pedagogies*. Bristol, UK: Multilingual Matters.

Reitz, J. G. (2001a). Immigrant skill utilization in the Canadian labour market: Implications of human capital research. *Journal of International Migration and Integration, 2*, 347–378.

Reitz, J. G. (2001b). Immigrant success in the knowledge economy: Institutional change and the immigrant experience in Canada, 1970–1995. *Journal of Social Issues, 57*, 579–613.

Schellenberg, G., & Maheux, H. (2007). Immigrants' perspectives on their first four years in Canada: Highlights from three waves of the Longitudinal Survey of Immigrants to Canada. *Statistics Canada*. Retrieved from: www.statcan.gc.ca/bsolc/olc-cel/olc-cel?lang=eng&catno=11-008-X20070009627 (accessed March 16, 2009).

PART 3

Personalizing the Public Space

11

LINGUISTIC LANDSCAPES INSIDE MULTILINGUAL SCHOOLS

Durk Gorter and Jasone Cenoz

Introduction: Linguistic Landscape Studies in Educational Settings

The functions of signage in multilingual education are the point of departure of this chapter. In the last years, the study of the use of languages on signs has focused on public spaces (Hélot, Barni, Janssens, & Bagna, 2012; Marten, Van Mensel, & Gorter, 2012; Shohamy, Ben-Rafael, & Barni, 2010; Shohamy & Gorter, 2009). Numerous researchers have investigated various aspects of multilingualism of the "decorum of the city walls." Investigations of institutional contexts, such as government buildings, libraries, museums, prisons, hospitals, laboratories, universities, or schools, are a possible future direction in linguistic landscape studies. Shohamy and Waksman (2009) point to education as one possible social institution for further promising linguistic landscape research. They argue for the use of linguistic landscape "as a powerful tool for education, meaningful language learning, [and] towards activism" (p. 326). The domain of education deserves to be treated in more depth because it has various implications for the study of the linguistic landscapes, in particular in areas where more than one language is taught and used. Studies of the signage of educational institutions can lead to a better understanding of what goes on inside the schools, and as such can also contribute to education research.

This chapter reports on a study of the linguistic landscape in schools in the Basque Country. We will first describe several earlier studies of the linguistic landscape related to education that inspired us to conduct the current study. Thereafter, we will briefly summarize the main characteristics of multilingual education in the Basque Autonomous Community in Spain in order to contextualize our discussion. In the main section, we present the design and main

152 Durk Gorter and Jasone Cenoz

outcomes of a study we carried out in a number of multilingual schools, where Basque, Spanish, and English are taught, which explored the functions, distribution, and authorship of the signs on the schools' walls. We summarize by drawing some conclusions on linguistic landscape research in educational contexts.

Linguistic Landscapes in Educational Contexts

Applying linguistic landscape as a pedagogical tool can be of great relevance to educators and students. For Shohamy and Waksman (2009), the linguistic landscape can be a "rich context for learning about the ways in which meanings are constructed and manipulated using a variety of devices" (p. 326). They utilize one specific linguistic landscape site, the *Haapala* in Tel Aviv, Israel, as an example of the possibilities of their approach. This site in public space is a resource "for in-depth learning about cultural and historical meaning" (p. 328). They clearly demonstrate that linguistic landscape items in public space have an educational function. Languages displayed in public space can also be useful for learning second languages as we concluded in a study of possibilities of signage for second language acquisition (SLA) (Cenoz & Gorter, 2008; Gorter & Cenoz, 2007). We looked at the potential use of language on signs in public space as a source of input in SLA in general, as well as in the acquisition of pragmatic competence in particular. Following Landry and Bourhis (1997), we considered the symbolic and informative functions of the linguistic landscape, and demonstrated that the texts used on signage can function as authentic input and can also enhance language awareness.

An interesting application of linguistic landscape ideas serving an educational purpose was carried out by Dagenais, Moore, Sabatier, Lamarre, and Armand (2009). In their study, they asked students in elementary schools in Vancouver and Montreal to document the linguistic landscape of their urban environment by means of disposable cameras. The project is relevant because it demonstrates that the linguistic landscape can be a possible way for teaching about language diversity and literacy practices from a critical perspective. In the politically and linguistically loaded context of Quebec, as well as in the socially diverse urban environment of Vancouver, the linguistic landscape can be a powerful educational tool. Children can understand the sociopolitical context where they live via their own investigations of the linguistic landscape in public space. A similar didactic strategy was examined by Clemente, Andrade, and Martins (2012) in a Portuguese primary school in a project called "learning to read the world, learning to look at the linguistic landscape." The researchers emphasized the importance of understanding the attitudes toward diversity and how linguistic and cultural competences can be developed through education, showing that the children achieved the ability to recognize and read the linguistic landscape.

Students also acted as language investigators in the research project by Sayer (2010) in Oaxaca, Mexico. For him, the linguistic landscape can serve as a pedagogical resource in the EFL classroom, where he used public signs to analyze the social meanings of English. The students' activities connect language in the streets to the language of the classroom. He looked into the purposes of the signs, the intended audiences, and different meanings of English on signs. He argued that a linguistic landscape project allows students to think creatively and critically about language. In a similar study, Rowland (2012) asked students to collect and analyze photographs of English as used on public signs, such as advertisements and road signs in Japan. These then find their way into L2 classrooms, used particularly for teaching English as a second language (ESL). He supports the idea that pedagogical linguistic landscape projects can be valuable to EFL students, particularly in the development of students' symbolic competence and literacy skills. Similarly, Hancock (2012) described a project where student teachers become researchers of the linguistic landscape. The students in Edinburgh, UK, took part in a "camera safari" to engage them in thinking about the multilingual community in which they live. Thus, the linguistic landscape is used as an awareness-raising technique "in order to prepare student teachers for the reality of multilingual schools" (p. 255).

In two other studies, researchers explored the linguistic landscape within an educational institution. Hanauer (2009) investigated the language posted in various places in a microbiology laboratory, which is part of a project where high school and undergraduate students are integrated in the process of learning about microbiological inquiry. He points out that the signs of the linguistic landscape on the laboratory walls are used for two functions: (1) facilitating a flow of knowledge throughout the laboratory; and (2) enhancing the procedural aspects of conducting scientific inquiry. He thus shows how the linguistic landscape promotes scientific and educational aims at the same time. In another study, Brown (2012) analyzed the re-emergence of the regional language of Võru inside "school spaces" based on anthropological fieldwork in Estonia. Local communities were formerly largely invisible in formal education due to the long absence of the regional language from schools, but now the schools provide a context of revitalization of the minority language. For Brown, the school space is a central but contested linguistic landscape where language ideologies are officially sanctioned and socially supported. The research includes signs in the classrooms but also in the entrance, foyer, and corridors, as well as in a school museum and in the curriculum. The two central themes of her "schoolscapes" are, on the one hand, the regional language as the enricher of national culture, and, on the other, the regional language as an historical artifact. The contested symbolic space of school leads to delicate negotiations over the reintroduction of the Võro language in the public schools. In our study of the Basque Country, we also consider the linguistic landscape as it is present inside the educational context itself. We have not involved teachers or students directly, but rather studied the signage inside the schools similar to the way we studied the linguistic landscape in public space (Cenoz & Gorter, 2006; Gorter, Aiestaran, & Cenoz, 2012).

154 Durk Gorter and Jasone Cenoz

Multilingual Education in the Basque Country

Multilingual education can be defined as the use of two or more languages in education provided that schools aim at multilingualism and multiliteracy (Cenoz, 2012). In the Basque Country, this implies the teaching and using of the three languages Basque, Spanish, and English, and in a few schools also French or German. The linguistic landscape inside the Basque schools that we investigate in this study has to be seen against the background of an educational system that went through an important transition with regard to the languages used in the schools. Over a period of 30 years, the Basque regional government has developed a robust policy of promotion of the Basque language. When the policy started in the late 1970s, Spanish was the dominant language in the education system, and less than 5 percent of all teachers were able to teach through the medium of Basque (Gardner, 2000). Teachers were given the opportunity for language study on a large scale, resulting in a rise in the percentage of qualified teachers, which currently reaches up to over 85 percent. Another policy outcome is that, nowadays, Basque is a language of instruction in over two-thirds of pre-primary, primary, and secondary schools (see also Cenoz, 2009).

The most prominent model is the D-model, where Basque is the medium of instruction and Spanish is taught for three or four hours per week. The schools also teach English from an early age onward (3 or 4 years) for a few hours a week, and many schools use English as a medium of instruction for one subject, such as history or social sciences. Education is thus multilingual because three languages are taught at the same time when society is becoming more multilingual, not only because of the spread of English, but also because of the arrival of immigrants from Latin America, Africa, and Eastern European countries. Almost 7 percent of the population are immigrants (INE, 2012), and those speakers of different languages create new challenges for schools that already teach three languages (Gorter, Zenotz, Etxague, & Cenoz, 2014).

Schools in the Basque Autonomous Community are very similar to schools anywhere in the world. A typical classroom is filled with desks and chairs, usually in neat rows, and the blackboard has a central place. The walls of a typical classroom can be full of signs with texts, can have just a few signs, or be empty. What we found in the Basque Country was a big difference between primary and secondary schools. In primary schools, there was usually a much higher density of signs, compared with secondary schools. This observation was confirmed by looking at linguistic landscapes inside schools in similar minority language areas in Friesland, the Netherlands, and in Wales.

Linguistic Landscapes in Basque Schools: An Explorative Study

Research Questions

In the first place, we wanted to find out about the use of the different languages in the signage in the schools. What functions do the signs have, and which languages are used for different functions? We also wanted to look at the distribution of the languages in the linguistic landscape of the schools. How often are the different school languages used, and in which combinations of languages? Finally, we wondered about the authors of the signs. Are they put up by the school authorities, or are the signs placed by the teachers or the students (top-down versus bottom-up signs)?

Methods and Data

We visited a total of seven different schools; of those, three are located in the city of Donostia-San Sebastián and four in surrounding smaller towns. During our school visits, we tried to obtain a reasonably complete overview of the signs in a school. We took pictures of the inside of the classrooms visited, but also of the corridors, other rooms (e.g. the library), and the immediate surroundings (in particular the school yard and the school front, e.g. its name). We coded 534 photographs of signs as identifiable units of analysis in our SPSS database (for the methodology, see Cenoz & Gorter, 2006).

Functions of Signs

The findings show that languages are used in different ways with different aims. Our analysis reveals the different communicative intentions conveyed by the texts. We broadly differentiate between an informative and a symbolic function of the signs (Landry & Bourhis, 1997), but we wanted to make a finer distinction, and thus we distinguish between nine different functions (see Table 11.1), as presented by the examples below.

We begin by looking into signs that are *informative*, and distinguishing three different uses.

1. Teaching content or language. One of the most obvious functions of the language used in the signs on the wall is to use them as a teaching aid. The use of the

TABLE 11.1 Functions of the signage inside the multilingual Basque schools

Functions	
1. Teaching of languages and subject content	Informative
2. Classroom management	Informative
3. School management	Informative
4. Teaching values	Symbolic
5. Development of intercultural awareness	Symbolic
6. Promotion of the Basque language	Symbolic
7. Announcing collective events	Informative and symbolic
8. Provision of commercial information	Informative and symbolic
9. Decoration	Informative and symbolic

156 Durk Gorter and Jasone Cenoz

language in the linguistic landscape inside a classroom can be part of a lesson plan, and will be employed as such by the teacher. Some signs are produced as learning materials and others are an extension of other materials. Maps are an example of a learning aid for geography that can be used for localizing a place. A nice example of the use of language on a sign as teaching material is given in Figure 11.1. The sign contains a short overview of music notation. A student can use the poster when given the task about music in class.

In our database, we found several other signs with similar language learning content.

2. Classroom management. An informative function is also carried out by signs that inform the students about how to behave toward their fellow students. These signs are intended to inform and remind the children about the dos and don'ts at school. They establish rules of etiquette. The example in Figure 11.2 provides a list (in Basque) that includes norms of behavior such as "do not hit or pull hairs," "do not shout," or "take good care of materials." We note that the handwriting is probably by the teacher. This list has 17 similar rules, and each child in the class has signed the rules to show their commitment and intention of living up to these rules. We call this the function of classroom management.

Other examples of classroom management can be name tags on shelves to indicate the location of materials, or to indicate students' ownership of a specific space.

3. School management. A third function is of a more general nature. There are signs that inform their readers, students, teachers, or visitors about locations: for example, designations of classroom functions (Figure 11.3; *zuzendaritza* = directorate, *idazkaritza* = secretariat), instructions to knock before entering (Figure 11.4; *atea jo eta sartu* = knock on the door and enter), or guides to what is located on which floor of the school building (Figure 11.5; *Salbatore Mitxelena Ikastola* is the name of the school, and the plaque indicates what is on each of the three floors = *solairua*).

These signs do not have a symbolic load, but they provide the reader, in straightforward terms, with information for orientation. They are intended as guides for visitors (or new students or teachers) rather than for the practicing teachers or students who are familiar with this information. They facilitate the flow of people through the school building (similar to the function identified by Hanauer, 2009). In quantitative terms, a great part of the signs could be classified as providing this type of general information.

A second broad category of signs can be characterized as *symbolic*, a less frequent category, which can also be useful as teaching materials. We distinguished three functions that are predominately symbolic.

4. Teaching values. There are signs that are used to bring a pedagogical message across to the students about values. One example was the slogan "*geroa alferraren leloa*" in Basque, which means "Later is the slogan of the lazy." In this school, the signs were written on the wall as a constant reminder to the students.

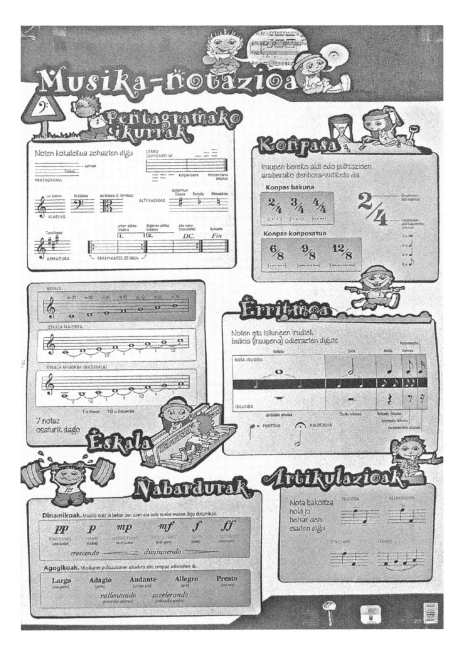

FIGURE 11.1 Example of teaching (music notation) through signage

- Ezin da jo eta iletik tira.
- Ezin da oihukatu.
- Hitz itsusirik ez dugu esango.
- Ez dugu burlatuko ez eta zirikatuko
- Gelan, pasiloan eta eskaileretan ezin da korrika egin.
- Baloia, pilota eta beste jostailuekin patioan bakarrik jolastuko dugu.
- Ezin dugu triklerik edo gozokirik jan.
- Txokoetan lan egingo dugu, eta ez jolastu eta kideak molestatu.
- Ondo portatuko gara eta irakasleei kasu egingo diegu.
- 2. mailakoek 1go mailakoei lagunduko die.
- Ez dugu inor bultzatuko.
- Lerroan isilik egongo gara.
- Antzokia antzerpenak egiteko bakarrik erabiliko dugu.
- Materiala ondo zainduko dugu.
- Mahaiak eta aulkiak ez ditugu marraztuko.
- Besteen lanak errespetatuko ditugu.
- Haserretzen garenean arnasa hartu eta lasaituko gara.

FIGURE 11.2 Example of classroom management through signage (arauak = rules)

FIGURES 11.3–11.5 Example of guiding signage (directorate/secretariat; knock on the door and enter; plate with explanation of the floors of the school building)

160 Durk Gorter and Jasone Cenoz

FIGURE 11.6 Example of teaching values through signage (translation from Basque: "Later is the slogan of the lazy")

This particular school had several pedagogical slogans written on the walls of the corridors, but we also found some similar "moral messages" in other schools.

5. *Developing intercultural awareness.* Other signs are related to the presence of immigrant children in the school. One example is in Figure 11.7. The sign says "*Ongi etorri*" (which is Basque for "welcome"), and then also the words for "welcome" in different languages (surrounded by the flags of the countries where the children are from). The presence of these words on the walls is a daily reminder for all the children of the diversity among the school population. The idea is to contribute to greater intercultural understanding among the children, and probably the teachers.

Other signs in this category reported on a field trip to another country, including details of its different culture, or work done by the students on different cultural celebrations.

FIGURE 11.7 Example of teaching intercultural awareness through signage

LL in Multilingual Schools **161**

6. Raising awareness about the Basque language. A special aspect of the schools in the Basque Autonomous Community is, of course, the minority position of the Basque language. We found several signs that represent a reference to efforts on behalf of the revitalization of the Basque language and culture so as to raise the awareness of the minority position of Basque or the efforts for the safeguarding of the language. It demonstrates a reflection in the schoolscape of the contested nature of the language in society, similar to Brown's (2012) notions, although Basque is in a different phase than Võru. A clear example is the handwritten slogan "*Guk euskaraz, zuk zergaitik ez?*" which can be translated as "We use Basque, why don't you?" (Figure 11.8).

Other signs refer to the use of Euskara for the future. The function of these signs is to make the students even more aware of the value of the minority language. They are a constant reminder of the endangered situation of Basque.

The last three functions we distinguish were found on signs that are not only informative or symbolic, but both.

7. Announcing collective events (non-commercial). Signs about events that would take place in the town, such as a theater play or a musical performance, were found on announcement boards. This included events that are specific for the promotion of the Basque language. The banner in Figure 11.9 was hanging on the facade of the school, and it announces the *Korrika*, an annual relay run that spans a distance of about 2,500 kilometers in which about 600,000 people

FIGURE 11.8 Example of stimulating Basque language awareness (translation: "We use Basque, why don't you?")

FIGURE 11.9 Example of announcing an event to support the Basque language

participate. Money is collected by selling each kilometer to an organization or individual to fund projects that support the use of Basque language (www.korrika.org).

Brown (2012) called these types of signs a reminder of the regional language as enricher of the culture.

8. *Provision of commercial information.* A small number of signs were related to commercial information from outside organizations or businesses, such as advertisements, similar to what one can find in the public space. However, the advertisements found inside the schools are not exactly of the same type or with the same diversity as in shopping streets, since all are related to education. There are examples of posters to prepare for commercial English language exams, because almost half of all secondary school students in the Basque Autonomous Community go to private English classes outside school hours (ISEI-IVEI, 2012, p. 114). It can also be an advertisement made by the students themselves for a fair inside the school, as in Figure 11.10.

9. *Decoration.* The final function we identify here is decoration. The purpose is perhaps more aesthetic than informative or symbolic. Of course, the choice of these decorative signs can also provide some insight into the messages that are implied, an indirect pedagogical device through which learning can be activated. Sometimes they are reproductions of famous paintings or announcements of museums, but quite often the materials produced by the students are also used for decorative purposes of the corridors, as can be seen in Figures 11.11 and 11.12. They can also be subsequently used by a teacher for instructional purposes.

By proving this open list of functions, we tried to give insight into the diversity of the linguistic landscape and the different communicative intentions present.

FIGURE 11.10 Example of advertisement (made by students about selling tortilla and pintxos)

Quantitative Distribution of Languages on Signs

We wanted to find out how multilingualism is reflected in the linguistic landscape of the schools, in particular because Basque, Spanish, and English are the languages taught in the schools. We know from previous studies in the Basque Country with a similar quantitative approach (Aiestaran, Cenoz, & Gorter, 2010; Cenoz & Gorter, 2006) that the linguistic landscape of public spaces is neither simply a reflection of the language composition of the population, nor of the proficiency or use of the different languages in a society. The distributive approach can give us some valuable insights in the constellation and the dynamics of languages.

First, we looked at the *number* of languages on each of the signs: how many are monolingual, bilingual, or multilingual? Of all the signs included in our sample, we found that a large majority were monolingual signs (see Table 11.2). The other signs were either bilingual (about one in six), and only a few were multilingual, with three or more languages. This demonstrates a rather large difference in comparison with the public space. For example, in one of our studies of the main shopping street of Donostia-San Sebastián, we found that 45 percent of the signs were monolingual, 37 percent bilingual, and 19 percent multilingual (Cenoz & Gorter, 2006, p. 72).

We subsequently looked at *which* languages were used. Because these schools have Basque as a medium of instruction, it is not surprising, as can be seen in

FIGURE 11.11 Example of decoration (wall poster made by a student)

LL in Multilingual Schools **165**

FIGURE 11.12 Example of decoration (corridor with posters made by students)

TABLE 11.2 Number of languages on signs inside the schools

Number of languages	Percentage (N = 534)
One	82%
Two	15%
Three or more	3%

Table 11.3, that Basque is the most common language used on 70 percent of all signs (monolingual and bi/multilingual signs combined). Spanish comes out second: it is used on 25 percent of all signs (monolingual and bi/multilingual signs combined). English figures on 16 percent of the signs on its own. The difference between the occurrence of Spanish and English is a bit of a surprise, given the dominant position of Spanish in society. In public space, Basque does not dominate in the same way, as only 12 percent of signs were monolingual in Basque and in combination with Spanish, English, or other languages. In total, Basque was present on just over 50 percent of all signs in the street. Spanish, in contrast, was on 36 percent of the signs on its own and had a total presence of 74 percent (Cenoz & Gorter, 2006, p. 73). Inside the schools, we also found

166 Durk Gorter and Jasone Cenoz

TABLE 11.3 Which languages are used on signs

Language	%
Basque only	58
Basque with Spanish or other language(s)	12
Spanish only	9
Spanish with Basque or other language(s)	16
English only	16
English with Basque, Spanish, or other language(s)	2
Other languages (e.g. Arabic, French)	3

some signs in other languages; most of those were in French or Arabic, and we also came upon incidences of Danish, Gaelic, and Chinese.

We also looked at the characteristics of the *multilingual* signs on their own to see how the different languages were represented. It turns out that half of the signs (53 percent) are bilingual with both languages represented equally. On one-third (31 percent) of the bilingual or multilingual signs, Basque is the most prominent language. On the remainder of the signs, the most prominent language is Spanish (6 percent), English (3 percent), or another combination of languages (5 percent). We can conclude that the bilingual and multilingual signs confirm the predominant position of Basque in the linguistic landscape of the schools.

Authorship of Signs

Our third research question concerns the classification of the signs in the school settings according to authorship. It turns out that the distinction between top-down and bottom-up is useful (Ben-Rafael, Shohamy, Amara, & Trumper-Hecht, 2006; Shohamy, 2006a), but at the same time, the dichotomy has to be qualified. We do find signs that have an obvious top-down character because they have been provided by the (regional) government. Examples are the sign plates that designate the name or function of the rooms (library, computer room, video room; see Figure 11.3). These name plates were the same, or very similar, in a number of schools, and they are standardized in terms of letters, colors, size, etc. The school directorate is another authority that decides top-down on several signs inside the school (such as the guiding signage in Figure 11.4). We also find materials that have been produced outside the school, as the example of the poster by a commercial publisher. Those can be considered top-down signs because they must be allowed or even hung by the school authorities or a teacher.

Quite a lot of signage material is produced by students during classwork, more in primary than in secondary school. These signs, produced by the students, can be characterized as bottom-up. Such signs are different from the ones produced by the authorities, even though most of those students would be inspired and controlled by their teachers (as in Figure 11.11). It seems that few signs were posted by teachers on their own, but some were obviously posted in combination with the students, such as the list of rules in Figure 11.2.

Conclusions

Our analysis reveals different communicative intentions conveyed by the texts on the signs in the schools. The linguistic landscape is a web of significances where languages are used in different ways, conveying different meanings and with different aims in mind. Some of the functions we identified are the teaching of subject content and language, the development of an intercultural awareness, the teaching of values, or establishing behavioral rules, but also providing practical guidance and commercial information. The signs can be a reminder of different cultures present among the students or a daily message to educate the children to behave in specific ways. Signs give directions or information about the function of a room, while others are related to the selling of a product or a service. We also observed signs that tell the students the dos and don'ts of their school life, and, taken together, we demonstrated that linguistic landscape can be used during lessons by the teachers.

Our study shows that Basque, the main language of instruction, has the most prominent role in the schoolscape, but other languages are not excluded. The study also shows that signs can be monolingual or multilingual, and that there are differences between signs in the public space and inside schools. By taking into consideration the earlier studies we carried out in the Basque Autonomous Community, we observed that the educational sphere has characteristics that are different from the public space. The multilingual signage probably also contributes to the multilingual competence of the students (Gorter, 2013). It also turned out that the signs produced by the students have a specific character, different from signs produced by authorities. Many student signs were obviously temporary and on display as the result of some specific activity, and only a few seemed to be posted by teachers. The fixed signs are those that are more often posted by the school authorities or the government.

Schools are meant to prepare students for the real world, and thus have to reflect a multilingual reality (Shohamy, 2006b). We have to make space for people, and the linguistic landscape inside schools can play an important role, because, as Shohamy (2006a) concludes, "language *is* like life" (p. 173, original emphasis).

Acknowledgement

We would like to acknowledge the funding by the Basque government for the Donostia Research Group on Multilingualism and Education (DREAM IT-714-13; UFI 11/54) and by the Spanish government (EDU 2012-32191).

References

Aiestaran, J., Cenoz, J., & Gorter, D. (2010). Multilingual cityscapes: Perceptions and preferences of the inhabitants of the city of Donostia-San Sebastián. In E. Shohamy, E. Ben-Rafael, & M. Barni (Eds.), *Linguistic landscape in the city* (pp. 219–234). Bristol, UK: Multilingual Matters.

Ben-Rafael, E., Shohamy, E., Amara, M. H., & Trumper-Hecht, N. (2006). Linguistic landscape as symbolic construction of the public space: The case of Israel. In D. Gorter (Ed.), *Linguistic landscape: A new approach to multilingualism* (pp. 7–30). Bristol, UK: Multilingual Matters.

Brown, K. D. (2012). The linguistic landscape of educational spaces: Language revitalization and schools in southeastern Estonia. In D. Gorter, H. F. Marten, & L. Van Mensel (Eds.), *Minority languages in the linguistic landscape* (pp. 281–298). Basingstoke: Palgrave-McMillan.

Cenoz, J. (2009). *Towards multilingual education: Basque educational research from an international perspective*. Bristol, UK: Multilingual Matters.

Cenoz, J. (2012). *Bilingual and multilingual education: Overview. The Encyclopedia of Applied Linguistics*. Hoboken, NJ: Wiley.

Cenoz, J., & Gorter, D. (2006). Linguistic landscape and minority languages. *International Journal of Multilingualism, 3*(1), 67–80.

Cenoz, J., & Gorter, D. (2008). Linguistic landscape as an additional source of input in second language acquisition. *International Review of Applied Linguistics in Language Teaching, 46*, 257–276.

Clemente, M., Andrade, A. I., & Martins, F. (2012). Learning to read the world, learning to look at the linguistic landscape: a primary school study. In C. Hélot, M. Barni, R. Janssens, & C. Bagna (Eds.), *Linguistic landscapes, multilingualism and social change* (pp. 267–285). Frankfurt: Peter Lang.

Dagenais, D., Moore, D., Sabatier, C., Lamarre, P., & Armand, F. (2009). Linguistic landscape and language awareness. In E. Shohamy & D. Gorter (Eds.), *Linguistic landscape: Expanding the scenery* (pp. 253–269). New York: Routledge.

Gardner, N. (2000). *Basque in education in the Basque autonomous community*. Vitoria-Gasteiz: Eusko Jaurlaritza.

Gorter, D. (2013). Multilingual interaction and minority languages: Proficiency and language practices in education and society. *Language Teaching* (first view article), 1–17. Available on CJO: DOI:10.1017/S0261444812000481.

Gorter, D., & Cenoz, J. (2007). Knowledge about language and linguistic landscape. In N. H. Hornberger (Chief Ed.), *Encyclopedia of language and education* (2nd ed.) (pp. 1–13). Berlin: Springer Science.

Gorter, D., Aiestaran, J., & Cenoz, J. (2012). The revitalization of Basque and the linguistic landscape of Donostia-San Sebastián. In D. Gorter, H. F. Marten, & L. Van Mensel (Eds.), *Minority languages in the linguistic landscape* (pp. 148–163). Basingstoke: Palgrave MacMillan.

Gorter, D., Zenotz, V., Etxague, X., & Cenoz, J. (2014). Multilingualism and European minority languages: The case of Basque. In D. Gorter, V. Zenotz, & J. Cenoz (Eds.), *Minority languages and multilingual education: Bridging the local and the global* (pp. 278–301). Berlin: Springer.

Hanauer, D. I. (2009). Science and the linguistic landscape: A genre analysis of representational wall space in a microbiology laboratory. In E. Shohamy & D. Gorter (Eds.), *Linguistic landscape: Expanding the scenery* (pp. 287–301). New York: Routledge.

Hancock, A. (2012). Capturing the linguistic landscape of Edinburgh: A pedagogical tool to investigate student teachers' understandings of cultural and linguistic diversity. In C. Hélot, M. Barni, R. Janssens, & C. Bagna (Eds.), *Linguistic landscapes, multilingualism and social change* (pp. 249–266). Frankfurt: Peter Lang.

Hélot, C., Barni, M., Janssens, R., & Bagna, C. (Eds.) (2012). *Linguistic landscapes, multilingualism and social change*. Frankfurt: Peter Lang.

INE (Instituto Nacional de Estadística [The National Statistics Institute]) (2012). *Statistical Office, Press bulletin, 19 April 2012*. Retrieved from: www.ine.es/prensa/np710.pdf (accessed 26 March, 2013) (in Spanish).

ISEI-IVEI (Instituto Vasco de Evaluación e Investigación Educativa [Basque Institute for Research and Evaluation in Education]) (2012). *Diagnostic evaluation 2011: Report with results and analysis of the variables in the 2nd grade of compulsory secondary education*. Bilbao: ISEI-IVEI (in Spanish).

Landry, R., & Bourhis, R.Y. (1997). Linguistic landscape and ethnolinguistic vitality: An empirical study. *Journal of Language and Social Psychology, 16*, 23–49.

Marten, H. F., Van Mensel, L., & Gorter, D. (2012). Studying minority languages in the linguistic landscape. In D. Gorter, H. F. Marten, & L. Van Mensel (Eds.), *Minority languages in the linguistic landscape* (pp. 1–15). Basingstoke: Palgrave MacMillan.

Rowland, L. (2012). The pedagogical benefits of a linguistic landscape project in Japan. *International Journal of Bilingual Education and Bilingualism, 16*(4), 494–505.

Sayer, P. (2010). Using the linguistic landscape as a pedagogical resource. *ELT Journal, 64*(2), 143–154.

Shohamy, E. (2006a). *Language policy: Hidden agendas and new approaches*. London: Routledge.

Shohamy, E. (2006b). Imagined multilingual schools: How come we don't deliver? In O. García, T. Skutnabb-Kangas, & M. Torres-Guzmán (Eds.), *Imagining multilingual schools* (pp. 171–183). Bristol, UK: Multilingual Matters.

Shohamy, E., & Gorter, D. (Eds.) (2009). *Linguistic landscape: Expanding the scenery*. New York: Routledge.

Shohamy, E., & Waksman, S. (2009). Linguistic landscape as an ecological arena: Modalities, meanings, negotiations, education. In E. Shohamy & D. Gorter (Eds.), *Linguistic landscape: Expanding the scenery* (pp. 313–331). New York: Routledge.

Shohamy, E., Ben-Rafael, E., & Barni, M. (Eds.) (2010). *Linguistic landscape in the city*. Bristol, UK: Multilingual Matters.

12

"WE ARE NOT REALLY A MIXED CITY"—A DE-JURE BILINGUAL LINGUISTIC LANDSCAPE

THE CASE OF JEWISH-ARAB MIXED CITIES IN ISRAEL

Dafna Yitzhaki and Theodorus du Plessis

What constitutes "successful" language planning? What are reasons for noncompliance to an official language policy in general and to one dealing with language visibility in particular? This chapter aims to answer these questions following an Israeli Supreme Court ruling that has conceded to the demands of an Israeli Arab organization (*Adalah*) to use Hebrew-Arabic bilingual signs in all public domains in four Jewish–Arab mixed cities (H.C. 4112/99). The ruling effectively requires the "bilingualization" of public signs under the jurisdiction of these municipalities.

In 2011, nine years after the ruling, the full-scale bilingualization of the linguistic landscape of the four municipalities has not been realized. Reflecting on this noncompliance enables the examining of where and how language-planning processes are situated between the judicial and political arenas and how the legal discourse about inclusive signage of the litigators and court differs from the administrative and political discourse of the policy implementers.

The study reported in the chapter is based on a series of interviews with decision-makers in the relevant cities and at the national level, supplemented by relevant public texts and additional public discourse resources.

Our analysis shows that the case at stake should be regarded as partly successful in terms of change of practice, but completely unsuccessful in terms of change of ideology.

The study builds on explanations provided for the apparent hesitance to bilingualize public signs in the four cities. In particular, it focuses on the tension between "the individual" and "the collective," realized in a dichotomy implementers make between instrumental and symbolic functions of public signs and eventually used as a mechanism to impede the realization of a bilingual landscape.

Introduction

Mixed Cities in Israel

According to the Israeli Central Bureau of Statistics (CBS), mixed cities in Israel are "Jewish cities/towns with a considerable Arab population" (CBS, 2011). The cities and towns that are recorded are the following (the number in brackets stating the percentage of Arab population): Jerusalem (36 percent), Tel Aviv-Jaffa (5 percent), Haifa (10 percent), Acre (29 percent), Ramla (22 percent), Lod (25 percent), Ma'alot-Tarshiha (19 percent), Upper Nazareth (17 percent), and Neve Shalom (50 percent).[1]

This list of cities and towns all fall within the CBS general definition; however, the list is by no means homogeneous. Some of the places differ rather significantly in terms of size, demography, socioeconomic profile, etc. Jerusalem (the capital), Tel Aviv-Jaffa, and Haifa are the largest cities in Israel, while the others are notably smaller and more peripheral. Moreover, the historical circumstances leading to their existence as "mixed cities" vary considerably. Some were originally Arab cities prior to the establishment of the state of Israel (e.g. Ramla and Lod), while others were established later (e.g. Upper Nazareth in the 1950s), or were formed out of two separate municipal units—Jewish and Arab (Ma'alot-Tarshiha). Neve Shalom (Hebrew for "Oasis of Peace") represents an additional category, as it is a unique cooperative village of Jews and Arabs established in the 1980s. The court case under discussion refers only to Lod, Ramla, Tel Aviv-Jaffa, and Upper Nazareth.[2]

Tel Aviv-Jaffa is the second most populated city in Israel (over 400,000 citizens) and centrally located. Founded in 1909, Tel Aviv was united with the port city Jaffa (with over 90 percent Arabs at that time) into one municipality in 1950. Arabs today constitute about 5 percent of the city's population, residing mostly in Jaffa. The three other cities are significantly smaller. Lod and Ramla, both originally Arab cities (al-Lud, ar-Ramlah), are also centrally situated, with about 70,000 citizens each and an Arab population of over 20 percent, mostly Muslims. Neighborhoods in both cities are traditionally either Jewish or Arab; however, Arabs have gradually moved into Jewish neighborhoods, which became "mixed neighborhoods." Finally, Upper Nazareth, located near the Arab city of Nazareth, was founded in 1957 as part of a larger project to establish Jewish towns in the northern area of Israel. Arabs today account for about 17 percent of the city's 40,000 residents.

The Court Case

The petitioners are two NGOs—*Adalah* (Legal Center for Arab Minority Rights in Israel) and ACRI (Association for Civil Rights in Israel). The petition's aim was to enforce a policy initiated during the British Mandate. Article 82 of the

Palestine Order in Council, 1922, adopted to Israeli legislation in 1948, requires, among other things, local authorities and municipalities in certain areas to publish notices in English, Arabic, and Hebrew (Drayton, 1934). Whether this section actually applies to the litigated areas became a debatable point in the court ruling (cf. Saban, 2003), but it nonetheless served as a starting point of the petition. The petitioners requested that all municipal signs (for street names, thoroughfares, intersections, public institutions, warning and safety signs, etc.) in the four cities be written in Arabic as well, and not only in Hebrew, as the convention was until then. Their arguments were broad, touching on both instrumental issues (such as allowing access to municipal services and information) and symbolic ones (e.g. strengthening the role of Arabic as a cultural and national identity marker). Additional arguments referred to implementing universal language rights as a basis for the demands.

Public Signs as Language Policy Actions

Public signage in this chapter refers to an element of the linguistic landscape (LL), or the scene where the public space is symbolically constructed (Shohamy & Gorter, 2009). The distinction between private and public signs as the two main components of the LL is usually attributed to Landry and Bourhis (1997) distinguishing between signage "of the authorities," such as road signs and public institution signs, and those issued by individuals and private bodies, such as shop signs.

LL studies have revealed the power relations between social groups and the various interests of each group, as well as highlighted the societal cleavages that stem from struggles over collective identities and ideologies. A series of recent case studies focus specifically on LL as a reflection of municipal and national language policies (cf. Shohamy, Ben-Rafael, & Barni, 2010). These studies all present a complex picture of three competing forces of language policy: language legislation, the language practices of communities, and the values attributed to languages and their users. An additional recurring issue is the almost inevitable gaps between policies and what actually occurs in the field.

Evaluating a (Language) Policy

Our question in this study is *whether the Adalah case can be regarded as a "successful" language intervention*. The component of assessing the extent to which a policy has been implemented and the changes it managed to create was not an integral part of the well-known Cooper (1989) model for studying language-planning actions—*"who plans what for whom and how."* Spolsky and Shohamy (1999) have extended this model to include several other components; among them is the one dealing with the evaluation of policies—*"with what effect."* In addition to more technical obstacles, such as the scarcity of reliable and quantifiable data provided by state authorities, Spolsky (2009) claims that when evaluations of language policies have been done, they were mainly in the field of educational language policies and focused more on the results of policy implementation and less on processes.

Though a language policy can be seen as similar to other social policies, it usually includes fundamental symbolic goals (e.g. creating a tolerant atmosphere or showing respect toward language minorities), which makes evaluation more challenging. The definition of "success" therefore depends on the initial goals in the first place, or the change that was "envisioned" (Hornberger, 2006, p. 30). It is evident that the goals of the policy action at stake, as reflected by both the petition and court ruling, clearly highlight symbolic elements as central (i.e. the way Arabic should be presented and valued in the LL of the mixed cities, as well as in Israeli society as a whole). Hence, in this study, we recognize both the change of practices and ideologies as greatly relevant to evaluating policy action. We are interested in evaluating not only what has been changed (in the actual LL), but also what kind of attitudes and perceptions the change represents.

The Current Study

Data

The study is based on a series of interviews with decision-makers (mayors, spokespersons, and chairpersons of municipal signage committees) in five mixed cities: Tel Aviv-Jaffa, Jerusalem, Ramla, Lod, and Upper Nazareth. Interviews were also done with stakeholders at the national level, such as the head of the government signage committee. The goal was twofold: first, to elicit accurate data about the extent to which the ruling was implemented; and second, to explore the discourse of policy implementation and to uncover obstacles that seem to impede implementation. The interviews were held at several occasions between December 2009 and December 2011. In addition to the interviews' transcripts, the data are supplemented by public texts and additional public discourse resources.

Analysis

We propose answering our question by using two criteria for "successful (bottom-up) policy action":

1. Did the policy effect change in practices?
2. What does the change represent (in terms of attitudes toward bilingualization)?

Our claim is that while the answer to the first question is partially yes, the answer to the second is that change represents a very narrow and limited understanding of a bilingual public sphere.

A Partial Change in Practice

The Supreme Court accepted the petition in July 2002 by majority decision and required the respondent municipalities to effect the addition of Arabic on municipal signs in their communities within four years (H.C. 4112/99). In terms of change in practice, the four municipalities exhibit different levels of implementation—three have changed the signs, to various degrees, while one (Upper Nazareth) has generally ignored the ruling. By 2009, only 4 percent of municipal signs in Upper Nazareth were in Arabic (Trumper-Hecht, 2009). In response to a request by the Supreme Court to submit a plan for immediate implementation of the 2002 ruling, the city reported in April 2011 that money would be allocated to this project in the following year (interview with city spokesperson, November 28, 2011).

The three cities that have indeed acted almost exclusively focused on bilingualizing street signs. One of the three (Ramla) has completed this change within one year, and in 2012, was in the process of changing other public signs such as road and instruction signs. In the two other cities, the process took longer. Due to budget problems, Lod has started replacing street signs only in 2008. By 2012, this stage was completed, and the process of replacing other municipal signs has begun. Tel Aviv-Jaffa has added Arabic to the majority of street signs by 2009 (interview with chairperson of the municipal Names Committee, December 12, 2009). All in all, this compliance can be referred to as partial implementation in terms of time span (change within four years after 2002) and the extent of the change (add Arabic to all public signs).

What Does (Partial) Implementation Represent?

The extent to which the 2002 ruling has been complied with and language visibility profiles of signs have changed is surely important. However, it does not tell the whole story. When looking deeper into what underlies these actions (or inactions)—particularly referring to the ideas and perceptions of decision-makers at the municipalities—the picture becomes more complex. Our analysis below confirms this.

Interestingly, even in places where the directive actually has been implemented (albeit not completely), implementation appears to be limited and in a primarily functional sense. Decision-makers apparently attach a rather limited meaning to the public use of Arabic in the municipal domain. More specifically, three main discourses can be identified. First, Hebrew-Arabic bilingual signage is not perceived as a realization of the notion of a mixed city. Second, the use of Arabic (in official domains) is not seen as a realization of official language status. Third, the public use of Arabic is not viewed as a (legitimate) symbolic element of social cohesion.

Discourse 1: Hebrew-Arabic signs are not a reflection of a Jewish-Arab city. Excerpts 1 and 2 are taken from interviews with the mayors ("Mayor A" and "Mayor B") of two "historical" Arab cities (after 1948, mixed cities). Our almost trivial question (Q) about the term "mixed city" did not receive a straightforward answer (A) from both:

Excerpt 1 (Mayor A):

Q: *Can I ask you, do you accept the term "mixed city"?*
A: *Yes, from my point of view, all Western world cities are mixed cities, in Germany, in France, cities are now mixed, US is officially an immigration state.*
Q: *Doesn't the definition here refer to having Jews and Arabs?*
A: *It's not just Arabs, even within the Arab community, it's not homogenous— there are Muslims and Christians.*
Q: *Of course, what we meant to ask is whether there is a concept here of being a Jewish-Arab mixed city?*
A: *It's a fact of life. We don't get a chance to choose whether we are a mixed city or not, it's our birthmark.*

Excerpt 2 (Mayor B):

Q: *What is the meaning of the term "mixed city" here?*
A: *I don't know what a mixed city is, here it's a mixed society, all should be respected, I don't ask them [the Arabs] to become Jewish and they don't ask me to become Muslim or Christian.*
Q: *Isn't this city considered to be a mixed city?*
A: *This represents, in my view, the right way to live together, separate but together, Jews with Jews, Arabs with Arabs, but in the city we are working together all of us with all the respect possible.*
Q: *The mere fact of having a large percentage of Arabs in the city, doesn't this technically turn the city into a mixed city?*
A: *This is a city that has an Arab population, the Muslims, for example, pray five times a day, the first time at 4:30 in the morning. It's better to have separate neighborhoods, in this way you can practice the rules of your religion.*[3]

Both mayors obviously recognize the large Arab population, but do not consider this reality as a central characteristic of the city. The presence of Arabs is a "fact of life" that should be "respected," but it does not define the city or turn it into a Jewish-Arab space. Using the term "mixed city" denotes the more general phenomenon of an ethnically diverse society, one that includes a variety of populations, including immigrants.

The two relevant cities have replaced most of their street signs and are in the process of replacing others. One of the two was the first municipality to start this process, and also the first to complete that stage. However, complying with the 2002 decision, even fast and in a committed fashion, by no means reflects a

176 Dafna Yitzhaki and Theodorus du Plessis

pro-bilingual position among decision-makers of consciously creating a Hebrew-Arabic LL, which represents a Jewish-Arab public space.

Moreover, the new signs in these two (and the other) cities that were studied actually are *trilingual* signs. All signs include Hebrew, English, and Arabic, and mostly in this order (occasionally with Arabic as the middle language), a changed language visibility profile. This strengthens the point that the new signs do not primarily intend to create a Hebrew-Arabic bilingual public sphere.

Discourse 2: The use of Arabic is not as a realization of its official status. The official status of Arabic was a major element of the court case. It was the founding argument of the petitioners and one of the main arguments of the majority opinion (cf. Pinto, 2010; Saban, 2003). Notably, the interviewees did not ascribe such role to Arabic, both in their cities and in the state as a whole. As can be illustrated by excerpts 3 and 4 below, the notion of official status is used either to support an exclusive use of Hebrew or to challenge the status of Arabic in Israel:

Excerpt 3 (Mayor A):

Q: *What do you do in terms of language at official events of the city?*
A: *Hebrew.*
Q: *No Arabic?*
A: *Hebrew is the official language of the state.*
Q: *Even when Arab citizens are present?*
A: *Hebrew is the official language of the state.*
Q: *Apart from the trilingual signs, you don't have any official use of Arabic?*
A: *No.*
Q: *You say that Hebrew is an official language, does that mean that the municipality does not see Arabic as an official language?*
A: *Arabic can be used as official if somebody is asking for it, we'll get someone to translate.*
Q: *For services, at a counter, etc.*
A: *Yes, we'll get someone to translate to or from Arabic. You have to remember that Arabs in this city have good Hebrew skills.*

Excerpt 4 (Mayor B):

Q: *You said all direction signs and street signs are trilingual, signs of public places too?*
A. *Yes. Today there are about 14,000 Russian speakers in our city—why not use Russian on signs? There are 4,000 Ethiopians—why not use Amharic on signs?*
Q: *But they are not official languages, right?*
A: *No, they are not official. If you go into details, you will probably find that Arabic is not official either.*

"We Are Not Really a Mixed City" **177**

Clearly, Arabic is perceived as an "ad hoc" official language at most. Services can potentially be given in Arabic, on demand. When Mayor B advocates for the public use of immigrant languages (Russian and Amharic—languages of immigrants from the former Soviet Union and Ethiopia pouring in during the 1990s), official status is not used as relevant criterion. Once the mayor is confronted with the notion of Arabic status, his reaction is to cast doubt on its official status as indeed a relevant criterion.

This position does not at all fall outside of general Israeli public discourse. In recent years, several proposals have been made to formally amend the status of Arabic, arguing that it is "not really" an official language. These attempts depart from various arguments, such as that the order dictating official status for Arabic dates from 1922 (see above) and was not legislated by Israel. Another argument claims the de facto situation of Arabic does not represent the broad bilingual conduct stipulated by the mandatory order and that official status therefore should be altered to match the current position of Arabic as a minority language (cf. Yitzhaki, 2013). Again, the idea of Hebrew-Arabic bilingualism is quite easily sacrificed for the sake of a (presumably) broader multilingual position, one wishing to add to the public space the resident Jewish immigrant languages. The status of Arabic as co-official language of the state is not seen as a policy element that underlies language arrangements at the municipal level.

Discourse 3: The functional/symbolic tension (or: "Arabs can read Hebrew well"). In addition to the above, when Arabic does get recognition—when the city uses Arabic—it is done in response to (Arab) citizens' demands for it, in a solely functional way. Arabic is perceived as an instrument to grant Arab citizens access to municipal services in their mother tongue, but not as a co-official language (of the city) that ought to be present in the public sphere regardless of functionality. Since public language visibility is not considered of symbolic value (e.g. displaying Arabic as an inclusive, unifying element), the apparent "good Hebrew skills" of Arabs (claimed by interviewees) makes its public presence superfluous. This point is further illustrated by the excerpt below. When asked what languages are used on municipal signs, Mayor A responded:

Excerpt 5 (Mayor A):

A: *All signs in the city are trilingual, Hebrew, English, and Arabic.*
Q: *English before Arabic?*
A: *Yes, but all three languages are the same size.*
Q: *Why did you make this decision about the configuration of the signs?*
A: *I don't know, the designer made this decision. But let me tell you something, here in the city, the young Arabs speak Hebrew better than Arabic.*

From the answers, we learn that the configuration of public signs is not important and, to some extent, even academic, since Arabs do not need Arabic on signs to find their way around the city, due to their good command of Hebrew. Again, the use of Arabic on signs is given a limited functional meaning, the message being that public use of the language is not needed for gaining "access and getting."

Yet, we do not wish to claim that the lack of, or the partial, compliance to the 2002 ruling is due primarily to this functional perception of language visibility. The symbolic element clearly plays a major role since Arabic is not perceived as the co-official language of a Jewish-Arab mixed city. Its public use does not confirm such (symbolic) status. More than that, in Upper Nazareth, as has been claimed by Trumper-Hecht (2009), the public use of Arabic is perceived as a threat to the Jewish identity of the city and even as "a concrete threat to the very existence of the Jewish state" (p. 244). Having no symbolic role in mixed cities, a functional role is all that is reserved. When this functional role is challenged by the claim that "Arabs have good Hebrew skills," the use of Arabic becomes largely redundant.

What Do the Three Discourses Tell Us about Public Signage as a Language Policy Action?

One clear issue arising from the analysis is the insignificant value assigned to *official status*. Corresponding to the claim by Shohamy (2006) that official status turns out to be a minor element in implementing language policies, the above cases show that the same applies to language use on public signage. City decision-makers do not regard Arabic's status as a co-official language of Israel as relevant policy dictum in determining criteria for language treatment on municipal signs. In places where Arabic has been added, no connection is made between such public use and co-official status. Co-official status is given a very limited scope at national level—raising the question whether Arabic is a de facto co-official language of the state. Given this limited scope, co-official status does not seem to privilege the language in any way on the municipal level.

The second issue to be highlighted is the dynamics of *bilingual versus multilingual policies*. Multilingual and multicultural arguments have been repeatedly claimed by respondents, advocating for the rights of various social groups to be recognized—usually immigrants—in one of the cities including the (Jewish) ultra-Orthodox community. The claim rests on a numerical issue—since immigrants are forming an increasingly larger percentage of the city population, they deserve to be represented in the city's landscape—in all respects, including language. This discourse obviously is important and valuable at both national and municipal level. However, its full meaning, and the potential outcomes of observing it, probably needs to be approached with caution.

In our discussion, three out of the four cities constitute "historical" Jewish-Arab mixed cities (i.e. Arab cities or cities that included a significant Arab population prior to the establishment of the state). Until the 1990s, Arabs in these cities were the largest minority population. Building on this reality and linking

"We Are Not Really a Mixed City" **179**

the co-official status of Arabic in Israel, an argument could be made for a bilingual Hebrew-Arabic municipal language model. The big waves of immigration during the 1990s changed the demographics of many Jewish-Arab mixed cities in such a way that the immigrant population became as significant numerically as the Arab population. The current multilingual/multicultural discourse therefore poses a dilemma for planning these cities' overall landscape—which criterion is more relevant, the "historical" or the "numerical"? In the meantime, if applying the prevailing logic, the Arab community is not (significantly) larger than the immigrant community, nullifying a justification for co-official status. This seems to echo the claims made by Rabinowitz and Monterescu (2008) about the need to extend the "dual-society paradigm" (p. 216) of the Jewish-Arab mixed cities and apply a view that sees them as a "fragmented and diversified . . . urban matrix" (p. 218) where national and local identities are constantly produced.

Finally, and beyond the ideological and attitudinal issues, a word should be said about bureaucratic matters, which seem to be tightly connected to language policy implementation at the municipal level. The interviews in all four municipalities revealed a lack of a clear system or mechanism, or agent responsible for implementing municipal policies on LL. There seems to be an overlap between different municipal committees (e.g. signage committee, names committee) dealing with public signage; also, there is an uncertainty regarding the responsibilities of elected officials and professional staff (e.g. city engineers, transport departments, etc.) working on such a mandate. This shortcoming creates great ambiguity as to the correct "address" for planning the public LL and to operationalizing policies. The fact that the Supreme Court gave the ruling but funds for implementation should have been allocated by municipalities creates a further obstacle. It is reasonable to assume that due to its more limited scope, policy implementation at the municipal level may be less complex than at the national level. However, one comparison with a related case reveals that it is not the case. A few years prior to the mixed cities case, the Israeli Court required the Public Works Department (*Ma'atz*) to add Arabic to all intercity road signs (H.C. 4438/97). Corrective, physical compliance to this ruling was near complete by the required date (Gavison & Babalfur, 2005). This relatively more successful case strengthens the need to take into account the unique and specific elements of language planning at the municipal level when evaluating language treatment in the public sphere.

Conclusion

In this chapter, we have asked what constitutes "successful" language planning. We have raised this question against the background of a 2002 court ruling instructing mixed cities in Israel to add Arabic to public signs. Reporting on significant changes in the LL, and therefore on increased language visibility for Arabic in the public sphere of these cities, would present the basis for a simple answer to the question. The addition of Arabic to intercity road signs that we have mentioned in our closing paragraph above confirms such a basis. However, our analysis has shown that a mere comparison of public signs including or excluding Arabic alongside Hebrew does not reveal the full picture. Implementing a policy directive, as such, does not necessarily constitute successful language planning. Our findings suggest that if this indeed was the case, we would have found evidence of a broader overall commitment to Arabic-Hebrew bilingualism in the four cities. As we did not—implementation was mostly ad hoc—and as the notion of Arabic-Hebrew bilingualism has not been integrated into overall municipal policies and plans, we have to reach the conclusion that there is more to measuring successful language planning than what is outwardly observable.

Therefore, the largest part of our study has dealt with a second question (i.e. the reasons for noncompliance, or incomplete compliance, with the ruling), specifically dealing with directives about language visibility on public signs. Our analysis has concentrated on how decision-makers and stakeholders at the four municipalities under investigation approach the notion of a bilingual LL, Hebrew-Arabic bilingualism, the notion of Arabic as co-official language, the notion of a mixed city as such, etc. In doing so, we have uncovered the crucial role of a language policy construct when evaluating language planning. This realization, we believe, points to the inadequacy of relating noncompliance to the court ruling simply to "ideology," as has become popular in many language policy critiques. A language policy construct could include or relate to ideology, but probably goes further. Most of the respondents in our interviews probably share similar ideological views on the state of Israel and on the position of Hebrew as de facto national language. However, the subtle differences that we find toward implementing the court ruling point to a variety of approaches to the language dispensation of the four cities. Specifically, we showed that: (1) ideological views often hide behind pro-multilingual positions; and (2) there are various bureaucratic issues quite specific to each municipality. Shared ideology does not necessarily relate to language-planning action in a predictable way.

We probably need to start paying more attention to thinking about solutions to language problems, mechanisms for implementation, budgetary support, demographic challenges and constraints, etc. It might help to steer us toward the uniqueness of each language-planning context and situation, recognizing the individuals involved.

Notes

1. Names of places are given in their English form (e.g. "Jaffa," not "Yaffo" in Hebrew or "Yaffa" in Arabic). Despite the political complexity of this issue, this is done in order to align with the language of the text.
2. The petition included additional mixed cities (e.g. Haifa), which were later removed when they declared they would add bilingual signs in their jurisdiction.
3. Apart from the introductory parts, the interviews were held in English. Excerpts from the interviews are quoted in their original form.

References

CBS (Central Bureau of Statistics) (2011). *Statistical abstract of Israel 2011, towns in Israel.* Retrieved from: www.cbs.gov.il/ishuvim/ishuv2011/info2011.pdf (accessed March 29, 2013).

Cooper, R. L. (1989). *Language planning and social change.* Cambridge: Cambridge University Press.

Drayton, R. H. (1934). *Laws of Palestine,* Vol. 3. London: Waterlow & Sons.

Gavison, R., & Babalfur, T. (2005). *Background document on minority collective rights.* Presented to the Constitution Committee of the Knesset, August 2005 (in Hebrew).

Hornberger, N. (2006). Frameworks and models in language policy and planning. In T. Ricento (Ed.), *An introduction to language policy, theory and method* (pp. 24–41). Malden, MA: Blackwell.

Landry, R., & Bourhis, RY. (1997). Linguistic landscape and ethnolinguistic vitality: An empirical study. *Journal of Language and Social Psychology, 16,* 23–49.

Pinto, M. (2010). Who is afraid of language rights? In O. Nachtomy & A. Sagi (Eds.), *Multiculturalism in Israel* (pp. 26–51). Brighton, MA: Academic Studies Press.

Rabinowitz, D., & Monterescu, D. (2008). Reconfiguring the "mixed town": Urban transformations of ethnonational relations in Palestine and Israel. *International Journal of Middle East Studies, 40,* 195–226.

Saban, I. (2003). A lone (bilingual) cry in the dark? *Tel-Aviv Law Review, 27*(1), 109–138 (in Hebrew).

Shohamy, E. (2006). *Language policy: Hidden agendas and new approaches.* London/New York: Routledge.

Shohamy, E., & Gorter, D. (Eds.) (2009). *Linguistic landscape: expanding the scenery.* New York/London: Routledge.

Shohamy, E., Ben-Rafael, E., & Barni, M. (Eds.) (2010). *Linguistic landscape in the city.* Bristol, UK: Multilingual Matters.

Spolsky, B. (2009). *Language management.* Cambridge: Cambridge University Press.

Spolsky, B., & Shohamy, E. (1999). *The languages of Israel: Policy, ideology, and practice.* Bristol, UK: Multilingual Matters.

Trumper-Hecht, N. (2009). Constructing national identity in mixed cities in Israel: Arabic on signs in the public space of Upper Nazareth. In E. Shohamy & D. Gorter (Eds.), *Linguistic landscape: Expanding the scenery* (pp. 238–252). London: Routledge.

Yitzhaki, D. (2013). The status of Arabic in the discourse of Israeli policymakers. *Israel Affairs, 19*(2), 290–305.

Legal Documents (in Hebrew)

H.C. 4438/97 *Adalah vs Ma'atz* (Public Works Department) (unpublished decision).
H.C. 4112/99 *Adalah et al., vs The Municipalities of Tel Aviv-Jaffa* 56(5) P.D. 393.

13

HEBRAIZATION IN THE PALESTINIAN LANGUAGE LANDSCAPE IN ISRAEL

Muhammad Amara

Introduction

The emerging importance of language landscape (LL) in the past two decades is related to various changes, primarily new technologies and globalization, and their impact on public space. The field of LL has risen to prominence following the publication of several important works on the topic, including Spolsky and Cooper (1991), Landry and Bourhis (1997), Gorter (2006), Backhaus (2007), Shohamy and Gorter (2009), Shohamy, Ben-Rafael, and Barni (2010), Jaworski and Thurlow (2010), and, most recently, a work on minority languages in the linguistic landscape (Gorter, Marten, & Van Mensel, 2012).

LL is a relatively new field. Landry and Bourhis (1997) were the first to elaborate on the notion of LL; accordingly, their work is considered to be a reference point for subsequent developments in the field (see Gorter et al., 2012). It is believed that within a few years, this field of study could attract additional researchers from various disciplines, such as political science (e.g. Sloboda, 2009), economics (e.g. Onofri, Nunes, Cenoz, & Gorter, 2008), and tourism (e.g. Kallen, 2009).

This article examines Hebraization in the Palestinian[1] linguistic landscape within Israel. Given the conflict-ridden nature of the region, the article explores the dynamic Palestinian linguistic reperoire in relation to Palestinian-Jewish contact within the state of Israel. At the core of this study are the language ideologies, which are outlined in more detail below.

Myhill (1999) has identified two ecologically based ideologies; the first associates language with individual identity, while the second connects language to a specific territory. Heller (2003) has identified a third ideology that links language with the economy. The connection between language and economy is understood to be related to the effects of globalization and "high" modernity

(Giddens, 1991). Leeman and Modan (2009) view the LL as ideologically charged and socially constructed representations of LL research. As Moriarty (2012) explains:

> To this end, the LL is seen not only to be reflective of language ideologies, but also a space where language ideologies can be indexed and performed, thus providing an apt tool for dealing with the multimodal nature of language ideologies.
>
> (p. 74)

Nelde (1998) contends that there "can be no language contact without language conflict" (p. 294). In the case of Hebrew-Arabic contact within the state of Israel, the linguistic conflict is very much alive due to the intense internal and external tensions described in more detail below. In light of this context, the question we raise is: What is the impact of this language conflict on the status and visibility of Hebrew within the Palestinian LL in Israel?

Hebrew in the Palestinian Linguistic Repertoire in Israel

Following the establishment of the state of Israel the sociolinguistic landscape changed dramatically, with Hebrew becoming the dominant language in the country. During this period, Arabic continued to be an important language within the Palestinian community. However, today, Arabic is almost completely absent from the national public sphere. This was not the case prior to the establishment of the state; indeed, the change is related to political and demographic changes within the region. The Jews became a majority and established a sovereign state in one portion of divided Palestine. They sought to establish hegemony within the country by making the Jewish identity of the state dominant, and—some might argue—the exclusive identity of the state. In accordance with this vision, Hebrew also took on added importance (Spolsky & Shohamy, 1999). Today, the linguistic repertoire of Palestinian citizens in Israel is complex and diverse. Arabic is the language of personal, cultural, and national identity. Hebrew is important for social mobility, for higher education, and for shared citizenship. English, as a global language, is a window into the wider world.

Hebrew among Palestinians in Israel is interesting not only from a linguistic perspective, but also because of its influence on the nature of Arabic in the country and its related effects on Palestinian culture and identity. In spite of similarities with other cases of language contact worldwide, Arabic-Hebrew contact lies within a unique sociopolitical context. The Palestinian minority in Israel is in conflict with the Jewish majority in relation to two central issues: the nature of the state and the geopolitical context. Within Israel, there is disagreement regarding the definition and perception of Israel as a Jewish-Zionist state. This has marginalized Palestinians in Israel on the civic and national levels. Externally, the ongoing

184 Muhammad Amara

struggle between the Arab states and Israel influences relations between the groups. Nevertheless, Palestinians are the largest non-Jewish minority within and outside of Israel holding proficiency in Hebrew. These factors affect the nature of contact between Hebrew and Arabic (Amara, 2007).

Palestinians in Israel learn Hebrew both formally within the school system and informally outside of school. Since Hebrew is one of Israel's two official languages, it is taught by schools as the language of the state (Hallel & Spolsky, 1993; Winter, 1981). Hebrew is taught in the Arabic-language stream of national education from third grade on, but the influence of informal education and normative contact on the acquisition of Hebrew is much greater (Reves, 1983). Palestinians of different ages are in contact with Israeli Jews in a variety of different settings and to varying degrees. Hebrew words, phrases, and expressions are commonly used by Palestinians in their spoken Arabic. The extent of this usage reflects their level of familiarity with Israeli Jewish culture (Amara, 1986, 1995; Amara & Spolsky, 1986).

For most Palestinians in Israel, Hebrew is their most important second language. It is regarded as even more important than English, and, at times and in some domains, it is even considered to be more important than Arabic (Amara & Mar'i, 2002; Shohamy & Donitsa-Schmidt, 1998). Not knowing Hebrew handicaps the Palestinian citizen in interactions with government offices, in finding suitable employment, and in pursuing higher education. Hebrew is now the main source of loanwords, not only for Hebrew words, but also for original English words. An examination of the various linguistic aspects that are borrowed from Hebrew into Arabic in Israel demonstrates that borrowing is not only motivated by need-filling, but also by taboo and prestige-related words. In other works, I have examined the various types of loanwords used: loanwords preserving original Hebrew form and meaning in Arabic, loan translations, and the borrowing of both single words and also phrases and expressions (Amara, 2006).

In light of the above, it is clear that Hebraization among Palestinians in Israel is pervasive in various domains of life. I use the term Hebraization, and not Hebrew, because Hebrew is the language itself, and Hebraization is a process through which Hebrew is given political and ideological character. Simply put, Hebraization is the highly charged ideologized Hebrew (Amara, 2010a).

How is Hebraization reflected in the Palestinian LL in Israel? The examination of Hebrew on Palestinian LL within Israel in this study is revealing, because it examines written texts (literacy) in comparison to the forms of contact reported in earlier studies, which are primarily based on the spoken language. In addition, the extensive use of signs within the Palestinian community only began over the past few decades when Palestinian society transitioned from being agriculturally based to wage based within the Israeli economy (see Ben-Porat, 1966; Ben-Shahar & Marx, 1972; Lewin-Epstein & Semyonov, 1986). Therefore, only recently and gradually has commerce became an important aspect of the Palestinian way of life in Israel. The following section explores the visibility of Hebrew on Palestinian signage in Israel, and its characteristics.

Hebraization in the Palestinian Landscape in Israel

First, we examine the visibility and predominance of Hebrew on Palestinian signs within Israel. Ben-Rafael, Shohamy, Amara, and Trumper-Hecht (2004, 2006) were the first to study the Israeli LL in various geographic locations, both Jewish and Palestinian. The findings reveal that within Jewish localities, Hebrew is predominant and appears—either with or without English—in nearly 100 percent of LL items. English is second, appearing in nearly 50 percent of LL items. Arabic, in contrast, appears in less than 6 percent of the LL items in Jewish localities. As to Palestinian localities (Nazareth, Tira, and Jaffa),[2] text that is exclusively in Arabic exists in less than 5 percent of the signs. Texts that are only in Hebrew surpass Arabic-only texts by appearing in 24 percent of the signs. Hebrew is also found in bilingual Arabic-Hebrew signs (44.6 percent of the signs), and in 24.1 percent of trilingual signs (Hebrew-Arabic-English). English plays more of a tertiary role; it appears in only 25 percent of all LL items.

The study of Ben-Rafael et al. (2006) reveals that Hebrew has a stronger presence than Arabic in the Palestinian localities investigated. Considering the contentious nature of Palestinian-Jewish relations in Israel, the results are surprising indeed. While this study illuminated some important aspects of the Palestinian language landscape in Israel, it did not provide us with a comprehensive picture, as it does not include a mapping of Palestinian localities, nor does it examine the social and religious elements of LL. More comprehensive studies by Amara (2010a, 2010b) examined the Palestinian LL in Israel and included a sample from a number of Palestinian localities in Israel (see Table 13.1 and Figure 13.1),[3] collecting 1,130 LL items located in commercial areas. The items included road signs, location names, street names, and names of institutions, while also capturing the linguistic diversity and mistakes.

TABLE 13.1 Sampling of LL items by localities, settings, and poplulations

Location	Type of locality	Population and demographic characteristics
Umm-el-Fahm	Arab Town; Little Triangle	All Muslim; 42,000 people
Rahat	Arab Town; Negev	All Muslim; 44,000 people
Dalyat Al-Karmel	Arab Druze Town; Haifa Region	Druze majority; 25,000 people
Nazareth	Arab City; Galilee	Both Muslim and Christian Arabs; 65,000 people
Haifa	Mixed City	Jewish majority, with a significant Arab minority of about 30,000 people
Sakhnin	Arab City; Galilee	Muslim majority, with a small Christian minority of about 25,000 people

Source: Basheer (2008)

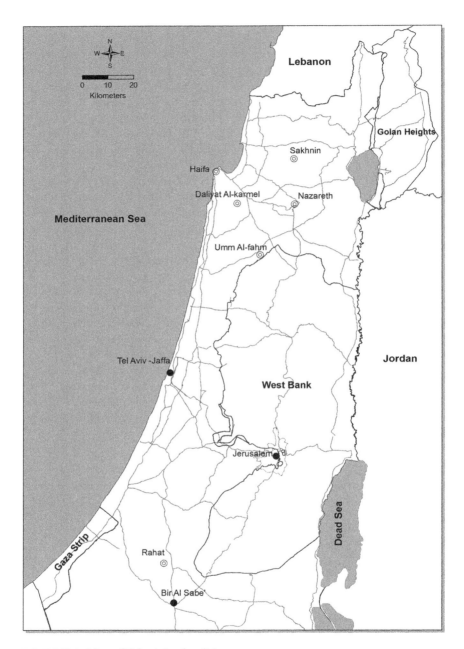

FIGURE 13.1 Map of Palestinian localities

Amara's studies reveal some similarities with the study of Ben-Rafael et al., but also some significant differences (see Table 13.2). Thus, unlike Ben-Rafael et al., Arabic was found in Amara's studies to be more visible as the primary language within the Palestinian LL. However, Hebrew is also prominent as a first language, and even more visible than Arabic as a second language. These findings mean that both Arabic and Hebrew enjoy visibility and dominance within the Palestinian LL, while English occupies third place. However, there is no doubt that Hebrew competes with Arabic within the Palestinian LL.

Moreover, Amara found significant differences between various Palestinian localities. In one group of localities (Umm-el-Fahm, Rahat, and Sakhneen), Arabic is more pronounced. Nevertheless, while less prevalent than Arabic, Hebrew is prominent in the LL, both in the private and public domains. In a different group of localities (Dalyat Al-Karmel, and some Arab neighbourhoods of Haifa, a mixed city), Hebrew has a more significant presence than Arabic. Hebrew appears in two-thirds of the LL as the exclusive language. In contrast, Nazareth is similar to the first group of localities, but also demonstrated an impressive English presence. We can infer from this study that Palestinian localities are not homogenous in their LL and significant differences exist in the presence and use of the Hebrew language.

In spite of the differences between the Palestinian localities, the above studies show that Hebrew is visible and competes with Arabic in the Palestinian LL in Israel. It appears even as the first or the only language in a significant number of signs. However, these studies do provide insights about the nature of Hebrew use in the Palestinian LL. Accordingly, we will qualitatively examine the essence of Hebrew. To this end, we will seek to answer the following questions: What is the nature of Hebrew in the Palestinian LL? What is the content of this Hebrew, and what does this tell us about the social and political landscape? Torkington (2008) argues that a qualitative account of a given LL allows for the:

> study of both the situational context in which the LL is embedded along with a more detailed examination of the interactional context of the signs themselves would help to reveal something about the collective identities and ideological orientations of social groups that make up the community in question.
>
> (p. 125)

TABLE 13.2 LL items by language (Arabic, Hebrew, and English) in all signs according to order of prevalence (%) ($N = 1,130$)

Order/language	First language	Second language	Third language
Arabic	51.1	28.3	17.2
Hebrew	38.9	54.2	13.3
English	9.8	9.8	66.4

188 Muhammad Amara

The distinction between commercial and government LL flows is important here. Ben-Rafael et al. (2006) and Amara (2010a) observed significant differences. The findings reveal that Hebrew as the exclusive language is particularly prominent in commercial signs. Bilingual signs (Arabic-Hebrew) and trilingual signs (Arabic-Hebrew-English) are pervasive in the LL of Palestinian localities, and have more visibility in the top-town LL. In all locations examined (Amara, 2010a), we see that street names are bilingual—Arabic-Hebrew, with Arabic first and with Hebrew transliteration (see Figure 13.2).

This is also true for all the signs prepared by local authorities. In bilingual signs, we see Arabic first and Hebrew second. In trilingual signs, Arabic appears first, Hebrew second, and English third. This is not the case when signs are established by national authorities. In bilingual signs, Hebrew is first and Arabic is second. In trilingual signs, Hebrew is first, Arabic is second, and English is third. However, an examination of the usage of the Hebrew in commercial signs is the most instructive because they reflect the motivations of the person hanging the sign and the varied reasons and interests for using Hebrew.

The Hebrew that appears on signs is not only confined to names of shops or institutions, but also reflects the kinds of activities in which people are involved. As such, they reflect Israeli values and cultural characteristics. We find, for instance, the following Hebrew expressions on signs:

- בשרים על האש (Barbeque)
- ספורט אלגנט (Sport elegant)
- חמישה כוכבים (Five stars)

FIGURE 13.2 Arabic-Hebrew sign with Hebrew transliteration (taken in *Tira*)

Hebraization in the Palestinian LL 189

- אוכל מהיר (Fast food)
- באישור משרד הבריאות (Authorized by the Ministry of Health)
- טעם פעם תבוא כל פעם (Eat once and you will always come)
- תקן ישראלי (Israeli standard)
- מספר 1 בישראל (No. 1 in Israel; see Figure 13.3)

Interestingly, sometimes Hebrew words are used even when the sign is written exclusively in Arabic. For instance, the words for *telephone* or *cellphone* in Hebrew are used even when the text is in Arabic (see Figure 13.4).

FIGURE 13.3 Hebrew-only sign

FIGURE 13.4 Arabic text with the word telefax in Hebrew

We have also observed cases where a shop logo is written either in Arabic-Hebrew or Hebrew-English, even when the entire text is in Arabic (see Figure 13.5).

Hebraization is not only reflected in the borrowing of items and expressions, but also in shop branches bearing Hebrew names. Thus, we found the following with Hebrew names: *Superpharm*, gasoline stations (such as *Sonol*, *Dor Alon*, and *Paz*), branches for cellphone companies (such as *Cellcom* and *Pelephone*), branches of banks (such as *Leumi* and *Hapoalim*), shops for clothes (such as *Delta*), and stores selling electronics (such as *Trakleen Hashmal* and *Bezek*), and many others.

The above examples represent Israeli values and habits (such as "do not give up," "barbeque"), reflecting in-depth understanding and involvement in Israeli society. Some aspects of this type of Hebraization and its characteristics were described by Amara previously (Amara, 1999a, 1999b, 2006); accordingly, they reflect the process of Israelization that Palestinian citizens are undergoing in Israel. The words and expressions on signs, not surprisingly, are frequently used by Palestinians in Israel in speech. In short, Hebraization, which reflects Israelization and its values, holds a significant space in the Palestinian LL not only quantitatively, but also in the versatile themes and values that it represents.

What we have described so far holds true regarding LL in predominantly Palestinian locations such as main shopping streets. In a study that explored the city of Umm-el-Fahm as a case study (Amara, 2010a), I examined other aspects of LL, documenting names of various locations and institutions. Names of mosques, street names (in this case, Hebrew transliteration is also provided), educational institutions (with Hebrew transliteration), and various geographic locations, such as valleys, springs, and mountains, were found to be only in Arabic and were based on Arab, Islamic, or local sources.

It can be argued that there are two different types of LL in Palestinian locations. The first type is found in the main shopping areas where Hebrew is

FIGURE 13.5 Arabic text with an Arabic-Hebrew logo

prominent and competes with Arabic. Signs of this nature connect Arab locations to modernity and globalization. The other type of LL is related to other aspects of life, not directly linked with the outside world, but rather reflecting the inner lives of Palestinians. And in this latter type, Arabic is the most salient and prominent feature in the language landscape.

Conclusions

Palestinian society in Israel has undergone two primary social transformations: modernization and changes in family patterns. We will elaborate on the first, as the latter is not relevant to this context. Contact with the Jewish population, constituting an important agent of modernization for Palestinians, has increased over the years (Amara, 1999a). At the same time, Palestinians have undergone a deep process of bilingualism (Arabic-Hebrew) and biculturalism (familiarity with the Jewish culture). This process has been associated with exposure to mass media in both Arabic (from the Arab world) and in Hebrew (Al-Haj, 1996; Smooha, 1989).

Our investigation of the Palestinian LL in Israel reveals the visibility and dominance of the Hebrew language in both commercial and government signage. Hebrew serves as both a symbolic and instrumental marker of modernity (Smooha, 1989). The intensive use of Hebrew on the Palestinian LL within Israel is not obvious, considering the ongoing Palestinian-Israeli conflict and the often contentious nature of relations between Arab and Jewish citizens within the state. As Shohamy (2006) notes, language space can be an arena for ideological battles. Yet, in the case examined here, perhaps somewhat surprisingly, in stark contrast to most other aspects of life between Palestinians and Jews, this is not the case. Why is this not reflected in language use in this Palestinian LL in Israel? Why do they choose Hebrew as a main language?

Spolsky (2009) rightly explains that choice of language in public signs in bilingual or multilingual urban space is a main feature of language landscape. In central shopping areas in Palestinians locations, Hebrew is prominent and competes with Arabic. Hebrew, in this context, could be explained by the link between language and economy as identified by Heller (2003). Indeed, use of Hebrew in central shopping districts is understood to be related to the effects of modernity (Smooha, 1989), as this is the arena where Palestinians mainly connect themselves to Israel and Israelization. Furthermore, this is an area that is rich with literacy, indicating Palestinians' transition from a traditional to a modern society. Accordingly, this reflects changes in the individual identities of Palestinians in Israel along with the extent and nature of contact they have with Israeli culture, in line with the notion of the ideology of language-and-identity (Myhill, 1999).

The adoption of Hebrew in commercial areas is, in a sense, similar to the use of foreign languages, mainly English and French, in the Arab world. Barhuma (2005) reports on extensive use of foreign names in commercial signs in Jordan,

192 Muhammad Amara

and Fayid (n.d.) regarding Cairo, a phenomenon interpreted as reflecting aspiration to modernity. Barhuma further reveals that foreign names imply high quality, refined aesthetic, and openness to the outside world. Usage of foreign names is perceived by some intellectuals as "linguistic pollution" (e.g. Fayid, n.d.), weaker loyalty to "indigenous culture and language," or an "inferiority complexity" (e.g. Barhuma, 2005). Shohamy (2006) points to an ideological battle between Arabic and foreign languages. Is this the case? Suleiman (2011) raises an important question in this context: "Could it be, therefore, that the anxiety about foreign names is an elite phenomenon?" (p. 217), claiming there is a need for further research to answer this question. Whatever the answer is, foreign names are widely used in the Arab world, reflecting modernity.

However, when other aspects of LL are examined—mainly those related to the internal communal life of Palestinians in Israel—Arabic is dominant, and when Hebrew is used, it is with transliteration. In contrast to language-and-identity ideology, this reflects individual identity and expresses the ideology of language-and-territory described by Myhill (1999). In other words, Hebrew is prominent when signs are related to economy and modernity, opening a window onto Israeli and other cultures. However, in relation to internal communal affairs involving Palestinians' unique identities—local, Arab, Islamic—Arabic dominates. This explains the differences in the usage of Hebrew in the language landscape.

This article demonstrated the pervasive use of Hebrew in the Palestinian LL. By observing the role of Hebrew in the Palestinian LL, the study also reflects the power relations between different national groups in Israel and sheds light on the collective identity of Palestinian citizens. Trumper-Hecht (2009) has clearly demonstrated this in her study of Upper Nazareth. As she explains, "The attempt to demand visibility of Arabic together with the continued immigration of Arabs into the city, are seen as an attempt to take away from Upper Nazareth its Jewish identity" (p. 240). It also reflects Hebraization and Israeli values, both social and economic. The Hebraization on Palestinian signage reveals ongoing Israelization in Palestinian localities—particularly in the realm of commerce. However, when examining internal aspects of life, Arabic remains the dominant language.

Notes

1. There are various ways to refer to Palestinians who became citizens of Israel, including: Israeli Arabs, Arab citizens of Israel, Israeli Palestinians, Palestinians in Israel, and Palestinian citizens in Israel. I prefer the last two terms because they are widely used by Palestinians themselves, and increasingly, also by Israeli Jews.
2. Nazareth is a city located in the Galilee region, in Israel's north. Tira is a town located in what is commonly referred to as "the Little Triangle," and is relatively close to the center of Israel. Jaffa is a mixed Jewish-Palestinian area that falls within the muncipal boundaries of Tel Aviv, in the center of Israel.
3. I thank Prof. Rassem Khamaisi, University of Haifa, for assisting with the preparation of this map.

References

Al-Haj, M. (1996). *Education among the Arabs in Israel—Control and social change.* Jerusalem: Magnes Press, Hebrew University (in Hebrew).

Amara, M. (1986). *The integration of Hebrew and English lexical items into the Arabic spoken in an Arab village in Israel.* MA Thesis, Bar-Ilan University, Ramat-Gan.

Amara, M. (1995). Hebrew and English lexical reflections of socio-political changes in Palestinian Arabic. *Journal of Multilingual and Multicultural Development, 16*(3), 165–172.

Amara, M. (1999a). *Politics and sociolinguistic reflexes: Palestinian border villages.* Amsterdam/Philadelphia, PA: John Benjamins.

Amara, M. (1999b). Hebrew and English borrowings in Palestinian Arabic in Israel: A social linguistic study in lexical integration and diffusion. In Y. Suleiman (Ed.), *Language and society in the Middle East and North Africa: Studies in variation and identity* (pp. 81–103). London: Curzon Press.

Amara, M. (2006). Ivrit loanwords in Arabic. *Encyclopedia of Arabic language and linguistics, 2* (pp. 464–467). Leiden: E. J. Brill.

Amara, M. (2007). Teaching Hebrew to Palestinian pupils in Israel. *Current Issues in Language Planning, 8*(2), 243–257.

Amara, M. (2010a). *Arabic language in Israel: Contexts and challenges.* Nazareth/Amman: Dar Al-Huda, Dirast and Dar Al-Fiker (in Arabic).

Amara, M. (2010b). *The Palestinian language landscape in Israel.* Final Report submitted to the Arabic Language Academy, Haifa (in Arabic).

Amara, M., & Mar'i, 'A. (2002). *Language education policy: The Arab minority in Israel.* Dordrecht: Kluwer Academic.

Amara, M., & Spolsky, B. (1986). The diffusion and integration of Hebrew and English lexical items in the Arabic spoken in an Israeli village. *Anthropological Linguistics, 28*(1), 43–58.

Backhaus, P. (2007). *Linguistic landscape: A comparative study of urban multilingualism in Tokyo.* Bristol, UK: Multilingual Matters.

Barhuma, I. (2005). *Language and communication: An example of the victory of foreign names in commercial signs in Jordan. Jordanian Language Academy* (in Arabic). Retrieved from: www.majma.org.jo/majma/index.php/2009-02-10-09-36-00/310-69-2.html (accessed July 6, 2013).

Basheer, N. (2008). *The Arab settlements in their local authorities in Israel: Comprehensive survey-2006.* Shaframr: Galilee Association, Rakaz Institute, and Al-Ahali Association (in Arabic).

Ben-Porat, Y. (1966). *Arab labor force.* Jerusalem: The Morris Falk Institute for Economic Research in Israel (in Hebrew).

Ben-Rafael, E., Shohamy, E., Amara, M., & Trumper-Hecht, N. (2004). *Linguistic landscape and multiculturalism: A Jewish Arab comparative study.* The Tami Steinmetz Center for Peace Research.

Ben-Rafael, E., Shohamy, E., Amara, M., & Trumper-Hecht, N. (2006). Linguistic landscape as a symbolic construction of the public space: The case of Israel. *International Journal of Multilingualism, 3*(1), 7–30.

Ben-Shahar, H., & Marx, I. (1972). *The Arab co-option: Economic social research, parts A-B (duplicated).* Tel Aviv: The Israel Institute for Research and Knowledge (in Hebrew).

194 Muhammad Amara

Fayid, W. (n.d.). *Studies in contemporary Arabic*. 'Alam al-Kutub (in Arabic).

Giddens, A. (1991). *Modernity and self-identity: Self and society in the late modern age*. Cambridge: Polity.

Gorter, D. (Ed.) (2006). Linguistic landscape: A new approach to multilingualism. *International Journal of Multilingualism, 3*(1), special issue.

Gorter, D., Marten, H. F., & Van Mensel, L (Eds.) (2012). *Minority languages in the linguistic landscape*. New York: Palgrave Macmillan.

Hallel, M., & Spolsky, B. (1993). The teaching of additional languages in Israel. *Annual Review of Applied Linguistics, 13*, 37–49.

Heller, M. (2003). Alternative ideologies of la francophonie. In R. Harris & B. Rampton (Eds.), *The language, ethnicity and race reader* (pp. 225–242). London: Routledge.

Jaworski, A. & Thurlow, C. (Eds.) (2010). *Semiotic landscapes: Language, image, and space*. London/New York: Continuum.

Kallen, J. (2009). Tourism and representation in the Irish linguistic landscape. In E. Shohamy & D. Gorter (Eds.), *Linguistic landscape: Expanding the scenery* (pp. 270–285). London: Routledge.

Landry, R., & Bourhis, R. (1997). Linguistic landscape and ethnolinguistic vitality: An empirical study. *Journal of Language and Social Psychology, 16*(1), 23–49.

Leeman, J., & Modan, G. (2009). Commodified language in Chinatown: A contextualized approach to linguistic landscape. *Journal of Sociolinguistics, 13*(3), 332–362.

Lewin-Epstein, N., & Semyonov, M. (1986). Ethnic group mobility in the Israeli labor market. *American Sociological Review, 51*, 342–351.

Moriarty, M. (2012). Language ideological debates in the linguistic landscape of an Irish tourist town. In D. Gorter, H. F. Marten, & L.Van Mensel (Eds.), *Minority languages in the linguistic landscape* (pp. 74–88). New York: Palgrave Macmillan.

Myhill, J. (1999). Identity, territoriality and minority language survival. *Journal of Multilingual and Multicultural Development, 20*(1), 34–50.

Nelde, P. (1998). Language conflict. In F. Coulmas (Ed.), *The handbook of sociolinguistics* (pp. 194–203). Oxford: Blackwell.

Onofri, L., Nunes, P. A. L. D., Cenoz, J., & Gorter, D. (2008). Language diversity in urban landscapes: An econometric study. *FEEM Working Paper, 40*. Retrieved from: http://ssrn.com/abstract=1131202 (accessed January 12, 2014).

Reves, T. (1983). *What makes a good language learner? Personal characteristics contributing to successful language acquisition*. Unpublished PhD thesis, The Hebrew University of Jerusalem.

Shohamy, E. (2006). *Language policy: Hidden agendas and new approaches*. London: Routledge.

Shohamy, E., & Donitsa-Schmidt, S. (1998). *Jews vs. Arabs: Language attitudes and stereotypes*. Tel Aviv: The Tami Steinmetz Center for Peace Research, Tel Aviv University.

Shohamy, E., & Gorter, D. (2009). *Language landscape: Expanding the scenery*. London: Routledge.

Shohamy, E., Ben-Rafael, E., & Barni, M. (Eds.) (2010). *Linguistic landscape in the city*. Bristol, UK: Multilingual Matters.

Sloboda, M. (2009). State ideology and linguistic landscape: A comparative analysis of (post) communist Belarus, Czech republic and Slovakia. In E. Shohamy & D. Gorter (Eds.), *Linguistic landscape: Expanding the scenery* (pp. 173–188). London: Routledge.

Smooha, S. (1989). The Arab minority in Israel: Radicalization or politicization? *Studies in Contemporary Jewry, 5*, 1–21.

Spolsky, B. (2009). Prolegomena to a sociolinguistic theory of public signage. In E. Shohamy & D. Gorter (Eds.), *Linguistic landscape: Expanding the scenery* (pp. 25–39). London: Routledge.

Spolsky, B., & Cooper, R. (1991). *The languages of Jerusalem.* Oxford: Clarendon Press.

Spolsky, B., & Shohamy, E. (1999). *Languages of Israel: Policy, ideology and practice.* Bristol, UK: Multilingual Matters.

Suleiman, Y. (2011). *Arabic, self and identity.* Oxford: Oxford University Press.

Torkington, K. (2008). *Exploring the linguistic landscape: The case of the "Golden Triangle" in the Algarve, Portugal.* Paper presented at the Lancaster Postgraduate Conference in Linguistic and Language Teaching. Retrieved from: www.ling.lancs.ac.uk/pg conference/v03.htm (accessed December 27, 2012).

Trumper-Hecht, N. (2009). Constructing national identity in mixed cities in Israel: Arabic on signs in the public space of Upper Nazareth. In E. Shohamy & D. Gorter (Eds.), *Language landscape: Expanding the scenery* (pp. 238–252). London: Routledge.

Winter, M. (1981). Basic problems in the educational system. In A. Lish (Ed.), *The Arabs in Israel: Continuity and change* (pp. 168–179). Jerusalem: Magnes Press (in Hebrew).

14

HEBREW IN THE NORTH AMERICAN LINGUISTIC LANDSCAPE

MATERIALIZING THE SACRED

Sharon Avni

When the Hebraist William Chomsky wrote in 1957 that Hebrew has been "the language of Judaism and intimately identified with the national and religious experiences of the Jewish people throughout the generations" (Chomsky, 1957, p. 3), he might never have anticipated how this intimacy would be refashioned in the irreverent movie *Borat: Cultural Learnings of America for Make Benefit Glorious Nation of Kazakhstan.* In this 2006 release, Sacha Baron Cohen, a religiously observant Jewish actor and Hebrew speaker, plays the anti-Semitic title character who employs Hebrew (for supposedly his native language of Kazakhstan) to engage in his outlandish sexist and homophobic antics. Though Chomsky, in this case, was echoing a centuries-old ideology that views language (Hebrew), culture (peoplehood), and religion (Judaism) as mutually constitutive, he (and perhaps Baron Cohen) also recognized the indeterminate, contested, and contingent nature of language in the linguistic landscape: that "when transposed from one experiential orbit into another . . . words change their 'meaning'" (p. 12).

In this chapter, I develop an approach to analyzing Hebrew that goes beyond the liturgical and canonical textual experiences of religious praxis. Instead, through an explanation of Hebrew sitings in the North American linguistic landscape (including how it is displayed, manipulated, and appropriated in a wide range of contexts), I offer a semiotics of Hebrew that takes into account the ways in which Hebrew materiality constructs new meanings and identifications for American Jews.[1] Employing theoretical tools from linguistic anthropology and the sociology of religion, this chapter analyzes how Hebrew enters into a complex constitutive relation with other categories of social meaning and materializes new and creative constructions of Jewishness. Within a broader framework, Hebrew as a material signifier of American Jewishness demonstrates how a language's iconicity and indexicality can be recruited in the service of constructing a repertoire of identity (Kroskrity, 1993).

My corpus of Hebrew materiality includes artifacts that I have amassed over the last several years. Aware of these items for some time, I only recently began to see them as folk poetry and culturally important. My initial interest stemmed from my research on the teaching and learning of Hebrew in a Jewish day school in New York City (Avni, 2011a, 2011b, 2012a, 2012b), which made me acutely aware of the different ways in which the students and teachers were exposed to Hebrew in and outside of the classroom. However, it was a confluence of events in 2009 that brought my simmering interest in Hebrew materiality to a level of scholarly focus. On the same day I finished reading Jeffrey Shandler's evocative chapter "Absolute Tchotchke" on the symbolic value—what he calls postvernacularity—invested in objects with Yiddish on them,[2] I happen to find myself at the Whole Foods supermarket in downtown Manhattan with a non-Jewish colleague who wanted to purchase some refreshments for a party. As she looked over the wide array of micro-brewed beers, she pointed to a bottle of He'brew beer with its Hebrew-ish lettering, and gleefully commented, "How cool!" From that moment on, it seemed as though I was seeing and hearing Hebrew everywhere, and I began my collection of Hebrew material objects. An important note about this collection is that it is completely serendipitous to my own Hebrew gaze. I have come across these material products while reading magazines, riding the subway, and browsing the Internet. Others were sent to me (or mentioned to me) by friends and colleagues who knew of my interest in Hebrew material culture. Though there are many other images of objects that I did not include in this chapter, I cannot quantify the prevalence of Hebrew materiality. My perspective is that these materializations emerge from many sources (institutional and individual), and while some may reach a wider audience, others remain primarily isolated to a small group of users. Finally, while some of these bumper stickers, pins, articles of clothing, advertisements, and tattoos may, at first hand, seem lowbrow, salacious, or trivial, the analysis shows that these materializations have deep semiotic complexity that rely on Hebrew's definitional ties to sacredness, even when the strict relationship between Hebrew/Judaism/sacredness is at times being subverted.

Theoretical Frameworks

The notion of linguistic landscape has come a long way since its coinage in Landry and Bourhis' (1997) seminal article in which they drew attention to the ways in which language use in the public space reflected the ethnolinguistic vitality of different groups of language speakers. Over the past two decades, theoretical and methodological work on linguistic landscape has expanded to include not only the signage of a particular geographical space, but also the sounds, images, objects, and texts by which public space is symbolically constructed (Shohamy & Gorter,

2008; Shohamy, Ben Rafael, & Barni, 2010). This chapter draws heavily from this analytic well, but offers an important theoretical shift. That is to say, while a great deal of research in linguistic landscape has examined how a particular space is occupied and made meaningful through linguistic and other semiotic means (Jaworski & Yeung, 2010), the focus of this article shifts the analytic frame to the circulating language and how it fulfills different social, cultural, religious, spiritual, and political functions. Hence, rather than focusing on how language(s) or genres (i.e. graffiti) constitute a specific context (i.e. an urban setting), this chapter offers a multilingual and multimodal analysis of the circulation of Hebrew as a type of material culture through which one can explore the varied ways in which people use language, including its orthography and iconicity, to imbue their actions with symbolic meaning.

This paradigmatic shift dovetails with recent calls in linguistic anthropology to consider language and materiality within the same analytic frame, and to look beyond the solely ideational and referential realm of language (Shankar & Cavanaugh, 2012). The dialectic relationship between language and materiality helps us to understand how words, ideologies, and objects shape meanings, and how these meanings are reproduced and challenged as they circulate across contexts (Keane, 2007). In this regard, the process of entextualization—the turning of discourse into replicable and transportable chunks of text that circulate and are recontextualized into new contexts—becomes analytically important (Briggs & Bauman, 1992). This propensity for language to move among contexts and be subjected to mimicry and humor can be problematic, and even morally troubling (Keane, 2007), particularly for Hebrew, believed by many to be a supernatural language through which God created the world. Entextualization processes, therefore, are a window into understanding how Hebrew is a site of contestation in negotiating the boundaries between the sacred and profane.

Examining how words and objects together shape meaning also informs an understanding of how people identify particular activities and signs as secular, religious, or spiritual (or some combination thereof). I am particularly interested here in combining the analytic lens of language materiality (Shankar & Cavanaugh, 2012) with *lived religion*, a notion that argues for studying religion not as it is defined by religious organizations, but as it is actually lived, understood, and practiced in people's everyday lives (Ammerman, 2007; McGuire, 2008). A focus on *in situ* practice moves attention away from the binary distinction between public and private, institutional and individual, religious and secular, and toward a closer analysis of the interactions between them (Bender, 2003, p. 6). For the study at hand, this analytic turn shifts attention to the ways in which Hebrew material-izations (outside of religious praxis) draw on, play with, and subvert notions of religion and spirituality in the process of constituting Jewishness. Put differently, Hebrew materiality is both a lens for analyzing the character of American Jewish identity and a privileged mode of its expression.

Hebrew and Jewish Publics

One might begin an analysis of the circulation of Hebrew in the American linguistic landscape with a simple question: *What Hebrew?* Indeed, in the highly multilingual palette of American society, Hebrew is not a commonly spoken language, nor is it widely taught to American children. Estimates are that there are approximately 215,000 Hebrew speakers in North America, and approximately 9 million throughout the world, including Israel. And, even within the North American Jewish community, the attachment to the language is often more ideological and affective than practical (Avni, 2011b). Most American Jews do not speak Modern Hebrew and may have limited proficiency in reading liturgical Hebrew. Yet, knowledge of the Hebrew alphabet has remained a dominant and crucial feature of American Jewish identification (Wirth-Nesher, 2006), and American Jews feel a deep sense of ancestral ownership of Hebrew, despite their limited competency in liturgical and communicative contexts (Avni, 2012a, 2012b).[3]

All the same, the persistent use of Hebrew as a synecdoche for Jewish religiosity and spirituality relies on naturalized correlations of the language with Judaism and sacredness, which are reaffirmed through formalized, repeatable, and symbolic performances of Hebrew in liturgical and other ritualistic practices (Avni, 2012a). For those individuals who define their Jewishness in terms of religious observance, the ability to decode sacred texts, pray, and engage in other Hebrew-related rituals is central to how they see themselves as American Jews (Avni, 2011a). This sense of codependency between Hebrew literacy and religiosity is played upon in Figure 14.1, in which the Hebrew letter *shin* has replaced the image of the gas pump, and the words *Jewish Studies* are substituted for gasoline on the sign alerting highway drivers to exits offering food, accommodations, and gasoline. The implication is

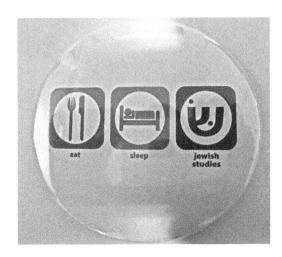

FIGURE 14.1
Eat, sleep; Jewish studies pin

clear: Jewish knowledge (as defined here by Hebrew literacy) is a type of fuel that is as essential as the physiological requirements of food and sleep.

The following two advertisements also draw on the interconnections of Hebrew learning and sustainability. The first (Figure 14.2) was produced by the National Jewish Outreach Program, an organization that offers free Hebrew language courses at synagogues and Jewish community centers across the US as part of its "literacy campaign to win back the hearts of North American Jews." Here, the letter *aleph* metonymically stands for Hebrew literacy, while the flag symbolically represents the American nation. Put together, this juxtaposition of language, religion, and place is discursively captured in the text "Read Hebrew America"—which, on closer examination, is ambiguous. While it can be read as an imperative (Americans must read Hebrew), its visual representation as a bow also suggests that reading Hebrew is a gift for American Jews to be unwrapped and enjoyed.

The second advertisement for a commercial language learning product (Figure 14.3) also plays on the language–heritage link, though the focus is on a particular methodology of language acquisition. By reading the text of the advertisement, readers can experience this pedagogical technique that intersperses Hebrew letters within English words, such that the letter *aleph* (in the words Can, Read, and Today) takes on the phonological characteristics of the letter A. This method also sells a sense of community and belongingness in that successful acquisition of this approach will enable the students to feel "at home in any synagogue, worldwide," and grant them access to their history ("3000 year old family") and their ancestral legacy ("priceless bequest: Hebrew!").

What do these advertisements have in common? Both rely on an indexical connection between Hebrew language learning and Jewish heritage and community. Both materialize Hebrew as a marketing tool to attract Jewish adults with limited Hebrew knowledge to learn decoding skills in order to (re)discover and (re)connect to Judaism. Both also make an implicit connection between

FIGURE 14.2
National Jewish Outreach Program Advertisement

FIGURE 14.3 Advertisement for Breidner Linguistic Method of learning Hebrew

202 Sharon Avni

learning Hebrew and being American, whether it is symbolized in the conjoining of the American flag and the letter *Aleph*, or explicitly conveyed in text ("English = Hebrew"). In short, these ads draw on ideological, affective, and historical attachments to the Hebrew language and materialize an American Jewish public that is largely defined by language-centric practices.

In summary, organized in parallel discursive and ideological ways, Hebrew materialization presents Hebrew literacy as a linguistic resource to be utilized (primarily by adults) in order to have a meaningful Jewish life. Hebrew is more than a purely linguistic activity; rather, it is deeply implicated in epistemological ways of identifying and practicing Judaism, locating Hebrew as a privileged site of Jewish authenticity. In this way, Hebrew materiality mobilizes Hebrew as a means of (re)connecting with Judaism.

Reimagining Jewishness

But what if the younger generation is not all that willing to reconnect to these traditional categories of Jewish authenticity? What happens to the conceptualization of Hebrew when Jewish identity is no longer ascribed or fixed, but rather fluid, contested, and complicated? What does Hebrew materialize in a society in which individual self-definitions and self-expressions of Judaism are distinct from one's adherence to religious praxis? These are not hypothetical questions. Research shows that Jewish youth today are quite different in tone, temper, and outlook from their parents and grandparents. Among Jews in the youngest generation of U.S. adults, the Millennials or American Jewish Gen Nexters are increasingly describing themselves as having no religion and identify as Jewish on the basis of ancestry, ethnicity, or culture, with a growing number claiming that it is not necessary to believe in God to be Jewish (Pew Research Center, 2013). Eschewing any religious affiliation and rejecting superimposed labels and boundaries, Jewish youth want to tell "a new American Jewish story" (Roth, 2007, p. 111). Hence, the question of how these youth and young adults actualize, articulate, and perform their Jewishness—or, how they understand Judaism and themselves as Jews—is crucially important to the sociology of contemporary American Jewry (Horowitz, 2002). Jacobs (2013), for example, argues that:

> [In a] postmodern, post-denominational, post-ethnic, post-Zionist, post-Diaspora, or what we may simply call a 'post-everything' phase ... the ways in which these youth identify Jewishly are complex, conditional, and increasingly individualistic, even as they still seek out ways to connect to their Jewish heritage.
>
> (pp. 39, 44)

The following section explores how Hebrew materiality imbues youth-centric American Jewishness with new meanings. This re-semioticization of Jewishness as hip, secular, and modern is accomplished by strategically and playfully co-opting and subverting Hebrew orthographies, meanings, and functions.

Self-conscious cultural productions linking Jewish identification and Hebrew use are not new. On college campuses, organizations such as Hillel have been producing apparel with the names of the university transliterated into Hebrew (Figures 14.4 and 14.5). In addition, popular sports organizations have transliterated their names in their popular logos and scripts (see Figure 14.6). Making meaning from the recognizable logo or color scheme, Hebrew is reduced to "tiny amounts of language . . . at the margins of text and talk units" (Androutsopoulos, 2007, p. 214) such that the symbolic, rather than the referential meaning, is privileged. This atomization of the language ensures that meaning making is possible even to those with limited or no Hebrew literacy (Shandler, 2006). Materializing Hebrew, in these ways, has as much to do with the actual content as it does with its performative value. It not only indexes overlapping identities (i.e. Jewish and a Jets fan), but it contextualizes Hebrew within popular and secular American culture.

In addition to contemporizing Hebrew, Hebrew materialization also commodifies the language and imbues it with social and economic value. One can see this in the case of He'brew beer (Figure 14.7), in which form and words transform the purchase of beer into an exercise of identification. The Schmaltz brewing company's caricature of the pious Jew (distinctively marked with head covering and beard) harks back to images of *Tevya*'s Eastern European *shtetl*. However, no longer teetering on a roof, this Jew is rejoicing in a modern city. Indeed, the juxtaposition of tradition with modernity links leisure alcohol consumption and Judaism, which, in turn, materializes a form of American Jewishness that is hip, secular, gendered, and modern. He'brew branding transforms being young and Jewish into quintessentially North American

FIGURE 14.4 University of Michigan at Ann Arbor T-shirt

FIGURE 14.5 Harvard University hat

FIGURE 14.6 Jets Football team bumper sticker

characteristics, and in some surprising ways, makes this form of Jewishness available to Jews and non-Jews alike.

Moreover, the He'brew logo utilizes a typeface that imitates the calligraphic curves and serifs of traditional Hebrew. This trick of the eye is an interesting case of bivalency—what Woolard (1997) refers to as the use of words that could "belong equally to both [linguistic] codes" (p. 8)—and exploits a type of multilingualism that relies more on orthographic knowledge than on the code itself. This Hebraized English is a commodity that has symbolic value to those consumers who can interpret these multimodal signs, appreciate their semiotic complexity, and are willing to put their money where their ethnicity is (Halter, 2000). They are willing to buy and buy into this re-semioticized Jewish "brand." He'brew, then, materializes a new narrative of what it means to be Jewish in America. What might be easily dismissed as *shtick* is actually a complex case of intertextuality that (re)appropriates, recontextualizes, and subverts traditional orthographic, discursive, pictorial, and religious forms and their meanings.

A type of subversion is also at work in Figure 14.8. The Hebraized English on this card suggests a scriptural text, but in fact, when it is read from bottom to top (and from right to left, as Hebrew is), the message is one of gross profanity. This type of subversion—that takes advantage of Hebrew calligraphic curves and directionality—depends heavily on the ability to recognize not only the orthography of Hebrew, but to associate it with sacredness. If the language were not ideologically and symbolically saturated (i.e. if its meaning did not rely heavily on a mutable chain of indexes that links Hebrew to sacredness), the subversive juxtaposition of the holy and profane would not be felicitous. Materialized Hebrew plays with the tension between the religious and secular, and the sacred and profane, drawing on precisely their permeability to reconstitute Jewishness as edgy and taboo.

No doubt, similar recontextualizing processes are at work in the growing trend among Jews (and non-Jews) to get tattoos of scriptural Hebrew words or expressions (Torgovnick, 2008). Inscribing a tattoo on one's body embodies multiple layers of meaning, particularly for many Jews who associate tattoos with enforced racial branding in Nazi-occupied Europe and/or recognize this practice as taboo in rabbinic Judaism. According to the documentary *Tattoo Jew*, the

FIGURE 14.7 Bottle label of He'brew beer

FIGURE 14.8
Card: Go F@$% Yourself

practice of Hebrew tattooing is an explicit act of subversion, in which Jews are not afraid to play with symbols that mark them as Other, inferior, or illegitimate (Figures 14.9 and 14.10). As a sign of defiance and alterity, tattoos enable Jewish individuals to resist hegemonic notions of Judaism that validate only particular forms of religious knowledge and practices by drawing on precisely those practices and visual significations, and using them to their own advantage in performing their Jewishness. Hebrew tattooing therefore enables individuals to access the spiritual (and brand themselves in the process), even if the Hebrew lettering is of a slangy register. In other words, tattoos of Hebrew scripture (and, for that matter, hosiery; see Figure 14.11) cross boundaries into the mundane everyday (secular) world of aesthetics, the body, and fashion to make meaningful connections with religiosity and spirituality. Materialized and embodied Hebrew, in this context, ritualizes a new Jewishness that respects and draws from tradition, but reappropriates its styles and discourse into a new genre of affiliation and pride.

Finally, this subversive act of purposefully secularizing the sacred as a means of expressing Jewishness is also at work in the circulation of Chai (חי), the Hebrew word that means "life."[4] Just as the Star of David, Chai is one of the most recognizable symbols in Judaism, and it is an icon of Jewish affiliation and religiosity. While in Modern (Israeli) Hebrew, it is pronounced as a pharyngeal consonant [ħai̯], the American pronunciation sounds like "hi" [χai̯]. In the latter case, Chai is a heterographic homophone (i.e. hi and high) that can be exploited for humorous and subversive purposes. Rather than seeing Chai on a necklace around a person's neck, in Figure 14.12 it is inscribed on a baby's bib, followed by the words "I'm new here," or entextualized on clothing as חי *achiever*, חי *roller*, or חי *maintenance*.

Its subversive function is also apparent in Figure 14.13, in which Chai is incorporated into the discourse of computers and modernity.

Furthermore, in Figures 14.14 and 14.15, the iconicity of Chai becomes a marker of rebellion and counterculture as it is embedded in discourses of

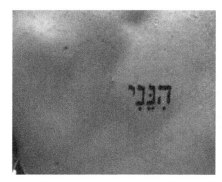 

FIGURE 14.9 Tattoo of biblical scripture: Genesis chapter 22:1–2 (Here I am)

FIGURE 14.10 Hebrew tattoo (*Shalom*)

FIGURE 14.11 Hosiery with Hebrew inscription *Ve'ahavta* (And you shall love: Leviticus 19:18)

FIGURE 14.12 Chai on baby's bib

FIGURE 14.13 Chai tech cap

FIGURE 14.14 I'm so Chai card

FIGURE 14.15 Gettin' Chai T-shirt

208 Sharon Avni

recreational marijuana use. This type of cultural jamming re-entextualizes and subverts the dominant semiotic resources of Judaism.

Finally, in the artifacts of American presidential elections, one can see how campaigns and their supporters use Hebrew to define a political Jewishness (i.e. an articulation of Jewish identity enmeshed in the American body politic that expresses support for a particular candidate or cause). The enlistment of Hebrew for political messaging on buttons and pins is not new (Schweitzer, 2008), nor is the creation of a Jewish political distinctiveness (what might be thought of as the transformation from the People of the Book to the People of the Vote). However, what is strikingly contemporary is the sophistication and creativity with which these objects of material culture have been put to use in recent election cycles, and their social effect.[5] For example, an Obama supporter in 2008 designed the poster in Figure 14.16, in which he mimics the official Obama slogan. The strategic use of Hebrew "ken" serves two functions. Its placement underneath the French word *Oui* transforms the slogan "Yes We Can" into "Yes Yes Yes." At the same time, in exploiting the sounds of *Oui* and *Ken* so that the former becomes "we" and the latter becomes "can," this new text not only portrays Obama as a cosmopolitan candidate willing to embrace cultural and linguistic diversity, but also positions its readers as sophisticated voters who have the linguistic and cultural knowledge to understand this multilingual and multimodal collage.

In Figures 14.17 and 14.18, Hebrew materializes a politically engaged Jewish public. In the 2012 highly mediatized presidential election, in which the "Jewish vote" was perceived to be up for grabs (Mahtesian, 2012), Hebrew materiality

FIGURE 14.16 Poster for the election of Barack Obama, 2008

FIGURE 14.17 Bumper sticker endorsing Presidential candidate Mitt Romney, 2012

FIGURE 14.18 Barack Obama campaign pin

FIGURE 14.19 Obama pin (2012)

signified a synecdochic representation of American Jewish presence and agency.[6] In the case of Romney, the Hebraized "Jewish Americans for Romney" may be read as a challenge to the political calculus of Jewish loyalty to Democrats. In both cases, Hebrew is recruited for persuasion and reassurance, and tacitly constructs a "new kind of mediated publicness" that does not involve individuals sharing a common locale, but an "openness and visibility" (Thompson, 1995, p. 236). As a result, these political artifacts materialize and constitute a Jewishness that no longer resists, but rather embraces syncretistic Americanism. It is no longer choosing between the religious and secular, but negotiating the in-between-ness. The syncretism is most revealing in Figure 14.19, in which the letter *aleph* replaces the "O" in Obama. Indeed, this provocative juxtaposition not only visually equivocates Obama with Hebrew (read: Jewish), but also erases other parts of his biography (i.e. his middle name Hussein) and counters discourses regarding his "Jewish" authenticity (Heileman, 2011). In short, materialized Hebrew therefore positions American Jews within a complex web of circulating national and political discourses that draw from religious and ethnic identifications, and also points to new ways of expressing religious and cultural syncretism and hybridity.

Conclusion

This chapter explores and theorizes the complex nature of the circulation of language in the linguistic landscape and its involvement in the construction of different social spaces and social identities. Rather than exploring how Hebrew constitutes a specific space, I reconceptualize Hebrew as material culture and explore the semiotic processes by which these cultural objects take on symbolic and social meanings across contexts for different social purposes. A close examination of Hebrew materiality reveals the creativity by which Hebrew is imagined and utilized. Individuals wear Hebrew, they consume Hebrew, they inscribe it on their bodies, and they stick it on their car bumpers. Moreover, Hebrew materiality is not limited to a strict graphic or referential representation. Instead, these materializations include words written in Hebrew letters, English words that mimic Hebrew orthography, multilingual and homophonic puns, and other word games. While in some cases, Hebrew materiality relies on an established chain of meaning to sacredness and Judaism in efforts to define Jewish authenticity, at other times its use extends these meanings for other purposes, often in the process subverting the strict relationship between Hebrew/Judaism/ sacredness. These semiotics of Hebrew materiality create opportunities to reimagine American Jewishness not as ascribed, fixed, and immutable, but rather as performative, creative, and open to change and transformation. In this sense, Hebrew materiality is but one means among many others in the re-semioticization of Jewishness as cool, young, trendy, and modern (Eisenberg, 2004). Yet, the emergence of the Jewish hipster, or Jews/z—the appropriation of the z itself a co-option of hip hop discourse (Baskind, 2007, p. 5)—does not exist in a cultural vacuum, but is part of a broader social trend of cultural syncretism in which difference is cool, ethnicity is trendy (p. 14), and "new is to Jew as hip-hop is to matzah" (Roth, 2007, p. 118).

To some, Hebrew materializations may be interpreted as a "hidden transcript" (Scott, 1990), a covert or differentiating language (Weinreich, 1973) that Jews use to mark cultural insider-ness and differentiate themselves from non-Jews. No doubt, these creative uses of Hebrew have value for those who are on the inside of the joke and/or are "speaking" to other cultural insiders. However, in our globalizing world, it is becoming impossible to know who exactly this speech community is and/or where they are located (Avineri, 2012). Put differently, this narrow definition of "hearers" or ratified members (Goffman, 1981) relies on an ideological artifact of sociolinguistic theory that sees language as a stable, bounded system linked with a bounded, homogenous community. Rather, the circulation of Hebrew materiality is analytically insightful and theoretically meaningful because it explores how individuals interact with multimodality and "opt in and opt out, how they perform or play with linguistic signs of group belonging, and how they develop particular trajectories of group identification throughout their lives" (Blommaert & Rampton, 2011, p. 6). The implications of this paradigmatic shift are profound, particularly for educators wedded to ideologies that perceive Hebrew language learning as a central means of ensuring Jewish continuity. However, in line with Rody's (2009) argument that "Jewishness has become part of the collective global inheritance . . . something fun to play around with, something that seems readily detachable from the exigencies of either Orthodox religious practice or Israeli national policy, an elastic and accommodating, even welcoming, condition for any experimental individual" (p. 124), I argue the same can also be said about Hebrew. In this sense, linguistic landscape, in its most radical conceptualization (Shohamy & Waksman, 2009, p. 328), is not only located in the midst of negotiation and contestation of the public space, but also in ideologies and publics themselves as they construct and refashion new social identities and social practices through linguistic and other semiotic means.

Notes

1. My focus on American Jews does not necessarily include American Orthodox communities that eschew popular culture and use Yiddish as their daily vernacular, reserving Hebrew as a language of sacred practice.
2. Shandler (2006) argues that since the Holocaust, Yiddish has been transformed from a language of daily communication to a "postvernacular language" of diverse and symbolic value. In many ways, the cases of Hebrew materiality presented here function as a postvernacular language for American Jews: the meta-level of signification is privileged over its instrumental value as a vehicle for daily communication. However, unlike Yiddish, Hebrew has never been the spoken and/or written language of American Jewry.
3. Hebrew encompasses four varieties from different historical periods: Biblical, Mishnaic, Medieval and Modern Hebrew. Modern Hebrew is an official language in Israel.
4. According to the *gematria*, a mystical tradition that assigns a numerological value to Hebrew letters, the letters *Het* (ח) and *Yud* (י) add up to the number 18, which represents good luck.
5. See Bloch (2000) for discussion about the use of political bumper stickers and pins in Israel.
6. The overt reliance on Hebrew in the political linguistic landscape underscores a semiotic complexity that perhaps other Jewish symbols, such as the Star of David or menorah, lack. As the revived language of the modern state of Israel, Hebrew not only indexes religiosity, but also Jewish nationalism and Israeli-ness.

References

Ammerman, N. (2007). Introduction: Observing religious modern lives. In N. Ammerman (Ed.), *Everyday religion: Observing modern religious lives* (pp. 3–20). New York: Oxford University Press.

Androutsopoulos, J. (2007). Bilingualism in the mass media and on the Internet. In M. Heller (Ed.), *Bilingualism: A social approach* (pp. 207–232). Basingstoke: Palgrave.

Avineri, N. (2012). *Heritage language socialization practices in secular Yiddish educational contexts: The creation of a metalinguistic community.* PhD dissertation. University of California Los Angeles.

Avni, S. (2011a). Hebrew-only language policy in religious education. *Language Policy, 11,* 169–188.

Avni, S. (2011b). Toward an understanding of Hebrew language education: Ideologies, emotions, and identity. *International Journal of the Sociology of Language, 2011*(208), 53–70.

Avni, S. (2012a). Hebrew as heritage: The work of language in religious and communal continuity. *Linguistics and Education, 23,* 323–333.

Avni, S. (2012b). Translation as a site of language policy negotiation in Jewish day school education. *Current Issues in Language Planning, 13*(2), 76–104.

Baskind, S. (2007). The Fockerized Jew? Questioning Jewishness as cool in American popular entertainment. *Shofar, 25*(4), 3–17.

Bender, C. (2003). *Heaven's kitchen: Living religion at God's Love We Deliver*. Chicago, IL: University of Chicago Press.

Bloch, L. (2000). Mobile discourse: Political bumper stickers as a communication event in Israel. *Journal of Communication, 5*, 48–76.

Blommaert, J., & Rampton, B. (2011). Language and superdiversity. *Diversities, 13*(2), 1–21.

Briggs, C., & Bauman, R. (1992). Genre, intertextuality, and social power. *Journal of Linguistic Anthropology, 2*(2), 131–172.

Chomsky, W. (1957). *Hebrew: The eternal language*. Philadelphia, PA: The Jewish Publication Society of America.

Eisenberg, C. (2004, February 7). Young, hip and "JEWCY." *Newsday*. Retrieved from: www.newsday.com/lifestyle/young-hip-and-jewcy-a-generation-weaned-on-irony-and-multiculturalism-defines-what-it-means-to-be-1.718335 (accessed March 1, 2014).

Goffman, E. (1981). *Forms of talk*. Philadelphia, PA: University of Pennsylvania Press.

Halter, M. (2000). *Shopping for identity: The marketing of ethnicity*. New York: Schocken Books.

Heileman, J. (2011). The first Jewish President. *New York Magazine* (September 18).

Horowitz, B. (2002). Reframing the study of contemporary American Jewish identity. *Contemporary Jewry, 23*, 14–34.

Jacobs, B. (2013). Problems and prospects of Jewish education for intelligent citizenship in a post-everything world. *Journal of Diaspora, Indigenous, and Minority Education, 7*(1), 39–53.

Jaworski, A., & Yeung, S. (2010). Life in the Garden of Eden: The naming and imagery of residential Hong Kong. In E. Shohamy, E. Ben-Rafael, & M. Barni (Eds.), *Linguistic Landscape in the city* (pp. 153–181). Bristol, UK: Multilingual Matters.

Keane, W. (2007). *Christian moderns: Freedom and fetish in the mission encounter*. Berkeley, CA: University of California Press.

Kroskrity, P. (1993). *Language, history and identity: Ethnolinguistic studies of the Arizona Tewa*. Tucson, AZ: University of Arizona Press.

Landry, R., & Bourhis, R. (1997). Linguistic landscape and ethnolinguistic vitality: An empirical study. *Journal of Language and Social Psychology, 16*(1), 23–49.

McGuire, M. (2008). *Lived religion: Faith and practice in everyday life*. New York: Oxford University Press.

Mahtesian, C. (2012, July 10). Is the Jewish vote really up for grabs? *Politico*. Retrieved from: www.politico.com/blogs/charlie-mahtesian/2012/07/is-the-jewish-vote-really-up-for-grabs-128477.html (accessed March 1, 2014).

Pew Research Center. (2013). *A portrait of Jewish Americans*. Washington, DC: Pew Research Center for the People & the Press.

Rody, C. (2009). *The interethnic imagination: Roots and passages in contemporary Asian American fiction*. New York: Oxford University Press.

Roth, L. (2007). Oppositional culture and the "New Jew" brand: From Plotz to Heeb to lost tribe. *Shofar, 25*(4), 99–123.

Schweitzer, D. (2008, October 12). People of the Button. *New York Times*. Retrieved from: www.nytimes.com/2008/10/13/opinion/13schweitzer.html (accessed March 1, 2014).

Scott, M. (1990). *Domination and the arts of resistance: Hidden transcript*. New Haven, CT: Yale University Press.

Shandler, J. (2006). *Adventures in Yiddishland: Postvernacular language and culture*. Berkeley, CA: University of California Press.

Shankar, S., & Cavanaugh, J. (2012). Language and materiality in global capitalism. *Annual Review of Anthropology*, *41*, 355–369.

Shohamy, E., & Gorter, D. (Eds.) (2008). *Linguistic landscape: Expanding the scenery*. New York: Routledge.

Shohamy, E., & Waksman, S. (2009). Linguistic landscape as an ecological arena: Modalities, meanings, negotiations, education. In E. Shohamy & D. Gorter (Eds.), *Linguistic landscape: Expanding the scenery* (pp. 313–329). New York: Routledge.

Shohamy, E., Ben-Rafael, E., & Barni, M. (Eds.) (2010). *Linguistic landscape in the city*. Bristol, UK: Multilingual Matters.

Thompson, J. (1995). *The media and modernity: A social theory of the media*. Palo Alto, CA: Stanford University Press.

Torgovnick, K. (2008, July 17). For some Jews, it only sounds like "taboo." *New York Times*. Retrieved from: www.nytimes.com/2008/07/17/fashion/17SKIN.html?page wanted=all (accessed March 1, 2014).

Weinreich, M. (1973). *The history of the Yiddish language*. Chicago, IL: University of Chicago Press.

Wirth-Nesher, H. (2006). *Call it English: The languages of Jewish American literature*. Princeton, NJ: Princeton University Press.

Woolard, K. (1997). Simultaneity and bivalency as strategies in bilingualism. *Journal of Linguistic Anthropology*, *8*(1), 3–29.

15

WELCOME

SYNTHETIC PERSONALIZATION AND COMMODIFICATION OF SOCIABILITY IN THE LINGUISTIC LANDSCAPE OF GLOBAL TOURISM

Adam Jaworski

Framing Sites of Sociality

Individualization is said to be one of the defining characteristics of late modernity, suggesting that, other things being equal, our lives now are more varied, discontinuous, and self-reflexive than they used to be (e.g. Bauman, 2000; Beck & Beck-Gernsheim, 2002; Beck, Giddens, & Lash, 1994; Giddens, 1991). Closely linked to the neoliberal free-market ideologies of egoistic entrepreneurship and personal lifestyle consumption, discourses of individualism permeate both the commercial sphere and, increasingly, the social sphere (Bourdieu, 2010). In this regard, Fairclough (1989) has proposed the term *synthetic personalization* to characterize the way that, for example, advertisers and politicians often use language to give the impression of "treating each of the people 'handled' *en masse* as an individual. Examples would be air travel (*have a nice day!*), restaurants (*welcome to Wimpy!*), and the simulated conversation (e.g. chat shows) and *bonhomie* which litter the media" (p. 62).

In tourism, the marketing of a unique, personal experience is often based on the promise of a "warm welcome" from, and "friendly" engagement with, local people. Tourists are ostensibly singled out for a personalized greeting that is extended by a specific local person or host community. These "personal" greetings can, of course, only ever be delivered as part of a commodified performance (Jaworski, 2009; Jaworski & Thurlow, 2010a). Tourists are always "mass" and locals always "imagined." With this in mind, I focus in this chapter on a specific, probably universal facet of the linguistic landscape of tourism—the *welcome* sign.

Spaces designated as "tourist" areas are likely to bear some semiotic marking framing them as such. *Welcome* signs are among the more prevalent ones, to the point of their *enregisterment* in the semiotic landscape of tourism. Agha (2003) defines "enregisterment" as "processes through which a linguistic repertoire becomes differentiable within a language as a socially recognized register of forms" (p. 231). Such is the expectation for us to see *welcome* signs framing tourist spots that, in their absence, "straightforward" information signs perform "an implicit welcoming act" (Kallen, 2009, p. 278).

Tourism is one of the agents commodifying and corporatizing space, which it subsequently redefines as "sites of sociality." According to Ash and Thrift (2007, p. 158), these sites of sociality have emerged as part of the contemporary, urban culture industry in the form of "corporate hospitality venues, airport lounges, and restaurant districts," with their expectations and conventions for agency and participation. As will become clear from my data, tourism discourse extends such sites of sociability to whole cities and states.

The main aim of the chapter is to problematize the ostensibly phatic function of *welcome* signs. I suggest that through the ubiquitous and frequently repeated placement of *welcome* signage, tourism operators stage a continuous *access ritual* (Goffman, 1971) for tourists visiting a country or city, and in innumerable other instances theme parks, museums, souvenir shops, hotels, restaurants, and so on. The synthetic personalization of the signs allows the tourists arriving at their destination *en masse* to be addressed as individuals. However, not all *welcome* signs necessarily belong to the same visual-spatial "discourse framework" (cf. Kallen, 2010). On the contrary, they appear to entextualize different cultural and commercial values, or *interpretive frames*, depending on the stances taken by their authors/principals and the "readings" by their intended audiences. Goffman (1974) explains "interpretive frames" as participants' definitions of social situations, of what goes on in strips of ongoing activities, built up in accordance with their subjective involvement in them. In other words, frames are part of the interpretive means that help participants understand or disambiguate utterances and other forms of communicative behavior. In this chapter, I identify five discursive frames through which different cultural and commercial values can be ascribed to public signage performing the act of "tourist welcome": (1) *the home (from home) frame*; (2) *the brand frame*; (3) *the spectacle frame*; (4) *the hedging frame*; and (5) *the multilingual display frame*. The list of these frames is not exhaustive. For reasons of space, I limit my discussion to some that I consider among the most common and prominent in staging the "synthetic access ritual" in contemporary global tourism (other linguistic landscape studies oriented to frame analysis include Coupland, 2012; Coupland & Garrett, 2010; Jaworski, 2010; Jaworski & Yeung, 2010; Kallen, 2010).

As will become apparent, one seemingly overarching function of all *welcome* signs is to create a sense of place for tourist destinations and places of mobility, which is most evident in the "brand frame." This styling of place is achieved

216 Adam Jaworski

through specific choices of the signs' language codes, visual motifs (fonts, color, images, etc.), their locations (or emplacements), and intertextual links with other discourses and genres (e.g. advertisements). It is in this way that I see *welcome* signs as particularly powerful in maintaining the (synthetic) sense of tourists as *individuals*—and the tourist experience as *singular*—while also being heavily ideologized semiotic resources for the positioning of tourist destinations and institutions involved in orchestrating and policing mobility in the global market of tourism.

Theoretically, this chapter is located within sociolinguistic approaches to "linguistic/semiotic landscapes" (e.g. Jaworski & Thurlow, 2010b; Shohamy & Gorter, 2009; Shohamy, Ben-Rafael, & Barni, 2010). Much of this work has been inspired by Scollon and Scollon's (2003) work on *geosemiotics*—"the study of the social meaning of the material placement of signs and discourses and of our actions in the material world" (p. 2)—with its focus on the analysis of displayed texts' multimodality, materiality, emplacement, and interaction order. Elana Shohamy's work lies at the center of theorizing linguistic landscapes as sites of symbolic construction of public space (Ben-Rafael, Shohamy, Amara, & Trumper-Hecht, 2006; Shohamy & Gorter, 2009). Far from treating it as benign or innocent, Shohamy has always argued for the view of emplaced texts as indicative of negotiation and contestation of different ideologies (including language ideologies), claims to ownership and preferred "meaning" of space, selective representation of different "voices," and the gatekeeping function of exclusion of various marginalized social actors (ethnic minorities, foreign workers, or anti-establishment groups) from full participation in the civic society (Shohamy, 2006; Shohamy & Waksman, 2009, 2010a). Shohamy has also been in the forefront of a methodological shift from examining a rather diffuse notion of "language" to a focus on linguistic and multimodal features, resources, and interdiscursive chains deployed strategically as markers of different group agendas, histories, and identities; means of resistance; and as instruments of social and political activism (Shohamy & Waksman, 2010a, 2010b).

Frames for the Tourist *Welcome* Signs

I now turn to illustrate how *welcome* signs and their variants are engaged in constructing different symbolic spaces of tourism, how they *position*, *interpellate*, or *hail* (Althusser, 1971) different publics, and how they organize tourist spaces as sites of agency and participation. My discussion is organized around the five interpretive frames suggested above.

The Home (from Home) Frame

Welcome signs constitute a global genre of texts deployed across most tourist areas, as well as numerous leisure, commercial, municipal, and other spaces. They probably originated as expression of domestic hospitality, and in the age of mass travel we find echoes of similar positioning of tourists as "guests" and destinations as "homes." This sentiment is expressed in the "Heathrow welcomes you home" sign (Figure 15.1), complete with the image of a typical, UK domestic doormat. Several identical signs are displayed around the arrivals area of Heathrow's Terminal 5, which almost exclusively services flights by British Airways, a "home" airline for many Heathrow passengers who may, in fact, take the signs at "face value" as ratified recipients.

FIGURE 15.1 "Heathrow welcomes you home," London Heathrow Airport, Terminal 5, May 2009

FIGURE 15.2 "Welcome," London Heathrow Airport, Terminal 1, May 2012

However, the participation framework (Goffman, 1981) of *welcome* signs is not always entirely clear. In Figure 15.2, for example, the represented *animator*, the person who is shown to be "uttering" the welcome, is named as one Crawford Butler, Beefeater, the Tower of London. Whether Butler—according to an Internet check, a real person—has actually written down the word "Welcome" enlarged on the poster next to his photograph—a typical "demand" image engaging his gaze with that of the viewers' (Kress & van Leeuwen, 1996) and spreading his arms in a "ready to embrace" gesture—cannot be known from just looking at the poster. Either way, the act of welcome is a representation or *performance* of a welcome ritual, a display of hospitality by a recognizable, named person who is also one of the iconic "Yeoman Warders" at the Tower of London. In this way, the poster creates a specific sense of place for London based on blending of heritage, distinction, and hospitality; it creates involvement between visitors and hosts through informal, personalized connotations of handwriting and implied contact (gaze, open arms gesture); and it plays into the expectations of many tourists of what they will or should "see" while visiting London. The fact that the welcome is mediatized and spectacularized (see below) requires from arriving passengers only temporary suspension of disbelief that it is not taking place face to face and in real time, and that all other passengers going past it are equally synthetically "addressed" by it.

The Brand Frame

The acts of welcome shown in Figures 15.3–15.7 demonstrate considerable variation in terms of their styling, content, and generic format. While the dominant,

FIGURE 15.3 "Welcome to Hong Kong," Hong Kong International Airport, April 2007

shared genre is that of the "tourist welcome," their styling and discourses vary (a common pattern across different global media formats, cf. Machin & van Leeuwen, 2007). The sign in Figure 15.3 doubles as an advertisement for a bank, fittingly for a city that is a major financial center. Put differently, the Royal Bank of Scotland appropriates the genre of *welcome* signs to colonize the semiotic landscape of the airport and to claim a stake in branding the city with its logo, albeit putting on an appearance of a friendly "host." Such conflation of *welcome* signs and advertisements is indeed quite common across different tourist and other commercial spaces.

FIGURE 15.4 "Welcome to Las Vegas," McCarran International Airport, Las Vegas, May 2007

FIGURE 15.5 "Welcome to Wonderful Copenhagen," Copenhagen Airport, April 2005

FIGURE 15.6 "Welcome to Los Angeles," Los Angeles International Airport, May 2007

FIGURE 15.7 "Welcome to Vancouver/Bienvenue à Vancouver," Vancouver International Airport, January 2005

Part of the "work" performed by the *welcome* signs is the aestheticization and authentication of travel destinations, especially providing visitors with an initial sense of arriving somewhere different from their mundane surroundings (cf. Kallen, 2009). The place names inserted into *welcome* signs—Hong Kong, Las Vegas, Copenhagen, Los Angeles, Vancouver, Israel/ישראל, Oslo, etc.—are quite redundant if we assume that most people "know" where they have arrived. Rather than as indexical place names, then, they function here as symbolic brand names, turning cities from places of dwelling and work into aestheticized, cultural objects

FIGURE 15.8 "Velkommen til Oslo Lufthavn/Welcome to Oslo Airport," Oslo Airport Gardermoen, June 2011

FIGURE 15.9 "Welcome to Israel/ברוכים הבאים לישראל," Ben Gurion Airport, January 2008

for tourist consumption (cf. Lash & Urry, 1994). *Welcome* signs equally create a sense of authenticity of place through display of "local" languages and, where necessary, a sense of security through their "translations" into the tourist lingua franca of English (cf. Kallen, 2009, p. 275). Displays of "local" art, regional and national branding of goods in duty free shops, and architecture of terminal buildings increasingly symbolic of their locations all add to the positioning of airports (and other transport hubs and tourist attractions) as metonyms of the cities, regions, and countries where they are situated.

The localizing of airports is, in great measure, achieved through the styling of their *welcome* signs. As seen in Figure 15.3, the sign creates a sense of Hong Kong as a "city of bankers," which is due to its styling as an RBS advertisement. "Welcome to Las Vegas" (Figure 15.4) is unmistakeably styled as signage reminiscent of amusement arcades and casinos. The multicolor neon is probably not as over the top as the frenzy of neon lights on the Strip that the cityscape of Las Vegas is best known for, but it certainly has a similar ring to it connoting gambling, nightlife, and hedonism. This is not miles away from the styling of the "Welcome To Wonderful Copenhagen" sign (Figure 15.5), which connotes informality and personalization with its stylized, handwritten font, nonstandard, emphatic capitalization of every word in the phrase, and the bright, if somewhat more "upmarket" than "Welcome to Las Vegas," blue neon light. "Welcome to Los Angeles" (Figure 15.6) stands in stark contrast to the "fun" connotations of the Las Vegas and Copenhagen signs. It may come as a bit of a surprise given the image of Los Angeles—the "City of Dreams"—as a major center of the cultural-products industries, with its entertainment sector (TV, film, music, theater), advertising, and architectural services. In fact, the commercial areas of the airport are completely saturated with the imagery of Hollywood as well as the "surf culture," sunshine and palm tree-lined boulevards on signage, packaging, themed souvenirs, and countless other products. However, the "Welcome to Los Angeles" sign seems to be indexing another side of the city that is indispensable to its status as a hub for cultural and creative industries: excellence in technology and design and its highly skilled labor force (Scott, 2000). The smooth, shiny, metallic, no-nonsense sans serifs connote just that: modernity, technocratic cool, and a potential for making money rather than for frittering it away at a gambling table. On the other hand, "Welcome to Vancouver/Bienvenue à Vancouver" (Figure 15.7) does not appear to "give away" much of the city's "character." The design of the sign is consistent with the rest of the airport signage, blending in seamlessly with its infrastructure and contributing to its textual cohesion. Yet, even some of the most banal aspects of the *welcome* signs, such as the name of the country (Israel) or city (Vancouver, Oslo), or appearance of a less familiar script (Hebrew), may give them an unusual, even exotic, feel for arriving tourists (cf. De Botton, 2002, p. 69; Jaworski & Thurlow, 2013), and a reassuring sense of familiarity to the travelers returning home.

The Spectacle Frame

In an earlier study (Jaworski, 2009), I suggested that greetings constitute a key speech act used in the tourism industry for the enactment of face-to-face encounters between tourists and hosts. However, due to the commodified nature of such encounters (service transaction, guided tour, theatrical performance, etc.), rather than constant reiterations of "greetings," these are repeated *performances* or *spectacles* of greetings, language displays that form part of the "tourist linguascape" (Jaworski, Thurlow, Lawson, & Ylänne-McEwen, 2003). Kallen (2009) captures the essence of this concept by suggesting that:

For the tourist who is in search of a feeling of being truly away from everyday experience, being greeted at the airport by signs in a foreign language is an immediate way to mark out the distance that has been travelled. The "foreign" language thus offers an immediate sense of transcendence from the mundane, and a token of authenticity in the new surroundings.

(p. 271)

Relative to other signage in their environment, *welcome* signs are often most prominent, large and towering over the people in their proximity (see Figures 15.8 and 15.9). These are Goffman's (1971) "platform events," spectacles performed on elevated stages for gathered or passing crowds (cf. Scollon & Scollon, 2003).

Figures 15.10 and 15.11 show a "Welcome to the United States of America" sign on the border between the US and Canada. This giant, multimodal sign stands in contrast to the formality of the border crossing once all the checks and formalities are out of the way. With the placement of the sign, the border undergoes a commodifying transformation (Debord, 1967/1995, p. 32); from a political and legal entity, it turns into a consumer-tourist spectacle, a theatrical metonym and gateway into the United States that is encapsulated in its composite landscape and cityscape of tourist attractions—to be proud of for Americans and to marvel at for visitors. This is the United States as a collage of patriotic heartlands or fun-filled playgrounds, where the economy of touring is intertwined with a culture economy vested with the task of regenerating post-industrial, late modern cities and regions (cf. Ash & Thrift, 2007). Rather than experiential, showing the United States "as it is," the multimodal content of the sign provides a way of imagining the United States as a historical, geographical, and cultural landmark to enhance the travelers' experience of border crossing, to heighten their excitement of anticipation, and to provide an aestheticized vision of the

FIGURE 15.10 "Welcome to the United States of America," US-Canadian border between British Columbia and Washington State, January 2005

FIGURE 15.11 "Welcome to the United States of America," US–Canadian border between British Columbia and Washington State (close-up), January 2005

"destination." All these features are consistent with Bauman's (1975) view of verbal performances as expressive acts focused on form and skill rather than referential content, dedicated to the audience's enhancement of experience, and subject to subsequent evaluation. The artful execution of the "Welcome to the United States of America" sign extends to modalities beyond language: (1) visual symbols and icons: the American flag positioned as the idealized backdrop to the composite landscape made up of the Statue of Liberty, the United States Capitol, the Gateway Arch, Mount Rushmore, Golden Gate Bridge, and Space Needle, all interspersed with images of "nature": trees and snow-capped mountains; (2) typography: a mixture of informal, cursive font vested with the job of "doing" the welcoming, giving it an aura of personalization, and the formal, solid, block letter forms reserved for the name of the country, giving it a sense of solidity and permanence; (3) color: the coloring of the letters rhymes with the red, blue, and white of the American flag, emphasizing the nationalist-patriotic connotations of the sign; and (4) materiality: combination of painted and "raw" wood makes the sign both durable and gives it a "natural" feel, with the stylized red ribbon on which the words "of America" are written, "softening" the overall impression and giving it a more celebratory appearance. Overall, the sign appears to be displayed to the passing audience (in a you-can't-miss-it-kind-of-way) to be *viewed* rather than to be read, to *entertain* rather than to inform (cf. Androutsopoulos, 2010).

The Hedging Frame

The signs in Figures 15.12–15.14, all located between the arrival gates and immigration control at Los Angeles International Airport, have clearly identifiable institutional principals: the U.S. Customs and Border Protection (Figures 15.12 and 15.13), and Homeland Security (Figure 15.14). In Figure 15.12, the act of welcoming appears to serve as a branding tool for the government agency. It is an aestheticized take on a nationalistic-patriotic theme, with a close-up of the American flag as background for the decorative, yellow-white, "3D" text. Overtly, the function of the sign may be phatic, but it also serves to inform the passengers that they are entering the U.S. Customs and Border Protection Agency-controlled space. The other two posters have a formalistic design, "sober" color schemes (predominantly white text on black in Figure 15.13 and blue text on white in Figure 15.14), and isotype-like pictograms, suggesting functionality rather than entertainment and playfulness.

The Homeland Security Agency uses a tagline that encapsulates its job of "Keeping America's Door Open and Our Nation Secure" (Figure 15.14), which plays on the notions of access and containment. Thus, it also projects a courteous, even friendly ethos while informing the visitors with visas of the requirement to provide "two digital fingerscans and a digital photograph." The phatic and informative elements of the poster are kept clearly separate. The "welcome" phrase is framed and contrasted with the rest of the text (cf. Kress & van Leeuwen, 1996) by the inversion of the background-font color scheme. The Agency's apparent "friendliness" is not to be mixed with its efficiency and main task at hand (see above). Interestingly, the Homeland Security "Welcome to the United States." sign is only one of very few with a full stop (period) at the end of the phrase. In my "collection" of approximately 300 *welcome* signs, no punctuation is typically used at the end of the "welcome (to)" formula. If a punctuation mark is present,

FIGURE 15.12 "U.S. Customs and Border Protection Welcomes You to the United States," Los Angeles International Airport, May 2007

FIGURE 15.13 "Welcome to Los Angeles," Los Angeles International Airport (U.S. Customs and Border Protection), May 2007

FIGURE 15.14 "Welcome to the United States," Los Angeles International Airport (Homeland Security), May 2007

it is more likely to be an exclamation mark connoting emphasis, excitement, and elation. With the full stop, Homeland Security appears to be more officious in its "welcome," giving it a pragmatic force of an emphatic statement and clear caesura—"we are done with the greeting, now let's move on to the business at hand." In sum, these last three examples demonstrate a shift in the function of the act of greeting from "merely" phatic to a hedging or mitigating device in the realization of face-threatening acts such as commands and directives (cf. Brown & Levinson, 1987).

The Multilingual Display Frame

As has been mentioned, "local" or "minority" languages can be used to create a sense of authenticity and distinction for a tourist destination (cf. Figures 15.8 and 15.9). However, multilingual displays (cf. Eastman & Stein, 1993) of tourist greetings often include a mixture of "local" and other national languages, orienting to or accommodating the visiting tourists. For example, at the Tourist Information desk at the Marco Polo International Airport in Venice, a large-format, Italian greeting *Ciao!* is accompanied by the phrase "welcome" displayed in no fewer than 20 different languages (Figure 15.15).

This composite sign functions both as part of the local linguascape, with the centrally emplaced *Ciao!*, and an "internationalizing" resource. Yet, it is reminiscent of Kelly-Holmes' (2005) notion of "fake multilingualism" dissociated from any sense of everyday, lived multilingualism. It is a playful and spectacular instance of linguistic commodification through which languages become "deterritorialized" and "detached" from their original environments and speakers,

FIGURE 15.15 "Ciao!" Marco Polo International Airport, Venice, September 2007

228 Adam Jaworski

challenging traditional notions of ethnolinguistic identity, language ownership, and authenticity. The light-heartedness of the display is emphasized by the different bright colors with which each "welcome" formula is written on the counter of the information desk.

Greetings and Welcomings in The Fleeting Sociolinguistics of Tourist-Host Relations

Throughout this chapter, I have used the terms "greetings" and "welcomings" as near-synonyms. This is consistent with Duranti's (1997) treatment of welcomings as (ceremonial) greetings, albeit in a rather different context. I am also in agreement with Duranti that there is more to greetings than a "'courteous indication of recognition' (Searle & Vanderveken, 1985, p. 216) or a conventional expression of pleasure at the sight of someone (Bach & Harnish, 1979, pp. 51–52)" (Duranti, 1997, p. 84). As this chapter has demonstrated, tourist greetings on *welcome* signs may fulfill a number of performative functions: create a "sense of place," add symbolic value of authenticity and distinction to destinations, or mitigate face-threatening acts.

In his study of greetings in Western Samoa, Duranti (1997) proposes six "universal" criteria for identifying greetings cross-linguistically and cross-culturally:

1. near-boundary occurrence;
2. establishment of a shared perceptual field;
3. adjacency pair format;
4. relative predictability of form and content;
5. implicit establishment of a spatio-temporal unit of interaction; and
6. identification of the interlocutor as a distinct being worth recognizing.

(p. 67)

As observed in my earlier study of tourist greetings (Jaworski, 2009), due to the inversion in tourism of everyday, mundane expectations and routines (Urry, 2002), this is where we can find a number of departures from Duranti's conditions for performance of greetings. Some have already been alluded to, including an important distinction between greeting exchanges versus displays, spectacles, and performances of greetings.

With masses of passengers, visitors, and locals passing through certain tourist areas, some individuals may filter out *welcome* signs from their attention structures (Jones, 2010). They may not "notice" them, or they may symbolically opt out from establishing a "shared perceptual field" attempted by the signs. On the other hand, a successful display of a tourist greeting or welcome does not require ratification from the tourist in an "adjacency pair format." Most of the *welcome* signs hanging "out there" are reminiscent of Mick Billig's (1995) "unsaluted" national flags staging and reinforcing a sense of banal nationalism(s) across the

Welcome **229**

globe, or—more to the point—they contribute to the semioscape of "banal globalism" alongside the images of globes (Szerszynski & Urry, 2002), airline tailfin designs (Thurlow & Aiello, 2007), or "new" typographic designs (Jaworski, 2013).

An exchange of greetings may occur on its own as a "minimal proper conversation" (Sacks, 1975), or it may mark the beginning of a new temporal unit or a subsequent shared activity (e.g. two colleagues may greet each other at the start of a new working day, and they may greet each other again at the start of a meeting later that same day). Tourist welcomings and greetings mediated by signage often remain just that—one-sided and unacknowledged displays followed in short succession by new instances of similar, fleeting acts of officious conviviality across adjacent or overlapping tourist areas.

Finally, and to return to my starting point, rather than acting as preludes to the "identification of the interlocutor as a distinct being worth recognizing," the commodified, mass-oriented greetings and welcomings mediated through signage seem to work predominantly as tokens of synthetic personalization, although, to repeat, they are only one of many discursive means of handling groups of tourists as individuals. Ron Scollon (1998, p. 19) argues that social interaction is organized around "three nested Maxims of Stance": (1) attention to the generic frame or "channel"; (2) once the channel is established, participants attend to their relationships and identities; and (3) when identities are established, participants attend to topics for discussion. In the fleeting sociolinguistics of tourism, and especially in the semiotic landscape of tourism dominated by *welcome* signs, much of the social interaction between "hosts" and "tourists" appears to begin and end with Scollon's first Maxim. While, following the second Maxim, destinations (and their principals) manage to express their stance of "warm welcome" and their identity ("sense of place") encoded in the signage, the tourists have no viable options of responding and asserting their identities in a reciprocal manner.

References

Agha, A. (2003). The social life of a cultural value. *Language & Communication, 23*, 231–273.
Althusser, L. (1971). *Lenin and philosophy*. New York: Monthly Review Press.
Androutsopoulos, J. (2010). Localizing the global on the participatory web. In N. Coupland (Ed.), *The handbook of language and globalization* (pp. 31–55). Malden, MA: Wiley-Blackwell.
Ash, A., & Thrift, N. (2007). Cultural-economy and cities. *Progress in Human Geography, 31*(2), 143–161.
Bach, K., & Harnish, R. M. (1979). *Linguistic communication and speech acts*. Cambridge, MA: MIT Press.
Bauman, R. (1975). Verbal art as performance. *American Anthropologist, 27*(2), 290–311.
Bauman, Z. (2000). *The individualized society*. Cambridge: Polity.
Beck, U., & Beck-Gernsheim, E. (2002). *Individualization: Institutionalized individualism and its social and political consequences*. London: Sage.
Beck, U., Giddens, A., & Lash, S. (1994). *Reflexive modernization*. Berkeley, CA: University of California Press.

Ben-Rafael, E., Shohamy, E., Amara, M. H., & Trumper-Hecht, N. (2006). Linguistic landscape as symbolic construction of the public space: The case of Israel. *International Journal of Multilingualism*, *3*, 7–30.

Billig, M. (1995). *Banal nationalism*. London: Sage.

Bourdieu, P. (2010). *Sociology is a martial art: Political writing by Pierre Bourdieu*. G. Sapiro (Ed.). New York: The New Press.

Brown, P., & Levinson, S. C. (1987). *Politeness: Some universals in language usage*. Cambridge: Cambridge University Press.

Coupland, N. (2012). Bilingualism on display: The framing of Welsh and English in Welsh public spaces. *Language in Society*, *41*(1), 1–27.

Coupland, N., & Garrett, P. (2010). Linguistic landscapes, discursive frames and metacultural performance: The case of Welsh Patagonia. *International Journal of the Sociology of Language*, *205*, 7–36.

Debord, G. (1967/1995). *The society of spectacle*. (D. Nicholson-Smith, Trans.). New York: Zone Books.

De Botton, A. (2002). *The art of travel*. London: Hamish Hamilton.

Duranti, A. (1997). Universal and culture-specific properties of greetings. *Journal of Linguistic Anthropology*, *7*, 63–97.

Eastman, C. M., & Stein, R. F. (1993). Language display: authenticating claims to social identity. *Journal of Multilingual and Multicultural Development*, *14*(3), 187–202.

Fairclough, N. (1989). *Language and power*. London: Longman.

Giddens, A. (1991). *Modernity and self-identity*. Cambridge: Polity.

Goffman, E. (1971). *Relations in public*. New York: Harper & Row.

Goffman, E. (1974). *Frame analysis: An essay on the organization of experience*. New York: Harper & Row.

Goffman, E. (1981). Footing. In E. Goffman (Ed.), *Forms of talk* (pp. 124–157). Oxford: Blackwell.

Jaworski, A. (2009). Greetings in tourist-host encounters. In N. Coupland & A. Jaworski (Eds.), *The new sociolinguistics reader* (pp. 662–679). Basingstoke: Palgrave Macmillan.

Jaworski, A. (2010). Linguistic landscapes on postcards: Tourist mediation and the sociolinguistic communities of contact. *Sociolinguistic Studies*, *4*(3), 469–594.

Jaworski, A. (2013). Indexing the global. *SemiotiX XN-10*. Retrieved from: http://semioticon.com/semiotix/2013/05/indexing-the-global/ (accessed March 1, 2014).

Jaworski, A., & Thurlow, C. (2010a). Language and the globalizing habitus of tourism: Towards a sociolinguistics of fleeting relationships. In N. Coupland (Ed.), *Handbook of language and globalisation* (pp. 255–286). Oxford: Wiley-Blackwell.

Jaworski, A., & Thurlow, C. (Eds.) (2010b). *Semiotic landscapes: Text, image, space*. London: Continuum.

Jaworski, A., & Thurlow, C. (2013). The (de-)centering spaces of airports: framing mobility and multilingualism. In S. Pietikäinen & H. Kelly-Holmes (Eds.), *Peripheral multilingualism* (pp. 154–198). New York: Oxford University Press.

Jaworski, A., & Yeung, S. (2010). Life in the Garden of Eden: The naming and imagery of residential Hong Kong. In E. Shohamy, E. Ben-Rafael, & M. Barni (Eds.), *Linguistic landscape in the city* (pp. 153–181). Bristol, UK: Multilingual Matters.

Jaworski, A., Thurlow, C., Lawson, S., & Ylänne-McEwen, V. (2003). The uses and representations of host languages in tourist destinations: A view from British TV holiday programmes. *Language Awareness*, *12*(1), 5–29.

Jones, R. H. (2010). Cyberspace and physical space: attention structures in computer mediated communication. In A. Jaworski & C. Thurlow (Eds.), *Semiotic landscapes: Language, image, space* (pp. 151–167). London: Continuum.

Kallen, J. L. (2009). Tourism and representation in the Irish linguistic landscape. In E. Shohamy & D. Gorter (Eds.), *Linguistic landscape: Expanding the scenery* (pp. 270–285). London: Routledge.

Kallen, J. L. (2010). Changing landscapes: Language, space, and policy in the Dublin linguistic landscape. In A. Jaworski & C. Thurlow (Eds.), *Semiotic landscapes: Language, image, space* (pp. 41–58). London: Continuum.

Kelly-Holmes, H. (2005). *Advertising as multilingual communication*. Basingstoke: Palgrave Macmillan.

Kress, G., & van Leeuwen, T. (1996). *Reading images: The grammar of visual design*. London: Routledge.

Lash, S., & Urry, J. (1994). *Economies of signs and spaces*. London: Sage.

Machin, D., & van Leeuwen. T. (2007). *Global media discourse*. London: Routledge.

Sacks, H. (1975). Everyone has to lie. In M. Sanches & B. G. Blount (Eds.), *Sociocultural dimensions of language use* (pp. 57–80). New York: Academic Press.

Scollon, R. (1998). *Mediated discourse as social interaction*. London: Longman.

Scollon, R., & Scollon, S. W. (2003). *Discourses in place: Language in the material world*. London: Routledge.

Scott, A. J. (2000). *The cultural economy of cities*. London: Sage.

Searle, J., & Vanderveken, D. (1985). *Foundations of illocutionary logic*. Cambridge: Cambridge University Press.

Shohamy, E. (2006). *Language policy: Hidden agendas and new approaches*. London: Routledge.

Shohamy, E., & Gorter, D. (Eds.) (2009). *Linguistic landscape: expanding the scenery*. New York: Routledge.

Shohamy, E., & Waksman, S. (2009). Linguistic landscape as an ecological arena: Modalities, meanings, negotiations, education. In E. Shohamy & D. Gorter (Eds.), *Linguistic landscape: Expanding the scenery* (pp. 313–331). New York: Routledge.

Shohamy, E., & Waksman, S. (2010a). Decorating the city of Tel Aviv-Jaffa for its centennial: Complementary narratives via linguistic landscape. In E. Shohamy, E. Ben-Rafael, & M. Barni (Eds.), *Linguistic landscape in the city* (pp. 57–73). Bristol, UK: Multilingual Matters.

Shohamy, E., & Waksman, S. (2010b). Building the nation, writing the past: History and textuality at the Ha'apala memorial in Tel Aviv-Jaffa. In A. Jaworski & C. Thurlow (Eds.), *Semiotic landscapes: Language, image, space* (pp. 241–255). London: Continuum.

Shohamy, E., Ben-Rafael, E., & Barni, M. (Eds.) (2010). *Linguistic landscape in the city*. Bristol, UK: Multilingual Matters.

Szerszynski, B., & Urry, J. (2002). Cultures of cosmopolitanism. *Sociological Review, 50*(4), 461–481.

Thurlow, C., & Aiello, G. (2007). National pride, global capital: A social semiotic analysis of transnational visual branding in the airline industry. *Visual Communication, 6*, 305–344.

Urry, J. (2002). *The tourist gaze* (2nd ed.). London: Sage.

PART 4

Placing People within Communities and Cultures

16

A RESEARCHER'S AUTO-SOCIOANALYSIS

MAKING SPACE FOR THE PERSONAL

Claire Kramsch

Shortly before his death, between October and December 2001, Pierre Bourdieu (1930–2002) decided to put into practice on himself the kind of reflexive sociology he had advocated throughout his career. His *Esquisse pour une autoanalyse* (2004), published first in Germany as *Ein soziologischer Selbstversuch* (2002), is a unique attempt to account for his intellectual trajectory and his choices as a researcher based on his experiences as a Béarnais, a son, a student, an academic, and a sociologist in the France of his time. He insists that it is not an auto-biography, a genre he repudiates as being self-indulgent and deceptive, but an objective account of subjective experiences that shaped his thinking and oriented him toward certain themes rather than others in his scholarly work. His fears that such an analysis would weaken his credibility as an objective sociologist in his own country were not unfounded, which is probably why he decided to have it first published in Germany. But what Bourdieu has given us with this book is a precious insight into the personal space of one of the most honest and rigorous scholars of our time. His little book has inspired me to write the following sketch of what he called an "auto-socioanalysis" of my own trajectory as an applied linguist. I dedicate it to Elana Shohamy, my multilingual companion in the linguistic landscapes of the heart.

A "French" Childhood

"*Vous êtes quoi, vous?—Je suis française*" (What are you?—I am French) I would have said in my youth with a certainty that surprises me, even today. So why did I leave? "*Pourquoi vous êtes-vous expatriée?*" (Why did you expatriate yourself?) The French word is so brutal—ex-patria, renouncing the land of your fathers—

236 Claire Kramsch

that I am taken aback. When asked of me in the intimate second person singular—
"*pourquoi t'es-tu expatriée?*"—it could make me cry.

For all my efforts to resist my mother's touted foreignness, I must have wanted
to make myself foreign. An immigrant. Not to be pinned down by any nationality,
language, religion, social class. To be just me. And yet dying to take root
somewhere, somehow; to be recognized and acknowledged as French, French
speaking, Catholic, middle class. Contradiction. Paradox. I made of paradox a
virtue and called it sophistication, originality, complexity.

My English mother emigrated to France when she married my French father,
as her mother had done when she emigrated from Hungary to England and married
my Polish grandfather, and as I later did when I emigrated from France to Germany
and married a German. Every time, marriage meant changing nationality,
language, religion, social class. Multilingualism came with the territory.

I must have been 11 or 12 on a visit to London just after the war. My Hungarian
grandmother is gabbing on the phone with her Hungarian friend. The guttural
Magyar inflections sound like hammers that are equally inflected with Danube
basin intonations, strong rolled "r"s, voiced sibilants, and singing nasals. I am totally
used to not understanding what is said around me. Suddenly, a call from the living
room: "Klär darrrling, poot ze teller in ze zink." I am starting to learn German
in school, so I recognize the word *teller* as meaning plate and I suppose *zink* means
sink. For my French ears, that is British English. I do not yet know that my
mother's family is of Jewish origin, and even if I had known, it would not have
made any difference. In my mind, I was French.

Back in Versailles, and throughout the 1950s, my mother is learning my
language. She still has a very recognizable English accent, but has made a virtue
of being foreign. "*Moi, mes enfants, je suis étrangère*" (As for me, children, I am a
foreigner), which would explain every odd pronunciation, excuse every
misunderstanding, glorify every violation of French social conventions. For the
life of her, she cannot get the French grammar and spelling straight. Every time
she has to write an official letter, she struggles with the agreement of her past
participles. I still hear her shouting from her desk in the living room to our
bedroom upstairs: "*la lettre que vous m'avez envoyée* (the letter that you sent me)—
does it take an e or not?" Today, at the dinner table, she recounts her story with
the fruit vendor at the market. "*Je lui demande: c'est combien les oranges?—Y m'dit:
trente francs l'kilo—alors j'lui dis: 'que-wah?'*" (I ask him: how much for the
oranges?—He tells me: thirty francs the kilo—so I tell him: w h a . . . t?). We
all burst out laughing and my father adds: "*de quoi de quoi?*" (what indeed!).
Language, always foregrounded, was always a source of merriment, irony, sarcasm,
ridicule. My English grandmother, who came especially from England to help
my mother deliver her sixth child at home, kept wandering around the house
desperately asking for "*une louche, une louche!*" (a ladle) when what she wanted
was "*une couche*" (a diaper). We children taught her the most inappropriate French
and made fun of her when she used French swearwords with my mother's well-

bred French friends. My mother's sister, who prided herself on her perfect native British English and was a teacher of English speech and diction, made fun of French whenever she came on a visit to Versailles. *Camembert* became "come 'n' push," *charcuterie* became "char-cuttery," and *Versailles* was forever "versyles." We accepted this mock French as part of my aunt's ability to at once love French food and denigrate the French. Like my mother, she had not learned any French in school, so could not speak French with my father, who had to use his school English in her presence. Not that our English was much better than his, but we were pitiless in our assessment of his accent. Statements of his such as "Ze childraine ave to poot on zeir clo-thes-es" could bring us into hysterics. My mother invariably came to the rescue: "Now don't you make fun of your father!" but they never spoke English together and my mother retained the splendid isolation of a British citizen stranded in a foreign country.

I only realized much later what it meant for my mother and her family to be "British citizens." As Jewish immigrants from Hungary and Poland at the turn of the century, and given the rampant anti-Semitism in the Britain of the time, acceding to British citizenship was a badge of distinction, a source of pride. The English-born generation made a point of speaking English to the utmost perfection, some members of the family exchanged their Polish-Jewish name for a British-sounding one, some even got a nose job. Their love of all things English was unsurpassed. Only surpassed by my own love of all things French.

Meanwhile, my mother has learned how to speak the French of the butcher, the house cleaner, and of Madame X next door. She has also learned to speak like her children. Upon leaving, she says: "*Bon ben moi j'me taille*" (roughly equivalent to "Well guys I'm beating it"), or "*J'vais m'tailler des clopinettes*" (God knows what she meant by that), or "*J'm'en fous*" ("Fuck you"), like any 12 year old would say, but it is hardly appropriate for a 40-year-old bourgeois mother of seven, and from Versailles, no less. We children are grateful that she has given up on what we called "the battle of Britain"—requesting that we say in English what we had just said to her in French, but I remain aware of the difference and of the impossible contradiction. I wish I had a mother who spoke French, like all the others, but when she speaks French it is not her language and she sounds like she is usurping my father's language—an imposture of sorts. Being the firstborn, I bore the brunt of her ambivalence. I still hear the way she pronounced sometimes my name the French way "Claire" and it always meant trouble. Whereas "Clare," pronounced the English way and sometimes followed by "darling," meant everything was OK. Unfortunately, when my mother spoke English, she was no longer part of my world, which I saw as French. An impossible conundrum.

Why was it so hard to be bilingual or even to admit that we were, to a certain extent, bilingual? For sure, I never took English in school, so until well into my twenties, I could not really read nor write in English, even though I could conduct simple conversations and enjoyed movies in English. But we children never did

238 Claire Kramsch

consider ourselves to be bilingual. The two worlds—the English and the French—were clearly delineated, with age-old suspicions and mistrust between them. Stereotypes were carefully groomed and maintained, an endless source of mirth and innuendos, and a sure way of preventing any potential hybridity. In the 1950s, the Channel was more than a sleeve (*La Manche*, as we would call it in French); it was an ocean. Once in France you were in Europe, whereas in England, you were already half in America.

German was still, in the 1950s in France, the language of science, philosophy, music. It was the language any student with academic ambitions would choose to learn. English was for secretaries and businesspeople. I took German. I was not particularly good at it: the grammar translation method, the endless conjugations, and case endings were deadly. But my adolescent yearnings were enthralled by the musicality of German poetry. While the pleasure of French was beaten out of me through the mechanical parsing of sentences and the desiccating *explications de textes*, German was the language that held the promise of answering my big questions about life and death, and my dreams of beauty and fulfillment. German remained, for me, a foreign language, but what made it attractive was precisely its foreignness. I later realized that part of that foreignness was that it was taboo: it was the language of the enemy. My falling in love with and then marrying a German broke my French grandmother's heart.

I tell this story in English with no small amount of trepidation, as I fear that Anglophone readers might not understand what I mean. *Apprendre l'allemand* is certainly a different experience from *learning German* and *der Sinn des Lebens* that Faust was seeking and that we had to read day after day in German classes is not translatable as *the meaning of life*. The first is metaphysical, the second is functional. Many of my writings as an applied linguist have stemmed from the despair of ever being able to be truly understood or to make myself understood, which is why I immediately identified with Kafka's characters and have always resonated to the paradoxes and the contradictions he expresses in his writings (Kramsch, 2008).

Discourse Analysis: My Way Out

I realize now that what attracted me to German was not the German language per se, but the historical paradoxes that it embodied, the impossible meanings it both constructed and expressed in the 1930s and 1940s. It is the binary oppositions: good guys versus bad guys, the French versus the Germans, capitalism versus socialism, that have obsessed me. This obsession has led me to distrust all the binaries that have come my way since then: French cartesianism versus Anglo pragmatism, language versus literature, the universal versus the particular, the exuberance versus the deficiency of meaning, morality versus functionality, individual agency versus institutional constraints. I find them at once intellectually useful and profoundly deceptive. I use them myself and am quick to deconstruct them.

The obsession to escape dubious dichotomies and bilingual binaries led me to always seek the third element in those impossible dialectics. In the same manner as German had become my language, which was neither the language of my mother nor that of my father, so I found myself yearning for a field of research that would be neither the philology nor the literary studies I had been taught in my studies at the Sorbonne. When I moved to the US in the early 1960s after completing my studies and was confronted with the realities of language teaching at MIT, I found that neither my philological nor my literary training was capable of resolving the problems I was facing teaching French and German to American engineers and scientists. While I was doing a good enough job as a language teacher, as a foreigner to the United States I could not identify with many of the ways of thinking I was encountering there. After 15 years teaching at MIT, I despaired at ever understanding my American students. They were intelligent and hard-working, but they did not seem to know anything about France and Germany, nor did they seem to care about the momentous events that had marked my life. Nor did I understand their views on life. Where to turn to for answers?

I got myself a Widener Library card and spent days in the Harvard stacks, trying to find wisdom in myth, folk tales, and historical narratives. I identified with the "hero with a thousand faces," who goes out into the world to seek his fortune and who discovers things he did not even know existed. I read and read, in a frantic search for clues. I devoured Roland Barthes (1957) and Erving Goffman (1959), Eric Havelock (1963) and Gregory Bateson (1972), Vladimir Propp (1968), Joseph Campbell (1949/1968), and Bruno Bettelheim (1975). Then, one day in Widener, I fell on a book by the sociolinguist Hugo Steger from the University of Freiburg titled *Heutiges Deutsch* (*Today's German*) (Steger, 1974). It contained transcripts of radio recordings of German native speakers in conversation on a variety of topics. Their discourse was filled with false starts, back channelings, repetitions, interruptions, repairs of various sorts. The transcriptions followed the conventions of today's conversation analysis. I was stunned. So that was what real conversation looked like! I had been teaching conversation courses for years and nobody had told me that there was a field of inquiry called conversation analysis! Maybe the reason I did not understand my students was because they had different ways of conducting conversations (Kramsch, 1987). From that moment on, I started reading everything I could put my hands on in the field of discourse and conversation analysis. The study of discourse was the perfect bridge between the study of language and the study of literature, the analyses of conversations and the interpretation of poems, between orality and literacy, storytelling and language teaching. It ultimately reconciled my interest in both the social sciences and the humanities. And critical discourse analysis hinted at a possible explanation for the inner turmoil I was experiencing.

My first little book, *Discourse Analysis and Second Language Teaching*, published by the Center of Applied Linguistics in 1981, was out of print hardly six months after its publication, but it was for me a first attempt to put into pedagogic practice

240 Claire Kramsch

the life-changing insights I had gained through discourse analysis. Those original epiphanies gave meaning to everything I read and wrote; they have sustained me over the years ever since. The ethical world they opened for me was radically different from the morality I had been inculcated in my primary habitus: that of the good daughter, who, like Simone de Beauvoir, was *une jeune fille rangée*, obeying the rules of proper French conduct; of the good student, who followed the rules of grammar and the French academic conventions of good writing; of the good citizen, who remained within the parameters of a French patriotic worldview. That morality was made of unquestioned a priori values. By contrast, the world of discourse revealed to me for the first time how historically constructed such a morality is and how it gets constructed differently in different languages. Through discourse, historicity was suddenly irrupting into my personal universe.

Painful memories of cultural clashes now made more sense. I remembered my mother ridiculing my efforts to glorify Napoleon, as I was taught in school to do by memorizing the battle plans of all his victories ("Nappy? That little dictator?" she would exclaim . . . in English). I understood now that she was only mouthing the understandable discourse of pride from those who had defeated Napoleon at Waterloo. I recalled my German mother-in-law telling me about her youth and mentioning almost in passing that September 1 was a school free day ("*schulfrei*") because it was "*Sedantag*" (Sedan day? The battle in which the Prussians defeated the French in 1870?). I now understood how the Franco-Prussian war that my French grandmother had suffered through could feel quite different on the other side of the Rhine on the part of Germans who had lived with the memory of Napoleonic wars. I remembered the foreman at the factory in Germany where I worked one summer after the war complaining to me that we, the French, had no business resisting German occupation ("*es war unfair*"). After all, we had been defeated, had we not? I had difficulty dealing with that remark, which shattered all my conceptions of aggressors and aggressed during three wars with the Germans. While these remarks were profoundly shocking, unsettling even, to me at the time, I now understood them not as mean or obtuse, but as so many discourses that speak through people, producing and reproducing the cultural habitus of citizens and their national ideologies. Norman Fairclough had not yet written *Language and Power* (1989), nor James Gee his *Social Linguistics* (1990), but I had already then intuited the potential of discourse studies to understand the awesome power of discourse to construct ideologies.

I found in the western Germany of the 1970s a remarkable nation without nationalism, indeed without ideology, and I took it as the promise of a Europe at last at peace with itself. I found in Germany, through the Goethe Institute, a large number of wise, experienced educators who were searching for democratic ways of teaching German as a foreign language on the backdrop of the total collapse of their nation and their national language. Strong in my new discoveries in the field of discourse studies, I embraced the then emerging field of second language acquisition and applied linguistics as the promise of a new way of learning and using language. The communicative approach to teaching foreign languages was the expression of that promise—a dream of dialogue with and openness to others with a healthy distrust of absolute truths and hegemonic nation-building. In the early 1980s, after a workshop I was invited to give in German at the Goethe Institute in Paris to French teachers of German, Daniel Coste invited me to write a book directly in French for a French readership in his collection *Langue et Apprentissage des Langues*. It felt like a return home. Expressing in French for my French compatriots what I had learned from American and German applied linguists was a greater joy than I would have ever imagined. The book, *Interaction et discours dans la classe de langue* (1984), gave me the opportunity to show the French educational system my gratitude by contributing to the teaching of foreign languages in my native country. It reconciled me with myself.

Ecological Landscapes of the Heart

Meanwhile, in the US, the 1980s were not a time of reconciliation of opposites, but, on the contrary, a hardening of the dichotomies that I had tried to escape. Not only did the Cold War exacerbate the us versus them mentalities, but American exceptionalism drew an irreducible line between the US and the rest of the world. The "America—love it or leave it" syndrome felt like an unbearable quandary. I had less and less tolerance for the gap between the lofty rhetoric of U.S. politicians and the realities on the ground, for the hypocrisies of capitalism clothed in democratic ideals, and for the increasingly blatant contradictions of American life. I found some comfort reading the work of Robert Bellah and his associates at UC Berkeley in their influential book *Habits of the Heart* (Bellah, Madsen, Sullivan, Swidler, & Tipton, 1985), which explained to me many of the contradictions between the call for individualism and the call for commitment in American life. And I gained incredible insights reading Pierre Bourdieu's *Ce que parler veut dire* (1982), which put in words the contradictions I had experienced between intellectual ferment and class prejudice in French academic life.

In his autoanalysis, Bourdieu has a phrase that captures well my feelings at the time. He talks about his *habitus clivé*, or "split habitus . . . inhabited by tensions and contradictions" (p. 127). His was a habitus divided between his academic success and his modest social origins. In my case, it was a habitus divided between European heritage and American citizenship, between a multilingual multicultural background and the expected allegiance to a fundamentally monolingual American ideology. This cleavage expressed itself, as it has done for Bourdieu, in a schizophrenic attitude toward academic achievements: on the one hand, French academic docility and success; on the other hand, a distaste of any American academic self-importance and a distinct conviction that I owed my success in the US merely to chance and to the support of key mentors in the course of my career. I did not have the disdain for the minutiae of language teaching that many of my fellow professors had in my department ("It is not below my dignity to teach first-semester German and schlepp the overhead projector across the hallways," I would say), but this very lack of disdain could have been seen as arrogance in reverse. I refused to play the academic power game (when I arrived at UC Berkeley, I had the graduate students call me Claire, to the great distress of my colleagues in the German department), even though I craved the recognition. Bourdieu was ambivalent toward the intellectual milieu of Parisian academics; I was ambivalent toward a country to which I owed so much professionally but that, by seeing itself as superior to all, devalued the very country that I came from and that had forever shaped the person I was.

My instinctive response was, once again, to objectify and historicize my divided subject position. Like Bourdieu, who chose as the topic of his inaugural lecture at the Collège de France a reflection on the very genre of the Collège-de-France-inaugural-lecture, my whole research has been an endless reflection on what it means to be a language teacher all the while that I write and teach about language and language teaching. Bourdieu called such a reflection "*une schizophrénie à demi contrôlée*" (semi-controlled schizophrenia; p. 139), and indeed that is what it might feel like. It is a process of objectivation or historicization that both establishes distance to language teaching practitioners and brings them closer as fellow travelers on the basis of our common concerns for education. It is a process that has made me gravitate more toward Pascal (1976) and the late Bourdieu (1997/2000), as well as to postmodern thinkers such as Bakhtin (1981) and Foucault (1970) than the Descartes of my youth. I retained this postmodern orientation as I later embraced ecological approaches to SLA (Kramsch, 2002) and complexity theory (Kramsch, 2012).

The new field of research on linguistic landscapes that emerged from the work of social psychologists Landry and Bourhis (1997) and sociolinguists (Gorter, 2006) must have seemed attractive to Elana Shohamy for exactly the same reasons as I had been attracted to discourse and ecolinguistics. Composed of the "linguistic tokens which mark the public sphere, including road signs, names of sites, streets, buildings, places and institutions as well as advertising billboards, commercials and even personal visit cards" (Shohamy & Gorter, 2009), linguistic landscapes are discourse in action, multimodal discourse, shaping our environment through signs that cry out in different languages. They interpellate us in different ways and force us to respond with our senses, our memories, and our imagination. As markers of the relative power and status of the linguistic communities that created them, they jostle for my attention, seek my recognition, challenge me to interpret them. As they vie for my personal space, they provide a window into the power relations among the discourses that I participate in. The fact that I can describe them, juxtapose them with other signs, in other languages, capture them on film, objectively interpret them within the historical context in which I found them, and take note of the effects of globalization on the languages themselves (Huebner, 2006) enables me to position myself as a multilingual researcher. But deep down,

A Researcher's Auto-Socioanalysis **243**

I know that those linguistic landscapes do not delineate only the geographic and social boundaries of neighborhoods. They are also the symbolic expressions, by the people who produced them, of personal memories, nostalgic expatriations, and hybrid hopes for the future. Just as I have attempted in this short essay to weave the threads of my linguistic landscape to make myself understandable to myself and to you.

In closing, I would like to use the notion of "habits of the heart," coined by Bellah et al. (1985), but inspired by de Tocqueville (1835/1969, p. 508), to characterize a habitus shaped by personal experiences and, in turn, shaping its environment. Linguistic landscapes are ultimately shaped by personal experiences. Foreign names, unfamiliar sounds, unexpected indexicalities, and historicities have shaped Elana's multilingual and multicultural landscapes as they have mine. In turn, these landscapes have made us into cosmopolitan researchers, but they have also made us leery of words, sensitive to hypocrisy, and aware of social injustice. They have delineated the affective boundaries of our allegiances, marked our transgressions and our unorthodoxies. In that respect, our respective linguistic landscapes find a common grounding in shared habits of the heart.

References

Bakhtin, M. (1981). *The dialogic imagination*. (M. Holquist & C. Emerson, Trans.). Austin, TX: University of Texas Press.

Barthes, R. (1957). *Mythologies*. Paris: Seuil.

Bateson, G. (1972). *Steps to an ecology of mind*. New York: Ballantine.

Bellah, R., Madsen, R., Sullivan, W., Swidler, A., & Tipton, S. (1985). *Habits of the heart: Individualism and commitment in American life*. Berkeley, CA: University of California Press.

Bettelheim, B. (1975). *The uses of enchantment: The meaning and importance of fairy tales*. New York: Vintage.

Bourdieu, P. (1982). *Ce que parler veut dire: L'économie des échanges linguistiques*. Paris: Fayard.

Bourdieu, P. (1997/2000). *Pascalian meditations*. (R. Nice, Trans.). Palo Alto, CA: Stanford University Press.

Bourdieu, P. (2002). *Ein Soziologischer Selbstversuch*. Frankfurt: Suhrkamp.

Bourdieu, P. (2004). *Esquisse pour une auto-analyse*. Paris: Raisons d'agir Editions.

Campbell, J. (1949/1968). *The hero with a thousand faces* (2nd ed.). New York: Bollingen Foundation/Pantheon Books.

Fairclough, N. (1989). *Language and power*. London: Longman.

Foucault, M. (1970). *L'ordre du discours*. Paris: Gallimard.

Gee, J. (1990). *Social linguistics and literacies: Ideology in discourses*. New York: Falmer Press.

Goffman, E. (1959). *The presentation of self in everyday life*. New York: Doubleday.

Gorter, D. (2006). *Linguistic landscape: A new approach to multilingualism*. Bristol, UK: Multilingual Matters.

Havelock, E. (1963). *Preface to Plato*. Cambridge, MA: Harvard University Press.

Huebner, T. (2006). Bangkok's linguistic landscapes: Environmental print, code mixing and language change. *International Journal of Multilingualism, 3*(1), 31–51.

Kramsch, C. (1981). *Discourse analysis and second language teaching*. Washington, DC: Center for Applied Linguistics.

Kramsch, C. (1984). *Interaction et discours dans la classe de langue.* Paris: CREDIF.

Kramsch, C. (1987). Classroom interaction and discourse options. *Studies in Second Language Acquisition,* 7, 169–183.

Kramsch, C. (2002). Introduction: "How can we tell the dancer from the dance?" In Kramsch, C. (Ed.), *Language acquisition and language socialization: ecological perspectives* (pp. 1–30). London: Continuum.

Kramsch, C. (2008). Multilingual, like Franz Kafka. *International Journal of Multilingualism,* 5(4), 316–332.

Kramsch, C. (2012). Why is everyone so excited about complexity theory in applied linguistics? In S. Bailly, A. Boulton & D. Macaire, (Eds.). *Didactique des Langues et Complexité. En hommage à Richard Duda. Mélanges CRAPEL* 33, 9–25.

Landry, R., & Bourhis, R. (1997). Linguistic landscape and ethnolinguistic vitality: An empirical study. *Journal of Language and Social Psychology,* 16(1), 23–49.

Pascal, B. (1976). *Pensées.* Paris: Garnier-Flammarion.

Propp, V. (1968). *Morphology of the Folktale.* (L. Scott, Trans.). Austin, TX: University of Texas Press.

Shohamy, E., & Gorter, D. (Eds.) (2009). *Linguistic landscape: Expanding the scenery.* New York: Routledge.

Steger, H. (1974). *Heutiges Deutsch.* München: Hueber Verlag.

Tocqueville, A. de. (Ed.). (1835/1969). *Democracy in America.* (J. P. Mayer, Trans.). G. Lawrence. New York: Harper & Row.

17

UNDERSTANDING THE HOLOCAUST

A PERSONAL HISTORY, CRITICAL LITERACY ANALYSIS OF A GESTAPO FILE

David I. Hanauer

Introduction: Language, Life, Death, and Academia

In the preface to her book *Language Policy: Hidden Agendas and New Approaches*, written in the aftermath of the tragic death of her daughter Orlee, Elana Shohamy (2006) wrote:

> There was just too big a gap between life and language; bridging it was not possible, it did not make sense. But it was at this very point that I began to see the connection between the two: when it comes to language one can see language in every life and life in every language . . . I see all things through language and within language, the world, society and my personal life.
>
> (p. xiv)

Elana's position, expressed above and exemplified in the actual writing of her book following personal loss, involved the intertwining of language, academia, writing, analysis, life, tragedy, and meaning. It is this avoidance of sterile boundaries between life and work, academia and phenomenology, and the constant recognition of the centrality of language for all that is human that has characterized Elana's career. I will, in this chapter, follow her lead and deal with issues that, for me, involve the same guidelines of life, death, familial tragedy, academia, language, and literacy. This is a chapter that explicates a research project into the meaning of the Holocaust and an analysis of the Gestapo file of my grandparents—Alfred and Helene Hanauer—who were murdered during the Holocaust in 1941. It is a personal paper, an essay, and an academic analysis.

246 David I. Hanauer

The investigation presented here is part of a larger personal research agenda to explore the meaning of the Holocaust for myself and for my family. The research question at the heart of this extended research project is: In what ways do my family and I understand our experiences of the Holocaust? This is a descriptive, qualitative, phenomenological research question aimed at understanding subjective positioning. The issue is not to understand the Holocaust in historical terms, but rather to address those aspects of the Holocaust that touch upon the cognition, affect, and consciousness of the members of a family. In one sense, the idea behind this project is to individualize, characterize, and personalize the Holocaust and its lingering effects; in another sense, the aim of this project is therapeutic and directed by the desire for salvation from the narrative of the Holocaust.

In a truly exceptional paper, the French psychoanalyst Nadine Fresco (1984) describes interviews she conducted with eight adult children of Holocaust survivors. I remember the first time I read this academic paper and shuddered as if I was reading my own story for the first time poetically expressed in the language of psychology. Through Fresco's words, I can explicate the underpinning impetus for the research agenda of which this current chapter is part. Fresco speaks of three intertwined aspects of the phenomenology and sociology of being a child of a Holocaust survivor: silence, inherited fear, and a deep sense of distance. As stated by Fresco, "The silence formed like a heavy pall that weighed down on everyone. Parents explained nothing, children asked nothing. The forbidden memory of death manifested itself only in the form of incomprehensible attacks of pain" (p. 421). It is the silence and the "forbidden memory of death" that construct the confusing consciousness of emotional pain for an event that one has not witnessed or experienced. Fresco speaks of parents who "transmitted only the wound to their children" without the memory, and eloquently describes the resultant consciousness as being "like people who have had a hand amputated that they never had. It is a phantom pain in which amnesia takes the place of memory" (p. 422). This phantom pain of a memory that one never had can be, as in my case, the impetus for a personal research project. The aim of this research includes the attempt to fill the void of silence by explicating historical family events and facilitating emotional attachment. After all, it is nearly impossible to grieve in the abstract. It is the possibility of concreteness and imagery that can allow grief to be directed at those who died before you were born.

I am aware that this is a different way of conceptualizing what being a researcher means. As in the title of this book, dedicated to the continuation of Elana's work, the individual is not just the subject of study, but the person who initiates and conducts the research. Developments over the last two decades of qualitative research have made it clear that the positioning of the researcher can never be ignored (Denzin & Lincoln, 2003). But I would like at this point to take this one step further. As applied linguistic researchers, we have an obligation to study those things that affect us most as human beings. Research, especially research at the nexus of language, psychology, and society, can and should be motivated by personal concerns and qualified by the use of appropriate and explicitly stated methodology. The aim is not to self-justify existing biased positioning, but rather to explore society and consciousness and reach conclusions that go beyond the a priori. Research of this kind can be ethical, honest, and socially valuable. As with any research project, both intention and methodology must be scrutinized for appropriateness and adequacy by the informed reader.

In all, over the last two years, I have conducted four studies from different perspectives and utilizing different literacy-based methodologies in the attempt to address the question: In what ways do my family and I understand our experiences of the Holocaust? The problems in addressing this question are obvious, but still worth explicating. First and foremost, there is only one living witness, my father, and he, for the majority of his life, preferred not to talk about his experiences at all. Second, as with any family that has undergone historic trauma, talking about events is painful and perceived as dangerous. The option always exists that if discussed and explored, the events of the past will lead to the dissolution of the present. The investigation of personal familial trauma has real dangers in psychiatric terms. Third, the existing material evidence is limited. Finally, I, as a researcher, am researching my own family, and there is no illusion of objectivity. This is clearly defined as a subjective research project.

The first study I conducted in relation to this research agenda consisted of a poetic rendition of a narrative interview concerning my father's Holocaust-Kindertransport experience (Hanauer, 2012a). The aim of the study was to elicit and present my father's subjective understanding of his wartime experiences. This narrative presentation was the first time my father had presented a full version of his experiences. The research methodology consisted of utilizing a narrative interview technique followed by transcription, thematic analysis, and rendition in poetic form (Hanauer, 2010; Richardson, 2003). The resultant poetic data provided access to the core aspects of my father's experience and, more broadly, understanding of the relatively little known Kindertransport events. A central theme of his narrative consciousness is the moment of parting from his parents. As presented in Hanauer (2012a):

We got to Frankfurt

I don't remember exactly whether we came

I do remember that it was then time for me to board the train.

And in front of the train which was a special train stood SA people
they're not stormtroopers
they're not the SS
    they were the brown shirts
    the uh SS wore the black shirts

248 David I. Hanauer

uh they stood there and had some dogs with them
because they'd had problems with parents
either trying to get on the train
or at the last moment trying to take their child

They didn't want everybody to see there
some of the parents and the children in one of the halls
that was there
I think it's a waiting room or something
I don't remember exactly what.

You got a little tag with your name on
and a number
and then when they were ready you were led out
by some young Jewish men
who were allowed to do it to the train
and put into compartments
and the compartments I remember had numbers on it
and I think if you had six you went into compartment six.

And said goodbye to your parents
and then you went into the compartment.

The compartment had other children
children little children of two years old
with some bigger girls there
who looked after them
the children in diapers
after you got into the compartment
the SA man came
and locked shut the door
and put a padlock on the door so that you couldn't get out
and all you could do is to look at the window

and look out and

and see your parents well in the distance

And the train left

(pp. 11–12)

As seen in this segment from the poem concerning my father's experiences, parting is a central emotional and thematic component of this particular Holocaust narrative.

Understanding the Holocaust **249**

The second study I conducted consisted of a poetic autoethnography of my own experiences growing up in a family that had a Holocaust-Kindertransport survivor in it (Hanauer, 2012b). The aim of the study was to explicate my own understandings and experiences of growing up in a family deeply affected by my father's unspoken story and thus to explicate a second-generation Holocaust-Kindertransport consciousness. This was an autoethnographic study that used two books of poetry I wrote in the 1980s as the core data and augmented these with contextualizing narrative memories and phenomenological description. Several themes emerged through this investigation concerning family and personal responses. First, the absence of a narrative and explicit understanding of what happened to my father and my grandparents in the Holocaust translated into a series of very vivid recurring nightmares and that these dreams were the point of personal contact with these past events. The second theme that emerged was the recognition that my father's story was silenced as a result of the fear of the emotional trauma of the narrative itself. Finally, the third theme that emerged was the recognition of the pain of my father and my own grief and mourning for the grandparents I never knew.

The third study I conducted involved an observational and interview study of an artistic performance by Kimi Hanauer that took place at the Maryland Institute College of Art (MICA) during a Process Gallery opening on November 17, 2011, in Baltimore, Maryland, and was entitled "In Memory of Hella and Alfred #2." The performance lasted for 25 minutes and consisted of the artist physically erasing sections of the drawn faces of Hella and Alfred Hanauer using sandpaper. The pictures themselves consisted of enlarged, charcoal drawings of my grandparents' passport photos. During the performance, the artist's hands bled on the pictures, and she stated, "I want to know you, feel you," echoing a poem I wrote in the 1980s. The aim of this study was to gain some insight into the transmission of familial trauma concerning the Holocaust to the third generation. The analysis of the performance and interview with the artist revealed the continuation of the traumatic consciousness found in previous generations, and in particular the need to emotionally engage with the experiences of great-grandparent Holocaust victims.

The fourth study in this series of investigations consisted of a linguistic landscape investigation of a Stolper Steine memorial dedication for Alfred and Helene Hanauer that took place in Wurzburg, Germany, in June 2011 (Hanauer, in press). The Stolper Steine memorial consists of placing small copper cobble stones engraved with the name of a person deported from Germany during the Nazi regime in the pavement in front of the former place of residence of the deported person. The Stolper Steines are paid for by local residents, and their placement is accompanied by a ceremony. The aim of this investigation was to understand the different ways in which the story of my grandparents, the Holocaust, and the memorial ceremony itself was conceptualized by different participants within a

250 David I. Hanauer

broader social frame. This study was conducted according to linguistic landscape research guidelines, and involved digital photographs of the site before and after the ceremony, documentation of all literacy products present at the ceremony, transcripts of speeches given, and limited interviews with the people involved. The findings pointed to three ways of constructing this memorial. Official understandings consisted of the political motive of signifying the difference between the "new democratic and multicultural Germany" and the Nazi regime, and to promote tolerance of minority populations currently living in the Wurzburg area. For the schoolchildren, the meanings of the Stolper Steine memorial involved the learning and personalization of local history (emotive, present, and concrete). For the family involved in this event, the Stolper Steine functioned as a gravestone and the ceremony as a funeral service in the absence of any other marker or ceremony designating what happened to Alfred and Hella Hanauer.

This collection of four studies presents a backdrop for the investigation presented in this chapter. The studies so far have explored the consciousness and experiences of the three living generations of Holocaust-Kindertransport survivors and the social ramifications of memory in the German context. The final piece in this set of studies consists of an understanding of what happened to my grandparents Alfred and Hella Hanauer, and it is to this study that we turn in the next section.

The Historical Analysis of the Gestapo File of Alfred and Helene Hanauer

The Gestapo file (see Figure 17.1), which is the collection of documents that will be analyzed here, came into my family's possession only in 2010 following a request by my sister (Elaine Alcalay) directed to the historian of the city of Wurzburg. My father had asked various international and German governmental institutions for information on his parents many times over the years since his parting from them. But in all cases, he was told that no files existed and that all evidence had been destroyed. But in 2010, through the diligent work of a municipality employee, the file was found, photocopied, and forwarded to the Hanauer family. As might be expected, the presence of the file caused deep distress. My father, who has impaired sight, spent many hours trying to read it. The German was difficult, and it was decided to have the file professionally translated. Alex Lapidus translated the file into English following the exact structure of each document in the file. The analysis presented here is based on the English version of the file.

The file was analyzed using a historiographic approach. Each document in the file was analyzed for its official function and historical evidence of the events related to my grandparents. The analysis was comprehensive and addressed all the documents in the file. Table 17.1 provides a timeline and a summary of the documents and historical evidence in the Gestapo file.

Understanding the Holocaust   251

FIGURE 17.1 Pages from the Gestapo file of Alfred and Helen Hanauer

As can be seen in the timeline and documents in Table 17.1, the process of deportation and ultimate murder of Alfred and Hella Hanauer in Jungfernhof death camp in Riga started, from a bureaucratic perspective, with the arrest of Alfred Hanauer in 1938 a few days after the extensive anti-Jewish pogroms across Germany known as the Kristallnacht. The arrest seems to have served several different purposes, including the criminalization of Alfred Hanauer, confirmation of his identity, specification of personal identifying characteristics, including photographs, and the documentation of all financial and material assets. During this forced incarceration, Alfred was also evaluated for his medical health and ability to work in a camp. During 1939 and continuing through 1941, a process of stripping of financial assets and properties from Alfred and Helene Hanauer was enacted. This included the forced sale of a business, the imposition of a "Flight Tax," the forced sale of furniture, and the imposition of fines for various violations during this period; further processes of criminalization were instigated in relation to a variety of "financial violations." The Hanauers were also forced from their apartment to a designated Jewish area. In 1941, Alfred and Helene Hanauer were given deportation orders and instructions. They were stripped of their citizenship, all papers were confiscated, all financial assets forcibly transferred to the state, and they were body searched. They were forced to pay for their own transportation and ordered into a train that deported them to Riga. Having read and analyzed the historical timeline of events, we now know some of the history of the last three years of my grandparents' lives.

TABLE 17.1 Gestapo file document summary and historical evidence

Date	Document and official function	Historical evidence
November 14, 1938	Announcement of protective custody (Secret Police and State Police)	Alfred Hanauer arrested and detained at the Wurzburg State Police Station
	Recording of personal information	Alfred Hanauer required to provide full disclosure of personal history
	Alfred Hanauer statement of personal history and financial assets	
November 15, 1938	Doctor evaluation for heart disease Release of personal items to Helene Hanauer	
November 17, 1938	Order of extension of detention (Secret Police)	Alfred Hanauer kept imprisoned and not allowed contact with anyone outside the prison
November 18, 1938	Request to the Director of Public Health to evaluate whether Alfred Hanauer is healthy and capable for work in a camp. Found to have limited ability due to war injury	Alfred Hanauer has leg injury from First World War German military service
November 21, 1938	Announcement of release from police custody	Alfred Hanauer released from Wurzburg Police Station
January 6, 1939	Announcement of name change. From Helene Hanauer to Helene Sara Hanauer	Helene Hanauer forced to add the name Sara to designate Jewishness
March 5, 1939	Announcement of forced acquisition of Hanauer Brothers White and Woolen Wares Wholesale Business to house servant Seebald	Alfred Hanauer forced to sell business without compensation
August 18, 1939	Affidavit that Alfred Hanauer is acquainted with farming work (Mayor of Wiesenfeld)	
September 20, 1939	Request to State Secret Police to allow Helene Hanauer to visit her aunt in another region for medical reasons	
November 10, 1939	Demand of payment of 10,000 Reichsmarks for Flight Tax as a result of the intent to "give up domestic abode" in Germany	Alfred Hanauer forced to transfer funds to Finance Office of Wurzburg
February 3, 1941	Investigation into Financial Violations: failure to report 100 Reichsmarks, underestimating monthly expenses, supporting relatives, and failure to hand in a gold-silver brooch	Instigation of criminal proceedings against Alfred Hanauer. New address—forced to leave apartment and move into Jewish-designated area
August 21, 1941	Request to State Secret Police to sell furniture of Alfred Hanauer	Forced sale of furniture
August 27, 1941	Announcement of transfer of furniture to auctioneer	
August 30, 1941	Sale of furnishings by auctioneer and bill	
October 11, 1941	Announcement of fine on Alfred Hanauer for financial violations	Alfred Hanauer found guilty of "financial violations" and fined

TABLE 17.1 continued

Date	Document and official function	Historical evidence
October 13, 1941	Search of Hanauer residence for "hoarded goods" of wealthy Jews	Secret Police, State Police, and tax investigators search Hanauer residence
	Announcement of fine and criminal proceedings against Alfred Hanauer for financial violations	Instigation of criminal proceedings against Alfred Hanauer for "hoarded goods"
	Announcement of confiscation of forbidden goods: sewing thread, pewter and copper plates	Confiscation of Hanauer household items
November 23, 1941	Deportation Order Alfred Hanauer and instructions from State Secret Police. Scheduled deportation date November 27, 1941, at which time all assets will be confiscated. A full statement of assets should be provided and apartment should be cleaned before departure. One travel bag allowed and foodstuffs for three weeks. Required to report to Guter Railroad Station and pay for transportation costs	Alfred Hanauer stripped of citizenship and deported by train to the Jungfernhof death camp in Riga, Latvia, on November 27, 1941
	Deportation Order Helene Hanauer and instructions	Helene Hanauer stripped of citizenship and deported by train to the Jungfernhof death camp in Riga, Latvia, on November 27, 1941
November 24, 1941	Statement of Assets Alfred Hanauer Statement of Assets Helene Hanauer	
December 2, 1941	Request from War Pension Department to State Secret Police for information on where Alfred Hanauer has been transferred to	
December 8, 1941	Request to War Pension Department to stop paying a pension to Alfred Hanauer as he has been "evacuated," "stripped of his citizenship," and his "entire fortune has been confiscated"	War pension of Alfred Hanauer ceased following his deportation
	Announcement of Evacuation to the East of Helene Hanauer by order of the Fuehrer. Body search and confiscation of identity papers	Confirmation of the deportation of Helene Hanauer and of a body search
January 29, 1942	List of documents confiscated from Alfred Hanauer during body search during deportation on November 27, 1941	Alfred Hanauer body searched before boarding train for deportation and papers confiscated

Additional Documents: Birth certificate Alfred Hanauer, Birth certificate Helene Leiter, Request for a Marriage License, Marriage License (Alfred and Helene Hanauer), Certificate of Military Service Alfred Hanauer, Military Class 3 Cross of Military Merit with Swords award to Alfred Hanauer for service during WWI, Announcement of military pension following war wounds

254 David I. Hanauer

A Critical Literacy Agenda

The outcome of reading and analyzing the file of my grandparents is a deepened sense of the events and what happened to them, but also pain and anger at the injustice. What does one do with these feelings? For a literacy researcher and an applied linguist, the answer seems to be to further explore this case so as to perhaps deter future events of this kind. An important feature of the file is that a wide range of functionaries and institutions were involved in the processes that led to deportation. While the State Secret Police (Gestapo) instigated and directed many of the proceedings documented in the file, the actions taken were, in many cases, those of regular state institutions, such as tax officials, local police, doctors, auctioneers, registrars, municipal officials, and transport officials. As seen in the file itself, the state, through its bureaucracy and officials, functioned in ways that allowed ordinary, law-abiding German citizens to be incarcerated, robbed, stripped of citizenship, and deported from the country to a death camp. There is a critical literacy agenda here. Understanding the role of literacy in this particular case may facilitate recognition of similar injustices in our present systems of governance. I agree with Denny Taylor (1996), when, in her discussion of how official literacies solidify poverty and entrap the poor, she states:

> I hold on to the possibility that if we can make visible the human rights violations that take place through the use of official documentation, we can interrupt the texts and hold bureaucratic institutions accountable. If we change the way official texts are used, we change the system.
>
> (p. 15)

The documents in this file fulfilled five specific functions: identification, criminalization, appropriation of assets, evaluation of health, and deportation. A modern state cannot function unless it is capable of clearly identifying its citizens (Matusov & St. Julien, 2004). Accordingly, a large part of the file just deals with documents that allow the state to be able to know who is Jewish, where they live, and what they look like. Within the Third Reich context, these ways of identifying were dictated by underpinning racial assumptions that combined physical traits and ancestry, and assumed social and psychological meanings in what Taylor (2004) has termed as race-thinking. The manifestation of these processes of identification is bureaucratic and conducted by regular state functionaries in addition to the secret police. In a governmental system directed by racial assumptions, the importance of the ability to identify specific segments of the population cannot be overstated.

Having identified an individual, the second function of these documents is to recreate the citizen as a criminal. This is easy enough to do. All one has to do is write laws that define people and specific acts as criminal. In the present case, most of these laws were based on racial guidelines and dealt with what was allowed or

Understanding the Holocaust **255**

not allowed for someone identified as Jewish. From 1933 through 1938, a series of anti-Semitic laws were enacted, designed to identify Jews, limit and ultimately stop their economic activity, destroy their civic participation, segregate Jews from other segments of the German population, revoke their citizenship, and, finally, present a legal basis for deportation to death camps (Edelheit & Edelheit, 1994). The importance of the legal basis for these racially directed discriminatory laws was that they allowed the activation of the complete apparatus of the state in fulfilling its intentions. This is a process of criminalization, and, of course, once instigated, changes the social perception and position of the person so defined.

A third aspect of these documents was the directed appropriation of all assets of the targeted person. This was enacted once again through the legal process, and went hand in hand with the process of criminalization. The documents for this included repeated requests for statements of assets followed by taxation, levying fines, forcing sale of property, and confiscation of goods and accounts. All of these actions were legal in the sense of following the law as defined by the state government. As with processes of personal identification, the seizing of financial assets was initiated through the identification of assets, and then followed by a legal process of seizing of assets through institutions such as tax collectors and customs officials. All of these acts were backed by the full force of the legal system and written and defined laws.

The last two functions of literacy are linked. Documents can establish the physical state of an individual, and this can be used to determine whether it is worthwhile to place someone in a situation of forced labor or have them sent directly to a death camp. In other words, the aim of a health evaluation document was not the well-being of the patient, but rather was used to help determine where you would be deported to. Deportation was once again a legal act, and consisted of both the taking away of German citizenship and the physical removal of the individual. In this sense, the documents enacted a physical and symbolic removal of citizens from the national entity. The documents for deportation required German Jewish citizens to sign that they understood (and agreed through signing) to the state's retraction of their citizenship and deportation. This document gave the illusion of legal compliance and de facto specified the state's intentions and directed the ultimate act of deportation to a death camp.

Countering Discrimination and Oppression

Shohamy (2006) has rightly pointed out that language (and, by extension, literacy) is not in itself either "good" or "bad"; literacy, in the case analyzed here, was used for the purposes of gross human rights violations, but this is not a damning criticism of literacy in all its aspects. Shohamy (2006) points out that:

> It is the duty and obligation of all linguists to make language users aware of these misuses of language and resist manipulations. Manipulations occur

256 David I. Hanauer

all the time but it is the extent to which the public is aware of these manipulations that makes a difference. Once they are aware, they can protest and resist.

(p. 172)

The question we need to pose at this time is whether literacy can also be used to counter genocidal intentions and not only facilitate human rights violations.

There is a history within applied linguistics exemplified in Elana Shohamy's research of using textual and linguistic analysis to explicate and raise awareness concerning the ways in which people are characterized, discriminated, and oppressed, and to act to change these situations. This history includes, among others, critical discourse analysis (Wodak & Meyer, 2001) and critical applied linguistics (Pennycook, 2001). In the present case, literacy clearly played a role in facilitating the Holocaust, and, as such, I endorse positions explicated within critical approaches to applied linguistics that researchers should use their knowledge and analytical abilities to critically investigate issues of discrimination, inequality, and oppression.

Two core avenues for potential action and interaction would seem to exist. First, as seen in the specifics of the transformation of Alfred and Helene Hanauer from law-abiding citizens of Germany into nameless, graveless, deported, and murdered people without any citizenship, literacy is, first and foremost, used to create the discursive and legal framework within which such atrocities can occur. Thus, as a first avenue of defense, racist discourse, in all its forms and manifestations, needs to be resisted. This relates to all levels of this form of discourse—propaganda, editorials, advertisements, pamphlets, political speeches, news, posters, everyday conversations, racist jokes, etc. Furthermore, and perhaps even more significantly, the legal disputes and written laws that construct legalized human rights violations must be contested. It is through these laws that, ultimately, state-sanctioned atrocity occurs and is justified.

A second important avenue through which literacy-based human rights violations may be countered is through literacy education. I am thinking about a very specific aspect of literacy education—the conceptualization of literacy pedagogy as humanizing practice (Hanauer, 2003, 2011). Literacy education can be used to make students explore their own histories, work out their own unique presence and position in the world, and appreciate and value the difference of others. Literacy can promote multiculturalism and tolerance. The atrocities of the Holocaust were facilitated through a decontextualized, literal, unfeeling acceptance of textual authority. Literacy was used to restrict personal interpretation and to enforce very specific outcomes that counter basic compassion and equality with other human beings. Literacy is always about communication between people, and there is always an interpretive act involved. However, literacy education can promote or restrict the degree of freedom an individual feels in countering and interpreting a written text. Unfortunately, most literacy education today around the world is designed to reinforce acceptance of existing genre conventions and accuracy in relation to structural components of written text. Thus, applied linguists should consider fighting for a different conception of literacy pedagogy and enact this difference in their classrooms and educational practices.

Final Comments

While we all know that life ends in death and parting, we all still hope for a positive ending. It is perhaps human nature to do so. But that positive ending, the march toward inclusive, equitable societies for all residents, is a constant challenge and struggle. One of the chilling aspects of this analysis of a Gestapo file that appears in this study is the very ordinariness of the documents that populate it. The vast majority of these papers are documents that you will find in every state bureaucracy: tax forms, police reports, doctor evaluations, financial transactions, travel papers, eviction orders, etc. What makes these documents different? Well, the historical context and the broad racist, societal discourse that underpinned them may be a difference. But there is a clear lesson here: human rights atrocities have a literacy basis and a gradual developmental trajectory. What starts as a racist political speech becomes a law of citizenship status, transforms into a written edict from a central government office, is enacted by a local policeman and tax official, and ends with deportation and murder. Racism does not start with violence, but rather with language. It is a symbolic act, and literacy allows that symbolic construction of humanity to become a social reality through the imposition of the authority of the written word. Concretized racism in the form of discriminatory documents is all around us, and it is the role of applied linguists to counter this at every opportunity. That is the legacy and the challenge of Elana Shohamy's collected work over the last two and a half decades, and something that we all must take very seriously.

Acknowledgments

I would like to thank Dr. Alex Lapidus of the University of Southern Maine for his careful and thoughtful translation of the original Gestapo file from German into English.

References

Denzin, N. K., & Lincoln, Y. S. (2003). The discipline and practice of qualitative research. In N. K. Denzin & Y. S. Lincoln (Eds.), *Collecting and interpreting qualitative materials* (pp. 1–45). Thousand Oaks, CA: Sage.

Edelheit, A. J., & Edelheit, H. (1994). Legislation, anti-Jewish. In *History of the Holocaust: A handbook and dictionary* (pp. 299–331). Boulder, CO: Westview Press.

Fresco, N. (1984). Remembering the unknown. *International Review of Psycho-Analysis*, *11*, 417–218.

Hanauer, D. (2003). Multicultural moments in poetry: The importance of the unique. *Canadian Modern Language Review, 60*(1), 27–54.

Hanauer, D. (2010). *Poetry as research: Exploring second language poetry writing.* Amsterdam: John Benjamins.

Hanauer, D. (2011). Meaningful literacy: Writing poetry in the language classroom. *Language Teaching: Surveys and Studies, 45*(1), 105–115.

Hanauer, D. (2012a). Living the Kindertransport: A poetic representation. *Shofar: An Interdisciplinary Journal of Jewish Studies, 31*(1), 18–33.

Hanauer, D. (2012b). Growing up in the unseen shadow of the Kindertransport: A poetic-narrative autoethnography. *Qualitative Inquiry, 18*(9), 845–851.

Hanauer, D. (in press). The discursive construction of the Stolper Steine memorial project: Official, educational and familial meanings. In R. Wodak & D. Seymour (Eds.), *Contested Memories.* New York: Routledge.

Matusov, E., & St. Julien, J. (2004). Print literacy as oppression: Cases of bureaucratic, colonial and totalitarian literacies and their implication for schooling. *Text, 24*(2), 197–244.

Pennycook, A. (2001). *Critical applied linguistics: A critical introduction.* Mahwah, NJ: Lawrence Erlbaum.

Richardson, I. (2003). Poetic representation of interviews. In J. F. Gubrium & J. A. Holstein (Eds.), *Postmodern interviewing* (pp. 187–202). Thousand Oaks, CA: Sage.

Shohamy, E. (2006). *Language policy: Hidden agendas and new approaches.* New York: Routledge.

Taylor, C. (2004). *Race: A philosophical introduction.* Cambridge: Polity.

Taylor, D. (1996). *Toxic literacies: Exposing the injustice of bureaucratic texts.* Portsmouth: Heinemann Trade.

Wodak, R., & Meyer, M. (2001). *Methods of critical discourse analysis.* Thousand Oaks, CA: Sage.

18

LANGUAGE EXPERIENCE CHANGES LANGUAGE AND COGNITIVE ABILITY

IMPLICATIONS FOR SOCIAL POLICY

Ellen Bialystok

Much of the research in psychology is based on the fiction that individual differences are noise in the data that interfere with the greater goal of describing human performance. Individuals are assumed to be equally good and interchangeable representatives of their designated groups: 5 year olds, French speakers, girls, and so on. This is a necessary simplification because the purpose of most psychological research is to uncover patterns that describe the "big questions": How do children learn language? How do adults make decisions? What kind of information can we retrieve from memory? But the simplification comes at a cost: we lose the ability to understand the myriad factors that make each of us unique and, with it, the ability to understand normal variation in the system. At the same time, much of psychological research is conducted in sterile laboratories, often housed in the windowless basements of dull buildings. Human behavior, in contrast, unfolds in a social context shaped by language, politics, and many other dimensions. These environmental features matter deeply for human behavior, but just as the individual difference variables that define us, they too are largely ignored in psychological research.

One way in which psychology is moving away from these models is by examining how intense experience modifies cognitive performance and brain structure. Systematic effects of experience have been found both in changes in brain structure and function and in behavioral performance. A famous example of brain response to experience is the case of London taxi drivers (Maguire et al., 2000). A unique feature of London taxi drivers is that they must pass "The Knowledge," a test demonstrating a detailed knowledge of every street and laneway in Greater London in order to be awarded a license. The region of the brain that is largely responsible for spatial navigation is a part of the hippocampus, and in the study by Maguire et al. (2000), this region was more enlarged in London taxi drivers than in a control group. More recently, a study by Suo et al. (2012) compared hippocampal volume for older adults who had held supervisory jobs with individuals of the same age who had not. They found that there was greater hippocampal density in those who had been supervisors, a difference they attributed to the cognitive demands of those jobs. Similar effects of experience have been reported using behavioral measures. Salthouse and Mitchell (1990) reported that professional architects outperform non-architects on tests of visuospatial ability. In a large research program, Bavelier and colleagues (e.g. Green & Bavelier, 2008) report significant modification of perceptual-motor ability in individuals who are intensely involved in video game playing. And finally, a recent study that compared professional football (soccer) players in two European leagues that differed in their level of competition found that players in the higher league demonstrated better performance on a design fluency test than did players in the lower league (Vestberg, Gustafson, Maurex, Ingvar, & Petrovic, 2012), and players in both leagues outperformed non-players. Design fluency requires rapid planning and execution, skills not dissimilar to those used in sport.

These examples all demonstrate the systematic effect of experience on the human mind, but all the examples suffer from problems of direction, selection, and extent. The direction problem is the inability to clearly attribute the outcome to the experience. There are very few training studies in which the outcomes can be calibrated to the experience or are tested prior to the experience, so the data are substantially correlational. There may be hidden factors that are responsible for the outcomes, but these are concealed by the group comparison. The problem of selection is related: it may be that individuals with excellent visuospatial skills choose architecture for a career and those with unusually sensitive finger control become string musicians; moreover, because these experiences tend to be chosen activities, it is possible that those individuals who are more suited to them persist, while those with less suitable skills drop out. Ultimately, individuals who are uniquely qualified for these activities are the ones who pursue them and become part of the experimental group comparisons. Finally, the problem of extent is that the outcomes are generally closely related to the training itself, so the evidence for modification in cognitive ability from experience is limited by the generalizability of those outcomes.

Bilingualism is an intense experience, but it is less vulnerable to these interpretative problems. The majority of bilinguals become so because of life necessity, such as immigration, and not by their choice to pursue an experience in which they have already demonstrated talent or interest. Although many people indeed decide to study language, it is not typically a choice for immigrants; geopolitical realities, by their nature, preclude selection at that level of individual difference. Our research is conducted in a culturally diverse city in which English is the community language but more than 50 percent of the population does not use English at home (Statistics Canada, 2007). Thus, people living in these homes, and their children, are naturally bilingual because the typical pattern is to maintain

Language Experience and Cognitive Ability **261**

the heritage language in the home (and local community, where there are sufficient numbers), but use English for work, school, and other social and larger community interactions. Because bilinguals are not preselected, comparisons between monolingual and bilingual individuals who are matched on other variables can be used to isolate aspects of cognitive and brain function that are different for the bilingual group. This possibility of finding relatively well-matched groups of monolingual and bilingual participants for research alleviates some of the problems of direction and selection.

The problem of the extent of these effects is also attenuated in bilinguals. Bilingualism is clearly a language experience, so evidence for its impact on nonverbal aspects of intelligence would demonstrate a broader range of effect than is typically found in this type of research. To summarize the research, bilingualism has been found to lead to enhanced executive functioning across the life span, although often in conjunction with poorer verbal processing than monolinguals, and contribute to "cognitive reserve" that protects against cognitive decline in both healthy aging and dementia.

Linguistic Effects of Bilingualism

Because bilingualism is a linguistic experience, it is not surprising that it has linguistic consequences; what is more surprising is that those consequences appear to be disadvantages. The differences between monolinguals and bilinguals in linguistic processing and verbal ability are found both in terms of vocabulary size and access to specific lexical entries. In two large-scale studies, each involving more than 1,600 participants, bilinguals had significantly smaller receptive vocabulary scores in English for both children between the ages of 3 and 10 years old (Bialystok, Luk, Peets, & Yang, 2010) and adults between the ages of 17 and 89 years old (Bialystok & Luk, 2012). The bilinguals in both studies were fluent in both languages, with the majority of them speaking the non-English language at home and English at school or work, and the non-English language included a wide variety of different languages. Nonetheless, the depth of their English vocabulary was, on average, less than it was for their monolingual counterparts, even though English was the language of work, school, and community.

Differences in lexical access as a function of language background are well documented: bilinguals typically take significantly longer to retrieve individual words than do monolinguals, such as in naming pictures (Gollan, Fennema-Nostestine, Montoya, & Jernigan, 2007). These effects are found equally when bilinguals are performing the naming task in their more dominant language (Ivanova & Costa, 2008). Bilinguals also perform more poorly than monolinguals on verbal fluency tests, standardized tests that are used as neuropsychological measures of brain functioning. There are two main versions of this task. In the first condition, category fluency, participants generate as many words as possible in 60 seconds that are members of a stated category, such as "animals."

262 Ellen Bialystok

Performance on this condition is an index of vocabulary size and semantic structure, and consistent with receptive vocabulary scores, bilinguals generally produce fewer words than monolinguals (e.g. Gollan, Montoya, & Werner, 2002). In the second condition, letter fluency, participants generate words that begin with a stated letter, usually F, A, and S. This task also relies on vocabulary knowledge, but it additionally taps executive control processes because our lexical networks are not organized according to initial letters or sounds, so effortful and strategic search processes are required to generate acceptable words. In this case, if monolinguals and bilinguals are matched for vocabulary size, bilinguals actually outperform monolinguals because of their superior executive control (Bialystok, Craik, & Luk, 2008). Thus, for performance on this task, the vocabulary deficit is outweighed by a more general advantage in executive control.

What is the connection between these linguistic processing costs associated with bilingualism and the idea that there are advantages in executive control? It is now well documented that both languages are activated, to some extent, when bilinguals are using one of them, creating a situation of perpetual conflict between language representations during any linguistic performance. There is evidence for this claim from behavioral (Kroll & de Groot, 1997), imaging (Martin, Dering, Thomas, & Thierry, 2009), and patient (Fabbro, Skrap, & Aglioti, 2000) studies. The fact that this competition does not impede performance—bilinguals are not prone to massive intrusions from the unwanted language in their speech production or comprehension—signals that the competition is resolved before it becomes a problem. Our speculation on the mechanism for resolving this conflict is that the domain-general executive control system, a network of brain regions and processes whose job it is to monitor and resolve conflict, shift attention, and manipulate working memory, is recruited into language processing (for review, see Bialystok, Craik, Green, & Gollan, 2009). This constant involvement of the general executive control network in language processing has two consequences: first, the network itself is reconfigured relative to that used by monolinguals (e.g. Luk, Anderson, Craik, Grady, & Bialystok, 2010), and second, the efficiency and power of the network is increased through massive practice (e.g. Gold, Kim, Johnson, Kryscio, & Smith, 2013).

Cognitive Effects of Bilingualism

Behavioral evidence for superior performance of bilinguals compared to monolinguals in nonverbal executive control tasks has been shown across the life span (Bialystok, Martin, & Viswanathan, 2005). The tasks used in this research are typically simple perceptual conflict tasks, such as the flanker task. Participants see a simple perceptual display, such as a row of five arrows, and are asked to press a key indicating the direction in which the center arrow is facing. The four irrelevant arrows can be facing in the same direction, creating congruent trials, or in the opposite direction, creating incongruent trials and requiring attentional effort to ignore those stimuli. Reaction times are always slower on incongruent trials. Studies of both children (Martin-Rhee & Bialystok, 2008) and adults (Costa, Hernández, & Sebastián-Gallés, 2008) have shown that reaction times for both congruent and incongruent trials are also slower for monolinguals than for bilinguals. There are no performance differences between groups when simple trials, such as congruent or neutral trials are presented in a single block, but the combination of both congruent and neutral trials, and the need to monitor and shift between them, leads to faster performance by bilinguals on the entire block of trials. This pattern of faster performance by bilinguals indicates that bilinguals have better ability than monolinguals on all aspects of executive control, not only the difficult incongruent trials. Thus, in this simple problem of resolving nonverbal perceptual conflict, a number of effortful processes that are part of the executive function system are implicated, and in all respects, bilingual participants perform more efficiently than monolinguals.

If it is bilingual experience that is responsible for these outcomes, then greater degrees of bilingualism should be associated with larger outcomes. To investigate this question, Bialystok and Barac (2012) studied children between 7 and 9 years old who were attending immersion programs, and so were in the process of becoming bilingual. All the children spoke English at home, but their education was being conducted in either French or Hebrew. Children were given a range of tests of language ability, metalinguistic ability, and executive control, as well as various background measures. In both programs, performance on linguistic and metalinguistic tasks was predicted by children's language proficiency and nonverbal intelligence, but performance on executive control tasks was predicted by how long they had been in the immersion program and how bilingual they were. Children who were in the program longer and were more bilingual showed larger gains in executive control.

The interpretation of these effects is that the use of the executive control system for language processing in response to the problem created by jointly activated languages strengthens that system more broadly so that performance on nonverbal problems that involve conflict is also enhanced. Support for that claim comes from a meta-analysis by Luk, Green, Abutalebi, and Grady (2012), in which they analyzed results from 10 different studies in which bilingual participants performed a language-switching task in fMRI. The tasks were different, but all included the requirement to switch between languages while producing verbal responses to stimuli. The results of their meta-analysis showed that overlapping brain networks were used for both language switching and task switching, suggesting that the domain-general network is indeed used to manage attention to two languages.

The constant recruitment of the domain-general executive control network for resolving competition between languages has the further effect of reconfiguring that network and improving its efficiency. A study by Abutalebi et al. (2012) identified the anterior cingulate cortex as the executive control region that is modified by bilingualism in that it is less activated by bilinguals than monolinguals in solving conflict tasks and that less activation is associated with better behavioral performance. Extending these results, Gold et al. (2013) demonstrated less activation by bilingual than monolingual older adults in a switching task that required executive control and crucially showed a significant negative correlation between the amount of activation in several regions involved in the executive control network and performance on the task. In other words, in both studies, bilinguals achieved better performance as a function of less effortful activation of the brain networks recruited for that task. Both studies conclude that the executive control network for bilinguals is more efficient.

Bilingualism and Cognitive Reserve

The research discussed to this point has focused on the impact of bilingualism that emanates from the joint activation of two languages and so requires the recruitment of the executive control system. Importantly, the benefits of bilingualism have been found through the life span including in older age, modulating the natural decline of cognitive function with healthy aging. This general notion of protection against cognitive decline is called "cognitive reserve" (Stern, 2002) and refers to the types of stimulating cognitive activities (crossword puzzles, formal education, social engagement) that are associated with the maintenance of cognitive function through aging. Thus, the protection of executive control for bilinguals is attributed to cognitive reserve. However, the complaints of aging are not generally described in terms of difficulty with executive control; instead, they are overwhelmingly documented as complaints of memory, but there is little research connecting bilingualism to memory function. Is there any evidence that bilingualism might mediate general cognitive decline with aging?

As an initial investigation of this possibility, we conducted two studies from the records of patients who had visited a memory clinic and had been diagnosed with either dementia (two-thirds of whom were diagnosed with Alzheimer's disease; Bialystok et al., 2007) or specifically with Alzheimer's disease (Craik, Bialystok, & Freedman, 2010). Together, the two studies included approximately 400 patients, about half of whom had been lifelong bilinguals. In both studies, bilingual patients experienced the onset of dementia symptoms about four to five years later than the monolingual patients who were largely comparable on other measures. This is a substantial and highly significant delay.

There are two possibilities for the mechanism by which cognitive reserve protects cognitive functioning, especially in the context of dementing disease. The first is a direct effect in which cognitive reserve enables the brain to resist the development of neuropathological changes underlying dementia, such as the deposit of beta-amyloid in the medial-temporal areas, which creates atrophy in those regions (e.g. Landau et al., 2012; Valenzuela et al., 2012). The second is a compensatory effect in which neuropathological changes continue to progress, but more intact aspects of brain function supplement impaired functions and permit the person to cope with the pathology (e.g. Bennett, Schneider, Tang, Arnold, & Wilson, 2006; Kidron et al., 1997). In support of the compensation hypothesis, we demonstrated that bilingual patients with Alzheimer's disease who were matched with monolingual patients on age and cognitive level at time of testing showed *more* atrophy in the medial-temporal regions than did the monolinguals (Schweizer, Ware, Fischer, Craik, & Bialystok, 2012). Thus, for the same cognitive level, bilinguals had more neurodegeneration, and therefore more advanced disease. Our interpretation is that preserved functioning for the bilinguals was achieved through compensation, a boost that presumably came from their enhanced networks and function of the executive control system. This research, showing protection against dementia by compensating for a compromised memory system with a more intact cognitive network, is powerful evidence for the reorganization of brain networks through experience.

Experience-Induced Plasticity from Bilingualism

Not long ago, it was assumed that the adult brain was a fixed structure, unable to generate new neurons, and locked into the levels and types of processing it had achieved when it was young and flexible. Research with both humans and other animals has categorically proven these assumptions to be false: brains are continually adapting to experience, changing in both their structural and functional organization, and constantly incorporating traces of their experience. This principle is easily proven with animals: rats raised in stimulating environments develop greater synaptic density (brain structure) and perform better on learning tasks such as mazes (brain function) than do rats that are raised in simple environments (e.g. Kolb et al., 2012), even when the experience is introduced in adulthood (Winocur, 1998). The interpretation of such experiments is straightforward because the rats that are randomly assigned to each of these two environments have no relevant measurable differences between them at birth, so all subsequent differences can be safely attributed to their experience. Therefore, the conclusion from this active body of research is that enriched experience for rats leads to enhancements in brain structure and function.

Investigating the role of experience in humans is infinitely more complex. Human babies are not interchangeably equivalent at birth, and random assignment to groups would challenge even the most liberal university Research Ethics Board! However, the kinds of experiences that have been studied for their effect on human performance, such as musical training and taxi driving in London, may conceal important individual differences between the types of people who chose to pursue these experiences; generally, we choose to engage in activities in which we have interest or talent. In this sense, bilingualism is a better test case for experience-induced plasticity: (1) the majority of bilinguals in our studies did not choose to

266 Ellen Bialystok

become bilingual, ruling out talent or predisposition; (2) the effects of bilingualism on executive control emerge gradually with increased experience (e.g. Bialystok & Barac, 2012); and (3) the most dramatic effects of bilingualism are not found in the domain of training, language, but in different domains that share processing with bilingual language use, namely nonverbal executive control (e.g. Bialystok et al., 2005). Together, these results support the conclusion that bilingualism modifies cognitive networks and enhances executive control functioning. Therefore, bilingual individuals do not have minds and brains that are identical to their monolingual counterparts. Accordingly, they will not perform the same on tests of language ability or executive control, they may express symptoms of cognitive disability or impairment differently from monolinguals, and they will likely produce different results from monolinguals on standardized neuropsy-chological assessments. Thus, bilingualism is not individual-difference "noise" in the data—it is an experience that has a systematic effect on cognitive systems.

Implications for Society

Evidence for different competences in bilinguals and monolinguals has large-scale social implications that follow from the tendency for interpretations of performance and policy decisions to be based on monolingual norms. Consider first the problem of assessment. It is standard procedure in education, clinical practice, and healthcare to evaluate individuals on the basis of test results and then make highly consequential decisions from those results (e.g. Kohnert, 2007). For example, children in school may be told they have learning problems, speech-language pathologists may describe a child as having a language impair-ment, or an older adult may be diagnosed with a condition such as fronto-temporal dementia based on word-finding problems. However, the tests typically used to reach these decisions are standardized on monolinguals, but as we have seen, there are significant differences in both verbal and nonverbal performance by mono-linguals and bilinguals. What happens when bilinguals complete tests that have been designed for monolinguals? Shohamy (2011) explains how this problem is compounded when social and political factors are included and further obfuscate actual performance levels. It is unlikely that we will turn away from our obsession with standardized testing, so it is incumbent upon us to guarantee that these tests are as fair and valid as possible.

The second social implication is more optimistic, although it emanates from a deeply unpromising fact: in spite of years of research, there are still very few pharmaceutical treatments for dementia, and those that exist have limited effect. Not surprisingly, therefore, increased attention has been devoted to persuading people to attend to the lifestyle factors that contribute to cognitive reserve and protect cognitive function as dementia progresses. The additional advantage of bilingualism as the cognitive reserve resource is that no extra effort is required:

the simple act of maintaining a heritage language in the home confers long-term benefits on cognitive function. Even a short postponement of cognitive impairment has enormous consequences for healthcare systems and families because individuals are able to live independently for a longer time, make fewer demands on expensive and scarce health resources, and enjoy quality of life for several more years.

It would be dramatic if these results that accrued from research with individuals could be extrapolated to societies. Nations differ in the degree to which they support bilingualism, so do more bilingual nations have lower incidence of dementia? Unfortunately, such comparisons are not possible; as much as individuals differ from each other, societies differ even more. The problem is that many factors converge on the comparative evaluation of societies, and the outcome depends on a range of factors that are not included in a simple count of the languages heard on the streets. Among these are questions concerning educational systems, healthcare systems, economic situation, and support for minority languages. And it is important to remember that cognitive reserve does not *prevent* dementia, so fluctuations in the incidence or prevalence of the disease across nations will be difficult to document.

There is an inherent tension between our concern with individuals who we acknowledge to have distinct profiles, some of it reflecting their unique experiences, and the social conventions around testing and assessment, including research in psychology, in which we assume the uniformity and equivalence of all the people we encounter. Although an approach to assessment and clinical practice that treats each person as individual and unique is impractical, a testing culture that fails to acknowledge systematic differences from experience is invalid. Accommodation from both sides of this divide is necessary to produce social structures that are appropriate and responsive to as many individuals as possible.

Acknowledgments

The research reported in this chapter was funded by grant R01HD052523 from the US National Institutes of Health, grant A2559 from the Natural Sciences and Engineering Research Council of Canada, and grant MOP57842 from the Canadian Institutes of Health Research.

References

Abutalebi, J., Della Rosa, P. A., Green, D. W., Hernandez, M., Scifo, P., Keim, R., Cappa, S. F., & Costa, A. (2012). Bilingualism tunes the anterior cingulate cortex for conflict monitoring. *Cerebral Cortex*, *22*, 2076–2086.

Bennett, D. A., Schneider, J. A., Tang, Y., Arnold, S. E., & Wilson, R. S. (2006). The effect of social network on the relation between Alzheimer's disease pathology and level of cognitive function in old people: A longitudinal cohort study. *Lancet Neurology*, *5*, 406–412.

268 Ellen Bialystok

Bialystok, E., & Barac, R. (2012). Emerging bilingualism: Dissociating advantages for metalinguistic awareness and executive control. *Cognition, 122*, 67–73.

Bialystok, E., & Luk, G. (2012). Receptive vocabulary differences in monolingual and bilingual adults. *Bilingualism: Language and Cognition, 15*, 397–401.

Bialystok, E., Craik, F. I. M., & Freedman, M. (2007). Bilingualism as a protection against the onset of symptoms of dementia. *Neuropsychologia, 45*, 459–464.

Bialystok, E., Craik, F. I. M., & Luk, G. (2008). Cognitive control and lexical access in younger and older bilinguals. *Journal of Experimental Psychology: Learning, Memory, and Cognition, 34*, 859–873.

Bialystok, E., Martin, M. M., & Viswanathan, M. (2005). Bilingualism across the lifespan: The rise and fall of inhibitory control. *International Journal of Bilingualism, 9*, 103–119.

Bialystok, E., Craik, F. I. M., Green, D. W., & Gollan, T. H. (2009). Bilingual minds. *Psychological Science in the Public Interest, 10*, 89–129.

Bialystok, E., Luk, G., Peets, K. F., & Yang, S. (2010). Receptive vocabulary differences in monolingual and bilingual children. *Bilingualism: Language and Cognition, 13*, 525–531.

Costa, A., Hernández, M., & Sebastián-Gallés, N. (2008). Bilingualism aids conflict resolution: Evidence from the ANT task. *Cognition, 106*, 59–86.

Craik, F. I. M., Bialystok, E., & Freedman, M. (2010). Delaying the onset of Alzheimer's disease: Bilingualism as a form of cognitive reserve. *Neurology, 75*, 1726–1729.

Fabbro, F., Skrap, M., & Aglioti, S. (2000). Pathological switching between languages following frontal lesion in a bilingual patient. *Journal of Neurology, Neurosurgery, and Psychiatry, 68*, 650–652.

Gold, B. T., Kim, C., Johnson, N. F., Kryscio, R. J., & Smith, C. D. (2013). Lifelong bilingualism maintains neural efficiency for cognitive control in aging. *Journal of Neuroscience, 33*, 387–396.

Gollan, T. H., Montoya, R. I., & Werner, G. A. (2002). Semantic and letter fluency in Spanish–English bilinguals. *Neuropsychology, 16*, 562–576.

Gollan, T. H., Fennema-Nostestine, C., Montoya, R. I., & Jernigan, T. L., (2007). The bilingual effect on Boston Naming Test performance. *Journal of the International Neuropsychological Society, 13*, 197–208.

Green, C. S., & Bavelier, D. (2008). Exercising your brain: A review of human brain plasticity and training induced learning. *Psychology and Aging, 23*, 692–701.

Ivanova, I., & Costa, A. (2008). Does the bilingualism hamper lexical access in speech production? *Acta Psychologica, 127*, 277–288.

Kidron, D., Black, S. E., Stanchev, P., Buck, B., Szalai, J. P., Parker, J., & Bronskill, M. J. (1997). Quantitative MR volumetry in Alzheimer's disease. *Neurology, 49*, 1504–1512.

Kohnert, K. (2007). *Language disorders in bilingual children and adults*. San Diego, CA: Plural.

Kolb, B., Mychasiuk, R., Muhammad, A., Li, Y., Frost, D. O., & Gibb, R. (2012). Experience and the developing prefrontal cortex. *Proceedings of the National Academy of Science, 109* (Suppl. 2), 17186–17193.

Kroll, J. F., & de Groot, A. M. B. (1997). Lexical and conceptual memory in the bilingual: Mapping form to meaning in two languages. In A. M. B. de Groot & J. F. Kroll (Eds.), *Tutorials in bilingualism* (pp. 169–199). Mahwah, NJ: Erlbaum.

Landau, S. M., Mintun, M. A., Joshi, A. D., Koeppe, R. A., Petersen, R. C., Aisen, P. S., & Jagust, W. J. (2012). Amyloid deposition, hypometabolism, and longitudinal cognitive decline. *Annals of Neurology, 72*, 578–586.

Luk, G., Green, D. W., Abutalebi, J., & Grady, C. (2012). Cognitive control for language switching in bilinguals: A quantitative meta-analysis of functional neuroimaging studies. *Language and Cognitive Processes*, *27*, 1479–1488.

Luk, G., Anderson, J. A. E., Craik, F. I. M., Grady, C., & Bialystok, E. (2010). Distinct neural correlates for two types of inhibition in bilinguals: Response inhibition versus interference suppression. *Brain and Cognition*, *74*, 347–357.

Maguire, E. A., Gadian, D. G., Johnsrude, I. S., Good, C. D., Ashburner, J., Frackowiak, R.S., & Frith, C. D. (2000). Navigation-related structural change in the hippocampi of taxi drivers. *Proceedings of the National Academy of Sciences, USA*, *97*, 4398–4403.

Martin, C. D., Dering, B., Thomas, E. M., & Thierry, G. (2009). Brain potentials reveal semantic priming in both the "active" and the "non-attended" language of early bilinguals. *NeuroImage*, *47*, 326–333.

Martin-Rhee, M. M., & Bialystok, E. (2008). The development of two types of inhibitory control in monolingual and bilingual children. *Bilingualism: Language and Cognition*, *11*, 81–93.

Salthouse, T. A., & Mitchell, D. R. D. (1990). Effects of age and naturally occurring experience on spatial visualization performance. *Developmental Psychology*, *26*, 845–854.

Schweizer, T., Ware, J., Fischer, C. E., Craik, F. I. M., & Bialystok, E. (2012). Bilingualism as a contributor to cognitive reserve: Evidence from brain atrophy in Alzheimer's disease. *Cortex*, *48*, 991–996.

Shohamy, E. (2011). Assessing multilingual competencies: Adopting construct valid assessment policies. *The Modern Language Journal*, *95*, 418–429.

Statistics Canada (2007). *2006 Census of Canada highlight tables: Population by language spoken most often at home and age groups, 2006 counts, for Canada, provinces and territories—20% sample data*. (Catalogue number 97-555-XWE2006002). Retrieved from: www12. statcan.ca/census-recensement/2006/dp-pd/hlt/97-555/T402-eng.cfm?Lang=E&T=402&GH=4&SC=1&S=99&O=A (accessed August 4, 2011).

Stern, Y. (2002). What is cognitive reserve? Theory and research application of the reserve concept. *Journal of the International Neuropsychological Society*, *8*, 448–460.

Suo, C., Leon, I., Brodaty, H., Trollor, J., Wen, W., Sachdev, P., & Valenzuela, M. J. (2012). Supervisory experience at work is linked to low rate of hippocampal atrophy in late life. *Neuroimage*, *63*(3), 1542–1551.

Valenzuela, M. J., Matthews, F. E., Rayne, C., Inco, P., Halliday, G., Kril, J. J., & Sachdev, P. S. (2012). Multiple biological pathways link cognitive lifestyle to protection from dementia. *Biological Psychiatry*, *71*, 783–791.

Vestberg, T., Gustafson, R., Maurex, L., Ingvar, M., & Petrovic, P. (2012). Executive functions predict the success of top soccer players. *Plos One*, *7*(4), e34731.

Winocur, G. (1998). Environmental influences on cognitive decline in aged rats. *Neurobiology of Aging*, *19*, 589–597.

19

STRATEGIES FOR THE SUPER-MULTILINGUAL IN AN INCREASINGLY GLOBAL WORLD

Andrew D. Cohen

Elana Shohamy has a fascination for language and for how people perform what it is that they know in their various languages. Of late, she is particularly interested in ways to assess the totality of what people know how to do in the various languages over which they have control. She has advanced the notion of having language tests that would assess at the same time respondents' abilities at *translanguaging* (i.e. their ability to communicate using more than one language as needed; Shohamy, 2011). This is an engaging notion, and one that has not been pursued to any great extent in the past. Our language assessment measures have tended to focus on performance in one language at a time. Fortunately, at present, Educational Testing Service has initiated a project to construct tests that assess communication involving translanguaging (Lopez, Guzman-Orth, & Turkan, 2014).

Elana is also keenly interested in efforts made to encourage or to restrict the use and spread of a given language in society—through educational policies regarding the languages taught, learned, and assessed at school, and language use in society. Her fascination with linguistic landscaping is one vehicle, and an effective one, for getting at how societies actually deal with multilingualism in their midst. So, what statement is being made, for example, if all street signs in South Yafo are written in Hebrew in what used to be an area where Arabic once prevailed? What does it mean if real estate ads on a store window in Tel Aviv are written in French and English?

While this chapter does not deal either with language assessment or with linguistic landscaping per se, it deals with a related issue. It deals primarily with a phenomenon that could be referred to as "super-multilingualism," and to the super-multilinguals who make up this special club. These people are also referred to as *hyperpolyglots* (i.e. those who can speak, read, write, or translate in at least 11 languages after the native language; Erard, 2012). The focus is not on speech communities, but rather on individuals, and especially those stellar individuals whose language performance is "over the top," such as Alexander Arguelles, whose learning of over 60 languages is showcased in Erard (2012).

Super-multilingualism is a dramatic departure from *bilingualism* in that the bilingual paradigm is, in many ways, dated. We used to get excited when referring to someone with skills in a *second* language. But these days, the college students that I taught at the University of Minnesota had studied perhaps two or three languages after the native one. It was not even so uncommon to find some with up to five languages. It is still very uncommon to find learners with a dozen languages after the native one, putting them into Erard's hyperpolyglot category. These are learners that, I would contend, are practitioners of what I am referring to as super-multilingualism. Learners of so many languages, predictably, are speakers, readers, and writers of different kinds of languages, so not only do they have numerous languages, but also experiences with a range of different types of languages.

The concern in this chapter, then, is with what it takes for an adult learner to achieve long-term success with at least three or more non-native languages from among the many that they have learned to some extent. In order to eliminate from our analysis those who are born into multilingual homes, let us consider only cases where the onset of second language (L2) learning for a language that they have become competent in does not occur in the very early years, but rather in high school or later. Success in this instance would mean being able to use the language as the vehicle of communication in a university course, being able to write academic papers in the language, and having control of L2 pragmatics, pronunciation, and grammar. The concern is with the issue of what it takes to be good enough in a series of especially unrelated languages to be able to:

- have people think your L2 pronunciation is native or nearly so;
- get the L2 pragmatics right in numerous speaking situations;
- have only negligible grammar errors in your oral language;
- have the L2 vocabulary trip off your tongue relatively effortlessly;
- take an active part in an academic meeting conducted entirely through the L2;
- read and critique academic work in your field of interest in the L2; and
- express yourself in written language at a professional level in the L2.

The main purpose of this chapter is to provoke thought about multilingual performance that is in some ways "over the top." As it turns out, my current efforts to learn Mandarin, the twelfth language that I have worked on after my native language, English, puts me in this hyperpolyglot category. I have now studied Mandarin since the fall of 2011. I started by doing a 150-hour DVD course of *Fluenz Mandarin*. I then added, in September 2012, tandem sessions with a native Chinese-speaking teacher from the Beijing University of Posts and

272 Andrew D. Cohen

Telecommunications, first while she was on a Fulbright teaching Chinese in Whittier, California, and then once she returned to her EFL teaching position at her institution in Beijing. We conducted well over 70 sessions over the Internet (using FaceTime for the audio and video, and Skype for the written communication). In addition, I have now had even more sessions with another Chinese female tandem partner living in Minneapolis (in a language exchange between English and Chinese).[1] The experience was tracked closely and written up, with an emphasis on my difficulties and achievement both from the perspective of the learner and the teacher, relating these to the variables of advanced age, hyperpolyglot status, and expertise at language strategies (see Cohen & Li, 2013).

I have found that it makes talking about language learning far more concrete for me if I am actively engaged in the learning of a language, and in this case, a very difficult one for me at a time in my life when language learning is more of a challenge than it was when I was a teenager tackling Latin and then French with relative ease. I find that I do not retain the vocabulary so easily and even if I remember the words in the *pinyin* form of Mandarin (not the characters), I am likely to forget which of the four tones apply to the given word. Fortunately, I can grasp the grammatical rules rather easily, so this gives me some control of the language. My experiences are consistent with the research findings for older language learners (Hale, 2005; Service & Craik, 1993).

Returning now to the general language-learning public, it is fair to say that dabbling in a variety of languages may not be all that difficult. It is my impression that many people can say enough words or phrases in a language so that the L2-speaking addressee will acknowledge them warmly for their effort. But then they would be hard-pressed to do anything more substantive with the language, so they quickly switch back to their first language (L1) or another language with which they are more comfortable. In addition, it would appear to me that the US can be characterized as a nation of language attritters, where little remains of what there once was when we were high school or college students fulfilling our L2 requirement. In an exhaustive review of language attrition, Bardovi-Harlig and Stringer (2010) point to numerous ways in which attrition is likely to take its toll on L2 abilities.

But what about getting really good in an L2 so that the skills remain for a lifetime—being good enough, for example, to successfully teach a university-level course through that language? My gratitude goes to Loraine Obler (CUNY Graduate School, Boston University School of Medicine, and Boston VA Medical Center) and Michael Erard (journalist and author of *Babel No More* (2012)), who assisted me in identifying the following four factors that contribute to an ability to function effectively at an advanced level in three or more languages:[2]

1. Issues specific to the languages themselves (e.g. the nature of the alphabet, the complexity of the morphology, the similarity of the languages to each other, and so forth).

Strategies for the Super-Multilingual **273**

2. Innate ability in learners—ability that is dependent on genetics, such as a brain that allows you to pick up a language later in life and retain the material.
3. Contextual factors relevant to the given learners at given moments in their lives.
4. Elements that can be developed.

Issues Specific to Learning a Given Language

The first issue specific to a given language is whether the language has an alphabetic or syllabic script, or logographic characters. Some English-speaking learners would consider it a challenge to learn Hebrew or Arabic since it involves an alphabet that is different from English and often is written without vowels, such that readers need to intuit what those vowels are. Logographic writing systems can pose another set of problems—such as having to learn a large number of radicals and other elements that make up the characters. Then there is a need to engage in careful analysis of the characters in order to distinguish one from another (for a review of studies dealing with Chinese learning, see Jiang & Cohen, 2012).

Next, Erard (personal communication) makes the case that morphological complexity helps in language learning, suggesting that the learning of numerous one-syllable homonyms can be more challenging than learning a series of more complex morphemes with two or more syllables. I am currently studying Mandarin, and find the morphological simplicity of many words that I need to learn puts a burden on the memory. Erard also argues that it can help if the languages are genetically related, such as the Romance languages. If the languages are not genetically related but at least share areal features by virtue of their contiguity of the years, that can help. Shared features is not, however, a given for contiguous languages. I studied two contiguous languages in Bolivia—first Quechua, the language of the Incas (thinking I would be placed in the Peace Corps in Cochabamba) and then Aymara, a language that appeared far earlier (the language I actually needed for my PC rural community development assignment on the High Plains in 1965–1967). I found remarkably few commonalities between these two languages, Aymara being far more difficult for me to learn.

Another issue is the similarity across languages, since similarity may make the learning and use of an L2 easier (Odlin, 1989). A speaker of Spanish, for example, should have far greater ease at learning Portuguese, say, than Chinese. The two Romance languages have numerous similarities—in grammar and vocabulary, with learnable differences in pronunciation, especially between continental Portuguese and Spanish.

Innate Ability in Learners

Second, there are the elements that are innate. One very helpful tool in being a super-multilingual is having solid neural hardware (i.e. having a robust innate

274 Andrew D. Cohen

ability to learn and use languages; Erard, 2012). This includes an ability to hear distinctions in speech sounds in the target languages, and, importantly, an ability to memorize and store learned material effectively. A successful multilingual can also keep the languages straight, calling on the needed language at the given moment. This would include knowing how to translanguage at a moment's notice when a word, phrase, or entire utterance in another language is deemed appropriate.

A challenge that adult multilinguals face is having to deal with the onset of language being considerably later than during the childhood period—when "picking up" languages could be accomplished with relative ease. This statement needs to be qualified, since children benefit from hours of repetition, while adults generally do not have anywhere near the same amount of contact with the target language. Hence, adults must rely more on their raw memory and on memory strategies if they wish to retain the target language. L2 learning processes and outcomes among elderly adults have been shown to differ from those of younger learners, taking into account individual differences among seniors, particularly with regard to working memory (see Mackey & Sachs, 2012).

The initial onset of Mandarin for me was at the age of 67, when my abilities to soak up language were long gone, when the learning of vocabulary was far more of an effort, and when attrition of learned material was rampant. As mentioned earlier, my most conspicuous problem involved efforts to learn the four tones associated with the words as I learned them in *pinyin*. I would learn the tones in order to perform them in speaking and to use them in writing, but then find myself forgetting them again, even in words that I had used many times. The Fluenz Mandarin course, for example, required that I get the tones correct on all *pinyin* that I used in written exercises in the lessons. Inputting this information took a good deal of the lesson time. I have found that in order to save time when writing sentences in *pinyin* for my tandem partners, I preferred to write without indicating the tones at all, except on certain new words.

Another factor in language learning success is the ability to monitor yourself through the brain's executive function. The *executive function* refers to a set of mental processes that help us connect past experience with present action (National Center for Learning Disabilities, 2008).

Problems with executive function may be manifested when a person has difficulty, for example, in memorizing and retrieving information from memory. A real problem can be keeping track of more than one thing at the same time since performing in a challenging L2 usually calls for the ability to multitask. The language learner is engaged in an awesome juggling feat, having to keep lots of balls in the air at the same time without dropping any of them. For me with Mandarin, it is retrieving the vocabulary words, which may be very similar to other words or actual homonyms of them, attaching the appropriate tone to each syllable, using the appropriate *measure words* (i.e. noun classifiers), if relevant, and checking to be sure the word order is appropriate. Needless to say, it means that

I am not producing Chinese utterances with the speed of summer lightning. Furthermore, my listening comprehension is poor because of the many homonyms and near homonyms in Chinese, and because I do not have frequent conversations with Chinese speakers in Chinese.

Memory for vocabulary is, in part, innate—a key element in a person's intelligence, since verbal skills play a significant role in determining how intelligent someone is. Some people have talent at retaining vocabulary, with some in fact having photographic memories, while for others their brains are like sieves and the new words are not easily retained. It is for this reason that the use of mnemonics such as the keyword mnemonic may be of value to some learners (for one of the early studies, see Cohen & Aphek, 1980; for a review of literature on the topic, see Cohen, 1987). Retention over time is, in part, a function of how proficient the learners became in the language when they were studying it—whether they got beyond the threshold level in the language so that their comprehension and production were relatively effortless. Unfortunately, language classes often do not provide rigorous recycling of vocabulary, so that material is introduced but might well be quickly forgotten after the quiz. In such cases, genuine language use undoubtedly poses a challenge. Even if learners get beyond the threshold level in a language, the question is the extent to which they have opportunities to perform their knowledge. If they do not, then this can be a further strain on the memory, ultimately resulting in language attrition, unless the learner creates effective memory links.

Another largely innate ability is that of being able to attend to specific details, not just to the gestalt, or larger picture. Ideally, learners can benefit from strategy instruction on how to attend to detail (Plonsky, 2011), but some of the ability to do so is inherited and not teachable. Some learners may simply be better at paying attention to detail than others. This can help them monitor for grammar as they use the language. Other learners seem, at times, to be impervious to the correct grammar patterns and to grammar rules.

Contextual Factors

Aside from the variables associated with the languages themselves and the innate abilities of the learners, there are contextual factors that can play a role in successful language acquisition. One highly significant factor can be the family that you are born into and its location. It is not surprising that when my colleagues Ulla Connor and Diane Belcher (2001) set about to describe success- ful multilinguals in the US, all of the contributors to their edited volume, except me, were people who had grown up in a multilingual context so that they were at least raised bilingually or even trilingually. In my case, I was raised monolingually and did not have my first onset with another language until 9th Grade—and a dead language at that, Latin. I studied Latin for four years, adding

276 Andrew D. Cohen

my first "living" L2, French, when I was a junior in high school (see my personal description in Cohen, 2001).

Another major contextual factor is that of living in contact with people for whom the target language is used regularly as an L2. Learners may find a living and working situation where this is the case—whether by going to a country where the language is spoken or by finding an enclave of target-language users locally. In addition to being in a context where the language is used, there is also the matter of the language skills that are needed in that context. For example, a study of soap factory workers in Wellington, New Zealand, found that a relatively high premium was put on knowing how to curse in English, and especially to use the f-word (see Daly, Holmes, Newton, & Stubbe, 2004). The study data, collected over a 15-year period, showed that an important ingredient in successful bonding with fellow workers was being able to engage in playful verbal jousting where the use of expletives was an important component. So Asian workers who had not had exposure to expletives in their language acquisition prior to coming to work at the factory were put at a disadvantage. True, working at the factory could now provide them this opportunity, if they did not get fired first for not fitting in. In this case, it would appear that cursing was socially and materially rewarded. I know from six years in the U.S. Army Reserves that cursing in that context had an important social role—such as in knowing how to use the f-word in most parts of speech.

Elements that Can be Developed

Now we arrive at the category of elements that learners can develop and nurture to improve their language learning, despite otherwise highly challenging conditions. For example, let us assume that the target language is not like any that you have learned before, your innate abilities at language learning are modest, and you have no contact with the language in any of your normal language contexts, so that learning and using the language is a real stretch.

Super-multilinguals, most predictably, are keenly aware of their learning style preferences and draw on these to the hilt. So, for example, if they are more concrete about their learning and enjoy learning in a sequential manner, then they undertake tasks that favor this style preference. In other words, they prefer to keep their language learning grounded with lots of practical activities and to learn things in a clear sequence so that they know what they are learning and when. For example, they may take step-by-step approaches in dealing with complex tasks in the L2, relying on visual organizational aids.

If you watch the YouTube eight-minute video of Alexander Arguelles describing what is required in this polyglot's daily workout in order to maintain his many languages, you are struck by how crucial time management is to him in this process.[3] Super-multilinguals may well create checklists and "to do" lists, estimating how long tasks will take, breaking down activities into chunks, and assigning time frames for completing each chunk. Such learners are probably very aware of their work environment and do their utmost to make it conducive to their learning. For example, they may do their best to eliminate environmental noises, minimize clutter, manage space and materials carefully, and harness numerous tools from the Internet, such as electronic flashcards for words and phrases, where they are stored in the cloud. I first created electronic flashcards for words and phrases using Flash My Brain (Mode of Expression, 2007; no longer in business). More recently I have created electronic flashcards using the BYKI Deluxe Software (Transparent Language, 2009; www.byki.com/products.html), where I enter the pinyin and an oral recording of each word as well.

In addition, super-multilinguals most likely possess a robust repertoire of language learner strategies and draw upon these strategies the way a carpenter skillfully accesses a whole array of tools as needed to get the job done. For these language learners, strategies are not abstractions, such as "using a dictionary," but rather the set of specific strategies that support them in actually obtaining a working sense of what a word or phrase means in context.[4] The accessing of their strategy repertoire may entail the use of up to five or more different strategies along the way—from the moment that learners start looking up the word to when they determine that they either have obtained from the dictionary the knowledge that they need or they have not. Their repertoire of language learner strategies would most certainly include:

- strategies for ensuring the learning, practice, and use of a new language in an already busy life;
- strategies for monitoring language learning and use; and
- strategies for remembering vocabulary deemed relevant and valuable.

We can also consider the strategies used by respondents in language assessment situations. As learners may be assessed in more than one language simultaneously, it means that they will need test-taking strategies that support this rather bold departure from conventional means of assessment into the realm of translanguaging (see Cohen, 2012; Lopez, 2013).

Next, they would have a highly refined sense of their language motivation, most likely with a sense of mission about learning languages, especially since language learning, at times, calls for perseverance in the face of what may appear as futility. For these learners, adding another language to their inventory would be akin to the way some people shop for clothes, to add a particular new shirt or dress. They would have numerous checks and balances to ensure that their motivation is rekindled in the face of inevitable circumstances working against language learning, such as an inordinate amount of work, family events such as a change in residence or employment, trips, and so forth.

In addition, the super-multilingual is willing to devote long hours to the hard work of memorizing vocabulary, working through the grammar, and practicing the language in numerous ways so as to make it real. This involves making the time for language learning, which not only entails setting aside the time, but also

278 Andrew D. Cohen

devoting enough energy to it so that there are tangible results. Some learners opt for language classes because a structure is already provided. However, the content may be relatively unsatisfying for learners who already have a string of successful language learning experiences and therefore already know what they would like to learn in this new language. Such learners may prefer some online learning experience, which involves tandem partners and the like, calling for organizational logistics to pull it off. These learners have more than likely identified a persona for themselves as language learners, much as others might identify themselves as artists, athletes, and the like.

At every step of the way, these learners are drawing from their strategy repertoire in order to sort out the logic behind some grammar rule, to search for a solution to an oral communication task perhaps involving finely tuned pragmatics so as not to offend the interlocutors, or perhaps to develop an argument in a written text.

These learners also have had numerous encounters with formal language instruction and have a sense of the advantages and disadvantages for them of studying through one or another of these approaches. In fact, it is likely that the methods used in a given language class will be aimed at the average student, and not at super-multilinguals, if there are any in the class. If these learners partake of conventional language instruction, they may well need to supplement it with private teachers, tutors, or tandem partners in order to learn words and phrases relating to their own interests, to check on their understanding and use of this material, and to troubleshoot with regard to their control of the grammar and pragmatics (see Cohen, 2005), among other things.

Over the years, I have relied to a great extent on tandem partners, both in my learning of German and Japanese, and now Chinese. Drawbacks with tandem partners include that they may not know how to best support you, that they may not have teaching skills to provide you with the information you need with regard to the target language, and that you may end up spending more than 50 percent of the time on your helping them learn the language in which you are strong (whether it is your L1 or another language), partly as a way to avoid the strain of sticking to the L2. So this then speaks to the benefits of having a paid instructor working exclusively with you, which is what I had for two months in my learning of Mandarin.

Actually, I am keenly aware that there are, in fact, numerous ways to learn an L2, and have even taught a freshman seminar several times at the University of Minnesota on this theme. The main goal of the seminar was to have wide-eyed and eager freshmen consider the various program alternatives that were available to them as entering college students at that time—including formal university offerings, non-university courses such as accelerated or crash courses, structured and independent Web-based courses, summer immersion camp experiences, study abroad, tandem partner programs, and other forms of independent language learning (home study through books, tutoring of non-natives, going to bilingual church services, and so forth; see Cohen & White, 2008).

When teaching the seminar for the second time in 2007, my then students asked what the aftermath had been for the freshmen who had taken the seminar in 2003, so I checked back with that group and got responses from three of them who were still at the University of Minnesota. The feedback on the impact of the seminar was heartening. The students were uniformly positive about the impact that awareness about how to become multilingual had had on their college experience. They reported that they had, in fact, benefited from the seminar in terms of the choices they made in their efforts to learn one or more languages. The seminar had helped to shape their language studies at the university.

Summary and Conclusions

This chapter has delved into the realm of super-multilingualism in an effort to identify what it takes to become a super-multilingual. Our current world is making increasing demands on language learners, often extending them beyond their comfort zone. Four areas relating to language learning were identified: issues specific to a given language, innate ability in the learners, contextual factors, and elements that can be developed. While few individuals will attain the status of super-multilinguals, an increasing number will attain functional skills in perhaps four or five languages over a lifetime. The journey to get there may be enhanced by greater awareness on the part of learners as to how they can be more proactive as language learners and language performers, focusing specifically on those elements that they can impact through their own efforts.

Notes

1. The Beijing tandem partner is Li Ping and the Minneapolis one is Yue Yang.
2. In preparation for a colloquium presentation on the good language learner that I gave at the IATEFL Convention in Harrogate, England, April 11, 2010.
3. Retrieved from: www.youtube.com/watch?v=Oudgdh6tl00 (accessed September 19, 2013).
4. Takac (2008) also found, among younger learners, that vocabulary had to be learned rather than simply being acquired through exposure, and that the systematic use of vocabulary strategies played a key role in this.

References

Bardovi-Harlig, K., & Stringer, D. (2010). Variables in second language attrition: Advancing the state of the art. *Studies in Second Language Acquisition, 32*(1), 1–45.

Belcher, D., & Connor, U. (Eds.) (2001). *Reflections on multiliterate lives.* Bristol, UK: Multilingual Matters.

Cohen, A. D. (1987). The use of verbal and imagery mnemonics in second language learning. *Studies in Second Language Acquisition, 9*(1), 43–61.

Cohen, A. D. (2001). From L1 to L12: The confessions of a sometimes frustrated multiliterate. In D. Belcher & U. Connor (Eds.), *Reflections on multiliterate lives* (pp. 79–95). Bristol, UK: Multilingual Matters.

Cohen, A. D. (2005). Strategies for learning and performing L2 speech acts. *Intercultural Pragmatics*, *2*(3), 275–301.

Cohen, A. D. (2012). Test-taking strategies. In C. Coombe, P. Davidson, B. O'Sullivan, & S. Stoynoff (Eds.), *The Cambridge guide to assessment* (pp. 96–104). Cambridge: Cambridge University Press.

Cohen, A. D., & Aphek, E. (1980). Retention of second-language vocabulary over time: Investigating the role of mnemonic associations. *System*, *8*(3), 221–235.

Cohen, A. D., & Li Ping (2013). Learning Mandarin in later life: Can old dogs learn new tricks? *Contemporary Foreign Language Studies*, *12*(5), 5–15.

Cohen, A. D., & White, C. (2008). Language learners as informed consumers of language instruction. In A. Stavans & I. Kupferberg (Eds.), *Studies in language and language education: Essays in honor of Elite Olshtain* (pp. 185–205). Jerusalem: The Hebrew University Magnes Press.

Daly, N., Holmes, J., Newton, J., & Stubbe, M. (2004). Expletives as solidarity signals in FTAs on the factory floor. *Journal of Pragmatics*, *36*(5), 945–964.

Erard, M. (2012). *Babel no more: The search for the world's most extraordinary language learners.* New York: Free Press/Simon & Schuster.

Hale, C. (2005). *Helping the older language learner succeed. ICCT Coachnotes.* Wheaton, IL: Wheaton College. Retrieved from: www2.wheaton.edu/bgc/ICCT/pdf/CN_older.pdf (accessed September 19, 2013).

Jiang, X., & Cohen, A. D. (2012). A critical review of research on strategies in learning Chinese as both a second and foreign language. *Studies in Second Language Learning and Teaching*, *2*(1), 9–43.

Lopez, A. A., Guzman-Orth, D., & Turkan, S. (2014). *A study on the use of translanguaging to assess the content knowledge of emergent bilingual students.* Paper presented at the Annual Conference of the American Association for Applied Linguistics, Portland, Oregon.

Mackey, A., & Sachs, R. (2012). Older learners in SLA research: A first look at working memory, feedback, and L2 development. *Language Learning*, *62*(3), 704–740.

National Center for Learning Disabilities. (2008). *Executive function fact sheet.* Retrieved from: www.colorincolorado.org/article/24880 (accessed September 19, 2013).

Odlin, T. (1989). *Language transfer: Cross-linguistic influence in language learning.* New York: Cambridge University Press.

Plonsky, L. (2011). The effectiveness of second language strategy instruction: A meta-analysis. *Language Learning*, *61*(4), 993–1039.

Service, E., & Craik, F. I. M. (1993). Differences between young and older adults in learning a foreign vocabulary. *Journal of Memory and Language*, *32*(4), 608–623.

Shohamy, E. (2011). Assessing multilingual competencies: Adopting construct valid assessment policies. *The Modern Language Journal*, *95*(3), 418–429.

Takac, V. P. (2008). *Vocabulary learning strategies and foreign language acquisition.* Bristol, UK: Multilingual Matters.

20

GENDER, SEXUALITY, AND MULTILINGUALISM IN THE LANGUAGE CLASSROOM

Lyn Wright Fogle and Kendall A. King

Elana Shohamy's work has dramatically advanced our understanding of how language, testing, identity, power, and public policy interact to produce differences in educational access and academic achievement across groups within multilingual societies. Shohamy's research has addressed a wide range of language assessment issues, including alternative assessment, oral testing, classroom and diagnostic assessment, and "washback," with a focus on the social and political dimensions of language tests (e.g. Shohamy 1994, 1995, 1996, 1997, 1998, 2001; Shohamy & Hornberger, 2008). Shohamy's most well-known contribution here concerns the power and misuses of tests, and in particular how tests impact teaching and learning practices, and thus serve as de facto language policies. This work has documented the negative consequences of tests in contexts of second language learning, migration, and, more recently, of language requirements for citizenship (e.g. Shohamy, 1998, 2001; Shohamy & Hornberger, 2008; Spolsky & Shohamy, 1999). Her book *Language Policy: Hidden Agendas and New Approaches* (Shohamy, 2006) introduced an expanded language policy framework that illustrated how everyday, often invisible mechanisms (e.g. tests, linguistic landscapes) create de facto language policies. These implicit policies, Shohamy has argued, lead to inequalities, violation of individual human rights, suppression of diversity, and marginalization of individuals and groups.

Although Shohamy's work is notable for its attention to the personal experiences of language learners, her research has not directly addressed gender. This might be due to her post-structuralist, critical stance toward established categories such as "citizen," "immigrant," or even "male"/"female." This might also be the case because gender has not been widely taken up as a central or worthy topic of investigation within the field of language testing. Yet Shohamy's emphasis on the ways that interaction between personal identity, on the one hand, and global migration forces, on the other, is expressed and enacted via language use, learning, and language policy demands attention to individual language learner characteristics, including gender. Here, we extend Shohamy's focus on the individual language learner's experience, and her concern with pedagogical and policy approaches that "make space for people," in particular by exploring how gender and sexuality are constructed in two ESL classrooms. Our intention here is not to make generalizable claims about the role of gender and sexuality in all ESL classrooms, but rather to point to some of the as of yet little-examined mechanisms through which individual learner identity is enacted in classrooms in ways that can privilege or marginalize students.

Past research indicates that gender impacts which learners participate in classroom tasks and accommodate to target language norms (Ohara, 2001), as well as learners' access to instruction and meaningful interaction in a second language (Teutsch-Dwyer, 2001). Few studies, however, have examined how gender and sexual identities emerge in classroom interactions, nor how classroom language learning itself serves to construct such identities (Fuller, 2009; O'Loughlin, 2001). Yet, such processes can play an important role for some learners. Liddicoat (2009), for example, has demonstrated how sexual identities are "policed" through teachers' corrective feedback and how learners resist heteronormative assignations by outing themselves as gay or lesbian in classroom tasks.

Through an analysis of code choice and interaction in two classrooms, this chapter discusses how gender and sexual identities emerge in classroom tasks and the implications for classroom language learning and politics. Here, we present a collection of "serendipitous" data excerpts that "occurred as spontaneous events in recordings or transcripts of classroom interaction" (Liddicoat, 2009, p. 193), in which gender and sexuality emerged as part of the classroom task. Such serendipitous data, according to Liddicoat, is important for the exploration of the reality and lived experience of certain "invisible" groups of students. These data allow us to explore the reality of women in migratory contexts of learning as they negotiate power, identity, and classroom language politics in vastly different contexts.

Together, these cases reveal how language competence and language learning intersect with women's gender and sexual identities, and provide insight into how individual identities and ways of being are socialized through collusion and resistance among students and teachers in classroom interactions. To illustrate these processes, this chapter draws on data collected in two different contexts. The first is a study of English language teaching in a private language school in Russia serving professionally oriented adult learners. The second study was conducted in an all immigrant high school in the US. Below, we provide a little background on each context and then examples and analysis from each site.

Post-Soviet Femininities in a Russian EFL Classroom

Study Context and Background

The data analyzed here were collected in fall 2008 at a supplementary English program in St. Petersburg, Russia that met in evenings and catered to university students and professionals. This particular pre-intermediate-level class was comprised of seven students, three of whom were enrolled in local universities or tertiary institutes and two of whom were older—one businessman (Ivan) and one stay-at-home mother (Alina). Ivan, who was 53, and Alina, 35, had had a variety of experiences in Western Europe and abroad, where they used English during their travels. These two students sat together and completed most of the pair work together.

Here, we discuss how pair work tasks and the resulting discussions facilitated by the instructor, Irina, opened spaces for the construction of new post-Soviet feminine identities for the female students in the class. Russian women in late modernity have experienced rapid transformations in possibilities and shifts from an ideal "working mother" identity, proscribed by the Soviet state, to multiple femininities (e.g. Temkina & Zdravomyslova, 2003). The women in this class-room grapple with the twenty-first-century identities available to Russian women outside of Russia and, through the English language-learning task, align themselves in relation to illicit topics and activities that were part of their international experiences.

The classroom teacher, Irina, audio- and videotaped this class five times over the course of three months. The first video was a focus group activity in which the students responded to prompts about using Russian in the EFL classroom. The four other videos were of entire class periods with no changes to the regular curriculum. These classes were structured around units in the textbook *New Headway*, and followed a communicative format, with about half the class time devoted to pair or small group work. In addition, the teacher (Irina) and researcher (Fogle) corresponded about language use in the class by e-mail and met for a week in the US to analyze the data together.

Interactional Spaces for Gender and Sexuality

The focus of the original study of the adult EFL classroom in Russia was on the ways in which students actively negotiated language choice during class time. Initial functional analyses found that code-switching to Russian in this classroom was used for a variety of purposes (e.g. explanations, instructions, jokes, etc. [Fogle & Grishenkova, 2010]); however, these functions intersected with more complex processes of identity construction and student positioning within the class environment. A second round of coding and analysis used nexus analysis (Scollon & Scollon, 2004), which focused on the actions of students, the stories

284 Lyn Wright Fogle and Kendall A. King

they told, and the identities constructed during class time to explain how one older male student's switches to Russian during class time were ratified by the teacher, Irina, and a younger male student's switches were rejected. The data presented here are moments when feminine identities and sexualities emerged and were constructed during the regular class activities. Examining such moments allows for an understanding of how these individual students' lived experiences influenced the learning context, as well as how this particular English language classroom became a site of negotiating and constructing new gendered identities in a post-Soviet reality.

In the following two excerpts, the students engage in a communicative task in which they interview each other about a recent vacation and report their partner's story back to the class. This activity constructs the classroom as a personal public space in which Liddicoat (2009) notes, "much of the questioning . . . is placed on the personal world of the learner" (p. 192), and gender and sexuality become relevant to the learning activity. Fuller (2009) further notes that gender identity is constructed on two levels in classroom tasks—the level of code choice and the level of collaboration. Below, the instructor collaborates with students through interactional strategies such as expansions and prompts, as well as code-switching, to talk certain gendered and sexual identities into being and resist others.

In Excerpt 1, Ivan, the older businessman, has just finished telling Alina's story about her recent vacation in Amsterdam. He mentions that she enjoyed "walking on the Red Light Street [District]" and going to cafes. Here, Irina takes up this topic and prompts Alina to discuss further:

Excerpt 1: Marijuana in Amsterdam

(words spoken in Russian in italics; translations to English are on the following line, also in italics)

1	Irina:	What about these coffee shops?
2		Uh huh.
3		What about these coffee shops or cafes, yes?
4		Or coffee shops.
5		So,
6	Alina:	We came here.
7		Bought some \<laughs\> sig –
8		*Как называется?*
		What is it called?
9	Ivan:	*Как же?*
		What?
10	Irina:	Cigarettes? Cigarettes? Drugs? Drugs? Drugs?
11		With drugs?
12		?: Cigarettes with /???/
13	Irina:	Drugs? With light drugs. With light drugs. Marijuana?

14	Alina:	*Что? Марья Иванна?*
		What? Maria Ivanna?
15	Ivan:	*Нервана.*
		Nirvana.
16	Irina:	\<laughs\>
17	Alina:	*Марья Иванна*
		Maria Ivanna
18	Irina:	\<laughs\>
19	Alina:	Yes we—*забыла, как будет*—*смеяться?*
		Yes we—I forgot how to say—smeyat'sya ((laugh))?
20	Irina:	Laugh
21	Alina:	We laugh after that like we –
22	Irina:	Like—like we do now, yes? Uh huh uh huh. Okay great.
23	Alina:	But I don't like it.
24	Irina:	You didn't like it.
25	Alina:	I didn't like this *состояние.*
		I didn't like this *sostayaniye.*
26	Irina:	This condition. Condition. Yeah. Good.
27	Alina:	I like to control –
28	Irina:	Yes.
29		The situation.
30	Alina:	The situation.
31	Irina:	Yes.
32		But you wanted just to taste to say that you have tasted it.
33	Alina:	Yes. First time in my life.
34	Irina:	Yes, yes, yes. Mm hm. So the, the condition, yes?
35		The state of yours was not very—very pleasant.
36		Okay. Good.
37	Alina:	I wanted to sleep and my head was hot
38	Irina:	Uh huh. I see. \<laughs\>

Alina recounts the experience of trying marijuana (illegal in Russia) for the first time. The instructor, Irina, who is slightly older than Alina and had also traveled abroad, prompts her to talk about this experience and provides the words she needs in English to discuss using drugs, and marijuana specifically. Irina's questions and laughter ratify the topic as acceptable for the classroom, and Irina's prompts encourage Alina to go deeper into the topic. Here, Irina supports Alina's telling of her experiences, and together they collaborate to construct a feminine identity in English of the traveler and tourist who is open to new things. The two women then negotiate the borders of this identity, as Alina states, "But I don't like it," and Irina goes on to suggest that she "wanted just to say that you have tasted it." Thus, the illicit activity of smoking marijuana as a continued pastime is rejected, but the notion of trying something new in a Western context and

286 Lyn Wright Fogle and Kendall A. King

learning how to talk about illicit topics (i.e. the words for drugs and marijuana, along with expressing states of being, or "conditions") in English are ratified. This conversation references new possibilities for Russian women that result from the construction of a new middle class and increased international tourism, and the participants here negotiate new norms in the "safe" space of the English language classroom.

In Excerpt 2, a very different feminine Russian identity is simultaneously invoked and constructed that shapes the classroom interaction. Here, a younger student, Eugenia (22), talks about her vacation with another young woman to Alanya, Turkey. Eugenia switches to Russian during the telling to refer to stereotypes about Russian women (sexually promiscuous or hypersexual) that circulate outside of Russia in regions where the prostitution of Russian-speaking women is prevalent.

Excerpt 2: "Natashas"

1	Irina:	And what was the place?
2		What was the name of the place?
3	Eugenia:	Sixteen kilometers of Alanya
4	Irina:	Uh huh. From Alanya. Uh huh.
5		Did you like, uh, your rest there?
6	Eugenia:	No.
7	Irina:	You didn't?
8	Eugenia:	No.
9	Irina:	Ah. Interesting.
10		Tell us why not. What was bad?
11	Eugenia:	Мм, *Как сказать, нам было –*
		Mm, how to say, it was for us –
12		*Мы просто из отеля не выходили, потому что Турки приставали*
		We simply did not leave the hotel because the Turks were hitting on us.
13	Alina:	Natasha ((derogatory term for Russian woman, "prostitute"))
14	Irina:	Russian—Russian Natasha.
15	Eugenia:	Leave the hotel.
16	Irina:	You couldn't leave the hotel because of this Turkish men.
17	Yes?	Mm hm mm hm. I see, I see.
18		And you were two of you, right? You were with your friend?

In lines 13 and 14, Alina and Irina collaborate to put a name on the problem Eugenia faced in her travels outside of Russia, "Natasha—Russian Natasha," referencing a common foreign stereotype of Russian-speaking women as whores or "Natashas" (Skapoulli, 2009). Eugenia then manages to accomplish part of the task in English in line 15, saying, "leave the hotel," to suggest why the vacation was so bad. Irina expands and translates Eugenia's Russian story to English, supporting the discussion of the topic and colluding to legitimize the story and Eugenia's problematic situation by making it part of the English language-learning task.

Incorporating women's histories is a part of feminist approaches to language teaching (Norton & Pavlenko, 2004). While Irina did not hold an explicit orientation to feminist pedagogy or state a commitment to these approaches, she does open space here for the two women in the class to explore their past experiences as Russian women outside of Russia and reinterpret their experiences through English. Irina's solidarity strategies (e.g. expansions, prompts) in Excerpt 1 encourage Alina to construct a positive identity as a woman who likes to try new things in the Western context. Her further collaboration with Alina to make sense out of Eugenia's story and reject hypersexualized stereotypes of Russian women empowers Eugenia to better understand the situation and lays the blame on the "Turkish men" rather than the young women themselves or the rampant sex trafficking industry (often orchestrated by Russian men) that has plagued post-Soviet life (Tverdova, 2011). Irina's facilitation of the classroom tasks and the rapport she established with her students led to interactional spaces for new identities to emerge and questions of nationality, language, and gender to be discussed and negotiated as part of English language instruction.

Authority, Gender, and Somali Language Expertise

Study Context

The second body of data comes from a study of English language learners at an all-immigrant U.S. high school, called Franken International. All students at Franken came to the US as adolescents or young adults, and for many, Franken is their first encounter with formal schooling. Students range in age from 14 to 21, and the majority have either Somali or Spanish as a first language. Franken International has 10 full-time teachers and enrolls about 150 students, 90 percent of whom are eligible for free or reduced-price lunch.

Ms. Mavis, the focal teacher, had lived in Africa as a Peace Corps volunteer, and spoke French and some Spanish. Ms. Mavis made a point of discussing and validating students' native languages in the classroom, although they were not used systemically for instructional purposes. Overall, she treated her students respectfully, as intelligent young adults; students frequently stated they learned a lot in her class. Both periods were focused on developmental literacy skills, and students included the most recent arrivals.

Across four months, the project yielded 59 hours of audio- and videotaped classroom observation, five hours of interviews, and 44 hours of individual or small-group tutoring sessions. Qualitative analysis focused on recordings of classroom interactions, students' written work, and 10 focal students' performance on elicited assessments in English and their dominant language. While the focus of the original study was on how students with limited formal schooling were socialized into "doing" school in an urban U.S. setting (King & Bigelow, 2012), our attention was also drawn to the ways in which native languages were used in the classroom, and how those uses established, or "thickened," students' gender and academic identities (Leander, 2002). Theoretically, this qualitative classroom approach is informed by insights from the field of linguistic anthropology (e.g. Bartlett, 2007), with a particular focus on how everyday rituals (e.g. native language translation routines) reflect and help construct student identities. For instance, while Spanish and French were often employed for quick academic translations by the teacher directly, she frequently asked Somali students to translate for less English-proficient Somali students, a practice that often led to extended discussion (in Somali). As highlighted below, these interactions, and the ratification of authority concerning the Somali language in particular, were often gendered in ways that potentially impact classroom language learning.

Somali Diaspora and Somali Language Authority

Somalis are one of the largest refugee populations worldwide, with more than a million Somalis living outside Somalia (Sheikh & Healy, 2009). This massive Somali migration started in 1991 due to civil war, and ongoing lack of political stability in Somali has contributed to ongoing migration and generations of children who grow up or were born in the Diaspora. Minnesota, the site of the research presented here, is estimated to have the largest Somali community in the US (32,000 by Census data, 70,000 by community estimates) ("State's Somali Population," 2011). Most Somali youths' lives are characterized by transnational emotional and familial ties to a Somali homeland (which many have never directly known or visited), but also grounded in everyday interactions and a media environment in which expressions of race, religion, and gender are interwoven, highly marked, and often controversial (e.g. Bigelow, 2010; Browning & Shaw, 2012).

The analysis here suggests ways in which the authority of one young woman (Ayan) as an expert speaker of Somali is undermined, while that of another male student (Saiful) is ratified. Across the scope of the study, these students' identities "thickened" (see Bartlett, 2007), with Ayan viewed as the less successful, distracted, and occasionally overtly oppositional learner, and Saiful as the respectful, older, mature, and "on task" student (Bigelow & King, in press).

As evident below, classroom translational practices—while well intended by the teacher—raise several tensions. First, we see how attempts to create equal access to curriculum (by providing translations in multiple languages) in fact served to establish or reify hierarchies *within* language groups. Second, our longer-term analysis of this local context suggests ways in which these within-language-group hierarchies are gendered. For many East African refugee youth, access to formal schooling prior to arrival to the US varied largely depending on gender. For

Gender, Sexuality, and Multilingualism **289**

instance, Abdi (2007), based on her visits to Dadaab refugee camps (Kenya), reported that in one year, only 69 of 675 high school students were girls; one reason for this is that as they reach marriageable age, they are at higher risk of sexual violence, and thus many families keep their girls home. While access to formal schooling in the US was more balanced, past inequities meant that boys were more likely than girls to arrive at school with first language literacy skills. This difference shaped how students were perceived by others, and potentially how they perceived themselves, as learners and individuals.

In the present case, while Saiful was highly literate in Somali, making rapid progress in his English literacy skills, and widely perceived as a "good student," Ayan was seen as struggling academically. This was Ayan's second year in Ms. Mavis' introductory English class, yet her English skills were among the weakest in the class. At the time of the study, she had been in the US for one year; Franken International was her first formal school experience. Ayan caught our attention immediately as she frequently sought support from the researchers, the teacher, and fellow students. She was often the target of Ms. Mavis' reminders and reprimands for talking out of turn or not staying on task. Ayan sometimes engaged in overtly oppositional resistance to teacher requests. She also, at times, seemed to push the boundaries of appropriate Muslim clothing (shorter, tighter, shinier) relative to other girls at the school. Her written work narrated accounts of resistance to gendered hierarchies in Somali and stressed personal agency (King & Bigelow, 2012).

Ayan had no previous access to written Somali or formal literacy instruction. In our informal written assessment activities, Ayan refused to look at the Somali tasks or materials, and was reluctant to do any of the written English work, completing these reading activities very slowly, with much sub-vocalization and little confidence. Saiful, in turn, had been in the US for only seven months. At 19, he was one of the older students in the classroom. Saiful reportedly attended school for 10 years prior to coming to the US. His informal literacy assessment in Somali indicated that he was very competent in reading and writing in Somali. Nearly all of the classwork we examined was complete, accurate, and had comments of "good!" by Ms. Mavis. Saiful had a serious, quiet, and respectful demeanor in class, and was always neatly and fashionably dressed. His writing frequently mentioned the importance of religion, respect, family, and school. He was usually focused and on task, and often helped other students in class.

As noted above, Ms. Mavis sometimes attempted to provide translations of key words or constructs. After providing support in Spanish (or French), presumably to balance out the level of native language support across all students, she often asked the Somali students to provide a translation as well. In Excerpt 3, Ms. Mavis is reviewing vocabulary words related to the folk tale that students had read earlier in the month. In this exchange, she is prompting them to recall the word "ground."

290 Lyn Wright Fogle and Kendall A. King

Excerpt 3: How do you say ground?

1	Ms. Mavis:	Where did Anasi plant the beans?
2	Ms. Mavis:	Where did he plant the beans? In the . . . (gesturing digging motion)
3	Luis Alberto:	Garden
4	Ms. Mavis:	In the garden but there's another word sounds a little bit like garden it starts with a g (writing "g" on document projector) starts with a "G" "R" "GR" (making grrr sound)
5	Ms. Mavis:	Ground (slowly enunciated)
6	Students:	Ground
7	Ms. Mavis:	Can you say ground? (looking around to left side of room)
8	Students:	Ground
9	Ms. Mavis:	Ground
10	Ms. Mavis:	Consebon, how do you spell ground? (poised to take dictation)
11	Consebon:	inaudible
12	Ms. Mavis:	Very good ground
13	Ms. Mavis:	(pause) You can plant many things in the ground, correct? Yea. Ground is like *la tierra.* How do you say ground in Somali? (looking in Saiful's direction)
14	Ms. Mavis:	Ground or dirt (walking toward Sahardid and sweeping desk). How do you say ground in Somali?
15	Ayan:	Dur dur (loudly)
16	Ms. Mavis:	Dur? Dur? Floor or ground?
17	Ayan:	inaudible
18	Ms. Mavis:	Dur?
19	Ms. Mavis:	So is "dur" floor or ground? (walking over to Saiful and making eye contact)
20	Saiful:	Dur is the earth
21	Ms. Mavis:	Dur, dur, OK sounds like dirt.

Ayan's clear and assertive translation was questioned three times by the teacher. Despite Ayan's apparent confidence that "dur" was the correct word, Ms. Mavis still "checked" the translation with Saiful. Indeed, Ms. Mavis only moves on to the next word once Saiful confirms (line 20). This interaction developed as such because Saiful was the de facto Somali expert in the class, despite the fact there were many speakers of Somali (and some who were more multilingual, competent in Somali as well as Amharic, Oromo, etc., and thus with potential to help translate across more languages to a greater number of students). This role as the expert was co-constructed by Saiful, together with younger female students such as Ayan (who often asked for help), but also, as evident in this example, by the teacher.

Ayan's identity in the classroom as a younger, less academically successful, at times oppositional, student undermined her expertise as a native speaker of Somali. Despite the teacher's welcoming stance toward students' native language use, Ayan's attempts to contribute and draw from her native language were minimized or overlooked. In turn, Saiful's identity as the older, more serious and successful academic learner, with literacy skills in Somali, anointed him as the expert speaker in the class. Thus, an informal classroom language policy enacted or sedimented hierarchies *within* language groups, in this case Somali. Further, the data here suggest the ways in which gendered inequalities outside the classroom (i.e. differential access to formal education and Somali literacy skills) live on inside the classroom in ways that intersect powerfully with student identities.

Discussion and Conclusion

A key principle in the study of language and identity is that identities are emergent in interaction and thus locally produced (Bucholtz & Hall, 2005). In the three excerpts we have analyzed here, interactions associated with language learning (e.g. communicative tasks and teacher-fronted explanatory episodes) present opportunities to construct, negotiate, and resist gendered and sexualized identities. Furthermore, the participants in these classroom activities collaborated with one another to afford or constrain opportunities for identity construction for themselves and others. In these examples, the teachers explicitly, and in some cases directly, ratify or reject certain students' contributions to the class in ways that construct student authority and agency or constrain it. In each case, broadly circulating gendered discourses, or identity categories, are taken up, enacted, rejected, or modified in everyday interactions. Our claim is not that the processes highlighted here are universal, but rather that these merit the attention of researchers and teachers.

More specifically, in both of these contexts, we see how circulating notions of gender constrain and simultaneously shape classroom interactions. In the Russian case, space is created for post-Soviet feminine identities, on the one hand, and rejection of sexualizing prostitute stereotypes, on the other. In the U.S. ESL context, in contrast, we see how gendered notions of what it means to be a successful student undermine authority in even one's *native* language. Concomitantly, the classroom itself affords agency for Ayan to resist, remodel, reformulate an assertive identity for herself, although one with mixed impact. These gendered identity categories impact not only how students perceive themselves and each other as individuals and learners, but also, we postulate, shape possibilities for interaction in the target language in the future, and hence opportunities for language learning going forward.

The implicit language policies at play in these classrooms intersected with the negotiation of women's identities, with gender playing an important role. In particular, the use of learners' first languages in the first study opened spaces for the introduction of difficult topics and experiences in narrative tasks that led to transformations in identity, but in the second study, L1 use reproduced constraining gender norms that intersected with being a good student and authority of one's native language. Thus, while gender and sexuality can shape or constrain learning processes, they are also constructed beyond the language-learning activity (O'Loughlin, 2001). The goals of the two different classrooms and varied activity types (e.g. a communicative task versus vocabulary exercise) in the data give rise to very different opportunities for identity construction. In the teacher-facilitated narrative tasks, the women are able to collaborate to talk about past experiences. However, in the more teacher-directed question-response sequence, authority is assigned in relation to norms for "good student" identities. The supplementary Russian English class, with its lower-stakes instructional goals, consistently offered the older students such as Alina a space to learn English while constructing new "cosmopolitan" Russian identities that connected with students' personal lives. In the U.S. setting, in contrast, students' academic identities as "good" academic English language learners are being constructed for the first time, with lasting implications for their educational trajectories.

These data thus suggest ways in which our analysis of implicit language policy, if such analysis aims to "make space for people," must take into account how individuals negotiate gender and sexuality as part of the learning process. If we take seriously Shohamy's (2006) argument that language must be analyzed as "open, dynamic, energetic, constantly evolving and personal" (p. 5) in order to avoid the manipulation of language as a "political instrument" (p. 23), we are obliged to critically analyze the multiple, fluid possibilities for gender identification that emerge in processes of language learning, teaching, testing, and policy creation, as well as the ways in which gendered and sexualized meanings shape these processes.

References

Abdi, C. M. (2007). Convergence of civil war and the religious right. *Signs: Journal of Women in Culture and Society*, *33*(1), 183–207.

Bartlett, L. (2007). Bilingual literacies, social identification, and educational trajectories. *Linguistics and Education*, *18*(3), 215–231.

Bigelow, M. (2010). *Mogadishu on the Mississippi: Language, racialized identity, and education in a new land*. New York: Wiley-Blackwell.

Bigelow, M., & King, K. A. (in press). The power of Somali script among Somali youth. *Writing Systems Research*.

Browning, D., & Shaw, A. (2012, October 19). Minneapolis man found guilty of aiding Somalia terrorist group. *Star Tribune*. Retrieved from: www.startribune.com/local/minneapolis/174834731.html?refer=y (accessed March 1, 2014).

Bucholtz, M., & Hall, K. (2005). Identity and interaction: a sociocultural linguistic approach. *Discourse Studies*, *7*(4/5), 585–614.

Fogle, L. W., & Grishenkova, I. (2010, March). *Language negotiation, student-led code-switching, and language policy in the EFL classroom*. Paper presented at the Teachers of English to Speakers of Other Languages (TESOL) Annual Convention. Boston, MA.

Fuller, J. M. (2009). Gendered choices: Codeswitching and collaboration in a bilingual classroom. *Gender and Language*, *3*(2), 181–208.

King, K. A., & Bigelow, M. (2012). Acquiring English while learning to do school: Resistance and accommodation. In P. Vinogradov & M. Bigelow (Eds.), *Low education second language and literacy. Proceedings of the 7th Symposium* (pp. 157–182). Minneapolis, MN: University of Minnesota.

Leander, K. (2002). Locating Latanya: The situated production of identity artifacts in classroom interaction. *Research in the Teaching of English, 37*(2), 198–250.

Liddicoat, A. J. (2009). Sexual identity as linguistic failure: Trajectories of interaction in the heteronormative language classroom. *Journal of Language, Identity, and Education, 8*(2/3), 191–202.

Norton, B., & Pavlenko, A. (2004). Addressing gender in the ESL/EFL classroom. *TESOL Quarterly, 38*(3), 504–514.

Ohara, Y. (2001). Finding one's voice in Japanese: A study of the pitch levels of L2 users. In A. Pavlenko, A. Blackledge, I. Piller, & M. Teutsch-Dwyer (Eds.), *Multilingualism, second language learning, and gender* (pp. 231–256). Berlin: Mouton de Gruyter.

O'Loughlin, K. (2001). (En)gendering the TESOL classroom. *Prospect, 16*(2), 33–44.

Scollon, R., & Scollon, S. W. (2004). *Nexus analysis: Discourse and the emerging internet.* New York: Routledge.

Sheikh, H., & Healy, S. (2009). Somalia's missing million: The Somali diaspora and its role in development. *Somalis in Maine Archive, 54*. Retrieved from: http://scarab.bates.edu/somalis_in_maine/54 (accessed March 1, 2014).

Shohamy, E. (1994). The validity of direct versus semi-direct oral tests. *Language Testing, 11*(2), 99–123.

Shohamy, E. (1995). Performance assessment in language testing. *Annual Review of Applied Linguistics, 15*, 188–211.

Shohamy, E. (1996). Test impact revisited: Washback effect over time. *Language Testing, 13*, 298–317.

Shohamy, E. (1997). Testing methods, testing consequences: Are they ethical? Are they fair? *Language Testing, 14*(3), 340–349.

Shohamy, E. (1998). Critical language testing and beyond. *Studies in Educational Evaluation, 24*(4), 331–345.

Shohamy, E. (2001). Democratic assessment as an alternative. *Language Testing, 18*(4), 373–391.

Shohamy, E. (2006). *Language policy: Hidden agendas and new approaches.* London: Routledge.

Shohamy, E., & Hornberger, N. H. (Eds.) (2008). *Encyclopedia of language and education (2nd Edition), Vol. 7: Language Testing and Assessment.* New York: Springer.

Skapoulli, E. (2009). Transforming the label of "whore": Teenage girls' negotiation of local and global gender ideologies in Cyprus. *Pragmatics, 19*(1), 85–101.

Spolsky, B., & Shohamy, E. (1999). *The language of Israel: Policy, ideology and practice.* Bristol, UK: Multilingual Matters.

"State's Somali population grows" (2011). *Star Tribune.* Retrieved from: www.startribune.com/local/132752328.html (accessed October 3, 2013).

Temkina, A., & Zdravomyslova, E. (2003). Gender studies in post-Soviet society: Western frames and cultural differences. *Studies in East European Thought, 55*(1), 51–61.

Teutsch-Dwyer, M. (2001). (Re)constructing masculinity in a new linguistic reality. In A. Pavlenko, A. Blackledge, I. Piller & M. Teutsch-Dwyer (Eds.), *Multilingualism, second language learning, and gender* (Vol. 6, pp. 175–198). Berlin: Mouton de Gruyter.

Tverdova, Y. V. (2011). Human trafficking in Russia and other post-Soviet states. *Human Rights Review, 12*(3), 329–344.

21

EXAMINING MARKERS OF IDENTITY CONSTRUCTION IN ENGLISH LANGUAGE LEARNING

SOME IMPLICATIONS FOR PALESTINIAN-ISRAELI AND JEWISH-ISRAELI LANGUAGE LEARNERS

Julia Schlam Salman, Elite Olshtain, and Zvi Bekerman

Introduction

Languages play a key role in how we construct understandings of ourselves, our social surroundings, our pasts, and our possibilities for the future (Norton & Toohey, 2004). Reorientations in language learning theory have shifted the focus away from understanding acquisition as primarily an isolated mental and individual process. Instead, more recent critical perspectives (Fairclough, 2001) support moving toward an interactionist view of language that focuses on input from the surrounding context and internal language processing (Ellis, 1997; Larsen-Freeman, 2011). This social turn in the understanding of acquisition recognizes language learning as a socially situated activity intricately tied to issues of power, identity construction, and the surrounding sociocultural context. According to Norton and McKinney (2011), "there is now a wealth of research that explores the relationship between identity and language learning, testament to the fact that issues of identity and power are being recognized as central to SLA" (p. 74).

How language learners recognize, perceive, interpret, and reconcile issues of power and identity within a particular contextual setting may directly affect how successful they are at acquiring the target language, how motivated they are to learn the language, and how readily they deal with identity negotiation processes that accompany language learning (Lee & Norton, 2009). In societies experiencing intractable conflict, issues of power and identity in language learning are particularly telling. Languages are symbolic representations of power, oppression, inequality, and, at times, outright conflict. They are also often associated with specific cultural, religious, and/or national identifications. These associations impact language learning, acquisition processes, and learners' ensuing successes or failures.

English language learning, in particular, carries multiple connotations with respect to identity markers, power relations, and the production/reproduction of power structures. English has acquired the status as a global or international language (Brutt-Griffler, 2002; Crystal, 2003) in a variety of settings throughout the world. This process of globalization has produced an area of research concerned with the re-examination of English language learning and its multiple effects. On the one hand, the unprecedented diffusion and use of English by speakers of other languages for local and global communication means that English marks a variety of social groups. It often functions as a language of wider communication (LWC)[1] and connects speakers from all over the world. On the other hand, alongside this "universal appropriation" emerges an array of uncharted consequences that have socioeconomic, political, cultural, and linguistic implications.

Additionally, in the framework of this study, English plays a particularly complex role as a language that is not directly associated with the enduring Israeli-Palestinian conflict, and yet is sometimes perceived as hegemonic and culturally/ ethnically deviant (Amara, 2003). English in the region remains tied to the legacy of colonialism and current political alliances alongside more favorable associations such as increased professional opportunities and social mobility.

Broadly speaking, this chapter involves an examination of the power structures and identity constructs that get named, produced, and reproduced (Bourdieu, 1977) when English is acquired and when local languages are acquired in juxtaposition to English. More specifically, building on discourse collected from a year-long qualitative study of Palestinian-Israeli and Jewish-Israeli English language learners, this article examines students' stated perceptions and understandings concerning issues related to power, identity construction, and the English language. In addition, when relevant, we discuss points related to the local languages of Arabic and Hebrew. Ultimately, collected discourse revealed points of intersection between the local and the global—demonstrating that issues of utility, symmetry, power, and identity, get constructed in sometimes unlikely circumstances.

The Study

This chapter builds on a larger study involving ninth-grade English-language learners in three secular state-run schools in Jerusalem; one is defined as a monolingual majority school (Hebrew-English), the second is defined as a monolingual minority school (Arabic-English), and the third is defined as an integrated, bilingual minority-majority school (Arabic-Hebrew-English). All three schools are located in Jerusalem and function partially or fully under the auspices of the Israeli Ministry of Education.

296 Julia Schlam Salman et al.

Participants

This study included L1 Hebrew, L1 Arabic, and bilingual Arabic-Hebrew speaking students studying English as a foreign language (EFL), between 14 and 15 years old. Table 20.1 delineates demographic and linguistic information concerning participants from all three schools.

Data Collection Instruments

This study involved the use of three qualitative research techniques, including: (1) weekly preliminary classroom observations; (2) in-depth semi-structured qualitative interviews; and (3) focus group activities in each class. Table 21.2 outlines the methods of data collection and the distribution of procedures in each school setting.

TABLE 21.1 Study participants

School	Class size	No.	Gender		Identified religion	Identified L1
			M	F		
Monolingual majority (Hebrew-English)	35	25	13	12	Jewish = 25	Hebrew = 23 Spanish = 1 German = 1
Monolingual minority (Arabic-English)	42	21	9	12	Christian = 3 Muslim = 18	Arabic = 21
Bilingual minority-majority (Arabic-Hebrew-English)	18	14	5	9	Jewish = 4 Christian = 4 Muslim = 6	Hebrew = 3 Arabic = 8 English = 2 Russian = 1

TABLE 21.2 Data collection breakdown

School	Preliminary classroom observations	Interviews	Focus groups
Monolingual majority (Hebrew-English)	Weekly from September–December 2008	10	4
Monolingual minority (Arabic-English)		12	3
Bilingual minority–majority (Arabic-Hebrew-English)		13	5
Total		35	12

Data Collection and Analysis

The data for the study were collected over the course of one academic school year. Initial contact with the principals and teachers commenced during the previous school year, and permissions and bureaucratic procedures vis-à-vis the Israeli Ministry of Education were arranged prior to the beginning of the school year. During the initial stages of the research, preliminary classroom observations were conducted in all three schools. The individual, semi-structured interviews and the focus group sessions then followed. All collected discourse was recorded using a digital voice recorder. Additionally, the focus group activities were videotaped and digitally recorded. The interviews were then fully transcribed and the focus groups were rewatched, with sections being selected for transcription. These data were then analyzed and coded according to qualitative and ethnographic principles (Tracy, 2001).

Study Limitations

Several limitations need to be acknowledged with respect to both the study population and the employed methodologies. Regarding the population, all participants resided in Jerusalem[2]—a fact that uniquely colors their perspectives and experiences. This may be particularly true for the L1 Arabic speakers, who have been part of distinct, outstanding historical/contextual processes not experienced by Palestinian Israelis residing in other parts of the country. With respect to the participants from the bilingual school, it is also necessary to acknowledge that their representation was less than that of the participants from the monolingual schools. This was especially true for the number of L1 Hebrew speakers and Jewish participants.

As concerns the limitations of the employed methodologies, two outstanding factors are worth mentioning. The first pertains to the decision to use English as the medium for the interviews and focus groups. Although the students were given the option to use their L1, most seemed to view the interviews and focus groups as extensions of their English classes and they chose to speak English. They exhibited a range of proficiency levels and some expressed themselves more fully than others. The second limitation pertains to the use of a translator for interviews and focus groups involving L1 Arabic speakers. At times, the translator took the liberty to rephrase a question or answer, or to inject additional comments. This added voice undoubtedly played a role in the conversation dynamic and the manner in which the interviews and focus groups unfolded.

Findings and Analysis

This chapter focuses on markers of identity construction articulated by English learners, including some of the meanings learners ascribed to issues related to

298 Julia Schlam Salman et al.

language, power, and identity. For the purpose of this chapter, each school is presented and analyzed independently. We then offer a comparative analysis, discussing some of the overlapping key points within the contexts of this study. Overarching implications are also addressed.

Markers of identity construction—monolingual majority students. Monolingual majority participants—students studying at the school that primarily served L1 Hebrew speakers—articulated several points with reference to English and identity markers. For the most part, these students awarded a high status to English and connected the language to power and influence. They described markers such as smart, educated, and successful to the kinds of people who know English, and these identifications translated into a correlation between English acquisition and social mobility. One student articulated this in the following way:

> I: *So what kinds of people know English?*
> S1Z: *Um, I don't know; smart people. People that—like in poor countries, not everybody can pay for English lessons so only the ones that can pay for it and are really from wealthy and from good families.*
> I: *Do you think that's true in Israel also?*
> S1Z: *I don't think that only some people can learn English. But I think that only people that are from good homes can learn a lot. You need this for success and university. So they learn it more seriously, they put more effort to this.*

A second student elaborated further:

> S5Z: *In Israel? What do they think about English speakers? Maybe they think they are sophisticated because they come from developed countries. Maybe when they see someone speak English they say, "Oh, he's educated, ah he's successful."*

Discourse showed that monolingual majority participants associated English with "*S6Z: intelligent people who work and who are educated.*" Moreover, they disconnected English from one specific culture and did not link English speakers to certain countries or places. Participants ascribed denationalized attributes to English language learners, stating that the identity of an English speaker spans a variety of cultures and ethnicities. The following excerpt illustrates this point:

> S4Z: *Hm—an English speaker? It can't—it's impossible to complete that sentence because an English speaker is someone who lives here, or an English speaker is someone who lives someplace else. An English speaker is simply someone who knows that language really really well but it's impossible to say what an English speaker is.*
> I: *So in your opinion, it's not connected to America? Or Britain?*
> S4Z: *No.*

Additionally, several students elaborated further, describing English as an international language and a language whose users adopt and localize the language. One participant described this in the following way:

> I: *Do you think there are customs or culture that's connected to English?*
> S8Z: *No. English as a language is not a culture because we can see that English has a lot of cultures together. For example the Indian, in India they speak English but they are acting a lot different than what they do in the United States or what they do in England. You see in England drinking tea and be very polite and in America they're eating junk food and hamburger. In India they're very traditional and they're eating their traditional food in India. The same language but different acts . . . English, specifically because it's an international language, it's not connected to any one culture.*

This process of cultural appropriation and subsequent identity acquisition extended to individuals within the local contexts. When asked what kinds of Israeli Jews and Israeli Palestinians know English, students also mentioned the educated and the elite. At times, they included themselves under the identity of English speaker. English acquisition and subsequent use functioned as an arbiter of identity construction in terms of the way participants viewed themselves. One student articulated this as follows:

> I: *. . . If I say to you, an English speaker is—how would you finish that sentence?*
> S10Z: *I don't know how to finish that sentence because I think about American or British people but I also think about other people that learn English.*
> I: *Okay. Like whom?*
> S10Z: *Like me.*
> I: *So you're also an English speaker?*
> S10Z: *Yes.*

Whether referring to themselves or to others in the Israeli context, appropriation of the perceived identity markers and power conferred by knowledge of English was not only feasible, but desirable. All people can potentially be English speakers, and the more they know and use English, the more others might perceive them as educated and successful. To a degree, then, the acquisition of English contributed to the construction of positive self-identifications, including markers associated with success and prestige.

In the end, identity constructions tied to English—such as power, social mobility, and success—appeared to be highly motivating, and participants indicated being able to successfully internalize these constructs. In describing why English was very important to his parents, one student articulated well the monolingual majority participant perspective: "*S10Z: . . . they know that if I know*

300 Julia Schlam Salman et al.

English I can manage better in my life." This ability to manage, to succeed, and to thrive was connected to markers associated with English and English language acquisition.

Markers of identity construction—monolingual minority students. Participants from the monolingual minority school (i.e. students studying at the school that primarily served L1 Arabic speakers) also addressed markers of identity construction and English. Discourse suggests that English acquisition contributed to ongoing identity negotiation processes, including students' perceptions of others and perceptions of self. These students had clear ideas about the identifications accompanying English speakers. They ascribed romanticized notions to English speakers such as good, kind, and well-mannered. According to some of the monolingual minority participants, a person was "good" simply by the virtue of knowing English. One of the participants articulated this as follows:

> I: *Okay. Um, now I'm going to ask you some questions about what you think an English speaker is. If I say to you, "an English speaker is?" How would you finish that sentence?*
>
> S11B: *Ah, a good person maybe—cause he talk a good language and he speak a language that everybody will know it in the future or in our time. So, it's a good language and he's a good person cause he know how to speak English and how to communicate with English people.*

Generally speaking, students put forth idealistic notions of English speaker identifications. In addition, like monolingual majority participants, they also associated markers such as educated and elite with English speakers. The following excerpt illustrates this point:

> I: *What kinds of people know English?*
>
> S3B: *People who learn more than one language and he studies. If you ask somebody who don't study and who don't do good in school, he won't know what you're saying. Cause he don't learn English or any languages.*

For the most part, monolingual minority students marked English speakers as people who are smart and who have studied a lot. That said, they did not tie these general traits to specific ethnicities or countries. Instead, like students from the monolingual majority school, they ascribed denationalized attributes to English speakers. One student described this as follows:

> S2bf1: *English is in every country I think.*
>
> I: *If I say to you, an English speaker, do you think of somebody specific?*
>
> S2bf1: *Like if I saw you, everyone says that oh she speaks English, she's American. So we go to ask from where you are and then we know that you are not American. English is not just for—I understand now that English is for*

everyone and not just for Americans. Like Arabs speak Arabic and Turkish speak Turkey and German—but English is for everyone.

To a degree, participants expanded their associations with English and were able to apply them to multiple cultural and ethnic groups. This included not only identifications they ascribed to others, but also identifications they ascribed to themselves.

All the participants from the monolingual minority school, except for one, identified themselves as L1 Arabic speakers. Nevertheless, there were a number of highly proficient English speakers, and discourse suggests that their knowledge of English contributed to their forming a positive self-identity. In other words, they assumed the previously mentioned identifications they ascribed to English speakers, such as smart, special, and successful. One student articulated this as follows:

> I: *Is it important to your parents that you study English?*
> S12B: *Yeah, because they want me to be, you know, smart, and know more languages. They want to feel proud of me.*
> I: *And somebody who knows English is someone who's smart, in your opinion?*
> S12B: *Yeah.*

Knowledge of English facilitated the construction of positive identities. Students mentioned that they were proud of themselves because they spoke English and that knowing English contributed to them feeling like they were special. Alongside these positive traits, a few students articulated cultural dissonance between their desire to know and use English and the expectation that, as Palestinians, they should primarily know and use Arabic. By demonstrating fluency in English, they were betraying their ethnic identity and were somehow less authentically Palestinian. The student who identified himself as fluent in English described this as follows:

> I: *How would you describe yourself?*
> S1B: *Well, hmm, something negative about me like I'm lost sometimes.*
> I: *Lost? Okay.*
> S1B: *I feel like I'm in a place where I don't really belong, you know.*
> I: *And you think part of that is because you're an English speaker?*
> S1B: *Yes, mostly because I mean like my first language now is English and um, well Arabic isn't like a priority for me. And like I'm not that great with Arab people and stuff. I am isolated and stuff so mostly yea. But like I also feel like I'm good at English so that's a positive. Um, I can make good friends sometimes and that's a positive too.*
> I: *So you don't identify as a Palestinian? Or?*

302 Julia Schlam Salman et al.

> *S1B:*   *Nationality wise, I do, of course. I mean, I can't change my heritage but if I could change my heritage I'd go umm, I don't know what I'd be. I mean . . .*
>
> *I:*   *It's interesting though because it's—your saying that your heritage is one thing and your language is another thing and that here—*
>
> *S1B:*   *It's a conflict!*

As will be addressed in the discussion section, some L1 Arabic speakers from both the monolingual minority school and the integrated bilingual school articulated cultural identity dissonance. This was particularly paramount for students who were highly proficient in English. L1 Arabic speakers wrestled with competing identity expectations, which, at times, resulted in discord.

Markers of identity construction—bilingual minority-majority students. Bilingual minority-majority students—students studying at the school that served bilingual Arabic-Hebrew speakers—also referenced markers of identity construction, as well as issues related to language and power. Discourse suggests that exposure to and acquisition of English contributed to ongoing identity negotiation processes related not only to language, but also to ethnicity, socioeconomic status, and education.

Bilingual minority–majority students mentioned positive attributes when articulating their perceptions of English speakers. Like students from the monolingual schools, they ascribed categorizations such as educated, successful, and smart to English speakers. Moreover, they tied knowledge of English to elitism and power. While the characteristics they awarded to English speakers were lofty, they did not connect them with a specific group or nation. Similar to students from the monolingual schools, bilingual students awarded denationalized attributes to English speakers. One student expressed this as follows:

> *I:*   *If I say to you an English speaker is—how would you complete that sentence?*
>
> *S6D:*   *An English speaker person is almost every person on the Earth. And I didn't think of it and it's not rare, it's not—it's something that you see almost every day. And it's a regular thing for me.*
>
> *I:*   *And so for you it's not connected to America or—*
>
> *S6D:*   *No, because I think like a lot of people here know English and almost in every country there is a big percent of people that know English.*

In particular, this process of "transnationalizing" English meant that students disconnected English from one particular culture or ethnic group. A second student elaborated further:

> *S4D:*   *English, it's become like one of the—it's more than one culture, it's more, it's all the cultures.*
>
> *I:*   *So there's no one culture that's English?*
>
> *S4D:*   *Yeah. Everyone.*

On the one hand, students perceived English as a language belonging to and representing many cultures. On the other hand, they perceived English as limited to those people who were educated and had money. Consequently, among students from the bilingual minority-majority school, a paradox emerged wherein, culturally, English belonged to everyone but, socioeconomically, English belonged only to the educated and the elite. In that respect, some students mentioned that Palestinians from Gaza or the West Bank might not identify or be identified as English speakers. Moreover, the Palestinian-Israeli participants who were highly proficient in English indicated that by speaking English well, other Palestinians viewed them as snobs and less authentically Palestinian.

The transnationalization of English facilitated the self-appropriation of the identifications participants ascribed to English speakers. Students indicated that knowing English was "good" for them and made them "a better person." One student elaborated as follows:

> I: *Okay. Um, now I'm going to ask you some questions about what you think about English. Do you think learning English is important? Why or why not?*
>
> S13D: *I think it's important because it can help you in a lot of places and it can, you can explore your language and you—you can be a better person. You will be more intelligent. You can learn things that you can't learn in your language. You can speak with other people from other countries and I think it's very important for our life now.*

Students ascribed positive identifications to themselves as English speakers. Nevertheless, this appropriation of the identifications accompanying English speakers—in particular for L1 Arabic speakers—appeared to come with a price.

In addition, students who identified themselves as fluent in English mentioned having to balance different aspects of their identity. For Jewish-Israeli students, there seemed to be an overriding sense of harmony and balance between their identification as Israelis/Hebrew speakers and their identification as English speakers. One student described this as follows:

> S3D: *. . . I was born here and I have lived here all my life. I mean I feel very American but I also feel kind of Israeli. So, I don't know.*
>
> I: *What does being Israeli mean to you?*
>
> S3D: *I guess living here, living here and kind of . . . feeling I guess like kind of you're home. Not just—yeah, that's kind of what I think.*

In contrast, Palestinian-Israeli students articulated a sense of dissonance between their identification as Palestinians/Arabic speakers and their identification as English speakers. They described being caught between different linguistic communities of practice and being perceived by other Palestinians as traitors to

304 Julia Schlam Salman et al.

their ethnicity and their people. The Palestinian Israeli who identified herself as a native English speaker described this in the following way:

> S10D: *I have friends from the LaSalle, you know it? And they only speak in English.*
> I: *You have friends from where?*
> S10D: *LaSalle School. They only speak in English. Like they are not ready to speak in Arabic. Like when we hang out with other friends who don't speak English. They are not like us in a way, different.*
> I: *Like you guys are snobs?*
> S10D: *I don't know. I'm always trying to be with them and with the other one, like speaking Arabic and English at the same time.*
> I: *So you're kind of split between different worlds?*
> S10D: *Yeah.*

Later in the interview, she elaborates further:

> I: *Do you think somebody from Nablus thinks differently about English speakers than somebody—than a Palestinian from Yaffo—*
> S10D: *Of course because I think in Nablus it's like, they don't speak English very well, I guess. I don't know. But um—like they even look at everyone in a different way. Just like why are they speaking in English and not speaking in Arabic. And you know like in Nablus and the problems there so they think of like we are less Palestinian or something.*

This sense of cultural identity dissonance—mentioned by both participants from the monolingual minority school and participants from the bilingual minority majority school—will be further addressed in the discussion section. Here, we simply reaffirm the point that English is not merely a neutralizing entity, but also a linguistic force that affects local/indigenous identity constructions and the equilibrium between different components of identity.

Discussion

Student discourse from all three schools showed that participants perceived language as a strong marker of identity. Languages demarcated ethnicity and, to a degree, religion—aligning speakers with a particular ethnic group. The identifications of Jew and Arab and their corresponding languages were particularly salient. On some level, all study participants perpetuated binary rhetoric in which Hebrew speakers were equated with being Jewish and Arabic speakers were equated with being Palestinian. In contrast, English was generally not linked to a specific ethnic/cultural group, but marked a variety of identity constructs related to education, status, and prestige. Similar statements were made across the ethnic and linguistic groups.

First and foremost, participants awarded a high status to English. They tied identifications such as smart, educated, and wealthy to the kinds of people who know English, and ascribed characteristics associated with power and influence to English speakers. Widespread English language usage in a variety of countries and settings (social, political, economic, technological, etc.) has contributed to this high positioning and unprecedented dominance of English in multiple arenas (Crystal, 2003). The identity markers articulated by participants were primarily related to education and socioeconomic status. As was evident in the collected discourse, participants generally did not equate English with specific cultures or nations.

This process of "internationalization" or "transnationalization" of English is in line with a relatively new body of research dealing with the reappropriation of English by speakers of other languages (e.g. Dissanayake, 2009). In describing English as an international language, McKay (2002) makes the following statement: "an international language is one that is no longer linked to a single culture or nation but serves both global and local needs as a language of wider communication" (p. 24). Ownership becomes "de-nationalized" or "re-nationalized," marking a variety of groups and cultures. To a certain extent, student discourse suggests that the process of denationalization and localization of English facilitated the emancipation of speakers from presupposed, locally imposed categorizations and encouraged them to reconstruct identities. At the very least, it may offer the possibility of self-identification where previously estrangement or disconnect proliferated. This process of denationalization appeared to facilitate participants' adoption of the identity markers they associated with English, in particular attributes associated with prestige, power, and social mobility. Nevertheless, to over-romanticize the transnationalization of English in the Israeli context and disregard local factors would be erroneous. Discourse also clearly showed that the legacy of colonialism in the region, as well as current political alliances between Israel and the United States, continues to impact the identity markers tied to English.

English language acquisition and accompanying identity negotiation processes sometimes stood in direct opposition with local or indigenous identities. This was particularly true for L1 Arabic speakers from both schools. For the most part, Jewish-Israeli participants from both the monolingual majority school and the bilingual minority-majority school articulated a sense of harmony between their identification as Israelis/Hebrew speakers and their identification as English speakers. They confidently marked Hebrew as the language of the Jewish people and the state of Israel, as well as the language tied to success in the local arena. Exhibiting competency in English, therefore, did not threaten Hebrew or mark participants as less Israeli or Jewish. Participants seemed to be able to successfully meld together competing ethnolinguistic identities and reach a state of balance and accord.

306 Julia Schlam Salman et al.

In contrast, Palestinian-Israeli participants expressed dissonance between their identifications as Palestinians/Arabic speakers and their identifications as English speakers. This was particularly true for L1 Arabic speakers who had achieved high levels of proficiency in English. This sense of cultural identity dissonance seemed to be further exacerbated by the fact that within the local context, English was strongly associated with Americans and the United States. Many participants, both Jewish and Palestinian Israelis, tied English to the United States and to a country that supports Israel. For some L1 Arabic speakers, they mentioned that this support came at the expense of the Palestinian people, and that the United States supported and facilitated Israeli occupation of Palestine. Within the Israeli context, then, at times there seemed to be an erosion of the espoused transnational or multicultural identifications previously ascribed to English and English speakers. Rather, the language symbolized Israeli and American-supported occupation and exploitation—hardly neutral or denationalized entities.

Often promoted as a "better" or more "neutral" alternative to Hebrew or Arabic, this study suggests that a more critical, nuanced perspective is warranted with respect to English. Constructed identity markers—regardless of the language —must be imbedded in the sociocultural contexts in which they transpire. Only then can we recognize and begin to legitimize the cohabitation of contradictory or competing identifications. In the Israeli milieu, discourse suggests that the identity markers associated with English ultimately function as both emancipating and colonizing forces—depending on the speakers, the accompanying circumstances, and the wider contexts.

Conclusion

In this chapter, we have considered some of the identity markers constructed by English language learners studying in three linguistically diverse communities of practice (Wenger, 1998) within the Israeli context. One of the central aims of this study was to explore the relationship between identity and language learning, and to investigate notions of power, identity, and investment in the language being learned—namely, English. Within the framework of this study, the markers articulated by participants reflected ambiguity and ongoing processes.

On the one hand, the markers participants ascribed to English increasingly bear resemblance to constructs associated with English as an international language (EIL). This includes using English as a language of wider communication and ascribing, to varying degrees, denationalized or transnationalized identifications to English speakers. On the other hand, English also marked political alliances, in particular those associated with the United States. When connected to the United States, English and its speakers became allies with Israel and the Israeli enterprise. This correlation was perceived as a force for propagating conflict, as well as identity discord.

The construction of new, other, or additional identity markers constitutes an outcome of language learning (Pennycook, 2000). The scope of these identity negotiation processes is intricately tied to social, dialogical encounters transpiring inside and outside the classroom setting. Moreover, languages are not learned in a void, but are an extension of "socially constructed relations among individuals, institutions, communities" and societies (Norton, 2000, p. 7).

Finally, this study demonstrates the need to contextualize English and to consider both historical legacy, as well as current political alliances, when examining its usage, accompanying identity constructions/negotiations and language learning outcomes. Additionally, this study highlights the need to avoid blanketed declarations of neutrality or lingua franca status, but instead to proceed cautiously and critically.

Notes

1. A language of wider communication can be defined as a tool for intra-communication between people who speak different languages. While the language often does not have an official status, it emerges as the primary means for communication between local individuals and speakers of other languages (see McKay, 2002).
2. The unique geopolitical climate within Jerusalem stems, in part, from circumstances surrounding the 1967 six-day war, in which Israel annexed East Jerusalem (from Jordan). In appropriating this land, Israel absorbed tens of thousands of Palestinians living in the area (for further information, see Oren, 2002; Segev, 2007). Although ostensibly under Israeli regime, for the most part these Palestinians have not been granted the same civil and inalienable rights as Palestinians from other parts of the country. Jerusalem Palestinians straddle different geopolitical spheres, which inevitably construct outstanding emotional, social, and political experiences (Kimmerling & Migdal, 2003).

References

Amara, M. (2003). Recent foreign language education policies in Palestine. *Language Problems & Language Planning, 27*(3), 217–232.

Bourdieu, P. (1977). Cultural reproduction and social reproduction. In J. Karabel & A. H. Halsey (Eds.), *Power and ideology in education* (pp. 487–510). Oxford: Oxford University Press.

Brutt-Griffler, J. (2002). *World English: A study of its development.* Bristol, UK: Multilingual Matters.

Crystal, D. (2003). *English as a global language* (2nd ed.). New York: Cambridge University Press.

Dissanayake, W. (2009). Cultural studies and discursive constructions of World Englishes. In B. Kachru, Y. Kachru, & C. Nelson (Eds.), *The handbook of World Englishes* (pp. 545–566). Malden, MA: Blackwell.

Ellis, R. (1997). *Second language acquisition.* Oxford: Oxford University Press.

Fairclough, N. (2001). *Language and power* (2nd ed.). Essex: Pearson Education.

Kimmerling, B., & Migdal, J. (2003). *The Palestinian people: A history.* Cambridge, MA: Harvard University Press.

Larsen-Freeman, D. (2011). A complexity theory approach to second language acquisition. In D. Atkinson (Ed.), *Alternative approaches to second language acquisition* (pp. 48–72). New York: Routledge.

Lee, E., & Norton, B. (2009). The English language, multilingualism, and the politics of location. *International Journal of Bilingual Education and Bilingualism, 12*(3), 277–290.

McKay, S. L. (2002). *Teaching English as an international language: Rethinking goals and approaches.* Oxford: Oxford University Press.

Norton, B. (2000). *Identity and language learning: Gender, ethnicity and educational change.* London: Pearson Education.

Norton, B., & McKinney, C. (2011). An identity approach to second language acquisition. In D. Atkinson (Ed.), *Alternative approaches to second language acquisition* (pp. 73–93). New York: Routledge.

Norton, B., & Toohey, K. (Eds.) (2004). *Critical pedagogies and language learning.* New York: Cambridge University Press.

Oren, M. (2002). *Six days of war: June 1967 and the making of the modern Middle East.* New York: Random House.

Pennycook, A. (2000). The social politics and the cultural politics of language classrooms. In J. Hall & W. Eggington (Eds.), *The sociopolitics of English language teaching* (pp. 89–103). Bristol, UK: Multilingual Matters.

Segev, T. (2007). *1967: Israel, the war, and the year that transformed the Middle East.* New York: Henry Holt & Company.

Tracy, K. (2001). Discourse analysis in communication. In D. Schiffrin, D. Tannen, & H. E. Hamilton (Eds.), *The handbook of discourse analysis* (pp. 725–749). Malden, MA: Blackwell.

Wenger, E. (1998). *Communities of practice: Learning, meaning, and identity.* Cambridge: Cambridge University Press.

22
INTEGRATIONAL LINGUISTICS AND L2 PROFICIENCY

James P. Lantolf

In this chapter, I consider a perspective on L2 proficiency grounded in an integrationalist rather than a segregationalist approach to language analysis. The consequences of the different perspectives are profound with regard to our understanding of human communication, in particular with regard to L2 proficiency and its assessment. The integrationalist orientation is represented in the writings of Roy Harris and his colleagues, while the segregationalist approach (Harris, 1998a) is represented in the work of structuralist theories of language beginning with Saussure (1959), extending to Bloomfield (1993) and eventually to Chomsky (1965).[1]

Integrationalist linguistics, with its origins in the writings of Malinowski (1927), brings communicative meaning (not decontextualized sentence meaning) to center stage. It is concerned with *parole*—people creating meaning in communicative activity—the study of which Saussure (and Bloomfield) relegated to disciplines other than linguistics. It approaches language study as one component of human communicative activity along with gestures, facial expressions, body movement, sighs, coughs, head scratching, etc. It recognizes, therefore, that from the perspective of real communicators, "whose humanity depends on social interaction . . . language is not an autonomous mode of communication and languages are not autonomous systems of signs" (Harris, 1998a, p. 9).

The chapter begins with a discussion of Saussure's solution to Locke's communicative skepticism—a solution that, on the positive side (perhaps?), gave rise to linguistics as a science, but, on the negative side (definitely!), came at the cost of reifying and fetishizing language, as people as real social entities were hidden from the gaze of linguistic researchers. The chapter next presents the integrationalist response to Saussure's approach that recovers people in communicative activity and what this means for how we understand language. The chapter then

310 James P. Lantolf

moves on to consider some of the implications of integrationalism for L2 use, in particular how we understand proficiency and its assessment. With this objective in mind, the chapter reanalyzes data from a study by Lantolf and Ahmed (1989) on the variable performance of an adult L2 speaker of English.

Integrational Linguistics

Atkinson (2002) expressed deep concern at the nature of the person positioned at the heart of the acquisition process in second language acquisition (SLA) research:

> I frequently find the reading of SLA research to be almost an exercise in surrealism—based, I believe, in the just-mentioned contradictory "present absence" of human beings. Human beings as I know them, whether people on the street, students I teach and work with, professional colleagues, or those I am close to and love, appear to act, think and feel in ways and for reasons entirely different than those most typically featured in SLA research.
> (pp. 535–536)[2]

The person that figures into most SLA research is a consequence of the collateral damage resulting from Saussure's project to create linguistics as the science of language and his response to the communicative skepticism raised by John Locke (1690) more than two centuries earlier.

Saussure: Dehumanizing Language

Saussure proposed the fixed-code model of language, whereby "all speakers of the same language link the same *signifies* with the same *signifiants* because that connection is arbitrarily imposed on them by the conventions of their language" (Taylor, 1998, p. 199). On this view, language is conceptualized as a fixed code whereby humans communicate with each other through telemention, a process in which A encodes a message in words and transmits these, via acoustic or light waves, to B, who, in turn, decodes or converts the words into the same semantic representation that A has in mind (Harris, 2003b). This ensures that all speakers of a language will understand each other in precisely the same way because meaning resides in language and not in speakers.

Saussure's approach resulted from his initial theoretical move designed to convert language into "a thing to be found in the world of other things" of "the same ontological order," and as such, it was "open to the methods of objective scientific study" (Crowley, 1996, p. 18). This move sanitized language by removing speakers from the equation, and, with them, speech, which linguistics, according to Saussure (1959, p. 9), did not have the methodological wherewithal to systematically study. Essentially, Saussure drew a circle around language—a "pure, clean, steel skyscraper rising above the chaos of the street" (Agar, 1994,

Integrational Linguistics and L2 Proficiency **311**

p. 37)—and proposed that inside-the-circle language, the proper and exclusive domain of linguistic science, was restricted to the study of form and "core meaning," or "the part of meaning that can be characterized formally and truth-conditionally," and therefore considered as "the only important and fundamental part of meaning" (Fauconnier & Turner, 2002, p. 15).

In one stroke, Saussure "simultaneously separated language from non-language and linguistics from all other investigations dealing with human behavior" (Harris, 2003a, p. 21). He created a dichotomy where there had been unity between speakers and their language. In effect, Saussure created the illusion of language as an entity with "mind-independent 'objective' existence" (Sfard, 2008, p. 44). Consequently, the metaphorical nature of reified language goes unnoticed, and we therefore treat it as we do "things-in-the-world that are not any less present and real than what we can see with our eyes or touch with our hands" (p. 44).

Saussure successfully alienated humans "both from the product of their activity and from their own creative powers" (Bakhurst, 1991, p. 193). Language was thus fetishized and imbued with a degree of agency that it does not deserve. For example, linguists (and teachers) often claim that "Spanish *requires* subjunctive with verbs expressing desire," "German *moves* inflected verbs to second position in main clauses," or "French uses *on* as a first-person plural pronoun." Spanish, German, and French do nothing of the sort, any more than hammers, saws, and screwdrivers self-modify their shapes to fit new purposes. Human beings create, shape, and manipulate language, just as they do physical tools, in order to meet specific communicative (or labor-related) goals.

Re-Humanizing Language

Integrational linguistics begins from the premise that "human beings do *not* live in a communicational world that is neatly and permanently compartmentalized into language and non-language" (Harris, 2003b, p. 67, original emphasis). It erases the Saussurean circle and reconceptualizes people as communicating beings. Strictly speaking, IL is not a theory of language as much as it is an exploration of the implications and consequences of (re)integrating language with speakers and their full communicative system, of which language is one component. Its project is to inquire "into the everyday mechanisms by means of which the reality of the linguistic sign as a fact of life is established" (Harris, 2003b, p. 50).

At least two significant claims emerge from IL. One is the indeterminacy of linguistic signs (i.e. signs do not preexist in some abstract decontextualized space, but are in fact constituted in purposeful communicating activity by virtue of the integrational role they fulfill). The other, perhaps more controversial claim is that "linguistic communication is a continuum of interaction which can be manifested both verbally and non-verbally" (Harris, 2003b, p. 45), and encompasses phenomena either ignored or marginalized in general linguistics. These

312 James P. Lantolf

include silences, pauses, grunts, tone of voice, facial expressions, eye gaze, touching, gestures, etc.

Indeterminacy. Harris (2003a) argued that what counts as a sign, in general, is dependent on the situation in which it occurs. He asked why linguistic signs should be an exception to the indeterminacy principle that holds for all other signs. Indeed, Saussure (1959), in laying the foundation for the field of semiotics, accepted the indeterminacy principle for all but linguistic signs—a special category in which meaning resides in the sign itself and not in its use.

For Harris, however, linguistic signs are indeed indeterminate, once we rescue communication from the Saussurean circle. Accordingly, the "exigencies of human communication demand" that linguistic signs must be indeterminate, unless of course humans are "some form of complex species of computer" that only accept "as input, signals drawn from a fixed inventory of invariant forms, and interpretable only by reference to a fixed inventory of invariant meaning" (Harris, 2003a, p. 24).

According to Harris (1998a), segregationalist (i.e. fixed-code) linguistics prioritizes "decontextualized" sentences and then attempts to explain how "social interaction works" (p. 11) once these sentences are inserted into particular social contexts. Integrationalists, on the other hand, assign priority to social interaction and argue that "meaning is inseparable from the language-game" (Wittgenstein, 1953, p. 11), and it is from social interaction that linguists create abstractions referred to as sentences. Another way of saying this is that pragmatics is all there is. There are no neutral abstract sentences that users acquire and deploy in this or that context. From the perspective of users, and this is what integrationalism attempts to understand, non-pragmatic language makes no sense.

Nonverbal linguistic signs and signals. The second implication of the integrationalist stance relates to the status of nonverbal signs. Consider the following interaction between individuals sharing a meal (Harris, 1998a):

> A: *Please pass the salt.*
> B: Extended gaze in A's direction accompanied by a sharp expulsion of air from the mouth.
> A: *Forget it* [with gritted teeth]. Stands up and walks to other side of table, picks up the salt and returns to seat.
>
> (p. 12)

A's initial utterance is a straightforward linguistic sign intended for B. However, as Harris (1998a) noted, the meaning of A's utterance as a request to B to move the salt shaker from near B to A cannot be built up from linguistic rules plus some kind of pragmatic information, but requires complex cultural knowledge of particular mealtime schemas and their function (e.g. that the salt is to remain inside the shaker rather than being shaken out into a napkin). Moreover, B's gaze and release of air has as much meaning as if B had said "No" or "Get it yourself,"

Integrational Linguistics and L2 Proficiency **313**

and therefore qualifies as a linguistic sign. A recognizes this, and indeed is able to interpret B's intended meaning, and does not assume, for example, that B has not heard or understood A's request. We know this because of A's verbal and nonverbal reaction to B's behavior, which is equally comprised of two linguistic signs, one involving verbal language and the other the body.

Voloshinov (1929/1973) made an important distinction between signal and sign that is relevant to the current discussion. Anticipating integrational linguistics by several decades, Voloshinov argued that the notion of language as an objective system is the outcome of the work of the linguist and not something that a speaker is concerned about with respect to the "immediate purposes for speaking" (p. 67). This means that rather than valuing the stability and identity of signs, speakers value the signs' "*changeable and adaptable*" properties (p. 68, original emphasis). Essentially, for listeners to understand speakers requires that instead of recognizing linguistic forms as familiar and identical, they must, on the contrary, interpret the novelty of the forms. Accordingly, signals are indeed recognized and acknowledged because they are singular and fixed and, most importantly, they do "not stand for anything else, or reflect or refract anything"; they are instead "a technical means for indicating this or that object, or this or that action" (p. 68). Thus, a red traffic light signals the action of stopping and a green traffic light signals the action of moving. These signals are invariant and demand nothing more than recognition. Signs require an orientation of the listener to variability "in the dynamic process of becoming" (p. 69).

According to Voloshinov, children born into a language community do not encounter language as a fixed, complete, full symbolic system that is passed on from one generation to the next. On the contrary, they enter into the communicative flow of a community through which their consciousness is formed as they appropriate fragments of the language as an inseparable component of lived experience. Voloshinov (1929/1973) pointed out that in at least one special, if not "abnormal" case, language is encountered as a fully prepared signal system: "Only in learning a foreign language does a fully prepared consciousness—fully prepared thanks to one's native language—confront a fully prepared language which it need only accept" (p. 81). He cautioned, however, that to master the language, the learner must overcome "signality and recognition," and unless and until this happens, the language is not fully a language (p. 69). The signality, he asserted, must be absorbed "by pure semioticity," and recognition "by pure understanding" (p. 69).

L2 Proficiency

I would now like to consider a piece of data from a case study originally published more than 20 years ago by Lantolf and Ahmed (1989). The purpose of the study was to investigate the variable performance of an L2 speaker across two tasks; one, the *bilingual syntax measure*, an instrument originally designed in

314 James P. Lantolf

1975 to assess children's proficiency in Spanish and English, was expected to produce a more grammatically correct performance than the other, an interview about the speaker's experience of American culture. Our assumption was that the participant (M), an L1 speaker of Arabic, would produce more grammatically accurate language on the BSM than in the interview, given the former's banal content, which would allow an adult speaker to focus cognitive resources on producing correct linguistic forms. The latter activity was open-ended, and as such was expected to bring meaning into greater focus at some cost to linguistic accuracy. In the original study, we were interested in M's performance on two high-frequency features of English—nominal plurals and *the/a* alternation. As anticipated, on the BSM, M produced correct noun plurals 96 percent of the time, while in the interview, his accuracy dropped to 53 percent. For article use, on the BSM, M's accuracy rate was 65 percent and decreased to 55 percent in the interview task.

Serendipitously, near the end of the interview, M raised the topic of comparative religion, resulting in an extended four-hour, wide-ranging conversation with the researcher (L) on Islam and Christianity. M had thought a great deal about the differences between the two religions since his early childhood. Lantolf and Ahmed (1989) compared M's performance during the conversation with that of the interview. We broadened the scope of linguistic features to include copula deletion, regular and irregular past tense verbs, and use of present for past morphology. We also considered M's use of pragmatic versus syntactic utterances, as well as his mean length of utterance (MLU) and mean length of turn (MLT) in both activities. Unfortunately, because the performances were audio-recorded only, we do not have any data on the interactants' nonverbal performance. Table 22.1 summarizes the data.

M's grammatical accuracy "deteriorated" as he moved from the interview to the conversation. Citing Yngve (1986, p. 102), who proposed a theory of "human linguistics" rather than a "linguistics of language," Lantolf and Ahmed (1989, p. 102) remarked that in order to account for M's performance, it was necessary to focus not on language, but on people and how they orient themselves to what they are doing through their language. While I believed that the analysis at the time was moving in a productive direction, I think it requires some sharpening in light of the position on language and communication I have outlined in the present chapter.

The specific question that I would like to address is: In light of IL, what can be said about M's English proficiency based on his differential performance in the two activities? From a segregationalist, linguistics-of-language perspective, one would surely want to argue that M's performance was less proficient in the conversation than in the interview. From an integrationalist, linguistics-of-people perspective, however, things look quite a bit different. In the conversation, even though M's grammatical accuracy declined, other aspects of his performance improved, as evidenced in the increase in his MLU and MLT from the interview

Integrational Linguistics and L2 Proficiency　**315**

TABLE 22.1 M's performance on interview versus conversation

Feature	Interview	Conversation
Noun plural –s	53%	36%
Article use	55%	35%
Copula deletion	8% (3/39)	32% (13/41)
Correct irregular past	66% (8/12)	30% (7/23)
Correct regular past	100% (4/4)	39% (7/18)
Present for past[a]	19% (2/16)	36% (23/64)
Pragmatic utterances[b]	6% (6/96)	31% (83/268)
MLU[c]		
M[d]	3.91	6.83
L[e]	7.3	8.6
MLT[f]		
M	7.5	16.09
L	11.8	9.7
Questions posed		
M	0	67
L	43	16
Topic shifts		
M	0	8
L	26	2

a　Examples of present for past
  Interview:
  L: Have you traveled around at all while you've been here?
  M: *I am going* to Washington, to France, and / ... to New York five times / ... to Niagara
     Falls, that's it.
  Conversation:
  When I was 15, I *think* I *can't* agreee with him.
  This, the second book about how the Christ *live*.

b　Examples of pragmatic utterances
  Interview:
  L: What about the food?
  M: The same food we have.
  Conversation:
  The rules, its exist.

c　MLU = mean length of utterance
d　MLT = mean length of turn
e　M = participant
f　L = researcher

316 James P. Lantolf

to the conversation, which, in both cases, surpassed L's performance. In addition, in the conversation, M asked more questions and initiated more topic shifts than L, whereas in the interview, M failed to ask a single question or initiate a single topic shift.

Relying on Vygotsky's (1987) theory of regulation, Lantolf and Ahmed (1989, p. 106) explained M's differential performances as emanating from a shift from *other-* to *self-regulation*. That is, the goal of the interview, as in most laboratory experiments, was predetermined by the researcher, who set the agenda with which the participant was expected to comply. The goal of the interview was for M to demonstrate to L his ability to speak English rather than to relate his experiences in American cultural settings, the ostensible topic of the interaction. That M was aware of the "unsaid" goal is attested by his remark toward the end of the interview session: "Do you think it's enough to make me speak (laughter). It's your turn" (p. 104). In terms of an oral proficiency interview (OPI), M had provided a ratable sample of speech, but had not engaged in a real conversation. Thus, Lantolf and Ahmed argued that in the interview, M was *other-regulated* by L much in the way an examinee's performance is other-regulated in an OPI (Johnson, 2001).

On the other hand, M was genuinely interested in the topic of the conversation, which he had initiated and asked to continue, as attested in the following comment made after the interaction had been going on for about two hours: "I have English class now. We can talk more after?" (Lantolf & Ahmed, 1989, p. 105). According to Lantolf and Ahmed, M's performance in the conversation was self-regulated because it complied with his interest in, and desire to discuss, comparative religion. They contended that the only way for him to achieve this goal was to produce speech that was less grammatical but at the same time more interactive than in the interview.

Expanding the Analysis

From an integrationalist perspective, I now believe that it is inappropriate to argue that in the interview M was other-regulated, while in the conversation he was self-regulated. It makes more sense to argue that both speakers co-regulated each other and themselves. In co-regulated activity, each participant is attuned not only to the self, but to the other as they construct a shared *definition of situation* (DOS), described by Wertsch (1984, p. 8) as the joint active creation of an interactive context. In the interview, M consented to a DOS that we might call "demonstrate my *linguistic* prowess in English." To achieve this commitment, he needed to produce the best-formed utterances he could.

In the conversation, the participants continued the activity of co-regulation; however, a new DOS, which might be labeled "a genuine dialogue on religion," was agreed to. As shown in Table 22.1, in this DOS, M's grammatical accuracy declined, while his MLU and MLT increased sharply, and at the same time L's MLU increased only slightly and his MLT decreased compared to his performance in the interview. Moreover, the disparity in the number of questions asked and the number of topic shifts initiated by each participant changed dramatically in M's favor.

A proposal by Taylor (1998) helps to better explain the circumstances of the two events. According to Taylor, in spoken communication, "communicational efficacy" and "grammaticality" can be, and often are, separated: "It is one thing to speak effectively, another to speak in conformity to the conventions for written language style" (p. 195). He argued that the most important goal of ordinary conversation is that the participants communicate to their "mutual satisfaction," and as such "the question of grammaticality of utterances produced is irrelevant" (p. 195). To assume that grammaticality is central to conversational communication is to accept the belief that in ordinary conversation, the grammatical standards that apply to formal written language, as is assumed in sentence-based, fixed-code, theories of grammar, underlie communicative interaction (p. 194). On this view, communication would be next to impossible unless hearers were able to access the supposedly well-formed sentences that underlie speakers' often grammatically problematic, discontinuous, and elliptical utterances. To argue that this must occur because of mutual understanding between interlocutors begs the question.

From the integrationalist perspective, there is no reason to require hearers "to transform an ungrammatical utterance into grammatical sentence form" in order for it to be understood (Taylor, 1998, p. 195). Brown (1980, p. 36) offered three reasons for why the transformation is not necessary: (1) conversations are fabricated as they proceed, and therefore a fair amount of planning happens on-line and in view of the interlocutor, who pays attention to this process, and therefore has at least a general idea of what the speaker is likely to say; (2) conversation deals with social, cognitive, and attitudinal meanings, and given that this is what an interlocutor listens for, if the meaning is coherent, grammatical form is not relevant either for the hearer or the speaker; and (3) conversation is an interactive (i.e. co-regulative) process whereby the speaker relies on the hearer's inferencing powers, which includes assigning meaning to the nonverbal linguistic signs the speaker is generating (e.g. gestures, gaze, coughs, puffs of air, clicks, etc.).

In the conversation, as the data in Table 22.1 show, M produced many more pragmatic than syntactic utterances. According to Ochs (1979) and Givon (1979), pragmatic speech is marked by overt planning, reduced morphological marking (e.g. tense endings), repetition, pauses, more coordination than subordination, and topic-comment rather than subject-predicate order. The following is an example of M's pragmatic speech:

> L: I don't remember what we were talking about?
> M: Talking about the way you, the way you, ah, the way you . . . fast
> . . . the way you fast your religion. I talk about my, the way we fast.
> (Lantolf & Ahmed, 1989, p. 98)

318   James P. Lantolf

Although M's utterance is grammatically problematic from the fixed-code point of view, from an integrationalist perspective it is communicatively effective. Indeed, L did not recast, nor did he request clarification. In fact, throughout the four-hour conversation, we encountered virtually no evidence of comprehension problems on the part of either participant.

Givon (1979) characterized pragmatic speech as "slapdash," and both he and Ochs (1979) agreed that it is a throwback to pre-syntactic communication of childhood that occurs when one is under communicative stress, or when one is completely relaxed, "where planning is simply NOT NECESSARY" (Givon, 1979, p. 105, original emphasis). Indeed, this was the position that Lantolf and Ahmed (1989), I now believe mistakenly, argued for. The problem with this position is that it assumes that syntactic speech is somehow more normal and adult-like.

Although pragmatic speech may be ontogentically prior to syntactic speech, it is inappropriate to characterize it as "slapdash" or "child-like" communication, because the central question that must be addressed is how a performance should be organized to make it communicatively effective—a very different matter from how a performance should be organized to make it grammatical (Taylor, 1998, p. 195). The effectiveness of an utterance is not determined by its appearance, but by how the interactants co-construct the communicative process, and this means that comprehending is no less creative than speaking. It also depends on the interactants' criteria for success as agreed upon in their consensual frame. According to Taylor (1998), there are "no fixed limits . . . determining what utterances must be like to be communicative" (p. 196). In light of the notion of Voloshinov's, rather than Saussure's notion, of linguistic sign, it is clear that "speakers and hearers can draw on a potentially limitless range of resources: From gesture to paralingusitics and poetic features and from situational context to assumptions of prior experience" (p. 196). Thus, the communicative efficacy of an utterance is neither determined by some abstract grammatical representation, nor by third-party observers. It is determined by the interactants themselves.

Taylor used the analogy of a tennis match to illustrate the difference between communicative efficacy and grammatical accuracy. One may engage in a tennis match with the goal of making a team or with the goal of winning a wager. In the first case, it is necessary to demonstrate one's full repertoire of shots, along with the ability to adapt to a variety of opponents and court surfaces. On the other hand, when free of this panopticon, and if a wager is riding on the outcome of the match, the only thing that matters is winning. The array of shots and adjustments one can make becomes irrelevant.

Ordinary conversation is analogous to winning the wager however one can. The grammaticality that applies in a fixed-code and segregationalist model of language simply does not come into play. If communication is achieved to the consensus of both parties involved, the wager is won. It would be "artificial and irrelevant to measure my style of play" (in this case, communication) against someone else's notion of the ideal style (p. 194), as occurs in the testing

Integrational Linguistics and L2 Proficiency **319**

panopticon, where one needs to demonstrate that one can comply with imposed criteria for playing the communicative game. This is precisely what M set out to do in the interview. In the conversation, his goal was to win the communicative wager by finding out as much as he could about another religion.

M's Proficiency?

If we judge M's performance in the interview only, we might conclude that he had a "reasonably advanced" level of proficiency. If we judge his performance in the conversation, we might conclude that he had a "reasonably low" level of proficiency. If we assess his proficiency in both activities, we would most likely conclude that his proficiency was variable (see Tarone, 1988). Over time, for the particular features under analysis, we would expect his proficiency to stabilize and his underlying competence to lose its variable nature, and one performance would transfer to another.

However, the fact that we expect someone's performance to transfer from one activity to another is, as Sfard (2008) noted, the consequence of "objectification that accompanies the metaphor of transfer" (p. 59). Given that knowledge is objectively present in the speaker's mind, it should be deployed when circumstances call for it. If this disappoints us, it is because of the objectification associated with the transfer metaphor—if something is actually present in one's mind, why is it not used when appropriate? In Sfard's view, objectification creates the illusion of "permanence and repetitiveness of patterns" (p. 56). Something that is permanent and objective is expected to be repeated, and therefore transfer from one activity to another; if it does not, then we assume that something is preventing the repetitiveness from occurring. To a language assessor, the two interactions that M participated in look suspiciously similar, and so we might expect the performances to be more or less equal, and when they are not we try to find an explanation grounded in monologic, inside-the-circle thinking. However, it is entirely possible that the two activities are completely different for M; one is a game of display and the other a game that has the goal of winning—achieving communicative satisfaction.

Returning to Voloshinov's notions of signality and sign, it is possible to understand M's performance in the interview as one where signality and recognition were foregrounded, while in the conversation he engaged in the manipulation and creation of mutable signs. Under the first scenario, he was invited and agreed to play a game where style mattered, and so rather than creating mutable signs, he deployed fixed signals. As in most situations when under the gaze of authority, correctness matters. Recognizing and agreeing to this DOS, M played the appropriate game. The game, however, was not played with signs, but with signals. In the conversation, on the other hand, the mutually agreed upon game, winning (comparing religions) trumped style, and correctness was no longer salient. This game was not played with signs.

320 James P. Lantolf

Rethinking Communicative Competence and Language Proficiency

Harris (1998b) argued that the concept of *communicative competence*, proposed by Hymes (1972), was an attempt to overcome the problems associated with segregationalism, while at the same time accepting its orientation to language. It was, he noted, a way of trying to integrate language into communication, but it continues to treat "communication as something extra to languages and thus presupposes the very separatism that an integrational approach must deny" (Harris, 1998b, p. 44). Successful communication depends on the interaction that unfolds between the interactants and cannot be explained on the basis of the participants following "a set program of rules" (p. 38). In real life, "experience is not neatly compartmentalized into the linguistic and the non-linguistic" (p. 44). Consequently, because it evokes rule-governed behavior, Harris dropped "competence" from communicative competence, and replaced it with "communicative proficiency," which can neither be "defined in advance" nor "legislated for by societies or by linguistic theorists," and instead is understood as "the ability to cope with the communicational demands and opportunities that situations present us with" (p. 44).

Kramsch (2006) also offered an important critique of communicative competence, but from a more pedagogically oriented perspective than Harris. She nevertheless arrived at a similar conclusion, observing that "human communication is more complex than just saying the right word to the right person in the right manner. Most of the time there is not even a right or wrong way of communicating" (p. 251). She suggested "symbolic competence" as an alternative concept, which encompasses not only communicative interaction, but also incorporates many of the features argued for in integrational linguistics, including the ability to produce and interpret written texts.

As appealing as the respective proposals offered by Harris and Kramsch may be, they each retain an element that, in my view, is problematic. Kramsch's use of "competence," for the reasons mentioned by Harris and Sfard, weakens her suggestion considerably. Substituting "proficiency" for competence, as Harris does, is also problematic, given how proficiency is usually construed in the L2 literature, especially when it comes to formal language assessment where successful communication supposedly hinges on accuracy in syntax, morphology, phonology, lexicon, and pragmatics. On the other hand, Kramsch's use of "symbolic" greatly broadens the notion that social interaction incorporates much more than what is traditionally understood by the term "communicative." It extends the notion to all types of communicative genres, whether written or oral, including the semiotics of respiratory exhalations, eye gaze, etc.

Widdowson (2003, p. 115 ff.), similar to Harris, suggested replacing the second element in "communicative competence" with *capacity* in order to avoid any of the baggage associated with Chomskyan linguistic competence. Although it may

Integrational Linguistics and L2 Proficiency **321**

not be fully satisfactory, I would like to propose a term that combines Widdowson's use of capacity with Voloshinov's notion of *sign* to capture the notion that humans are able to create, appropriate, and manipulate signs (verbal, nonverbal, textual, contextual, etc.) in the service of their communicative need that includes L1 and additional languages and does not establish clear boundaries among these: *sign-making capacity*.

Notes

1. I realize that Chomsky argued against Saussurean and Bloomfieldian structuralism on several grounds, including that their approaches were unable to account for such phenomena as ambiguity. Nevertheless, Chomsky continues to privilege structure over meaning, and therefore maintains the tradition proposed by Saussure that the proper study of language (*langue*) requires excising it from the world of human communication (i.e. performance).
2. Lantolf and Pavlenko (2001) expressed a similar view when they argued that a person is most decidedly not an autonomous rule-processing device, but is instead a flesh-and-blood entity engaged in, and inseparable from, a collectively organized world—a world where dialogic interaction is the usual way of doing business.

References

Agar, M. (1994). *Language shock: Understanding the culture of conversation.* New York: Quill.

Atkinson, D. (2002). Toward a sociocognitive approach to second language acquisition. *The Modern Language Journal, 86,* 508–525.

Bakhurst, D. (1991). *Consciousness and revolution in Soviet philosophy: From the Bolsheviks to Evald Ilyenkov.* Cambridge: Cambridge University Press.

Bloomfield, L. (1933). *Language.* New York: Holt, Rinehardt, & Winston.

Brown, E. K. (1980). Grammatical incoherence. In H. W. Dechert & M. Raupach (Eds.), *Temporal variables in speech: Studies in honor of Frieda Goldman-Eisler* (pp. 25–37). The Hague: Mouton.

Chomsky, N. (1965). *Aspects of the theory of syntax.* Cambridge, MA: MIT Press.

Crowley, T. (1996). *Language in history: Theories and texts.* London: Routledge.

Fauconnier, G., & Turner, M. (2002). *The way we think: Conceptual blending and the mind's hidden complexities.* New York: Basic Books.

Givon, T. (1979). From discourse to syntax: Grammar as a processing strategy. In T. Givon (Ed.), *Syntax and semantics, vol. 12: Discourse and syntax* (pp. 81–114). New York: Academic Press.

Harris, R. (1998a). Language as social interaction: Integrationalism versus segregationalism. In R. Harris & G. Wolf (Eds.), *Integrational linguistics: A first reader* (pp. 5–14). Oxford: Pergamon.

Harris, R. (1998b). Making sense of communicative competence. In R. Harris & G. Wolf (Eds.), *Integrational linguistics: A first reader* (pp. 27–49). Oxford: Pergamon.

Harris, R. (2003a). Critique of orthodox linguistics. In H. G. Davis & T. J. Taylor (Eds.), *Rethinking linguistics* (pp. 16–26). London: Routledge.

Harris, R. (2003b). On redefining linguistics. In H. G. Davis & T. J. Taylor (Eds.), *Rethinking linguistics* (pp. 27–68). London: Routledge.

322 James P. Lantolf

Hymes, D. (1972). On communicative competence. In J. B. Pride & J. Holmes (Eds.), *Sociolinguistics: Selected readings* (pp. 269–293). Harmondsworth: Penguin.

Johnson, M. (2001). *The art of non-conversation. A re-examination of the validity of the oral proficiency interview.* New Haven, CT: Yale University Press.

Kramsch, C. (2006). From communicative competence to symbolic competence. *The Modern Language Journal, 90*, 249–251.

Lantolf, J. P., & Ahmed, M. K. (1989). Psycholinguistic perspectives on interlanguage variation: A Vygotskyan analysis. In S. Gass, C. Madden, D. Preston, & L. Selinker (Eds.), *Variation in second language acquisition: Psycholinguistic issues* (pp. 93–108). Bristol, UK: Multilingual Matters.

Lantolf, J. P., & Pavlenko, A. (2001). (S)econd (L)anguage (A)ctivity: Understanding learners as people. In M. Breen (Ed.), *Learner contributions to language learning: New directions in research* (pp. 141–158). London: Pearson.

Locke, J. (1690). *An essay concerning human understanding.* J. Manis (Ed.). The Pennsylvania State University. Retrieved from: www2.hn.psu.edu/faculty/jmanis/locke/humanund. pdf (accessed March 1, 2014).

Malinowski, B. (1927). The problem of meaning in primitive languages. In C. K. Ogden & I. A. Richards (Eds.), *The meaning of meaning* (2nd ed.) (pp. 451–510). New York: Harcourt, Brace & Company.

Ochs, E. (1979). Planned and unplanned discourse. In T. Givon (Ed.), *Syntax and semantics, vol. 12: Discourse and syntax* (pp. 51–80). New York: Academic Press.

Saussure, F. de. (1959). *Course in general linguistics.* New York: McGraw Hill.

Sfard, A. (2008). *Thinking and communicating: Human development, the growth of discourses, and mathematizing.* Cambridge: Cambridge University Press.

Tarone, E. (1988). *Variation in interlanguage.* London: Edward Arnold.

Taylor, T. J. (1998). Do you understand? Criteria of understanding in verbal interaction. In R. Harris & G. Wolf (Eds.), *Interactional linguistics: A first reader* (pp. 198–208). Oxford: Pergamon.

Voloshinov, V. N. (1929/1973). *Marxism and the philosophy of language.* New York: Seminar Press.

Vygotsky, L. S. (1987). *The collected works of L. S. Vygotsky. Vol. 1: Problems of general psychology including the volume thinking and speech.* New York: Plenum.

Wertsch, J. V. (1984). The zone of proximal development: some conceptual issues. In B. Rogoff & J. V. Wertsch (Eds.), *Children's learning in the "zone of proximal development"* (pp. 7–18). San Francisco, CA: Jossey-Bass.

Widdowson, H. G. (2003). *Defining issues in English language teaching.* Oxford: Oxford University Press.

Wittgenstein, L. (1953). *Philosophical investigations.* Oxford: Blackwell.

Yngve, V. (1986). *Linguistics as a science.* Bloomington, IN: Indiana University Press.

ABOUT THE CONTRIBUTORS

Muhammad Amara is an Associate Professor at Beit Berl Academic College, Israel. His academic interests include language education, language policy, sociolinguistics, language and politics, and collective identities. He has published widely on those issues.

Sharon Avni is Assistant Professor of ESL at BMCC, CUNY. Combining ethnographic fieldwork and discourse analysis, her research examines how Hebrew, in its discursive, textual, ideological, and material forms, is a constitutive element of Jewishness in the American context.

Monica Barni is Professor in Educational Linguistics at the Università per Stranieri di Siena. Her research deals mainly with issues of language policy in plurilingual societies and in educational contexts, specifically in relation to the presence of immigrants and their languages and cultures.

Zvi Bekerman, PhD, teaches anthropology of education at the School of Education and the Melton Center, Hebrew University of Jerusalem. His main interests are in the study of cultural, ethnic, and national identity, including identity processes and negotiation during intercultural encounters and in formal/informal learning contexts.

Ellen Bialystok is Distinguished Research Professor of Psychology at York University in Toronto, Canada. Her research uses both behavioral and neuroimaging methods to examine the effect of experience, in particular bilingualism, across the life span, including patients with cognitive impairment and dementia.

324 About the Contributors

Lindsay Brooks is currently an Instructor in the TESOL Certificate Program, Woodsworth College, University of Toronto, where she teaches courses on curriculum planning and assessment, and second language theory. Her research interests include second language assessment, writing, and strategy use.

Jasone Cenoz is Professor of Research Methods in Education at the University of the Basque Country, UPV/EHU. Her research focuses on multilingual education, bilingualism, and multilingualism. She has published a large number of articles, book chapters, and books, and the award-winning monograph *Towards Multilingual Education* (Multilingual Matters, 2009).

Andrew D. Cohen was Professor of ESL at UCLA, Professor of Language Education at the Hebrew University, and Professor Emeritus of Applied Linguistics at the University of Minnesota. He co-edited *Language Learning Strategies* with Ernesto Macaro (Oxford University Press, 2007), *Teaching and Learning Pragmatics* with Noriko Ishihara (Longman/Pearson, 2010), and, most recently, authored the second edition of *Strategies in Learning and Using a Second Language* (Longman/Pearson, 2011).

Alan Davies is Emeritus Professor of Applied Linguistics at the University of Edinburgh. His most recent book is *Native Speakers and Native Users* (Cambridge University Press, 2013).

Bessie Dendrinos is Professor at the Faculty of English, National and Kapodistrian University of Athens. Interested in socially accountable applied linguistics, she has researched and published widely in the areas of foreign language pedagogy, language education policy, and language politics. Her book *The Hegemony of English* (co-authored with D. Macedo and P. Gounari) received the 2004 American Educational Studies Association Critics' Choice Award.

Theodorus du Plessis is Professor in Language Management and Head of the Department of Linguistics and Language Practice at the University of the Free State. He is involved in language management activities in South Africa and is Editor-in-Chief of the Van Schaik Publishers series *Language Policy Studies in South Africa*, and Associate Editor of the journal *Studies in the Languages of Africa*. He is also co-editor of several books and articles on language politics in South Africa and a member of the International Academy of Linguistic Law.

Catherine Elder is Associate Professor, Principal Fellow, and former Director of the Language Testing Research Centre in the School of Languages and Linguistics at the University of Melbourne. She was the co-editor of the journal *Language Testing* (2007–2012), *The Dictionary of Language Testing* (Cambridge University Press, 1999), *The Handbook of Applied Linguistics* (Blackwell, 2004), and is the

About the Contributors **325**

co-author of *Implicit and Explicit Knowledge in Second Language Learning, Teaching and Testing* (Multilingual Matters, 2009). She has a particular interest in issues of fairness in language assessment for specific populations including minority language learners.

Lyn Wright Fogle is an Assistant Professor of Linguistics and TESOL at Mississippi State University. She is the author of *Second Language Socialization and Learner Agency: Adoptive Family Talk* (Multilingual Matters, 2012).

Kellie Frost is a PhD student and Researcher at the Language Testing Research Centre in the School of Languages and Linguistics at the University of Melbourne. Her PhD is investigating the impact of language test requirements on migrants seeking permanent residency in Australia. Her research interests include language testing and immigration, test impact, and the relationship between social justice and test validity.

Ofelia García is Professor in the PhD programs in Urban Education and Hispanic and Luso-Brazilian Languages and Literatures at the Graduate Center of the City University of New York. She has published widely on issues of bilingualism, bilingual education, and sociolinguistics.

Durk Gorter is Ikerbasque Research Professor at University of the Basque Country, UPV/EHU, Donostia-San Sebastián, Spain. He researches multilingual education, European minority languages, and linguistic landscapes, on which themes he has published widely. He is also the editor of *Language, Culture and Curriculum (ISI)* and leader of the Donostia Research Group on Education and Multilingualism (DREAM).

Voula Gotsoulia, PhD in Linguistics, is a Research Fellow at the Research Centre for Language Teaching, Testing and Assessment, National and Kapodistrian University of Athens. Her work and interests focus on aspects of meaning representation and the syntax–semantics interface, representation of language competences, corpus-based descriptions of language proficiency, lexical resources, and ontologies. As a computational linguist, she has developed and evaluated language technology software for large commercial houses.

David I. Hanauer is Professor of Applied Linguistics/English at Indiana University of Pennsylvania and the Assessment Coordinator of the PHIRE program in the Hatfull Laboratory at the Pittsburgh Bacteriophage Institute. He has published widely on issues of literacy in first and second languages, with an emphasis on poetry, graffiti, and scientific writing. He is currently the journal editor of *Scientific Studies of Literature* and the book series editor for *Language Studies in Science and Engineering*.

326 About the Contributors

Nancy H. Hornberger is Professor of Education and Chair of Educational Linguistics at the University of Pennsylvania, USA. Her research interests include linguistic anthropology of education, bilingualism and biliteracy, language policy, and Indigenous language revitalization. Author of more than 100 articles and chapters, she is also a prolific editor; recent books include the 10-volume *Encyclopedia of Language and Education* (Springer, 2008), *Can Schools Save Indigenous Languages? Policy and Practice on Four Continents* (Palgrave Macmillan, 2010), and *Sociolinguistics and Language Education* (with Sandra McKay, Multilingual Matters, 2010).

Ofra Inbar-Lourie lectures on language education and heads the unit for teacher education at the School of Education in Tel Aviv University. Her areas of research are language assessment, language policy, and language teachers.

Adam Jaworski is Professor of Language and Communication at the School of English, University of Hong Kong. His research interests include language and globalization, display of languages in space, nonverbal communication, and text-based art. With Nik Coupland, he edits the Oxford University Press book series *Oxford Studies in Sociolinguistics*.

Kamran Khan completed his joint PhD at the University of Birmingham and University of Melbourne. His research interests include citizenship, language testing, integration, belonging, and multilingualism. He is currently a Research Associate at the University of Leicester and the University of Birmingham.

Kendall A. King is Professor of Second Languages and Cultures Education and Director of Graduate Studies at the Department of Curriculum and Instruction at the University of Minnesota, where she teaches and conducts research on language policy, sociolinguistics, and multilingualism. Her work has been widely published in scholarly journals such as *Applied Linguistics*, *Discourse Studies*, and *Journal of Language, Identity and Education*, as well as in edited collections published by Cambridge University Press, Routledge, and others. Together with Elana Shohamy, she is an editor of the journal *Language Policy*.

Claire Kramsch is Professor of German and Affiliate Professor of Education at UC Berkeley, where she teaches courses in German and applied linguistics. She is the author of numerous books and articles on foreign language learning and teaching, including *The Multilingual Subject* (Oxford University Press, 2009), *Teaching Foreign Languages in an Era of Globalization* (*Modern Language Journal*, Special Issue, in press), and, with Ulrike Jessner, *Multilingualism: The Challenges* (de Gruyter, in press). She is past President of AAAL and current Vice President of AILA.

James P. Lantolf is the Greer Professor in Language Acquisition in the Department of Applied Linguistics at Penn State University. His research focus is on sociocultural theory and second language development. His most recent book, co-authored with M. Poehner, is *Sociocultural Theory and the Pedagogical Imperative: Vygotskian Praxis in L2 Education* (Routledge, 2014).

Elizabeth Lanza is Professor of Linguistics at the Department of Linguistics and Scandinavian Studies, and Director of the Center for Multilingualism in Society across the Lifespan, University of Oslo, Norway. Her main field of research is multilingualism, and her work is sociolinguistically oriented. She has published on language ideology, linguistic landscape, language policy, identity in migrant narratives, language socialization of bilingual children, and research methodology.

Tim McNamara is Professor in the School of Languages and Linguistics at the University of Melbourne. His main areas of research are in language testing (particularly specific purpose language testing, Rasch measurement, and the social context of language tests) and in poststructuralist perspectives on language and identity.

Kate Menken is an Associate Professor of Linguistics at Queens College of the City University of New York (CUNY), and a Research Fellow at the Research Institute for the Study of Language in Urban Society at the CUNY Graduate Center. Recent books are *English Learners Left Behind: Standardized Testing as Language Policy* (Multilingual Matters, 2008) and *Negotiating Language Policies in Schools: Educators as Policymakers* (with Ofelia García, Routledge, 2010).

Elite Olshtain, PhD, University of California, 1979, is Professor Emerita of Language Education at the Hebrew University of Jerusalem. Her research and teaching focuses on second language acquisition, discourse analysis, course design and policymaking, and classroom-oriented research and reading.

Thomas Ricento is Professor and Chair of English as an Additional Language at the University of Calgary, Canada. His current research and publications focus on language policy, political economy, and English in a global context. Recent publications include *Political Economy and English as a "Global" Language* (Critical Multilingualism Studies, 2012) and *Language Policy and Political Economy: English in a Global Context* (Oxford University Press, forthcoming).

Julia Schlam Salman is a Lecturer and Teacher Trainer at the David Yellin Academic College of Education in Jerusalem. She also teaches English at the Max Rayne Hand in Hand School for Jewish-Arab Education and is interested in critical pedagogies, learning technology, and language learning.

328 About the Contributors

Bernard Spolsky is Professor Emeritus of English at Bar-Ilan University. His most recent book is *The Languages of the Jews* (Cambridge University Press, 2014).

Merrill Swain is Professor Emerita at the Ontario Institute for Studies in Education of the University of Toronto, where she taught and conducted research for 40 years. She was President of AAAL, and Vice President of AILA, and was presented AAAL's 2004 Distinguished Scholarship and Service Award. She has published widely, and has recently co-authored a textbook, *Sociocultural Theory in Second Language Education: An Introduction through Narratives* (Multilingual Matters, 2010).

Michal Tannenbaum is a Senior Lecturer and the Head of the Language Education Program, School of Education, Tel Aviv University. Her research interests include linguistic patterns of minority groups, psychological and emotional aspects of immigration and language maintenance, inter-group relations, and translingual writing.

Hirut Woldemariam is Associate Professor of Linguistics at the Department of Linguistics, Addis Ababa University, Ethiopia. Her focal area of research has been descriptive linguistics, historical-comparative linguistics, and sociolinguistics. Her research focuses on Omotic languages of Ethiopia, and her research interests include language ideology, language policy, and the linguistic landscape in Ethiopia, as well as aspects of the phonology and morphology of Ethiopian languages.

Dafna Yitzhaki is a Research Associate at the Department of Linguistics and Language Practice at the University of the Free State and a Lecturer at Tel Aviv University. Her research interests include sociolinguistics, language policy, and multilingualism.

INDEX

Locators to plans and tables are in *italics*.
The abbreviation "LL" means language or linguistic landscapes, viz. North America LL.

Abdi, C. M. 289
Abutalebi, J. 263–264
Academic English 117
academic speaking 68, 70–75
accents 88
achievement 56, 58, 60
Adalah (Legal Center for Arab Minority
　Rights in Israel) 171
Addis Ababa (Ethiopia) 113
Addis Ababa University 117
additive approaches 98
adults 272, 274
advertisements *163*, 200–201, 219
African Language Clusters 129
Agha, A. 214–215
aging 264, 274
Ahmed, M. K. 313, 314, 316, 317–318
airports 217–222, 225–228
Alderson, C. 89
Alina (EFL student) 284–285, 287
Amara, M. 185, 187, 188, 190
American Educational Research
　Association (AERA) 85–86
American exceptionalism 241 *see also*
　North America LL; United States
　(US)
American Jewishness 202–204, 208–211
　see also Hebrew; Jews
Amharic (language) 110–112, 114,
　115–117, 118–119

Amsterdam (the Netherlands) 284–285
Andrade, A. I. 152
anti-Semitic laws 254–255
applied linguistics 256
Arabic: and Hebrew signs 170–180, 188;
　learning 273; monolingual school
　studies 300–302, 305; and Palestinian
　LL 183–192; population 171; and social
　cohesion 174 *see also* Palestinian LL
Arabic-Hebrew: bilingualism 170,
　174–176, 177, 179, 180, 302–304;
　shop logos 190; signs 185, *188, 189*;
　sociopolitical context 183–184
architects 260
Arguelles, A. 271, 276
Armand, F. 152
artefactualization 44–45
Ash, A. 215
Asian languages 56–57, 60 *see also*
　Chinese; Mandarin
assessment practices 44–45 *see also* tests
Association for Civil Rights in Israel
　(ACRI) 171
Association of Language Testers in Europe
　(ALTE) 82, 83
asylum seekers 88–90 *see also* refugees
Atkinson, D. 310
Attali, Y. 66, 76
Australia 12–16, 20, 54–56, 61, 87
authorship, of signs 166–167

330 Index

autoethnographic studies 249
"auto-socioanalysis" (Bourdieu) 235
Ayan (student) 289–291
Aymara (language) 273

Bachman, L. F. 87
background language learners 58–59, 60
  see also language learning
Bakhtin, M. 17–18, 21
Barac, R. 263
Bardovi-Harlig, K. 272
Barhuma, 'I. 191–192
Baron Cohen, S. 196
Basque Country (Spain) 151–152
Basque language 154, 160–161, 163–165
Basque schools 154–167
Bauman, R. 224
Bavelier, D. 260
Belcher, D. 275
Bellah, R. 241, 243
Ben Gurion Airport (Israel) *221*
Ben-Rafael, E. 185, 187, 188
Bialystok, E. 263
biculturalism 34, 191
bilingual education 34, 95–96, 98, 103
bilingual intercultural education (EIB) 125
bilingualism: Arabic-Hebrew 170,
  174–176, 177, 179, 180, 302–304;
  cognitive effects 262–266; ESL
  programs 103; executive functioning
  260–261; French-English 235–242;
  language fluidity 99; linguistic effects
  261–262; multilingual policies 178;
  Palestinians 191; schools 98, 302–304
  see also multilingualism; second
  language (L2)
bilingual signs 170–180, 188 *see also*
  multilingual signs
bilingual syntax measure (BSM) 313–314
Billig, M. 228–229
bivalency 204
Blackledge, A. 12, 89
Blommaert, J. 114, 145–146
Bloomfield, L. 309
Bo (student) 75
Bogale, B. 116
Borat (Baron Cohen) 196
bounded languages 42
Bourdieu, P. 235, 241, 242
Bourhis, R. Y. 152, 172, 182, 197
brain structures 259–260, 265–266
brand frames 215–216, 218–222
branding 202, 203–204, 220
Breen, M. P. 61

Breidner Linguistic Method 200, *201*
British Mandate for Palestine 171–172
British political discourses 12
Brooks, L. 68
Brown, E. K. 317
Brown, K. D. 153
Butler, C. *217*, 218
Butler, J. 20–21
Byram, M. 34, 41, 43–44

Calgary (Canada) 137–138, 143
Canada 135–146, 152, 223
Cavafy, Constantine 8
Ce que parler veut dire (Bourdieu) 241
Chai (life חי) 206–208
Chen, I. 55
children, language learning 274
Chinese 54–58 *see also* Mandarin
Chomsky, N. 309
Chomsky, W. 196
citizenship 12, 17, 89, 90, 254, 255 *see also*
  identities
Citizenship and Immigration Canada 136
City University of New York—New
  York State Initiative on the Education
  of Emergent Bilinguals (CUNY-
  NYSIEB) project 95–105
classroom interactions 282, 287–288,
  289–291, 291–292 *see also* schools
classroom management 156, *158*
Clemente, M. 152
clothing 203, *207*
Clyne, M. 55
codemeshing 99
Codes of Ethics (CoE) 84–85
Codes of Practice (CoP) 82, 84–85, 90
cognitive abilities 259–267 *see also*
  memory
cognitive reserve 264–265, 266–267
Cold War 241
collaborative descriptive inquiry (CDI)
  101
College of Physicians and Surgeons of
  Alberta (Canada) 138, 139
Colombia 138–139
colonialism 111, 295, 305
commercial LL 162, 188, 191–192 *see also*
  signage
Common European Framework of
  Reference (CEFR) 16, 24, 26,
  40–49, 52
common metadata values 33
communicative: activities 284–287, 309;
  approaches 241; competence 14, 24,

26–27, 43, 320–321; efficacy 317, 318–319
"communicative proficiency" (Harris) 320
community support 102–103, 144–145
competence standards 49 *see also* language competence; standards
comprehension 26, 318
conflicts 183–184, 294, 295
congruent trials 262–263
Connor, U. 275
contextual factors 56, 275
continuum of competence 43
conversations 317–319
Cooper, R. L. 124
Copenhagen Airport (Denmark) *219, 222*
co-regulated activities 316
corpus-status-acquisition typology (Cooper) 124
Coste, D. 241
critical applied linguistics 256
critical discourse analysis 256
critical language testing (CLT) 81 *see also* tests
cross-language descriptors 33
cultural appropriation 299
cultural diversity 40, 47
cultural identity: Arabic 183; dissonance 302, 304, 306; English speakers 302–303; Hebrew materializations 210; and language 125–126, 152, 294–295; multilingual curricula 34 *see also* identities
curricula 23, 34–35, 53, 56
cursing 276
Cusco (Peru) 126–127

Dadaab refugee camp (Kenya) 289
Dagenais, D. 152
Dalyat Al-Karmel (Israel) *185, 186*
Davidson, F. 86, 87, 90
death, forbidden memory 246
de Beauvoir, S. 240
decoration, and signage 162, *164, 165*
definition of situation (DOS) 316
De Mauro, T. 42
Democratic Republic of the Congo 139, 142
deportations 254, 255
Derrida, J. 20
design fluency tests 260 *see also* tests
de-skilling 137
destinations, *welcome* signs 217
developmental bilingual education programs 98

dialects 88
Diaz, F. 139–142
Dictation Test (Australia) 87
direct testing 66 *see also* testing
Discipline and Punish (Foucault) 11
"discitizenship" 142
Discourse Analysis and Second Language Teaching (Kramsch) 239
discourses: authoritative 17–18; linguistic landscapes 242; organization 28, *30*; studies 239–240
distributive approaches 163–166
diversity 42, 152
domain-general executive control network 263
domestic hospitality, *welcome* signs 217
Donostia-San Sebastián study (Basque Country) 163
dual language bilingual programs 98
Duranti, A. 228
dynamic bilingualism 105 *see also* bilingualism

economy, the 182–183, 191
Edinburgh (UK) 153
educated elites 112, 114
Educational Testing Service (ETS) 88
Elder, C. 55
Emergent Bilingual Leadership Teams (CUNY-NYSIEB) 101–102, 103, 104
emergent bilinguals 95, 98, 99
employment, barriers to 138, 142
Encyclopedia of Language and Education (Shohamy & Hornberger) 124
engagement 102–103
English: in Basque schools 154, 165–166; in Ethiopia 109–120; Hebraized 204, *205*; and Hebrew speakers 298–300; identity markers 295; international language 112, 295, 305, 306; Israeli-Palestinian conflict 295; language learners classification 96–97; medium of instruction (MOI) 109, 111, 118, 154; monolingualism 95, 103; multilingualism 236–238; proficiency 118, 142; in Singapore 119; speaker identifications 298–304, 305; Zulu-ized 129
English as a foreign language (EFL) 283–287, 295–304
English as a second language (ESL) 54, 61, 96, 103, 145, 153
enregistrement 214–215
entextualization 198

332 Index

equality of opportunity 135–136
Erard, M. 271, 272–273
Esquisse pour une autoanalyse (Bourdieu)
  235
ethics 81–90
Ethiopia 109–120
Ethiopian National Language Academy
  118
ethnic federalism 114
ethnic identities 301–302, 304
Ethnologue: Languages of the World (Lewis,
  Simons, & Fennig) 110
Eugenia (EFL student) 286–287
European Association for Language Testing
  and Assessment (EALTA) 82–84
European Union (EU) 40
events, signage 161–162, *162*
examiners, sanctions against 85, 86
exclusion 14
executive functioning (control) 260–264,
  274
experience, cognitive performance
  259–260, 265–266
Extra, G. 41

face-to-face testing 66 *see also* tests
Fairclough, N. 240
fairness, language tests 88–89
Fairness Review Guidelines (ETS) 88
"fake multilingualism" (Kelly-Holmes)
  227
family engagement 102–103
Faraz (student) 70, 73
Fayid, W. (n.d.) 192
feminist approaches 287 *see also* women
Fennig, C. D. 110
Fernandez, S. 55
Finland 130–132
first language (L1): Arabic-Hebrew study
  296–307; learning 56, 58, 59, 60–61;
  South Africa 128 *see also* second
  language (L2)
Flash My Brain, learning programme 277
Fluenz Mandarin course 271, 274
football players 260
foreign: languages 23–25, 25, 34–35, 60,
  112–113; names 192; professionals 137
"foreignness" 136
Foucault, M. 11
frames, *Welcome* signs 215–228
Franco-Prussian war 240
Franken International school 287
French 235–243
Fresco, N. 246

Fulcher, G. 53, 86, 87, 90
functional descriptors 26–27

Gamo-Gofa zone (SNNP, Ethiopia)
  115–116, 117
García, O. 99, 104, 117
gatekeeping mechanisms 15–16, 45–46
Gee, J. 240
gender 282, 284–285, 291–292 *see also*
  women
generic standards frameworks 60 *see also*
  standards
geosemiotics (Scollon & Scollon) 216
German language 238–239, 241
Germany 240–241, 250–251, 256
Gestapo files 250–253, 257
Givon, T. 317, 318
globalization *see* international languages
Goffman, E. 215
Gold, B. T. 264
good practice 86
government LL 188, 191
grammar 29–31, 48, 56, 263, 317–318
Greece 23, 25–26
Green, D. W. 263
"greetings" 228 *see also welcome* signs
guests, tourists as 217
Guide for Professional Development
  (CUNY-NYSIEB) 101
guiding signage *159*
Guzmán Valerio & Kleyn CUNY-
  NYSIEB team 104

Haapala (Tel Aviv, Israel) 152
Habits of the Heart (Bellah) 241, 243
habitus clivé (Bourdieu) 241
Haifa (Israel) *185, 186*
Hanauer, Alfred and Helene 245,
  247–254
Hanauer, D. I. 153
Hanauer, K. 249
Hancock, A. 153
Hanyu Pinyin Romanization 59
Harris, R. 309, 311–312, 320
Harvard University hat *203*
Heathrow airport (UK) 217
Hebraization: English 204, *205*;
  Palestinian LL 182–192
Hebrew: language learning 200–202, 273;
  materialization 202–211; monolingual
  school studies 298–300, 303, 305;
  North American LL 196–211; and
  Palestinian LL 183–184, *185*, 187,
  190–191; political messaging 208; signs

188–189, 190; tattooing 204–206 *see also* American Jewishness; Israel; Jews
Hebrew-Arabic: bilingualism 170, 174–176, 177, 179, 180, 302–304; signs *188, 189*, 190; sociopolitical context 183
He'brew beer 203–204, *205*
hedging frame 225–227
Heller, M. 182, 191
heritage languages 55–56, 267 *see also* regional languages
Herrera and Ebe CUNY-NYSIEB team 103
Heugh, K. 114
Heutiges Deutsch (*Today's German*, Steger) 239
hierarchies 291
Hillel (organization) 203
hippocampus 259–260
historic trauma 247
Holocaust, the 245–257
Holocaust-Kindertransport 247–248, 249
home (from home) frame 216–218
Homeland Security Agency (US) 225–227
home languages 98–99, 100, 102 *see also* mother tongue
homogenization, language standards 54
Hong Kong International Airport *218*, 222
Hornberger, N. H. 95, 124
hospitality 217–218
House of Lords (UK) 89
Huan (student) 70
Hudson, T. 53
human rights 256
Hymes, D. 320
hyperpolyglots 270–271
identities: exclusive 183; and language 182, 192; sexual 282, 292 *see also* citizenship; cultural identity; national identity
identity construction 291–292, 294–307
ideologies: language and territory 180, 191–192; language tests 44–45
immigration *see* migrants
in-class speaking 71–72, 74
incongruent trials 263
indeterminacy of linguistic signs 311–312
Indigenous languages 123–132
inequality 135–136, 294
informative signs 225–227 *see also* signage
"In Memory of Hella and Alfred #2." (Hanauer) 249

Integrated Foreign Languages Curriculum (IFLC) 5, 24–28, 33, *36–37*
integration 12, 40, 46, 146
integrational linguistics (IL) 309–321
Interaction et discours dans la classe de langue (Kramsch) 241
interactionist theory 294
interactions 76–77 *see also* interviews
interculturality 34, 126–127, 160
interlingualism 34–35
internally persuasive discourses (Bakhtin) 17, 21
International English Language Testing System (IELTS) 13
International Language Testing Association (ILTA) 82, 84–86, 90
international languages 40, 112, 295, 299, 305, 306
interpretive frames 215
interviews: communicative tasks 284–287; "M" L2 proficiency 314–319; study methodology 297
isiZulu 127–130
Israel: English learners 299–307; Jewish-Arab mixed cities 170–180; Jewish-Zionist state 183; language landscape (LL) 185–192; values and culture 188–190 *see also* Hebrew
Israeli-Palestinian conflict 183–184, 295
Israel-Palestinian LL 170–180, 185–191
Italy 45–49

Jacqueline (refugee) 139, 142–145
Jaworski, A. 222–223
Jerusalem 295–304
Jets Football team bumper sticker *204*
Jewish-Arab mixed cities 170–180
Jewish Studies Pin 199–200
Jews: heritage 200–202; identity 183, 208–209; religiosity 199 *see also* American Jewishness; Hebrew
Jungfernhof death camp (Riga) 251

Kafka, F. 238
Kelly-Holmes, H. 227
Kiddle, T. 66
Kim, S. H. O. 61
Kindertransport 247–248, 249 *see also* Holocaust, the
King, M. L. 102
Kloss, H. 124
Kormos, J. 66
KPG 23–24, 25–26, 35

334 Index

Kramsch, C. 320
Kristallnacht 251

L1 (first language): Arabic-Hebrew study
296–307; learning 56, 58, 59, 60–61;
South Africa 128
L2 (second language): adults learning
271–273, 278–279; Chinese learners
55, 58–59, 60; English as 112;
proficiency 313–316; proficiency
interview 314–319; South African 128
see also bilingualism
Lamarre, P. 152
Landry, R. 152, 172, 182, 197
Language and Power (Fairclough) 240
language background 58
language communities 313
language competence: integration 47–48;
migrants 12, 13, 44; monolingual 42;
representation 28–32; standards 49 see
also proficiency
language: components 33; contact, and
conflict 183; education 34, 184;
ideologies 42, 110–111, 113
Language Instruction for Newcomers to
Canada (LINC) 140, 145
language landscapes (LL) 182; and the
economy 191; ideologically charged
183; and policy implementation 179 see
also linguistic landscapes (LL)
language learning: abilities 273–274;
assessments 60; Australia 54–56;
backgrounds 58; difficulties 53;
experience of language 43; gender and
sexuality 292; and identity 281–282,
294; and power 294; strategies 270–279
see also schools; students
language policies (LP): Ethiopia 110–114,
118–119; EU 40–41; hidden agendas
110, 124; implementation 179–180;
Israel 172–173, 180; multilingual
127–130, 178; rating scales 45; and
social policies 173; Sweden 130–131
Language Policy: Hidden Agendas and New
Approaches (Shohamy) 245, 281
language processing 262, 263–264
language proficiency see language
competence; proficiency
language revitalization 125, 126
languages: and the economy 182–183;
and ethnicity 304; fixed-code model
310–311; and "foreignness" 136;
functions 29, 30; and heritage links
200–201; and identity 182, 192,

295–307; and materiality 198; objective
system 313; power/political
domination 111, 294; and territory 182
language school advert (Addis Ababa) 113
Languages of New York, The (CUNY-
NYSIEB) 102
languages of wider communication
(LWC) 295
languages other than English (LOTEs) 96
language space 191
language standards see standards
language tests see tests
language use, norms 42
Langue et Apprentissage des Langues (Coste)
241
Lantolf, J. P. 313, 314, 316, 317–318
Lanza, E. 113, 116
Lapidus, A. 250
Las Vegas airport (US) 219, 222
Leeman, J. 183
letter fluency tests 262 see also tests
Leung, C. 45
leveled descriptors 25, 26, 33
Lewis, M. P. 110
Lewkowicz, J. 45
lexical access 261–262
lexical types 31, 32
Lian (student) 75
liberal democracies 135–136
Liddicoat, A. J. 282, 284
life (Chai חי) 206–208
Life in the UK: A guide for new residents
(TSO) 17
Life in the UK test (LUK) 16–19
lifestyle 266–267
linguistic: anthropology 198; competence
see language competence; conflict 183;
distance 53; diversity 41, 42, 96; effects
261–262
Linguistic Human Rights Tribunal (South
Africa) 130
linguistic landscapes (LL): Basque schools
154–166; "camera safari" study 153; as
discourse in action 242–243;
educational contexts 151–153; Ethiopia
113–114; Palestinian 185; public space
124, 172; Stolper Steine memorial
249–250; theoretical work 197–198;
urban environments 152 see also
language landscapes (LL); signage
linguistic resources, bilinguals 99
linguistic science 311
linguistic signs (Voloshinov) 318
linguistic types 29–32

literacy education 152, 256–257
Literacy in Sápmi research project 131–132
lived religion 198
Li W. 117
loanwords 184
localizing, airports 221–222
Locke, J. 309, 310
Lod (Israel) 171, 174
logographic writing systems 273
London 218, 259–260
Los Angeles International Airport (US) *220*, 222, 225–226
Luk, G. 263

"M," L2 proficiency interview 314–319
McCarran International Airport (Las Vegas, US) *219*, 222
McKay, P. 61
McKay, S. L. 305
McKinney, C. 294
McNamara, T. 87–88, 89
Maguire, E. A. 259–260
Malinowski, B. 309
Mamani, N. 125–127
Mandarin 55, 271–272, 273, 274 *see also* Asian languages; Chinese
Marco Polo International Airport (Venice) 227
markers of identity construction 298–304 *see also* identity construction
Martins, F. 152
Marxism 135
mass-oriented greetings 214–229
materiality 198, 210
Mavis (focal teacher) 287, 289
Meänkieli (language) 131
mediums of instruction (MOI): Basque country 154; English 109, 111, 118, 154; Ethiopia 109, 110, 111, 114, 115–116, 117–118; South Africa 127–128
Mei (student) 77
memory 246, 274–275 *see also* cognitive abilities
Messick, S. 86
metrolingualism 99
microbiology laboratory LL 153
migrants: Dictation Test (Australia) 87; language competence 12–13, 20, 40–41, 44, 46–47 *see also* refugees
Millennials 202
minorities 130–131
Mitchell, D. R. D. 260

mixed cities, Israel 173–179
mnemonics 275
mobility 40
Modan, G. 183
Modern Standard Chinese 55 *see also* Mandarin
monoglossic language policies 35
monolingual approaches 41–42, 45, 47, 95
monolingual linguistic processing 261
monolingual studies 298–302
mono-normative, concept of language 44–45
Monterescu, D. 179
Montreal (Canada) 152
Moore, D. 152
Moriarty, M. 183
morphology 273, 317
mother tongues 60–61, 111, 116 *see also* home languages
multilingual competence 34, 167
multilingual curricula 23, 34–35 *see also* curricula
multilingual display frames 227–228
multilingualism: benefits 126; French-English-German 235–242; as a resource 40–41; in schools 95–105, 154–167; and societies 270; standards 23–38; US 275–276 *see also* bilingualism; super-multilingualism
multilingual policies 127–130, 178 *see also* language policies (LP)
multilingual signs 166, 167, 227–228, 242 *see also* bilingual signs
multi-literacies perspectives 34
multimodal discourses 242
multiple femininities 283
multiple inheritance ontological schema 31
municipal signs 174
Myhill, J. 182, 192

Napoleonic wars 240
"Natashas" dialogue 286–287
National Curriculum Profile (Australia) 54
national identity 183, 294–295 *see also* identities
nationalism: Germany 240–241; language tests 44; *welcome* signs 228
National Jewish Outreach Program 200
national languages, obligation to learn 41
National Minority Languages (Sweden) 130
native languages 43, 56, 287–288
Nazareth (Israel) *185, 186*
Nazreth (Oromia, Ethiopia) 117

336 Index

Ndimande-Hlongwa, Nobuhle 127–130
Nelde, P. 183
neo-capital theories 135
New York City (US) 95
No Child Left Behind policy (US) 52
non-European immigrants, Canada 137
non-refugee immigrant population 136
nonverbal linguistic signs and signals
    312–313
normative language: standards 52–53; use
    42, 44–45
North American LL 196–211 *see also*
    United States (US)
Norton, B. 294

Oaxaca (Mexico) 152–153
Obama, B. *208–209*, 209
Obler, L. 272–273
Ochs, E. 317, 318
official languages 174, 176–177, 178
older language learners 272, 274 *see also*
    language learning
ontology 29–32
oppression 294
oral proficiency, TOEFL iBT 76
Oromia region (Ethiopia) 116–117
Oslo Airport Gardermoen (Norway) *221*
Outakoski, Hanna 130–132
outcomes-based frameworks 52–53 *see also*
    standards
out-of-class speaking 71–72, 74
"outsiders" 136
ownership, international languages 305

Palestine Order in Council 1922 171–172
Palestinian LL: English language 303–305;
    Hebraization 182–192; mixed cities
    170–180 *see also* Arabic
Palmer, A. 87
parallel monolingualism 34
Parmenter, L. 41, 43–44
participation frameworks 218
pedagogies 99, 104, 152, 153
pediatric surgeons, as refugees 139–142
perceptual-motor ability, video games 260
performance *see* proficiency
performances: artistic 249; theatrical
    222–224
permanent resident status, benefits 139
personal familial trauma research 247
personal identity *see* identities
personalized greetings 214
personal language policies 125
person-to-machine testing 66

phantom pain 246
phatic signs 215, 225–227
place names 215–216, 220
plurilingualism 24, 41, 44–45, 48
poetic autoethnography 249
policy implementation: 179–180 *see also*
    language policies (LP); tests
political domination 111, 295, 305
political messaging 208
politics, language tests 45, 47, 86, 90
polylingualism 99 *see also* multilingualism
Portugal, primary school project 152
post-Soviet femininities 283–287
poverty 143–144, 145
power 20–21, 294
Power of Tests, The (Shohamy) 65, 81
pragmatic speech 317–318
pre-entry language tests debate, House of
    Lords (UK) 89
private signs, and public signs 172
procedures, language testing 82, 86
PROEIB-Andes master's program 125
professionals: credentials 142; ethics
    89–90; as refugees 137–138
proficiency: descriptors 26–27, 44;
    Ethiopia 117; in interviews 314–319;
    refugees 140–142, 146; in tests 66,
    74–75 *see also* language competence;
    tests
public cultural practices 126
public language visibility 177–178
public signs 172, 215 *see also* signage
public space 152, 172, 197–198, 216

Qian, D. D. 66
Quebec (Canada) 143
Quechua language 125–126, 273

Rabinowitz, D. 179
race-thinking (Taylor) 254
racism 257
Rahat (Israel) *185, 186*
Ramla (Israel) 171
rating scales 45
reaction times 263
real-life speaking 74–76, 77, 78
receptive vocabulary 261
reflexive sociology 235–242
refugees 88, 136–146 *see also* asylum
    seekers; migrants
regional languages 88, 153 *see also* heritage
    languages
regulatory institutions, and refugees
    138–139, 139–140

religious identity 294–295, 304
research: refugees 137–138; society and consciousness 246–247; test taking 66–68
residency, and language tests 14, 47
retention 275
Robert (refugee) 139, 142–145
Rody, C. 210
Roever, C. 87–88
Romance languages 273
Romney, M. *208*, 209
Rowland, L. 153
Royal Bank of Scotland (RBS) *218*, 219, 222
Russia 283–287

Sabatier, C. 152
Saiful (student) 289–291
Sakhnin (Israel) *185*, *186*
Salthouse, T. A. 260
Sámi (language) 130
Sami (student) 71, 76
sanctions 85, 86
San Simón University (Bolivia) 125
Sápmi people (Scandinavia) 130
Sara (student) 73–74
Saussure, F. de 309–312
Saussurean circle 311, 312
Sayer, P. 152
Scarino, A. 53
Schiffman, H. F. 124
School of IsiZulu Studies 129
schools: Basque country 154–167; CUNY-NYSIEB project 95–105; curricula 23, 25; Ethiopia 117–118; Israel 295–307; linguistic landscapes 152–153 *see also* classroom interactions; language learning; students
Scollon, R. 216, 229
Scollon, S. W. 216
second language (L2): adults learning 271–273, 278–279; Chinese learners 55, 58–59, 60; English as 112; proficiency 313–316; proficiency interview 314–319; South African 128 *see also* bilingualism; first language (L1)
Second Life distance learning 130
secularizing, sacred words 206
segregationalist approaches 309, 312, 314
Selassie, Haile 110
self-assessment checklists 82, 83
self-identity 301, 305 *see also* identities
semi-direct testing 66, 76

sexuality 282, 292
sexual violence 289
Sfard, A. 319, 320
Shan (student) 76
Shandler, J. 197
Shohamy, E.: bilingualism 96, 99; democratic assessments 57, 132; *Encyclopedia of Language and Education* 124; language manipulation 255–256, 292; language policies (LP) 95, 111, 118–119, 120, 124, 172–173, 178; *Language Policy: Hidden Agendas and New Approaches* 245, 281; language space and ideology 191; language standards 53–54; linguistic landscapes 113, 151, 152, 185, 216; *The Power of Tests* 41, 65, 81; standardized tests 266; test contexts 77; tests and ethics 90–91; tests and policy agendas 12, 45, 49, 281; tests and teaching and learning practices 281–282; tests as gatekeeping mechanisms 11, 15; translanguaging 270; work of 1–8
shops 113, 190
Sidama (SNNP region Ethiopia) 116
signage: authorship 166–167; Basque Country 163–166; functions 155–162; Israel-Palestinian LL 170–180, 185–191; linguistic landscapes 152–153; *welcome* signs 214–229 *see also* commercial LL; linguistic landscape (LL)
signality 313, 319
sign-making capacity 321
Simons, G. F. 110
simulation, real life speaking 76
Singer, P. 89
sites of sociality 215
SLA (second language acquisition) 152, 310
soccer players 260
social capital 136–146
social cohesion 12, 40–41
social goods 135
social identity 87–88
social interaction 312
Social Linguistics (Gee) 240
social networks 144–145
social services 139
socioeconomic integration 136
"sociolinguistic consumption" (Stroud and Wee) 119
Sofia (student) 69, 74–75
Somali Diaspora 288

338 Index

South Africa 127–128
South Africa-Norway Tertiary Education
    Development Program (SANTED) 128
Southern Nations, Nationalities and
    Peoples (SNNP, Ethiopia) 115–117
Spanish 97, 154, 165
spatial navigation 259–260
speaking tests 65–66 *see also* tests
spectacle frame 222–224
Spolsky, B. 113, 124, 172–173, 191
standards 14, 49, 52–62, 85–86 *see also*
    outcomes-based frameworks
standards-based multilingual curricula 34
Star of David 206
Steger, Hugo 239
Stoddart, J. 118
Stolper Steine memorials 249–250
St. Petersburg (Russia) 283
Stricker, L. J. 66, 76
Stringer, D. 272
Stroud, C. 119
structuralist theories 309
Student Achievement in Asian Languages
    study (SAALE) 56–61
students: linguistic landscapes 152–153;
    multilingualism 102; signage 166–167;
    TOEFL iBT speaking test 68–78 *see
    also* language learning; schools
subjection 20–21
subtractive bilingualism 98
subversion 204–206
Suleiman, Y. 192
Summo O'Connell, R. 55
Suo, C. 260
super-multilingualism 270–279 *see also*
    multilingualism
supervisors 260
survival jobs 140
Suyin (student) 76
Swain, M. 68
Sweden 130–131
symbolic brand names 220 *see also* branding
"symbolic competence" (Kramsch) 320
symbolic expressions 243
synthetic personalization 214, 229

Tala (student) 74
tandem partners 274, 278 *see also* language
    learning
Tao (student) 73
tattooing 197, 204–206
Tattoo Jew (documentary) 204–206
taxi drivers 259–260
Taylor, D. 254

Taylor, T. J. 317, 318
teachers: narrative tasks 292; proficiency
    in English 114
teaching: and assessment strategies 61;
    communicative approaches 241;
    emergent bilinguals 105; Ethiopia 114,
    115–116, 117–118; feminist approaches
    287; research into 242; Sápmi people
    (Scandinavia) 131–132; using signage
    155–156, *157*, 160
Tel Aviv-Jaffa (Israel) 171, 174
Tel Aviv University 8
territory, and language 182
Test of English as a Foreign Language
    internet-based Test (TOEFL iBT)
    69–78
tests: Australia 12–16; consequences 87;
    contexts 66, 77; design 49, 82; ethics
    81–90; fairness 88–89; gatekeeping
    mechanisms 15–16, 45–46;
    immigration and citizenship 12; Italy
    47–48; misuses 281; as policy
    instruments 41–42; politics 44–45, 86,
    90; principles 82, 86; real-life academic
    speaking 72; and social identity 87–88;
    standardized 266; study 65–77;
    translanguaging 270 *see also* proficiency
text types 28, 31, *32*
theory of language 28
theory of regulation (Vygotsky) 316
Thrift, N. 215
Tigray (Ethiopia) 116
Tigrinya (language) 116
tourists 214–229, 284–285
training policies 119
transidiomatic practices 99
transitional bilingual education 98, 103
    see also bilingual education
translanguaging 34, 99, 104, 117–118,
    270
Translanguaging Guide (CUNY-
    NYSIEB) 104
translating 288–291, 297
transnationalization 305
travel destinations 220
trilingual signs 188
Trumper-Hecht, N. 185, 192
two-way bilingual programs 98

Umm-el-Fahm (Israel) *185*, *186*, 190
unemployment 12, 136 *see also* working
United Kingdom (UK) 16–19
United States (US): bilingual programs 98;
    border signs 223–224; Customs and

Border Protection Agency 225–226;
elections 208–209; English as a second
language (ESL) 291; Somali Diaspora
288; students 239 *see also* North
American LL
University of Athens (Greece) 23, 35
University of Kwazulu-Natal (UKZN,
South Africa) 127–130
University of Michigan (US) *203*,
278–279
University of Umeå (Sweden) 130
Upper Nazareth (Israel) 171, 174, 192

Vancouver (Canada) 152
Vancouver International Airport *220*,
222
verbal fluency 261
verbal jousting 276
video games 260
visitors, engagement with hosts 218
visuospatial abilities, architects 260
vocabulary 262, 274–275
Voloshinov, V. N. 313, 318, 319, 321
Võru (Estonia) 153
Vygotsky, L. S. 316

Waksman, S. 151, 152
Wee, L. 119
welcome signs 214–229
Wenyan (student) 72, 76
Wertsch, J. V. 316
Western influences, Indigenous people
126–127
Widdowson. H. G. 320–321
Williams, C. 99
Woldemariam, H. 113, 116
women: feminism 287; histories 287, 292;
identities 283; sexual violence 289 *see
also* gender
Women's Association (Calgary) 144
working: as refugees 138–139 *see also*
unemployment
Wu, S.-M. 55

Xiao, Y. 56

Yagmur, K. 41
Yngve, V. 314
youth-centric culture 202–203

Zulu 129